SL06

# Royal College of Speech & Language Therapists

# Clinical Guidelines

First published in 2005 by

**Speechmark Publishing Ltd**, Telford Road, Bicester, Oxon OX26 4LQ, UK

Telephone: +44 (0) 1869 244 644    Fax: +44 (0) 1869 320 040

**www.speechmark.net**

**002-5179**/Printed in the United Kingdom/1010

**British Library Cataloguing in Publication Data**
A CIP catalogue record for this Book is available from the British Library.

ISBN-10: 0 86388 505 5
ISBN-13: 978 086388 505 1

# Contents

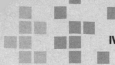

# Introduction

1

## 1.1 SCOPE OF THE GUIDELINES

In 1998, The Royal College of Speech & Language Therapists published *Clinical Guidelines by Consensus for Speech & Language Therapists* which contained eight clinical guidelines.

In 1999, the second edition of *Clinical Guidelines for Speech & Language Therapists* was commissioned. This current edition updates and expands upon the first edition in several ways with:

- The addition of a further five clinical guidelines;
- The addition of an overarching core guideline;
- The inclusion of tables of evidence;
- The addition of suggestions from service users.

This revision was initially supported in part by funding from the Department of Health, which was subsequently transferred to the National Institute for Clinical Excellence (NICE).

In this edition there are 12 clinical guidelines, which are underpinned by a core guideline. Although each clinical guideline can be considered as an individual document, it is of greater benefit to view each guideline as only part of the complete whole. Inevitably, there is a certain amount of overlap between the clinical guidelines and this demonstrates the close interrelationship between each clinical area.

Most of the guidelines are relevant for both children and adults. However, a few are predominately either child or adult focused. The following provides an outline of the clinical guidelines divisions.

### Children

- Pre-school Children with Communication, Language & Speech Needs
- School-aged Children with Speech, Language & Communication Difficulties

### Children & Adults

- Autistic Spectrum Disorders
- Cleft Palate and Velopharyngeal Abnormalities
- Clinical Voice Disorders
- Deafness/Hearing Loss
- Disorders of Fluency
- Disorders of Feeding, Eating, Drinking & Swallowing (Dysphagia)
- Disorders of Mental Health & Dementia
- Dysarthria

### Adults

- Aphasia
- Head & Neck Cancer

## 1.2 PURPOSE OF THE GUIDELINES

The aim of these clinical guidelines is to provide clinicians and managers with explicit statements regarding clinical management that are based on the current evidence, where available. They can assist in the clinical decision-making process by providing information on what is considered to be the minimum best practice. The focus of a clinical guideline is the content of the care provided. Expert opinion and professional consensus have also been included within the evidence base.

Clinical guidelines are an important tool in attempting to provide equity and quality of service provision.

Although these guidelines are uni-professional and directed primarily at practising Speech & Language Therapists it is anticipated that they will contribute to multi-professional documents as appropriate. Throughout the document there is a strong emphasis on multi- and interdisciplinary team-working.

The guidelines will also inform health, social and educational purchasers and other agencies that may become involved with individuals who have a communication or swallowing disorder.

Each guideline contains recommendations that are explicit statements providing specific clinical guidance on the assessment and management of each area. Each recommendation is supported by evidence from the literature or is based upon the consensus of clinical experts.

## 1.3 CONTEXT AND USE

These guidelines should be used within the prevailing context of the clinical governance agenda. The recommendations made should not be viewed as rules; rather, they should be taken as statements that assist the clinician in decision-making. They are not restrictive but empowering, providing guidance for the assessment and management of specific disorders/populations. They are written from the viewpoint of minimum best practice as opposed to a perceived idealistic 'gold standard'.

In order to demonstrate where and how the clinical guidelines contribute to the full clinical governance agenda within the Royal College of Speech and Language Therapists, the schematic drawing in Figure 1 places them in context.

The clinical guidelines should be read and interpreted in accordance with the Speech & Language Therapist's clinical judgement. It is recognised that not every recommendation will be clinically appropriate in every case, which is understandable.

It is expected that the Speech & Language Therapist will need to refer to one or more of the clinical guidelines for each individual. For example, for an individual with cerebral palsy the following clinical guidelines are likely to be of relevance:

- Pre-school Children with Communication, Language & Speech Needs
  *or*
- School-aged Children with Speech, Language & Communication Difficulties
  *or*
- Dysarthria
  *and*
- Deafness/Hearing Loss
  *and*
- Clinical Voice Disorders
  *and*
- Disorders of Feeding, Eating, Drinking & Swallowing (Dysphagia)

**Figure 1: Context Guidelines**

**CLINICAL GUIDELINES**
Interpret the evidence base into recommendations for details of clinical management.

**COMMUNICATING QUALITY**
Recommended parameters for the process of service delivery.

**CLINICAL JUDGEMENT & DECISION MAKING WITH THE CLIENT**

**MODEL OF PROFESSIONAL PRACTICE**
Highlights key dimensions of competence.

**CLINICAL COMPETENCIES**
Support the process of giving definition to the individual's scope of clinical practice & responsibility for client care.

## 1.4 ORGANISATION OF THE CLINICAL GUIDELINES

The majority of the clinical guidelines are based upon the presenting disorder or condition, for example, Dysarthria. Two are written with a specific population in mind, for example, 'School-Aged Children with Speech, Language & Communication Difficulties'. It is recognised that this type of division, indeed almost any division, will impose certain restrictions upon the content and this is true in this case. In particular, those clinical guidelines that are population based do not address the specifics of every condition and/or disorder which may arise, but rather provide the minimum best practice for any school-aged child.

The rationale for adopting both approaches, and not concentrating on disorder-based clinical guidelines is that a multitude of guidelines, would be required to cover the vast amount of specific disorders found within pre-school and school-aged populations. In addition, there would be a tremendous amount of overlap, with each clinical guideline most likely supported by little evidence. In particular, disease- or condition-based clinical guidelines benefit from multidisciplinary input.

A key feature of this document is the interrelatedness of one clinical guideline to another, for example, 'Head & Neck Cancer' and 'Disorders of Feeding, Eating, Drinking & Swallowing (Dysphagia)'. Where this is the case, the reader should consult the related guideline or guidelines.

The core guideline must be read in conjunction with each individual clinical guideline. It contains the core clinical recommendations that are pertinent across all populations, disorders and conditions.

## 1.5  FORMAT

The majority of the guidelines follow a consistent format:

- Introduction
- Use of clinical guideline
- Recommendations, accompanied by a rationale and evidence
- Table of evidence

For each recommendation the evidence has been graded according to the methodological design, and after the title of each recommendation this grading is indicated by the letter A, B or C in brackets. The level, eg, I–IV, assigned to each paper is indicated at the end of each reference. An explanation of this system is given in section 3.4.

## 1.6  SERVICE DELIVERY OPTIONS

The delivery style of Speech & Language Therapy provision is dependent upon many factors and Speech & Language Therapists deliver their care using a variety of approaches. No one approach is better than another – rather, it is essential that the chosen approach is appropriate to the client group and prevailing culture of the working environment. The Speech & Language Therapist may work alongside, and collaborate with, other professionals in order to affect the communication and swallowing skills of the individual.

## 1.7  ADULTS WITH LEARNING DISABILITY

This volume does not include a Clinical Guideline for Adults with Learning Disability. A Position Statement on Adults with Learning Disability is available on the RCSLT website, www.rcslt.org.

## 1.8  ACKNOWLEDGEMENTS

The Royal College of Speech and Language Therapists (RCSLT) wishes to express its thanks to all those involved in developing these clinical guidelines.

These guidelines are a reflection of the commitment, energy and progressive thinking which is ingrained within the speech and language therapy profession.

Many colleagues throughout England, Scotland, Northern Ireland, Wales and the Republic of Ireland contributed to the text, each bringing a unique perspective to a document that outlines the expected minimum best standards of practice.

The expert groups and the advisory group have been a source of knowledge and support throughout the project.

Users of speech and language therapy services make a particularly valued contribution to the core clinical guideline.

The support of Dr Marcia Kelson was invaluable for her knowledge and input during the development of the consultation with service users.

A wide range of professional organisations, voluntary agencies and national bodies have added their perspective and given support throughout the project. In particular, we are grateful to the Scottish Intercollegiate Guideline Network and the Royal College of Nursing for permitting the reproduction of their checklists for reviewing of the evidence.

The National Institute of Clinical Excellence's initial financial support was extremely valuable in the development of the project.

Finally, thanks to the staff at the RCSLT. Their organisational skills and patience have ensured that this project has come to fruition.

Sylvia Taylor-Goh
**Editor**

# Methodology

## 2

The project leading to this edition of the *Clinical Guidelines* commenced in 1999. The following outlines the methodology employed.

## 2.1 PROJECT ADVISORY GROUP

A Project Advisory Group was created and the membership represented a wide variety of relevant skills and multi-professional backgrounds. For a variety of reasons, it was not possible for all members of the group to come together when meetings were convened. Discussion with individual members was very helpful and valuable input was received, in particular, with regard to consultation with service users. Some members of the group assisted with the editing process in order to ensure that the final document presented a consistent format across all the clinical guidelines.

## 2.2 IDENTIFICATION AND RECRUITMENT OF 'EXPERTS'

The professional membership of the Royal College of Speech & Language Therapists (RCSLT) was asked to nominate therapists whom they considered to have the relevant skills and knowledge to contribute to this project. Requests were distributed to all RCSLT Clinical Advisors, Special Interest Groups and Institutes of Higher Education. Over 200 names were proposed. Each person nominated was asked to submit his or her curriculum vitae. Not all nominees returned their curriculum vitae and some indicated that they wished to be involved with the project by correspondence only. From this process, between 8 and 15 'experts' were selected per clinical guideline. Expert groups were thus formed. Throughout the project, additional members were asked to join the individual groups if it was felt that there was a gap in the necessary skills and knowledge.

## 2.3 LITERATURE SEARCH

A systematic review of the literature was commissioned and searches using specified key words were carried out. This search was subsequently expanded and further refined. Full details are available in section 3.1.

## 2.4 APPRAISAL OF THE EVIDENCE

In order to ensure a certain level of rigour, each paper was critically appraised. In order to facilitate critical appraisal, seven checklists were provided, each reflecting a different methodological design. During this process, some papers were discarded as they failed to reach the accepted level of rigour required.

For those that were used for the guidelines, the Agency for Healthcare Policy and Research (AHCPR) 1992 system was used to assign levels of evidence and grades to the recommendations.

## 2.5 WRITING OF THE GUIDELINES

Each 'expert group' was invited to meet on at least three occasions during which the bases of the clinical guidelines were created and subsequently amended. At the first meeting, the basic format and content for each clinical guideline was agreed and drawn up. The first draft of all the clinical guidelines was written up and distributed for comment to the expert group members, Chairs of Special Interest Groups, Institutes of Higher Education, RCSLT Clinical Advisors and members of the profession who requested copies. There was an iterative process as members and colleagues reviewed the documents, consulted colleagues and discussed them at meetings. Comments received were integrated as appropriate and this became the second draft. From each expert group a sub-group was identified, who continued to meet and make changes. This iterative process occurred at least three times with each draft of the document.

A final meeting of each expert group was held where the final draft was discussed, amended and agreed.

## 2.6 CONSULTATION WITH THE PROFESSION AND OTHER PROFESSIONAL BODIES

The profession was made aware of the project and kept up to date via the RCSLT monthly publication, *Bulletin*, and was invited to review each draft and make comments. Copies of each draft were also sent to Chairs of Special Interest Groups, RCSLT Clinical Advisors and Institutes of Higher Education. In addition to consulting with the non-Speech & Language Therapy colleagues on the Advisory Group, professional bodies were sent copies of the various draft documents. Copies of the final draft were circulated around a wide group of associated health, social and educational professions.

## 2.7 CONSULTATION WITH VOLUNTARY ORGANISATIONS

There was a substantial amount of consultation with voluntary bodies, primarily with regard to consulting with service users. However, as with the professional bodies, voluntary organisations were sent copies of the various draft documents, and copies of the final draft were widely circulated.

## 2.8 CONSULTATION WITH SERVICE USERS

This was a significant aspect of the project. There were three main approaches to consulting with the users:

- Inviting representatives from voluntary organisations to attend meetings of the expert groups
- Focus groups with service users or their parents/carers
- Postal questionnaire

The information obtained from this consultation was incorporated into each clinical guideline.

# Clinical Guidelines

# 5

# 5.1 Core Clinical Guideline

These recommendations are relevant for every area of speech and language therapy, regardless of clinical speciality. They form the absolute basis of minimum best practice. They are principles that underpin practice and should be read in conjunction with each of the clinical guidelines and the Speech & Language Therapist should exercise clinical judgement with regard to their application.

## Information Prior to First Appointment (C)

Prior to the first appointment the Speech & Language Therapist will have read and be familiar with all available, relevant information regarding the client, including the reason for referral. This may include any assessment of risk undertaken previously in relation to the case.

*Rationale*
A variety of information may be available to the clinician prior to the first appointment – including other professionals' opinions, the reason for referral, and certain biographical/case-history details. In order to present a professional impression and to engender confidence in the health-care system as a whole, it is important that preparation for the first appointment is complete. This enables the effective use of the consultation time without necessitating the individual's repetition of previously known information. It also prepares the Speech & Language Therapist to deal with any particular areas of risk or concern.

*Evidence*
Professional consensus.

## Clinical History Taking (C)

A case history must always be taken, in order for the Speech & Language Therapist to establish a complete picture of the individual, their communication disorder and the environments in which they function. Consideration must be given to each of the following areas (although some may not be applicable for every individual):

## COMMUNICATION
- Comprehension/receptive skills
- History of language development
- Expressive language skills
- Fluency
- Hearing evaluation results
- Interaction
- Listening and attention skills
- Languages used or exposed to regularly
- Non-verbal communication skills
- Oromotor skills
- Preferred mode of communication, eg, gestural, cued speech, sign, writing
- Pre-morbid language skills
- Prosody
- Resonance
- Respiratory status
- Speech
- Use of augmentative/alternative communication
- Voice

## EATING AND DRINKING
- Feeding history and current status
- Hydration level
- Nutritional status
- Oromotor functioning
- Respiratory status

## HOME AND FAMILY
- Activities of daily living
- Family history, especially of stammering, learning or language difficulties
- Cultural background
- Parental/carer concerns

## PERSONAL
- Activities of daily living
- Cognitive skills
- Confidence
- Insight
- Perception of the difficulty
- Memory skills
- Presence of distress and emotional well-being

## SOCIAL

- Activities of daily living
- Current social circumstances
- Play skills

## EDUCATIONAL

- Activities of daily living
- Educational history
- Concerns of teaching staff
- Literacy skills
- Phonological awareness skills

## EMPLOYMENT

- Activities of daily living
- Employment history

## MEDICAL/PHYSICAL

- Concurrent or relevant investigations
- Current psychiatric state
- Developmental history, including general milestones
- Etiological information
- Hospitalisations
- Motor skills
- Pre-natal history
- Psychiatric history
- Surgical status
- Vision

### Rationale

Taking a clinical history gives the individual the opportunity to introduce the situation from their own point of view. It provides information about the individual, their preferences and interests, their perception of their difficulties and areas of concern. It gives a picture of the individual as a whole, including the areas where communication skills are important – building a picture of strengths, weaknesses and areas of need. How the difficulties are perceived by the client and their family is important, and has been shown to be an accurate indicator of a need for intervention. It also gives an indication of the motivation and commitment to change.

A wide range of information is vital for accurate clinical decision-making – firstly as a basis for assessment and hypothesis formulation, and secondly in relation to the appropriateness, method and areas of intervention.

It is important to gain the individual's perspective on how the disorder affects all aspects of their life – enabling the therapist to undertake a comprehensive approach to management.

### Evidence
Professional consensus.

### Assessment (B)

As a framework for practice, the World Health Organisation (WHO) classification system (ICIDH-2) is a helpful model.[1] Therefore, for each individual, assessment must take into account the following:

1. *Body functions and structures:* The relevant physiological and psychological body functions and anatomic structures, including level of any impairment.

2. *Activity (person as a whole in a uniform level – individual level):* The communicative and/or eating and drinking skills of the individual, identifying their strengths, needs and difficulties.

3. *Participation (person in current environment – societal level):* The individual's use of functional skills in communication/eating and drinking within the current and likely environments (including different settings, routines and relationships) and the opportunities and need for communication use in everyday life.

4. *Contextual factors (environmental and personal factors):* The individual's (and/or carer/significant other's, where appropriate) perception of the impact of the disorder on their life; the physical, social and attitudinal environment in which people live; personal factors such as age, race, gender, educational background and lifestyle.

### Rationale

The aim of assessment is to form a complete picture of the individual, their skills (including strengths and weaknesses), the activities they undertake, and the areas of participation in life that are impaired by their difficulty. The nature of

---

1 *International Classification of Functioning, Disability and Health (ICIDH-2)*, World Health Organisation, 2001 http://www.who.int/classification/icf/

communication requires that the environment and communication partners are a part of this process, having a significant effect on the communicative effectiveness of the individual concerned. Frequently these people will be involved (with the individual's consent) in the ongoing work of therapy, and their potential for this should also be evaluated.

A detailed assessment should provide information to enable diagnosis of a speech and language disorder, and to formulate a hypothesis relating to the disorder and its treatment. It should also contribute significantly to any discussion related to the formulation of treatment goals, should therapy commence.

The assessment should (at least in part) contribute to a measurable baseline for treatment against which the outcome of any intervention can be measured.

*Evidence*
- Raaijmakers MF, Dekker J, Dejonckere PH & Zee J van der (1995) Evidence Level III
- Raaijmakers MF, Dekker J & Dejonckere PH (1998) Evidence Level III

## Assessment and Bilingualism (B)

1  Assessment procedures should aim to examine skills in all languages.

2  Assessments should be carefully matched both to the language/dialect and cultural and religious profile of the client.

3  Assessment of bilingual children should include observation in a variety of social settings.

4  Assessment should take a holistic view of the individual's social communication. In addition to a case history, a language usage profile should be created. This will include information on:
   - The language code(s) understood and used by the client, including specific information on dialects.
   - The length of time these languages have been used by the client.
   - The language code(s) understood and used by the client's family, friends and social circle.
   - The written language(s) the client understands/uses.
   - The communicative context — places where specific language(s) are used.
   - The attitudes the client has to their language(s).
   - The attitudes the carer(s) have to the client's languages (where applicable).

*Rationale*

Liaison with bilingual personnel will assist the Speech & Language Therapist in differentiating linguistic and cultural diversity from disorder.

Assessment of the individual's complete communication system will prevent confusion of normal bilingual language acquisition with communication disorders in bilingual children.

Cultural and linguistic bias have in the past led to the misdiagnosis of language and learning difficulties in bilingual populations. Bilingual children from ethnic minority populations may be unfamiliar with assessment procedures, may expect to speak a certain language in one situation and may respond only minimally to adult questions.

Assessment of an adult's complete communication system will identify which elements are language specific and which elements are affected across the whole system. Informed therapy targets can then be devised.

Increasing evidence is emerging that, for phonological disorders, the central underlying disorder may be expressed as differing surface patterns for each language.

Reference should be made to 'Good practise for Speech & Language Therapists working with clients from linguistic minority communities' (RCSLT, 1998).

*Evidence*
- Holm A, Dodd B, Stow C & Pert S (1999) Evidence Level III
- De Houwer A (1999) Evidence Level IV

## Differential Diagnosis (C)

Following initial assessment, a differential diagnosis of communication, feeding, eating, drinking and swallowing

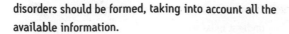

disorders should be formed, taking into account all the available information.

*Rationale*
There should be a clear working hypothesis or diagnosis of the communication and/or eating and drinking disorder which will facilitate the planning of intervention, and give an indication of the prognosis. This diagnosis will enable literature/evidence supporting effective treatment to be accessed, as well as enabling the individual and/or carers to access information and support relating to the disorder as appropriate.

*Evidence*
Professional consensus.

## Working in Partnership (B)

- A clear explanation of the behaviour/disorder will be offered to the individual and their family, with written information to reinforce this.
- There will be sharing of assessment findings with other relevant professionals (subject to the individual's consent).
- There will be sharing of assessment findings with the individual (and carers where appropriate) in a manner which facilitates understanding, discussion and joint decision-making.
- Decisions relating to the need, appropriateness, type, timing and frequency of intervention should be made in consultation with the individual, their carer and other professionals involved in their care.
- A bilingual professional will be central to the assessment and management of a bilingual individual. Interpreters or co-workers should be matched to the individual as closely as possible, with consideration given to language/dialect, gender, national heritage and religion. Where possible, the same interpreter or co-worker should be involved throughout the therapy process to ensure smooth continuity of care. Relatives and friends should not be encouraged to take the role of formal interpreters as this may compromise confidentiality; place undue stress on younger family members; or place unreasonable linguistic and emotional demands on a person close to the individual. Planning time and de-briefing time must be arranged

with the interpreter/co-worker to review the aims and outcomes of the session.

*Rationale*
The sharing of information and assessment findings is important to developing partnership with the individual and/or their carer, in order to develop understanding and joint decision-making. It has been demonstrated that better outcomes are achieved where there is openness of information and a willingness to actively involve the individual in management decisions. With bilingual relatives, the key difference between them and the role of the bilingual personnel is that their role is supportive rather than primary.

*Evidence*
- Glogowska M, Campbell R, Peters T J, Roulstone S & Enderby P ( 2001) Evidence Level III
- Langhorne P & Pollock A (2002) Evidence Level III
- Pollack MR & Disler PB (2002) Evidence Level IV

## Timing of Intervention

Timing of intervention should be determined by an evaluation of the individual's readiness and ability to change (or the potential to change the environment). This should also take into account the individual's motivation to change and the level of support available.

*Rationale*
An individual's ability to respond to therapy can be affected by many factors, both internal and external, and it is important to give consideration to these during the period of care.

*Evidence*
Please refer to individual clinical guidelines for specific evidence.

## Hypothesis-driven Management (C)

Management will be planned, based on the following:

- Results of information gathering/assessment and consequent hypothesis formation.
- Understanding of the theoretical frameworks relevant to the behaviour/disorder.

- Knowledge of the different approaches to intervention/management.

*Rationale*
The Speech & Language Therapist should plan management from a hypothesis-driven model. A clear and detailed hypothesis of the underlying barriers to effective communication should be made explicit. Progress can then be measured against the hypothesis.

*Evidence*
Professional consensus.

## Management Planning and Goal Setting (C)

A management plan, with timescales, will be drawn up in consultation with the individual. It will be shared with their carer and other professionals and will detail the aims, objectives and expectations of intervention/management.

Goals should be identified relating to the individual's activity, participation and well-being.

*Rationale*
Discussion with service users indicates that the therapeutic relationship is more effective when there is openness of information and willingness to actively involve the family/individual in management decisions.

*Evidence*
- John A (1998) Evidence Level IV

## Multidisciplinary Team-working

The Speech & Language Therapist will work as a core member of the multi- or interdisciplinary team. The composition of the team is likely to vary across specialities.

*Rationale*
The multidisciplinary management of individuals ensures a timely, efficient, integrated and holistic period of care.

*Evidence*
Please refer to individual clinical guidelines for specific evidence.

## Contribution to Assessment of Capacity (C)

The Speech & Language Therapist is in a position to provide clinical expertise by assessing the language of an individual, which can contribute to a team decision regarding their capacity. The Speech & Language Therapist's assessment may highlight requirements for further assessment from other professionals.

The Speech & Language Therapist's assessment should include:

- Assessment of comprehension of verbal information of differing complexity.
- The individual's ability to retain information for sufficient time to process the information.
- The individual's ability to express themselves sufficiently.
- The individual's ability to evaluate information in order to understand the consequences of action/lack of action.

*Rationale*
Assessment of capacity is based upon input from the relevant multidisciplinary team members. The Speech & Language Therapist can assist in this process by providing the information as outlined in the recommendation.

*Evidence*
Professional consensus.

## Cross-agency Working (C)

Where intervention is undertaken across agencies (eg, into education or social services settings) it will, where possible, be tailored for delivery within the culture/working practices of that environment/organisation.

Where intervention tasks are delegated to speech and language therapy assistants, other team members, parents or carers, it is the Speech & Language Therapist's responsibility to ensure that person has the competence to carry out the required task, understands their limitations and any risks, and that there is clear guidance for ongoing

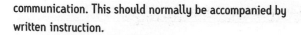

communication. **This should normally be accompanied by written instruction.**

*Rationale*
A clear link from assessment, through diagnosis, to planning of intervention ensures that intervention is client-centred and tailored to maximise the individual's potential.

A clear negotiated goal-setting process ensures clear aims of therapy, which are understood by all those involved. This facilitates joint working, building mutual trust and respect, and ensures an integrated comprehensive and holistic approach to the individual's care. It facilitates shared decision-making, improves outcomes of care, and encourages client satisfaction through full involvement in the programme of care. Agreed aims and involvement of carers allows carry-over of therapeutic intervention into other settings – a vital part of effecting change in communicative patterns.

*Evidence*
Professional consensus.

## Reflective Practice (C)

**Management aims and objectives must be reviewed regularly and frequently. If anticipated progress is not achieved the therapeutic intervention should be reviewed.**

*Rationale*
In order be effective and efficacious, the Speech & Language Therapist needs to respond to the individual's needs appropriately.

*Evidence*
Professional consensus.

## Evaluation of Outcome (C)

**Outcomes of therapy should be routinely measured, reflecting the range of interventions delivered and the aims agreed for therapy.**

*Rationale*
Monitoring of progress is important in establishing the effectiveness of intervention – enabling goals to be adjusted

or the approach to be modified in order to maximise therapeutic gain.

Lack of change may be an indicator of one of a variety of barriers, including incorrect diagnosis/hypothesis, lack of motivation or readiness to change, or poor support for the programme of intervention. These issues must be identified and addressed for successful intervention to be achieved.

Monitoring of progress encourages clinicians to reflect and revise their own intervention and to learn from their experience, as well as facilitating the ongoing involvement of the client in therapy through honest feedback on progress and achievement.

It is through this ongoing monitoring that decisions can be made regarding the achievement of goals, the potential for further improvement, and the appropriate and timely closure of episodes of care.

*Evidence*
Professional consensus.

## Themes Identified from the Consultation with Service Users

This was a significant aspect of the project. There were three main approaches to consulting with the users:

- Inviting representatives from voluntary organisations to attend meetings of the expert groups.
- Focus groups with service users or their parents/carers.
- Postal questionnaire.

The following themes are based upon a sample of individuals' experiences and their perception of what a Speech and Language Therapy Service should offer. Full details of the process undertaken are outlined in the 'Consultation with Service Users', section 4.

- Familiarity with client details and relevant information prior to initial appointment.
- Provision of information
  - The normal process of speech and language development.
  - Provision of a working diagnosis to aid the individual/ parent/carer in accessing relevant information.
- Working in partnership with the Speech & Language Therapist.

# 5.2 Pre-school Children with Communication, Language & Speech Needs

## Introduction

This guideline addresses the speech and language therapy management practice for children from birth to full-time school entry. Children may be preverbal and/or have difficulty with communication, language, fluency and speech. The range, complexity and severity of the underlying impairments of these children will vary and will include the full range of intellectual and physical abilities. The effect of a child's communication, language and speech impairment will impact on current and future functioning. It is not limited to the child involved, since for parents/carers the presence of speech and/or language difficulties in their child is probably one of the most common single causes of concern about child development.

Included within this group will be the very young infant (or very sick infant or young child) for whom issues of speech and language therapy management will mainly concern feeding and/or the impact of medical, neurological and sensory disorders or structural abnormality. In these circumstances the role of the Speech & Language Therapist will be to liaise, inform, support and, if possible, lessen the impact of the impairment by their interventions.

This period of life is the time of greatest developmental change and developmental vulnerability. Intervention needs to take account of these changes and adapt accordingly. The role of the primary carers as the most influential factors in the child's world will influence intervention.

The Speech & Language Therapist needs to be aware, and to ensure that others are also aware, of the child's changing sensory/medical/psychological status and the impact that this may have on the ability to communicate.

## Using the Guideline

This guideline addresses the speech and language therapy management practice for children from birth to full-time school entry and not the knowledge and skills needed by the Speech & Language Therapist working with this client population. Such skills are outlined in the parallel 'Underpinning knowledge and skills framework' – a product of the Competencies Project – and should be read in conjunction with this and with *Communicating Quality*.

This guideline should be read alongside the 'Core Guideline' and in combination with any of the following that may be relevant:

- Aphasia
- Autistic Spectrum Disorders
- Cleft Palate & Velopharyngeal Abnormalities
- Clinical Voice Disorders
- Deafness/Hearing Loss
- Disorders of Feeding, Eating, Drinking & Swallowing (Dysphagia)
- Disorders of Fluency
- Disorders of Mental Health & Dementia
- Dysarthria
- Head & Neck Cancer
- School-aged Children with Speech, Language & Communication Difficulties

## ASSESSMENT

### Assessment (B)

Assessment will include a view of the whole child whatever their mode of production (speech, sign, AAC) and their interaction with primary carers and educators in a range of settings and across time. Where appropriate to age and circumstances, this will also include the child's peers and siblings.

A combination of structured observation and formal assessment will take into account the following:

## 1 Communication skills

A full profile of the effectiveness of the child's communication skills within the differing environments in collaboration with all significant others will include:

- The communicative skills of the child – strengths, needs and opportunities;
- Preferred modality or modalities of communication;
- The use of communication;
- The impact of the environment upon communication;
- An identification of any disadvantageous or helpful factors within the environment;
- The impact of the child's communication within the environment;
- The opportunities and need for functional communication;
- The impact of any other concomitant disorders.

## 2 Interaction

Consideration will be taken of the development from pre-intentionality to intentionality, the quality and the sustainedness of the child's interactions, and the emergence of joint attention and declarative interaction.

## 3 Attention

Consideration will be taken of the development from distractibility, through single channelled attention, to a more flexible pattern of sustained attention, both auditory and visual.

## 4 Object Concept

Consideration will be taken of the development of play from people-centred, through object-centred, to imaginative/social.

## 5 Comprehension

Consideration will be taken of the development from emotional atunement, through recognition of patterns of routine, situation and associated language, to true verbal comprehension.

## 6 Expression

Consideration will be taken of the development of the form, content and use of expressive skills from preverbal to narrative.

## 7 Oromotor Structure and Function

Consideration will be taken of the development of oromotor structure and function.

## 8 Phonology

Consideration will be taken of the development of the child's phonological processes and production of speech or sign.

*Rationale*
Impairment in any of the above impedes the development of effective communication, language and/or speech.

*Evidence*
- Law J, Boyle J, Harris F, Harkness A & Nye C (1998) Evidence Level IIa
- Gathercole S, Willis C & Bradley A (1992) Evidence Level III
- Gathercole S & Adams AM (1993) Evidence Level III
- Dockrell JE & Messer D (1998) Evidence Level III
- Bloom L & Lahey M (1978) Evidence Level IV
- Goldin-Meadow S (1998) Evidence Level IV
- Parkinson A & Pate S (2000) Evidence Level IV

## Differential Diagnosis (C)

Differential diagnosis(es) will be made on the basis of ongoing assessments and management.

*Rationale*
The purpose of differential diagnosis is to identify other associated disorders which may be pervasive in order to:

- Target intervention appropriately
- Inform parents
- Ensure access to full and appropriate resources and services.

*Evidence*
Professional consensus.

### Evenness of Development (C)

An evaluation will be made of the evenness of the child's communicative developmental profile in comparison with their overall development.

*Rationale*
Children's communication, language and speech are expected to be in line with general cognitive development. Intervention will be more effectively targeted if this is recognised.

*Evidence*
- Bloom L & Lahey M (1978) Evidence Level IV
- Sheridan MD, Frost M & Sharma A (1997) Evidence Level IV

## MANAGEMENT

In the management of the pre-school child, collaboration with the primary carers and educators in the context of the child's environment, culture and language is paramount.

### Collaborative Working (B)

The clinician will work collaboratively within the multi-agency/disciplinary team, recognising the skills and contribution to a child's communication development offered by the range of other agencies.

*Rationale*
If a child of such a young age has been identified as having a communication impairment of any type then it is important to consider other possible difficulties, and the reasons/aetiology may be associated with social and emotional factors. It is in the best interests of the child and the family that the wider context is considered and supported. Work from other professionals and support workers to alter support systems or parental skills, and to meet the wider needs of the family, may be more effective in improving the child's attainments in all of its development than the change that a Speech & Language Therapist can effect alone.

*Evidence*
- Glogowska M & Campbell R (2000) Evidence Level III

### Management Approaches

There are a variety of possible approaches to management that may be used concurrently. Their use will be continuously reappraised during the management process. Decisions governing their use will be influenced by the assessment of the child and consideration of the following factors:
- The chronological age and developmental level of the child.
- Any medical diagnosis and prognosis for the child.
- The cultural, language, social and emotional environments of the child.
- The emotional factors influencing the child.
- The motivation and capacity of the carers to engage in facilitation of the child's communication development.
- The motivation and capacity of the child to engage in therapy.

These approaches are:

### 1 Health Promotion/Prevention of Future Difficulties (A)

- Training of and advice to referral agencies and parent/carer.
- Production and dissemination of information.

*Rationale*
A young child's difficulties may be in the context of wider developmental problems, and the child may live in a family or community where the chances of other children having similar difficulties are higher than the average. In these circumstances the child's problems will not be alleviated without attention being paid to the knowledge and support of those around them. The effect of such intervention may prevent further developmental disadvantages, not only for this child, but also for other children in contact with those personally and professionally involved.

*Evidence*
- Feldman MA, Sparks B & Case L (1993) Evidence Level Ib
- Girolametto L, Pearce PS & Weitzman E (1996) Evidence Level Ib

- Gibbard D (1994) Evidence Level Ib
- Law J, Boyle J, Harris F, Harkness A & Nye C (1998) Evidence Level IIa
- Barber M, Farrell P & Parkinson G (2001) Evidence Level IV

## 2 Maximising Communication Environments to Increase Potential for Participation and Activity

This may occur by:
- Training of parents/carers in lessening the effect of potential distractors.
- Training of parents/carers in enabling development of attention and listening.
- Training of parents/carers in selection and use of appropriate toys and activities.
- Training of parents/carers in enabling development of sound awareness, discrimination.

*Rationale*

Much is known about the normal acquisition of communication, language and speech, and the influence of the family and primary carers. Therapists should ensure that similar opportunities are available for children with impairments in these areas. Parents, carers and educators may need training to tailor interaction to the specific developmental and personality needs of each child.

*Evidence*
- Peterson C, Jesso B & McCabe A (1999) Evidence Level Ib
- Coulter L & Gallagher C (2001) Evidence Level III

## 3 Reduce Impact of Impairment by (C)

- Selection of appropriate alternative or augmentative communication (AAC) system(s) in close cooperation with parents/carers.
- Training of parents/carers in the use of selected AAC.
- Collaboration with other involved allied health professions in adapting equipment to enable ease of access to selected AAC.

*Rationale*

Communication impairment in young children impacts on their experiences of interaction, and affects their learning. The introduction of AAC systems, such as signing, enables children to receive and use communication and language. This can moderate the skewing effect on development and may prevent difficulties in later skills acquisition.

*Evidence*
Professional consensus.

## 4 Improve the Child's Level of Functioning by (A)

- Implementing therapy aimed at fostering development of age-appropriate communication skills.
- Implementing therapy aimed at fostering development of age/ability-appropriate language comprehension.
- Implementing therapy aimed at fostering development of age/ability-appropriate language use.
- Implementing therapy aimed at fostering development of age/ability-appropriate phonology.

All of these can be delivered in group settings, either speech and language therapy specific or multidisciplinary/agency settings.

*Rationale*

Intervention which addresses skill acquisition in the areas of interaction, attention, play, comprehension and expression will support development of an even profile. The acquisition of key developmental skills not only supports the later development of communication, language and speech but also enhances emotional, social and academic development.

*Evidence*
- Peterson C, Jesso B & McCabe A (1999) Evidence Level Ib
- Robertson SB & Weismer SE (1999) Evidence Level Ib
- Glogowska M, Roulstone S, Enderby P & Peters TJ (2000) Evidence Level Ib
- Girolametto LE (1988) Evidence Level IIa
- Hesketh A, Adams C, Nightingale C & Hall R (2000) Evidence Level III

### Themes Identified from the Consultation with Service Users

This was a significant aspect of the project. There were three main approaches to consulting with the users:

- Inviting representatives from voluntary organisations to attend meetings of the expert groups.
- Focus groups with service users or their parents/carers.
- Postal questionnaire.

The following themes are based upon a sample of individuals' experiences and their perception of what a speech and language therapy service should offer. Full details of the process undertaken are outlined in the 'Consultation with Service Users' section.

- Collaborative working
  - Required between all the disciplines involved.
- Provision of information
  - The normal process of speech and language development.
  - General strategies that enhance communication.
  - Specific strategies that form part of the therapeutic programme.

# 5.3 School-aged Children with Speech, Language & Communication Difficulties

## Introduction

This guideline refers to all school-age children who have difficulty with speech, language, disorders of fluency and communication. These children will attend a variety of educational placements. They will present with a range of difficulties and levels of severity. The underlying causes of the communication difficulties found within this population are many and may include delayed development, genetic, environmental, acquired and congenital disorders.

School-based learning is a major and fundamental part of the school-aged child's life, and communication is intrinsic to learning and accessing the curriculum. Assessment and management must take into account children's life in school and their ability to access and learn from the curriculum. In order to assess these areas for the individual child, enabling access may mean making adaptations to the linguistic, physical, organisational, social and psychological environment, both in school and out. Specific consideration should be given to relevant legislation, eg, The Code of Practice, National Curriculum and others.

Although the recommendations of this guideline are divided into four main headings, it is important to recognise that language issues underlying the entire school curriculum need to be addressed.

The four main areas are:

- Recommendations for all children
- Communication
- Language
- Phonology and articulation

## Using the Guideline

This guideline addresses the speech and language therapy management practice for school-aged children and not the knowledge and skills needed by the Speech & Language

Therapist working with this client population. Such skills are outlined in the parallel 'Underpinning knowledge and skills framework' – a product of the Competencies Project – and should be read in conjunction with this and with *Communicating Quality*.

This guideline should be read alongside the 'Core Guideline' and in combination with any of the following that may be relevant.

- Aphasia
- Autistic Spectrum Disorders
- Cleft Palate & Velopharyngeal Abnormalities
- Clinical Voice Disorders
- Deafness/Hearing Loss
- Disorders of Fluency
- Disorders of Feeding, Eating, Drinking & Swallowing (Dysphagia)
- Disorders of Mental Health & Dementia
- Dysarthria
- Head & Neck Cancer
- Pre-school Children with Communication, Language & Speech Needs

## RECOMMENDATIONS FOR ALL CHILDREN

### 1 Collaboration (B)

Collaboration should, as far as possible, reflect a shared perspective and should build, wherever possible, mutual understanding and agreement.

At a minimum, this will mean:

- Where the service is school-based (which should be the primary choice) the Speech & Language Therapist will seek information from, and provide information to, the family. The Therapist will also plan the child's management jointly with the educational professionals.

■ Where the service is not school-based, the Speech & Language Therapist will seek information from, and provide information to, the school.

It is recommended that the service should be school-based and a non-school based service should not be viewed as equal.

Where a Statement of Special Educational Needs exists, the Speech & Language Therapist will contribute to Individualised Education Plans (IEPs) and target setting, and will consider the speech, language and communication needs of the child within the context of the curriculum.

*Rationale*
Ensures that goals are identified and that any gains impact upon the child's learning in a wide context.

*Evidence*
■ Law J, Lindsay G, Peacey N, Gascoigne M, Soloff N, Radford J, Band S & Fitzgerald L (2000) Evidence Level III
■ Reid J, Millar S, Tait L, Donaldson M, Dean EC, Thomson GOB & Grieve R (1996) Evidence Level III

## 2 Assessment (B)

Communication ability in a range of contexts should always be addressed. However, it may not be necessary in every case to assess phonology, articulation and language.

*Rationale*
Communication ability dictates the extent to which the individual child can participate in the wider school and social environment. This ability cannot be predicted solely from direct assessment of phonology, articulation and/or language, therefore the impact of the child's speech, language and communication difficulties on learning and socialisation must always be considered. During the course of the assessment information should be gathered from education professionals regarding the child's functioning in school and their ability to access the curriculum.

*Evidence*
■ Law J, Lindsay G, Peacey N, Gascoigne M, Soloff N, Radford J, Band J & Fitzgerald L, (2000) Evidence Level III

## 3 Management (B)

The Speech & Language Therapist will work collaboratively within the multi-agency/disciplinary team, with parents and carers, recognising the skills and contribution to a child's communication development offered by the range of other agencies/opinions.

There are a variety of possible approaches to management that may be used concurrently. Their use will be continuously reappraised during the management process. Decisions governing their use will be influenced by the assessment of the child and consideration of the following factors:

■ The chronological age and developmental level of the child.
■ Any medical diagnosis and prognosis for the child.
■ The cultural, language, social and emotional environments of the child.
■ The emotional factors influencing the child.
■ The motivation and capacity of the carers to engage in facilitation of the child's communication development.
■ The motivation and capacity of the child to engage in therapy.

*Rationale*
Working collaboratively will ensure that the child's needs are being met in a holistic manner and that communication is perceived as fundamental to the child's well-being.

*Evidence*
■ Doherty KM & Masters R (1996) Evidence Level III

## ASSESSMENT OF COMMUNICATION

## 1 Communication Ability (C)

Assessment of communication will give consideration to the following areas:

■ Non-verbal communication
■ Conversation and discourse
■ The relation of language to context
■ Use of the social rules of communication

■ Strategies the child uses to compensate for linguistic or communicative deficits

Care must be taken to elicit information from all relevant others and to cover a range of contexts and different modalities, eg, signing, symbols, writing and communication aids.

*Rationale*
Communication includes social, cognitive and linguistic components. Therefore all these areas need to be considered.

*Evidence*
Professional consensus.

## 2  Environmental Factors (C)

Assessment of the school environment will consider the following aspects:

■ Physical – demarcation of areas within the classroom and organisation of available space and positioning of the child.
■ Social – ratio of staff to children and number of children in class.
■ Sensory – sources of visual and auditory distraction, acoustic environment and lighting.
■ Linguistic – classroom language and ease of access to the curriculum.
■ Organisation of the school day.
■ The type of educational placement and the strengths of other staff in the placement to meet the specific needs of the child.

*Rationale*
Such assessment will identify the management needs of the child within the classroom. Modification of the environment and thereby removal or reduction of barriers can impact on the child's communicative potential.

*Evidence*
■ Picard M & Bradley JS (2001) Evidence Level IV

## MANAGEMENT OF COMMUNICATION

### 1  Communication Ability (C)

Consideration will be given to developing communication skills and/or alternative strategies to support learning and socialisation within an appropriate context that is relevant to the child's everyday experience.

*Rationale*
It is important to foster the application of knowledge and skills in meaningful social exchanges.

*Evidence*
Professional consensus.

### 2  Modification of the Environment (C)

The Speech & Language Therapist will work with others to adapt the physical, social, sensory and linguistic components of the environment, and to look at the demands being placed on the child in order to maximise successful communication and learning.

*Rationale*
Ensures removal or reduction of barriers to communication.

*Evidence*
■ Picard M & Bradley JS (2001) Evidence Level IV

## ASSESSMENT OF LANGUAGE

### Assessment (C)

The Speech & Language Therapist will need to assess comprehension and expression of language including grammar and vocabulary. A wide range of assessment procedures are available and the Speech & Language Therapist should select from these, bearing in mind the child's cognitive, physical and perceptual abilities. A combination of formal and informal procedures will be used to assess the impact of any difficulties on the child's learning and socialisation.

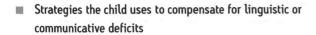

*Rationale*
- Grammar and vocabulary form the core components of language.
- Cognitive and/or perceptual difficulties may prejudice performance and therefore clinical interpretation.
- There is evidence that reliance on formal testing in these areas provides an incomplete or inaccurate profile.

*Evidence*
Professional consensus.

## MANAGEMENT OF LANGUAGE

Language is central to the learning process. It is the main tool for teaching and learning. The role of the Speech & Language Therapist is to help children become active participants in their learning, and to use language effectively. The purpose of speech and language therapy involvement is to facilitate the acquisition and maintenance of new speech and language skills in order to support the learning process. Acquiring effective spoken language involves the development of a range of processing skills, which utilises multi-sensory information, and the development of phonology and articulation.

To understand spoken language the typically developing child will perceive speech; understand word meaning; have grammatical knowledge; understand sentences in real time; integrate language and context; and develop an understanding of the social aspects of language. This will include the use of verbal and non-verbal cues such as body language and intonation. A Speech & Language Therapist may work on facilitating development of language skills in any of these areas. Collaborating with school staff in teaching strategies to manage communication needs will reduce the impact of the language difficulties on both the child's learning and their access to the curriculum. A range of strategies is available to the Speech & Language Therapist, including the use of visual supports such as objects of reference, photographs, gesture, signs and symbols. School-aged children are expected to access the curriculum via the written word. The Speech & Language Therapist should consider the impact of a child's ability to develop and understand written language as part of their intervention strategies. This may include working collaboratively on phonological awareness, sentence formulation and written grammatical conventions.

### Speech Perception (B)

Speech perception is the ability to process the sounds that are heard, discriminate the sounds accurately and interpret them correctly. The Speech & Language Therapist should consider the child's ability to process speech as a critical skill for speech and language development.

*Rationale*
To lay down an accurate representation of the sequence of sounds to enable intelligible speech, word learning, expressive language and literacy skills. Some children with normal hearing acuity may be unable to accurately process speech and may therefore learn words inaccurately.

*Evidence*
- Tallal P, Stark RE & Mellits ED (1985) Evidence Level IIa

### Vocabulary (B)

Vocabulary knowledge should be considered in terms of conceptual, semantic and phonological knowledge. This applies to all parts of speech: nouns, adjectives and especially verbs. The vocabulary required to access the curriculum should be considered; both core vocabulary and vocabulary specific to subject areas or topics. It may be necessary to target understanding of basic concepts that may underpin this vocabulary. The child should be given access to strategies for learning and recalling words, including signing (both for whole words and for phonology) and memory aids.

*Rationale*
- Difficulties with vocabulary are manifest at many different levels: understanding of the concepts, semantic connections between items, and storage and retrieval of phonological representations.
- Difficulties with verbs could lead to further difficulties with grammar, as sentences are constructed around verbs.
- Children need to access the curriculum to the best of their ability in order to improve long-term educational outcomes.
- Children need to become independent learners as vocabulary continues to be acquired throughout life.

*Evidence*
- Constable AJ, Stackhouse J & Wells B (1997) Evidence Level III
- Easton C, Sheach S & Easton S (1997) Evidence Level III
- Hyde-Wright S, Gorrie B, Haynes C & Shipman A (1993a) Evidence Level III

## Grammar (B)

Both comprehension and production should be considered for all areas of grammar. Particular attention should be paid to the following:

- Word order
- Argument structure
- Morphology, especially tense and aspect inflections
- Syntactic movement, especially passives and 'wh' questions
- Coordinating and subordinating conjunctions
- Expanded noun phrases

Intervention should always establish comprehension of structures before or in conjunction with work on production. Correct syntactic rules should also be established. A Speech & Language Therapist may work on developing the skills in these areas using supports such as colour and shape coding.

The Speech & Language Therapist may also work on teaching strategies to overcome skill deficits and support teaching staff in reducing the impact of a child's difficulties with comprehension and expression of language on the child's access to the curriculum. The therapist should ensure that other symbolic forms of communication (signs, objects of reference, photographs, symbols and communication aids) are used appropriately to improve comprehension and expression where necessary.

*Rationale*
- Any forms produced by a child that are not comprehended by the same child are likely to be based on incorrect rules.
- Intervention needs to be structured for the individual child, and modification of intervention requires a good understanding of the underlying rules by the therapist.
- Children require strategies to access the curriculum both in written and oral forms to the best of their ability.

*Evidence*
- Hirschman M (2000) Evidence Level IIa
- Ebbels S & Lely H van der (2001) Evidence Level III
- Bryan A (1997) Evidence Level IV

## Narrative Structure (B)

Children who struggle with the process of developing expressive language frequently have problems acquiring literacy skills and require specific teaching. The Speech & Language Therapist should target oral language skills as a prerequisite to the development of written narrative skills.

Methods to be used by the Speech & Language Therapist can include:

- Explicit teaching of story grammar using story maps
- Retelling
- Role play
- Close activities using story picture cards
- Story frameworks
- Use of discourse in giving coherent accounts in everyday situations.

*Rationale*
The Framework for Teaching for the National Literacy Strategy (NLS) provides an explicit developmental model for the teaching of written language acquisition and it assumes that the child has oral language competency. Text-level working in the NLS covers aspects of narrative such as:

- Sequencing
- Story setting
- Character descriptions and feelings
- Problem-solving
- Using language to reason
- Figurative language
- Different genres – processes include describe, explain, instruct, argue, narrate.

The definition of text in the NLS is 'language organised to communicate – includes written, spoken to electronic forms'. The term 'narrative' can be interpreted as 'story' or can be referred to as a type of text. Narrative and conversational forms share many similarities but there are differences. Narratives have an orderly

presentation of events with a logical resolution. As children progress through school, the written word increasingly becomes their primary means of learning. Access to written language in turn influences spoken language by building up knowledge of vocabulary, concepts and complex sentence structures.

*Evidence*
- Camarata SM, Nelson K & Camarata M (1994) Evidence Level III
- Catts H & Kamhi A (1999) Evidence Level IV
- Grove N (1998) Evidence Level IV

## Understanding of connected speech/narrative (B)

The Speech & Language Therapist will need to consider the child's ability to understand connected speech and oral narratives, and devise ways to enable them to interpret correctly.

*Rationale*
- Strong implications for emergent literacy (in pre-school population).
- Link to literacy and other areas of language development.
- Importance for conversational skills/life skills.
- Ability to use narrative may be related to learning and academic success.

*Evidence*
- Bishop DV & Adams C (1992) Evidence Level IIa
- McFadden TU & Gillam RB (1996) Evidence Level III
- Hayward D & Schneider P (2000) Evidence Level III

## Understanding of figurative language (B)

Strategies should be employed to develop the child's skills at interpreting figurative language (both spoken and written) as this forms a substantial part of understanding language.

*Rationale*
Children with language impairments find understanding this form of language difficult and need specific help in learning to interpret and use this sort of language.

*Evidence*
- Kerbel D & Grunwell P (1998) Evidence Level IIa

## Understanding of Social Aspects of Language (B)

Children with language impairments have difficulties interpreting non-verbal communication and verbal language in social contexts. The Speech & Language Therapist should provide strategies to facilitate the child's understanding of social aspects of language.

*Rationale*
Children with language difficulties, particularly those with pragmatic impairments, do not develop social understanding and need specific teaching in this area.

*Evidence*
- Rowe C (1999) Evidence Level III

## Organisation and learning strategies (C)

Children make sense of the world through the language they use. Difficulties with language can contribute to problems with self-organisation and can limit the use of strategies for learning.

The Speech & Language Therapist should suggest or provide:

- Learning strategies – 'thinking skills' programmes such as mind mapping
- Memory strategies – memory files
- Strategies for understanding and using timetables, and use of organisers
- Study skills – identifying key information
- Revision strategies

*Rationale*
Information needs to be securely held in the automatic long-term memory and to be recalled. If information is not reviewed, on average only 20 percent of new or unfamiliar information is remembered the next day. Children with speech, language and communication needs generally have problems with auditory memory. They are likely to benefit from additional systems to support and organise their learning.

*Evidence*
Professional consensus.

## Classroom Management (B)

The Speech & Language Therapist can advise on appropriate strategies for classroom management to enable pupils to access the curriculum. Language within the classroom should be interactive, and the correct questioning will develop thinking skills. The classroom environment can be modified and strategies used to enable pupils with speech, language and communication needs to access the curriculum and to reach their potential.

Modifications of methods of information presentation include:

- Practical experience of handling equipment to provide kinaesthetic information
- Visual support
- Mind maps to highlight vocabulary, establish semantic links within topics and aid organisation of information
- Modifying the language of instruction, eg, simplifying vocabulary or rephrasing
- Asking questions at varying levels (Bloom's Taxonomy of Thinking Skills)

Development of a range of tools to aid organisation may include:

- Writing frameworks for report writing
- Use of ICT
- Symbol systems

Different methods of delivery:

- The Speech & Language Therapist will work collaboratively with the teacher and plan lessons that may include whole class delivery, small group, paired and individual work.
- The Therapist will provide a consultation service for school staff, which may include the provision of language programmes.
- The Speech & Language Therapist should advise on appropriate strategies for classroom management to enable pupils to access the curriculum. Language within the classroom should be interactive and the correct questioning will develop thinking skills. The classroom environment can be modified and strategies used to enable the pupils with speech, language and communication needs to access the curriculum and to reach their potential.

*Training of staff*

Training sessions for school staff, including support assistants, to enable them to:

- Understand the pupils' difficulties.
- Meet the needs of the pupils though modification of classroom delivery.
- Carry out language programmes under the direction of the therapist.

*Rationale*

The Code of Practice for Special Educational Needs (DfES 2001) states '... since communication is so fundamental in learning and progression, addressing speech and language impairment should normally be recorded as educational provision unless there are *exceptional* reasons for not doing so'. This statement confirms that speech and language therapy should be embedded within the curriculum and take the child's educational context and environment into consideration.

*Evidence*

- Law J, Lindsay G, Peacey N, Gascoigne M, Soloff N, Radford J, Band S with Fitzgerald L (2000) Evidence Level III
- McCartney E (ed) (1999) Evidence Level IV
- Martin D & Miller C (1999) Evidence Level IV
- Wright JA & Kersner M (1998) Evidence Level IV

## Use of Signs and Symbols with Language Impaired Children (B)

Children with speech, language and communication needs have been shown to benefit from the use of sign language and/or symbols. The Speech & Language Therapist needs to consider the development of opportunities for the child with these needs to use signs and symbols to communicate, with training and support for school staff, peers and parents as communication partners.

*Rationale*

The visual nature of gestures, signs and symbols enables children who understand visual information more easily than verbal to understand and develop spoken and written language. A child's use of gestures, signs or symbols can facilitate the development of their language and communication.

*Evidence*

- Hurd A (1995) Evidence Level III

## ASSESSMENT OF PHONOLOGY & ARTICULATION

### Phonological Processing (B)

In addition to phonological production, consideration will be given to phonological processing and development of literacy skills. This should be assessed where there are overt speech difficulties and also where there are vocabulary problems, whether or not these coexist with speech problems.

*Rationale*

Phonological processing is causally related to the acquisition of speech, vocabulary and literacy.

*Evidence*

- Bird J, Bishop DVM & Freeman NH (1995) Evidence Level IIb
- Gillon G & Dodd BJ (1994) Evidence Level IIb

### Discrete Phonological Difficulty (B)

Where the child has a discrete production problem, the clinician will need to assess both phonological processing and articulation.

*Rationale*

An articulation problem may exist in isolation or in combination with other speech, language and communication difficulties, and is not thought to have an impact upon literacy. Such a problem requires different remediation techniques from those required for a phonological problem.

*Evidence*

- Stackhouse J (1982) Evidence Level III

## MANAGEMENT OF PHONOLOGY & ARTICULATION

### Phonology & Articulation (C)

Within an appropriate context, consideration needs to be given to the development of the child's:

- Phonological system
- Phonological processes
- Intelligibility
- Phonetic system
- Phonetic errors
- Self-monitoring
- Pre-literacy skills
- Literacy skills

Specific consideration should be given to relevant government legislation, eg, The Code of Practice, National Curriculum and others.

*Rationale*

Phonological processing is causally related to the acquisition of speech, vocabulary and literacy.

*Evidence*

Professional consensus.

### Themes Identified from the Consultation with Service Users

This was a significant aspect of the project. There were three main approaches to consulting with the users:

- Inviting representatives from voluntary organisations to attend meetings of the expert groups.
- Focus groups with service users or their parents/carers.
- Postal questionnaire.

The following themes are based upon a sample of individuals' experiences and their perception of what a speech and language therapy service should offer. Full details of the process undertaken are outlined in the 'Consultation with Service Users' section.

- Collaborative working
    - Required between all the disciplines involved, and in particular, between the Speech & Language Therapist and the class teacher.
- Provision of information
    - The normal process of speech and language development.
    - General strategies that enhance communication.
    - Specific strategies that form part of the therapeutic programme.
- Documentation of need
    - The need for, and details of, speech and language therapy provision to be included within the child's Individualised Education Plan (IEP).

# 5.4 Autistic Spectrum Disorders

## Introduction

*An autistic spectrum disorder is a complex developmental disability that affects the way a person communicates and relates to people around them. The autistic spectrum included the syndromes described by Kanner and Asperger, but is wider that these two subgroups.*

*The whole spectrum is defined by the presence of impairments affecting social interaction, communication and imagination, usually known as the 'triad of impairments', often accompanied by a narrow, repetitive range of activities.*

*Other physical or psychological disabilities can occur in association with an autistic spectrum disorder. These included cerebral palsy, Down's syndrome, dyslexia, language disorders and generalised learning disabilities. Epilepsy occurs in about one third of those with 'typical' autism.*

*The Autism Handbook*, 2000
National Autistic Society

## Using the Guideline

This guideline primarily describes the content of care being offered to pre-school and school-aged children who present with an autistic spectrum disorder and not the knowledge and skills needed by the Speech & Language Therapist working with this client population. Such skills are outlined in the parallel 'Underpinning knowledge and skills framework' – a product of the Competencies Project – and should be read in conjunction with this and with *Communicating Quality*.

Aspects of this guideline are also relevant for adolescents and adults. It should be read alongside the 'Core Guideline' and in combination with any of the following which may be relevant.

- Aphasia
- Cleft Palate & Velopharyngeal Abnormalities
- Clinical Voice Disorders
- Deafness/Hearing Loss
- Disorders of Feeding, Eating, Drinking & Swallowing (Dysphagia)
- Disorders of Fluency
- Disorders of Mental Health & Dementia
- Dysarthria
- Head & Neck Cancer
- Pre-school Children with Communication, Language & Speech Needs
- School-aged Children with Speech, Language & Communication Difficulties.

## Multidisciplinary Team (C)

**The diagnosis and management of autistic spectrum disorders (ASD) should always be multidisciplinary and multi-agency to achieve optimum benefit. It should, therefore, include anyone involved with the care of the individual. In addition to the family/carers this may include child psychology, child psychiatry, clinical psychology, paediatrician, educational psychology, occupational therapy and teaching staff.**

*Rationale*
Autism is a complex and variable disorder impacting upon many areas of development and functioning.

*Evidence*
- National Autistic Society Guidelines (2002) Evidence Level IV
- Public Health Institute of Scotland – Needs Assessment Report Evidence Level IV
- Charman T & Baird G (2002) Evidence Level IV

## Collaboration (B)

**Working collaboratively with parents, teachers and others involved in the day-to-day care of the individual will significantly improve the consistency of intervention and ensure generalisation and maintenance of emerging and newly acquired communication skills.**

*Rationale*

Collaboration in intervention programmes and joint working practices will facilitate consistency of management which, in turn, will maximise progress and promote the generalisation of skills.

*Evidence*

- Reid J, Millar S, Tait L, Donaldson M, Dean EC, Thomson GOB & Grieve R (1996) Evidence Level III
- Law J, Lindsay G, Peacey N, Gascoigne M, Soloff N, Radford J, Band S & Fitzgerald L (2000) Evidence Level III
- Miller C (1999) Evidence Level IV
- Howlin P (1998) Evidence Level IV
- Hart C (1995) Evidence Level IV

## ASSESSMENT

### Triad of Impairment (B)

During assessment, consideration must be given to the triad of social impairments, as well as theories relating to the triad, for example sensory sensitivity and integration; intersubjectivity; executive functioning deficits; motivation; memory and central coherence.

*Rationale*

The triad of social impairments is fundamental in the diagnosis of autism. Individuals with an ASD have difficulties in the three major aspects of social development, which encompass relationships, communication and flexibility of thought and action. In able individuals, the evidence can be very subtle. In addition, they have difficulty in understanding the perspective of others, as well as extracting what is meaningful in the world about them.

*Evidence*

- Wing L & Gould J (1979) Evidence Level III
- Frith U (1989) Evidence Level IV
- Baron-Cohen S, Tager-Flusberg H & Cohen D (1993) Evidence Level IV

### Joint Attention (B)

An evaluation of the individual's ability to direct and maintain shared attention with another individual should be completed.

*Rationale*

Difficulties in this area are among the earliest signs of an autistic spectrum disorder. Lack of reciprocity is a key indicator.

*Evidence*

- Baron-Cohen S, Allen J & Gillberg C (1992) Evidence Level III
- McArthur D & Adamson LB (1996) Evidence Level III
- Mundy P, Sigman M & Kasari CA (1990) Evidence Level III
- Charman T (1998) Evidence Level IV
- Trevarthen C & Aitken KJ (2001) Evidence Level IV

### Readiness to Focus and Shift Attention (B)

An evaluation of the individual's readiness and ability to focus and shift attention will be made. This is the baseline for determining which type of intervention and management would be appropriate.

*Rationale*

Stages of a child's readiness to attend have been well documented. They extend from extreme distractibility to well-established integrated attention.

*Evidence*

- Pascualvaca DM, Fantie BD, Papageorgiou M & Mirsky AF (1998) Evidence Level III
- Cooper J, Moodley M & Reynell J (1978) Evidence Level IV

### Social Interaction (B)

It is essential to make a qualitative assessment of the individual's social interaction skills. This should be carried out in a variety of social settings such as a school, nursery or day centre.

*Rationale*

Deficits in social interaction are intrinsic in ASD. Depending upon the individual's level of development and the severity of autism, interactive skills will range from extreme remoteness, through passivity, to active interest with but with restricted social awareness and inappropriate social interaction.

*Evidence*

- Dawson G, Meltzoff AN, Osterling J, Rinaldi J & Brown E (1998) Evidence Level III
- Wing L & Gould J (1979) Evidence Level III
- Wimpory DC, Hobson RP, Williams JM & Nash S (2000) Evidence Level III
- Frith U (1989) Evidence Level IV
- Happe F (2001) Evidence Level IV
- Baron-Cohen S, Wheelwright S, Cox A, Baird G, Charman T, Swettenham J, Drew A & Doehring P (2000) Evidence Level IV

## Communicative Strategies (B)

An evaluation of the individual's use of communicative strategies should be undertaken.

*Rationale*

Individuals with autism show delayed or deviant strategies depending on their developmental level. These range from screaming, using an adult's arm as a tool, repeating learned phrases that may be out of context, to talking at other people without reciprocal intent.

*Evidence*

- Brady NC & Halle JW (1997) Evidence Level III

## Play Skills and Interests (B)

An evaluation of the child's play and how they occupy themselves must be undertaken which includes an assessment of the type and range of activities.

*Rationale*

Abnormalities of play feature prominently in diagnostic criteria for ASD. Play may be absent or may consist of apparently meaningless and repetitive activity. Functional play, which consists of learned play sequences, may be present but does not extend into creative and imaginative scenarios. Social play, when present, is likely to be confined to chasing and rough-and-tumble pursuits. Older children may show a preference for PC or video games, or develop circumscribed, possibly unusual, interests.

*Evidence*

- Libby S, Powell S, Messer D & Jordan R (1998) Evidence Level IIa
- Charman T (1997) Evidence Level III
- Jarrold C, Boucher J & Smith P (1993) Evidence Level IV
- Williams E, Costall A & Reddy V (1999) Evidence Level IV

## Learning Potential and Preferred Learning Style (C)

Information about learning potential should be obtained, including consideration of particular learning strategies and a cognitive profile. A visual learning style and rote memory are common features and should be evaluated.

*Rationale*

Due to the wide variety of abilities found in ASD, there is a clear need to ensure that the individual's learning style and potential are assessed. A large proportion of the ASD population has additional learning difficulties. Many children with ASD learn more readily through rote learning and the visual modality.

*Evidence*

- Howlin P (1998) Evidence Level IV
- Schopler E (1998) Evidence Level IV
- Powell S (2000) Evidence Level IV

## Mental Health (C)

The impact of the individual's mental health (eg, anxiety and depression) should be taken into consideration.

*Rationale*

Individuals with autism are prone to mood changes that may affect their performance in standardised assessments. Typically, anxiety and sensory processing differences are much in evidence, especially in younger and more seriously affected children. Older children with an ASD may present mental health problems including depression and challenging behaviour. However, it is important to bear in mind that these symptoms may be manifestations of the underlying ASD, and may be ameliorated by appropriate management. Autism can coexist with a range of psychiatric disorders.

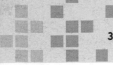

*Evidence*
- Bailey A, Phillips W & Rutter M (1996) Evidence Level IV
- Wolff S (1991) Evidence Level IV

## APPROACHES TO MANAGEMENT

### Early Intervention (B)

Early intervention is likely to be beneficial in fostering the development of communication skills in children with ASD.

*Rationale*
Early intervention ensures appropriate management decisions are made at the optimum time for skills development.

*Evidence*
- Rogers SJ (1996) Evidence Level IIa
- Salt J, Shemilt J, Sellars V, Boyd S, Coulson T & McCool S (2002) Evidence Level IIa
- Jordan R, Jones G & Murray D (1998) Evidence Level IV
- Salt J, Sellars V, Shemilt J, Boyd S, Coulson T & McCool S (2001) Evidence Level IV

### Support and Training of Primary Caregivers (C)

Following diagnosis it is important to enable primary caregivers to access specialist services that offer support and opportunities to acquire skills and strategies for managing children with autism.

*Rationale*
The success of specialist programmes, such as the NAS Early Bird Help Project and the Hanen Project 'More than Words', which combines group training sessions for parents with individual home visits, has reinforced the importance of involving caregivers at the outset.

*Evidence*
- Klinger L & Dawson G (1992) Evidence Level IV
- McDade A & McCartan P (1998) Evidence Level IV
- Shields J (2001) Evidence Level IV

### Social Communication Programme (B)

Approaches that focus on social functioning should be introduced as an on-going intervention strategy from early years to adulthood.

*Rationale*
Social skills approaches for individuals with ASD have been shown to be beneficial and provide opportunities for collaboration among professionals.

*Evidence*
- Kamps DM, Leonard BR, Vernon S, Dugan EP, Delquadri JC, Gershon B, Wade L & Folk L (1992) Evidence Level III
- Hall L-J & Smith KL (1996) Evidence Level III
- Aarons M & Gittens T (2003) Evidence Level IV

### Alternative Augmentative Communication (B)

Consideration should be given to the use of alternative and augmentative communication systems (low and high technology). The level of symbolic understanding and communicative intent are critical.

*Rationale*
Object, picture or symbol exchange systems such as Objects of Reference or PECS are beneficial in helping some children to understand their environment, and may reduce anxiety and encourage communication.

*Evidence*
- Schepis MM, Reid DH, Behrmann MM & Sutton KA (1998) Evidence Level III
- Light JC, Roberts B, Dimarco R & Greiner N (1998) Evidence Level III
- Bondy AS & Frost LA (1994) Evidence Level IV
- Jordan R, Jones G & Murray D (1998) Evidence Level IV
- Park K (1997) Evidence Level IV

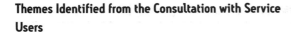

## Themes Identified from the Consultation with Service Users

This was a significant aspect of the project. There were three main approaches to consulting with the users:

- Inviting representatives from voluntary organisations to attend meetings of the expert groups
- Focus groups with service users or their parents/carers
- Postal questionnaire

The following themes are based upon a sample of individual's experiences and their perception of what a speech and language therapy service should offer. Full details of the process undertaken are outlined in the 'Consultation with Service Users' section.

- Collaborative working
    - Required between all the disciplines involved, and in particular, between the Speech & Language Therapist and the class teacher.
- Provision of information
    - The normal process of speech and language development.
    - General strategies that enhance communication.
    - Specific strategies that form part of the therapeutic programme.
- Training Courses
    - For parents regarding the normal process of speech and language development and general strategies which enhance communication.
- Documentation of need
    - The need for and details of speech and language therapy provision to be included within the child's Individualised Education Plan (IEP).

# 5.5 Cleft Palate & Velopharyngeal Abnormalities

## Introduction

This guideline has been written for the assessment and management of syndromic and non-syndromic cleft palate and velopharyngeal abnormalities. While velopharyngeal dysfunction is often associated with cleft palate, it can also present as a separate disorder.

## Using the Guideline

This guideline addresses the speech and language therapy management practice for those with syndromic and non-syndromic cleft palate and velopharyngeal abnormalities and not the knowledge and skills needed by the Speech & Language Therapist working with this client population. Such skills are outlined in the parallel 'Underpinning knowledge and skills framework' – a product of the Competencies Project – and should be read in conjunction with this and with *Communicating Quality*.

This guideline should be read alongside the 'Core Guideline' and in combination with any of the following that may be relevant.

- Aphasia
- Autistic Spectrum Disorders
- Clinical Voice Disorders
- Deafness/Hearing Loss
- Disorders of Feeding, Eating, Drinking & Swallowing (Dysphagia)
- Disorders of Fluency
- Disorders of Mental Health & Dementia
- Dysarthria
- Head & Neck Cancer
- Pre-school Children with Communication, Language & Speech Needs
- School-aged Children with Speech, Language & Communication Difficulties

## Interdisciplinary Team Working (B)

**The Speech & Language Therapist will work within the framework of an interdisciplinary cleft palate team, extending its network into the community.**

*Rationale*
The CSAG Report (1998) recommends that 'a fully integrated multidisciplinary approach centred on a patient's needs from before birth through infancy, childhood, adolescence and to the end of facial growth is required. In the best teams the key individuals are the cleft surgeon, orthodontist, and speech and language therapist.'

*Evidence*
- Bearn D, Mildinhall S, Murphy T, Murray JJ, Sell D, Shaw WC, Williams AC & Sandy JR (2001) Evidence Level III
- CSAG Report (1998) Evidence Level IV

## Speech Outcomes of Primary Surgery – Timing of Speech and Language Therapy Intervention and Surgery (B)

**The Speech & Language Therapist is responsible for reporting speech outcomes that inform surgical decisions regarding the timing and techniques of primary palate surgery.**

*Rationale*
There is evidence that there is great variability in the techniques, sequence and timing of palatal surgery. These can significantly influence the quality of speech outcomes. Therefore speech is considered as one of the primary outcome measures of palatal surgery.

*Evidence*
- Bardach J, Morris HL & Olin WH (1984) Evidence Level IIb
- Shaw WC, Semb G, Nelson P, Brattstrom V, Molsted K & Prahl-Andersen B (2000) Evidence Level III
- Lohmander-Agerskov A, Friede H, Lilja J & Soderpalm E (1995) Evidence Level III
- Witzel MA, Salyer KE & Ross RB (1984) Evidence Level IV

# ASSESSMENT

## Early monitoring (B)

Routine assessments of pre-speech, speech and emerging language should begin after palate repair with particular reference to nasal tone, consonant repertoire, hearing and oral structure.

*Rationale*
Early identification of problems facilitates the implementation of appropriate management, including referral to other members of the interdisciplinary team.

*Evidence*
- Chapman KL (1993) Evidence Level III
- Harding A & Grunwell P (1998) Evidence Level III
- Grundy K & Harding A (1995) Evidence Level IV
- Harding A & Grunwell P (1996) Evidence Level IV
- Russell J & Grunwell P (1993) Evidence Level IV
- Golding-Kushner KJ (2001) Evidence Level IV

## Assessment of speech (B)

Systematic assessments of speech should take place at predetermined times. Clinically, the recommended speech assessment protocol is GOS.SP.ASS '98. CAPS is recommended for audit and inter-centre comparison.

Phonological interpretation of speech should inform management decisions and therapy planning.

Particular attention is given to the following:

- Presence and degree of hypernasal resonance
- Presence and degree of nasal airflow (nasal emission and nasal turbulence) and its effect on consonant production
- Nasal/facial grimace
- Voice quality
- Cleft-type characteristics in consonant production
- Contributing factors: eg, oral structure, hearing, dental occlusion, dentition, lip closure, nasal airway, social and emotional issues, associated conditions/syndromes

*Rationale*
Assessment findings inform differential diagnosis, which determines management decisions. Identification of specific cleft-related characteristics provides essential information, both about the hypothesised function of the velopharyngeal sphincter, and other structural constraints on articulation. Since speech is one of the main outcome measures of surgical management, distinction must be made between cleft-type speech characteristics and non-cleft developmental delay or disorder. It is important for management and therapy planning to determine the nature and prevalence of atypical and/or delayed speech characteristics and to determine to what degree these result from phonetic and/or phonological bases.

*Evidence*
- D'Antonio LL, Muntz HR, Province MA & Marsh JL (1988) Evidence Level III
- Harding A & Grunwell P (1998) Evidence Level III
- Sell D, Harding A & Grunwell P (1999) Evidence Level IV
- Harding A & Grunwell P (1996) Evidence Level IV
- Trost JE (1981) Evidence Level IV
- Kuehn DP (1982) Evidence Level IV
- McWilliams BJ & Philips BJ (1979) Evidence Level IV

## Hearing (B)

The Speech & Language Therapist will work in close collaboration with colleagues in Audiology and Ear, Nose and Throat (ENT), especially when there are concerns that hearing deficits may be affecting communication development.

*Rationale*
In children with cleft palate the almost universal occurrence of otitis media with effusion (OME), due to Eustachian tube malfunction, leads to fluctuating conductive hearing loss which may seriously affect auditory skills and communication development. The presence of a hearing loss in addition to the structural anomaly compounds speech and language problems.

*Evidence*
- Grant HR, Quiney RE, Mercer DM & Lodge S (1988) Evidence Level IIb
- Broen PA, Devers MC, Doyle SS, Prouty JM & Moller KT (1998) Evidence Level III

- Rach GH, Zielhuis GA & Broek van den P (1988) Evidence Level III
- Teele DW, Klein JO & Rosner BA (1984) Evidence Level III

## Language (B)

When screening indicates delayed or deviant language development, further in-depth assessment should be carried out.

### Rationale

It is recognised that cleft palate children are at risk of delays in linguistic skills, particularly in the development of expressive language. When the cleft is part of a syndrome there may be associated language, learning and hearing difficulties.

### Evidence

- Chapman KL, Graham KT, Gooch J & Visconti C (1998) Evidence Level III
- Neiman GS & Savage HE (1997) Evidence Level III
- Broen PA, Devers MC, Doyle SS, Prouty JM & Moller KT (1998) Evidence Level III
- Golding-Kushner KJ, Weller G & Shprintzen RJ (1985) Evidence Level III
- Scherer NJ & D'Antonio LL (1995) Evidence Level III

## Assessment of Velopharyngeal Dysfunction (C)

The perceptual assessment of speech has a central position in the assessment of velopharyngeal dysfunction. Hypernasality and/or excessive nasal emission/turbulence and/or certain characteristics of consonant production are usually indicative of velopharyngeal dysfunction and should prompt referral to the regional cleft palate team for investigations of velopharyngeal function.

### Rationale

The perceptual assessment is the gold standard for evaluating hypernasality. Velopharyngeal dysfunction and its associated speech disorders occur in all surgical series of primary palate repair, with a highly variable incidence (5–40 percent) across studies based in the western world. It is also associated with some neurological conditions, post-adenoidectomy, submucous cleft palate, congenital box-like pharynx, phoneme-specific

nasality, severe hearing impairment and some syndromes. Historically, cleft teams have developed the expertise to deal with such speech problems.

### Evidence

- Witt PD & D'Antonio LL (1993) Evidence Level IV
- Kuehn DP & Moller KT (2000) Evidence Level IV
- CSAG Report (1998) Evidence Level IV

## Evaluation of Velopharyngeal Dysfunction (B)

Differential diagnosis of velopharyngeal dysfunction based on direct and indirect methods of visualisation of the velopharygeal sphincter should usually include as a minimum: videofluoroscopy and perceptual evaluation. Nasendoscopy, acoustic and airflow measurements should also be carried out wherever possible.

### Rationale

Velopharyngeal dysfunction presents physically and perceptually in different ways and the choice of management strategy needs to be based on comprehensive information and differential diagnosis.

### Evidence

- Henningsson GE & Isberg AM (1986) Evidence Level III
- Dalston RM, Warren D & Dalston E (1991a) Evidence Level III
- Dalston RM, Warren D & Dalston E (1991b) Evidence Level III
- Dalston R & Warren D (1986) Evidence Level III
- Witt PD & D'Antonio LL (1993) Evidence Level IV

# MANAGEMENT

## Early Advisory Role (C)

The Speech & Language Therapist will explain to parents about the function of the velopharyngeal mechanism in speech. The Speech & Language Therapist will monitor communication development in relation to the cleft palate and hearing, and will offer advice and support until speech and language are established. The target for the majority of children should be normal speech by school entry, or earlier if possible.

*Rationale*
Early intervention aims to monitor and influence developing speech patterns in order to prevent any atypical speech patterns becoming established in babble and early speech. Golding-Kushner maintains that parents working at home are able to elicit normal sound production in their children so that the need for speech therapy can be avoided. Up to 60 percent of children with cleft palate may require therapy during speech acquisition.

*Evidence*
- Golding-Kushner KJ, Weller G & Shprintzen RJ (1985) Evidence Level III
- Russell J & Harding A (2001) Evidence Level IV
- Golding-Kushner KJ (1994) Evidence Level IV
- Golding-Kushner KJ (2001) Evidence Level IV
- Hahn E (1989) Evidence Level IV

## Partnership with Parents (A)

The Speech & Language Therapist equips parents to monitor and influence babble, language and speech. Expert information and advice on communication will be available to parents so that they can share responsibility for their child's development as a confident and competent communicator.

*Rationale*
Historically, management of children with cleft palates follows a medical model leaving parents and children as passive recipients of the treatment offered. Current philosophies of patient care recognise the need to involve parents in management decisions affecting their children. Parents are more likely to carry out the follow-up activities if involved in objective setting.

*Evidence*
- Pamplona MC, Ysunza A & Jimenez-Murat Y (2001) Evidence Level Ib
- Pamplona MC, Ysunza A & Uriostegui C (1996) Evidence Level Ib
- Pamplona MC & Ysunza A (2000) Evidence Level IIa
- Golding-Kushner KJ (2001) Evidence Level IV

## Feeding Support (A)

Where a Speech & Language Therapist is involved in feeding support, he/she will work in collaboration with the specialist nurse or dysphagia specialist with regard to all aspects of an individualised feeding programme.

*Rationale*
The incidence of feeding difficulties in cleft lip and palate are reported to be as high as 63 percent, although the nature and physiological basis of these difficulties are poorly described. Children with other medical problems are particularly at risk of complex feeding difficulties.

*Evidence*
- Brine EA, Rickard KA, Brady MS, Liechty EA, Manatunga A, Sadove M & Bull MJ (1994) Evidence Level Ib
- Shaw WC, Bannister RP & Roberts CT (1999) Evidence Level Ib
- Clarren SK, Anderson B & Wolf LS (1987). Evidence Level III
- Choi BH, Kleinheinz J, Joos U & Komposch G (1991) Evidence Level III

## Phonology and Articulation (A)

The therapy programme for cleft palate children is based on a comprehensive assessment and tailored to the individual. This may include articulatory, phonological or combined articulatory and phonological approaches. Objectives may target normal or adaptive articulation. Intervention may be necessary from a very young age into adulthood. Extended periods of therapy input may be necessary. Intensive therapy has been shown to be effective in both individual and group therapy contexts.

*Rationale*
Speech problems associated with cleft palate and/or velopharyngeal dysfunction require therapy that is distinct from approaches used with the non-cleft population. Clients may need to learn new articulatory movements in order to achieve accurate consonants, and a phonological approach may then be appropriate in order to establish the new sound/s in the client's phonological system. Using specific therapy

techniques, normal or nearly normal speech can often be achieved despite structural limitations.

*Evidence*
- Albery L & Enderby P (1984) Evidence Level Ib
- Grunwell P & Dive D (1998) Evidence Level III
- Golding-Kushner KJ (1994) Evidence Level IV
- Golding-Kushner KJ (2001) Evidence Level IV
- Russell J & Harding A (2001) Evidence Level IV

## Electropalatography Intervention (B)

**Electropalatography should be a treatment option for school-aged children and older patients with persistent articulatory disorders.**

*Rationale*
Electropalatography (EPG) is a technique designed to record details of the timing and location of tongue contacts with the hard palate during continuous speech. It is effective in the treatment of children with cleft palate, because it makes tongue position and movement explicit and helps develop conscious control of such clues. It is appropriate for individuals who have abnormally broad or increased posterior tongue placement, often identified as palatal or velar articulation, lateral/lateralised articulation and abnormal double articulations.

*Evidence*
- Michi K, Suzuki N, Yamashita Y & Imai S (1986) Evidence Level III
- Gibbon F, Cramplin L, Hardcastle W, Nairn M, Razzell R, Harvey L & Reynolds B (1989) Evidence Level IV
- Dent H, Gibbon F & Hardcastle W (1992) Evidence Level IV

## Management of the Speech Consequences of Velopharyngeal Dysfunction with Surgery (B)

**The Speech & Language Therapist working as an integral member of the cleft team contributes to the surgical decision-making process. Assessment pre- and post-operatively should occur routinely and the results used in the joint recommendations to determine the nature of surgery.**

*Rationale*
Surgery can improve soft palate function, and/or reduce the size of the velopharyngeal orifice during speech, thereby reducing or eliminating the speech consequences of velopharyngeal dysfunction. Speech outcomes determine the success of the surgical procedures.

*Evidence*
- Sommerlad BC, Henley M, Birch M, Harland K, Moiemen N & Boorman JG (1994) Evidence Level III
- Witt PD & D'Antonio LL (1993) Evidence Level IV
- Sommerlad BC, Mehendale FV, Birch M J, Sell DA, Hattee C & Harland K (2002)

## Management of the Speech Consequences of Velopharyngeal Dysfunction: Therapy Aimed at Muscle Activities (C)

**Therapy aimed at reducing or eliminating hypernasality/ nasal air emission using non-speech activities, such as articulation and palatal exercises, palatal massage, blowing, sucking, icing, interrupted swallowing, cheek puffing and gagging, are inappropriate for most patients with velopharyngeal problems.**

*Rationale*
These non-speech activities do not address the underlying aetiology, which is usually a result of insufficient tissue or a reflection of a problem in the timing of velopharyngeal closure. Velopharyngeal closure is a three-dimensional activity involving the soft palate, and the lateral and posterior pharyngeal walls. Focusing on one part of the mechanism, such as the soft palate, only, as advocated in the above exercises, is unlikely to be effective.

*Evidence*
- Ruscello DMA (1982) Evidence Level IV
- Starr CD (1990) Evidence Level IV

## Management of the Speech Consequences of Velopharyngeal Dysfunction: Therapy aimed at Speech Production Modification Techniques (C)

**Techniques using oral-nasal auditory discrimination, increased speaking effort, greater mouth opening and reduced speaking**

rate may have a place, but only when the patient is capable of achieving velopharyngeal closure. This must be established by direct visualisation of the velopharyngeal mechanism using nasendoscopy/videofluoroscopy.

*Rationale*
These techniques will be ineffective if velopharyngeal dysfunction is present and delay decision-making regarding appropriate management of velopharyngeal dysfunction.

*Evidence*
- D'Antonio LL (1992) Evidence Level IV
- Sell D & Grunwell P (2001) Evidence Level IV

### Management of the Speech Consequences of Velopharyngeal Dysfunction using Visual Biofeedback (A)

Visual biofeedback, although still experimental, may be a useful technique in therapy where there is inconsistent velopharyngeal closure.

*Rationale*
Fibre-optic nasopharyngoscopy, videofluoroscopy and nasometry have been used as techniques to encourage the patient to increase or change velopharyngeal closure. Such techniques provide visual cues not usually available in traditional speech therapy techniques which largely emphasise auditory feedback. Visual feedback is usually only appropriate when the patient is capable of achieving velopharyngeal closure. This must be established by direct visualisation of the velopharyngeal mechanism using nasendoscopy/videofluoroscopy.

*Evidence*
- Ysunza M, Pamplona T, Femat I, Mayer A & Garcia-Velasco M (1997) Evidence Level Ib
- Kawano M, Isshiki N, Honjo I, Kojima H, Kurata K, Tanokuchi F, Kido N & Isobe M (1997) Evidence Level III
- Siegel-Sadewitz VL & Shprintzen RJ (1982) Evidence Level III
- Witzel MA & Posnick JC (1989) Evidence Level III
- Golding-Kushner KJ (1994) Evidence Level IV

### Management of Velopharyngeal Dysfunction with Speech Therapy for Consonant Production (B)

Therapy for consonant production may be appropriate when there is excessive nasal airflow/hypernasal resonance as a result of velopharyngeal dysfunction. Therapy is aimed at establishing correct oral placements, albeit with nasal airflow/hypernasal resonance. Where there is a diagnosis of phoneme-specific nasality, this is an indication of velopharyngeal mislearning and should be eliminated with therapy and not surgery or prosthetics.

*Rationale*
In the context of non-oral articulation, including glottal and pharyngeal articulation, speech therapy techniques aimed at eliminating such errors may improve soft palate and lateral pharyngeal wall movements, which may have an impact on the subsequent management of hypernasality. Improving speech intelligibility through working on consonant articulation in the presence of velopharyngeal dysfunction can be effective. Velopharyngeal mislearning represents an abnormal and unusual pattern of producing consonants with abnormal nasal airflow, which can be effectively treated with therapy.

*Evidence*
- Harding A & Grunwell P (1998) Evidence Level III
- Peterson-Falzone S & Graham MS (1990) Evidence Level III
- Hoch L, Golding-Kushner K, Siegel-Sadewitz VL & Shprintzen RJ (1986) Evidence Level IV

### Management of Velopharyngeal Dysfunction with Prosthetics (B)

Velopharyngeal dysfunction resulting in hypernasality/nasal airflow can be effectively managed with a palatal lift or speech bulb obturator. It is an appropriate option to consider where surgery and/or therapy have failed or are contraindicated, such as where there is severe tissue deficiency, anaesthetic contraindications to surgery exist, and in some neurological cases. The team approach is essential in this treatment which is usually only possible in school-aged children and older clients.

*Rationale*

Both appliances have been shown to be effective in eliminating abnormal nasal airflow and excessive nasal resonance. The palatal lift works by lifting the soft palate in a posterior and superior direction through the use of an acrylic extension from the back of an oral plate. The speech bulb consists of an oral plate with an extension which courses up behind the soft palate and terminates in an acrylic ball positioned in the velopharynx, physically blocking the velopharyngeal mechanism and preventing abnormal nasal airflow and excessive nasal resonance.

*Evidence*

- Witt PD, Rozelle AA, Marsh JL, Marty-Grames L, Muntz HR, Gay WD & Pilgram TK (1995) Evidence Level IIb
- Golding-Kushner KJ, Cisneros G & LeBlanc E (1995) Evidence Level IV
- Sell D & Grunwell P (2001) Evidence Level IV

## Themes identified from the Consultation with Service Users

This was a significant aspect of the project. There were three main approaches to consulting with the users:

- Inviting representatives from voluntary organisations to attend meetings of the expert groups
- Focus groups with service users or their parents/carers
- Postal questionnaire

The following themes are based upon a sample of individual's experiences and their perception of what a speech and language therapy service should offer. Full details of the process undertaken are outlined in the 'Consultation with Service Users' section.

- Collaborative working
  - Required between all the disciplines with particular focus upon the individual's physical and psychosocial needs.
- Provision of information
  - The normal process of speech and language development.
  - The impact of cleft palate upon speech development.

- Training courses
  - For educational staff and other professionals regarding the normal process of speech and language development and the impact of cleft palate.
- Continuity of care
  - Incorporates a process for regular communication for the family.
- Group therapy
  - Would decrease the feeling of isolation for the child.

# 5.6 Clinical Voice Disorders

## Introduction

A clinical voice disorder (dysphonia) is the term applied to a voice which is characterised by an abnormality of pitch, volume, resonance and/or quality, and/or to a voice that is inappropriate for the age, gender or culture of the speaker. It may be intermittent or constant, mild or severe. The resultant voice may not be capable of meeting the occupational, professional, educational or social needs of the individual. Aphonia refers to the complete absence of voice, which may arise from a number of underlying causes. Dysphonia or aphonia may be caused by a variety of aetiologies. In some instances it may be the manifestation of a complex neurological or systemic disease process.

## Using the Guideline

This guideline primarily describes the content of care being offered individuals who present with a clinical voice disorder and not the knowledge and skills needed by the Speech & Language Therapist working with this client population. Such skills are outlined in the parallel 'Underpinning knowledge and skills framework' – a product of the Competencies Project – and should be read in conjunction with this and with *Communicating Quality*.

This guideline should be read alongside the 'Core Guideline' and in combination with any of the following that may be relevant.

- Aphasia
- Autistic Spectrum Disorders
- Cleft Palate & Velopharyngeal Abnormalities
- Deafness/Hearing Loss
- Disorders of Feeding, Eating, Drinking & Swallowing (Dysphagia)
- Disorders of Fluency
- Disorders of Mental Health & Dementia
- Dysarthria
- Head & Neck Cancer
- Pre-school Children with Communication, Language & Speech Needs
- School-aged Children with Speech, Language & Communication Difficulties

## ASSESSMENT

### ENT Examination (C)

**Each individual must have an examination by an Ear, Nose and Throat (ENT) Surgeon prior to or simultaneously with speech and language intervention in order to identify disease, assess structure and contribute to the assessment of function. The Speech & Language Therapist should also refer back for a re-examination if there is concern regarding lack of progress or deterioration in the individual's progress.**

*Rationale*
Accurate and detailed description of laryngeal structure and function is necessary to plan effective therapy. A percentage of dysphonic individuals will present with organic disease without associated muscle tension or psychological factors, and the ENT surgeon may manage these without the need for speech and language therapy. Dysphonia, with associated symptoms, can be a manifestation of a complex neurological or systemic disease process. The ENT surgeon is trained in the identification and management, eg, pharmacological treatment, of these disease processes.

*Evidence*
Professional consensus.

### Voice Clinic (C)

**It is in the individual's best interest to be assessed in a Joint ENT/Speech and Language Therapy Voice Clinic. The Joint ENT/Speech & Language Therapy Clinic is valuable for several reasons:**

- To formulate a diagnosis and to plan management using the joint and complementary skills of the ENT surgeon and Speech & Language Therapist.
- In addition to the surgeon's knowledge of vocal tract pathology and of medical and surgical approaches, the

Speech & Language Therapist has knowledge of the physiological presentation and perceptual parameters of dysphonia and the suitability of the patient for voice therapy.
- It provides a greater range of laryngeal imaging, including stroboscopy for the examination of the mucosal wave.
- The availability to the Speech & Language Therapist of laryngeal images will inform clinical management.

According to the British Voice Association (BVA) Position Document, the minimum requirements for a voice clinic include:

- An ENT Surgeon with a special interest in laryngology.
- A specialist Speech & Language Therapist.
- A range of laryngeal imaging equipment, including stroboscopy.

*Rationale*
The combination of these factors provides the opportunity for increased accuracy of diagnosis and appropriate management.

*Evidence*
- Casiano RR, Zaveri V & Lundy DS (1992) Evidence Level III
- Woo P, Colton R, Casper J & Brewer D (1991) Evidence Level III

## Perceptual Assessment (B)

A perceptual assessment of vocal and respiratory behaviours will be made in order to acquire an accurate vocal profile for analysis.

*Rationale*
The main aim of the perceptual assessment is to provide a description of voice on which to base therapy and measure change. It enables:

- A study of the interrelation between speech subsystems.
- The highlighting of those parameters of voice which are contributing to the dysphonia.
- Evaluation of each speech subsystem and the potential for change.
- Establishment of a baseline and a measure of overall severity.

*Evidence*
- Dejonckere PH, Remacle M, Fresnel-Elbaz E, Woisard V, Crevier L & Millet B (1998) Evidence Level III
- Carding P, Carlson E, Epstein R, Mathieson L & Shewell C (2000) Evidence Level IV

## Instrumental Evaluation (C)

A good quality audio recording is essential. Access to additional instrumentation for the measurement of respiratory and vocal parameters such as aerodynamics, pitch, intensity resonance, vibratory cycle and/or aspects of vocal quality, is recommended.

*Rationale*
An audio recording provides a reproducible record of the patient's voice that can be used for the perceptual evaluation of change and as input to other instrumental tools. The complexity of the speech signal results in auditory misperception, which can be clarified through instrumental assessments.

*Evidence*
- Baken R & Orlikoff R (2000) Evidence Level IV

## Client Self-assessment (A)

A record will be completed of the perceptions of the individual, carer and, where appropriate, significant others, of the impact of the voice disorder and its symptoms.

*Rationale*
The individual's perceptions influence the management approaches adopted and specific joint goal-setting for therapy. They also provide a valid baseline from which to measure change in well-being. The level of handicap experienced may be disproportionate to the level of impairment.

*Evidence*
- MacKenzie K, Millar A, Wilson JA, Sellars C & Deary I (2001) Evidence Level Ib
- Benninger MS, Ahuja AS, Gardner G & Grywalski C (1998) Evidence Level III
- Jacobson B, Johnson A & Grywalski C, Silbergleit A, Jacobson G, Benninger MS & Newman CW (1997) Evidence Level III

■ Smith E, Verdolini K, Gray S, Nichols S, Lembe J, Barkmeier J, Dove H & Hoffman H (1996) Evidence Level III

### Palpation of the Extrinsic Laryngeal Musculature (C)

Palpation of the extrinsic laryngeal musculature may be completed as part of the Speech & Language Therapist's voice assessment and in addition to the ENT surgeon's own evaluation of the neck for disease.

*Rationale*
This part of the speech and language therapy assessment provides information about the status of the extrinsic laryngeal musculature, and the position of the laryngeal cartilages at rest and during phonation. It assists the identification of muscle tension disorders and acts as a guide to therapy.

*Evidence*
■ Lieberman J (1998) Evidence Level IV
■ Roy N, Ford C & Bless D (1996) Evidence Level IV

### Differential Diagnosis (C)

The combined assessment findings will be analysed so that the clinician can formulate a differential diagnosis of the voice disorder.

*Rationale*
It is necessary to interpret all assessment findings in order to determine the causal and maintaining factors that constitute the dysphonia and so develop a working hypothesis on which to base management.

*Evidence*
Professional consensus.

## MANAGEMENT

Education, vocal-tract care and voice conservation will be appropriate to most cases. The choice of therapy approaches is determined by the assessment findings and may involve a direct approach (physiological) and/or an indirect approach (psycho-social). A physiological approach is one which works directly on changing specific aspects of the function of the

subsystems (articulatory, respiratory, laryngeal and resonatory). The psychosocial approach aims to address the emotional, environmental and/or social factors that may underlie a dysphonia. The goals for therapy also differ, depending on the assessment findings, and may be curative, preventative, facilitative, rehabilitative or supportive.

### Education & Explanation (B)

An explanation of the normal anatomy and physiology, especially of the vocal tract, for voice production will be provided. In addition, an explanation of the causal and maintaining factors that make up the voice disorders will be discussed.

*Rationale*
Improved understanding of the vocal mechanism and associated factors gives the individual a rationale for active participation in therapy.

*Evidence*
■ Chan R (1994) Evidence Level IIa
■ Drudge M & Philips B (1976) Evidence Level III

### Vocal Tract Care and Voice Conservation (B)

An explanation of voice care and conservation will be provided that will include hydration, environmental factors, voice use and lifestyle.

*Rationale*
Care and conservation improve vocal-tract health, which will optimise efficient voice production. In cases of vocal misuse and abuse, and following phonosurgery, it will assist recovery and prevent recurrence.

*Evidence*
■ Verdolini-Marston K, Sandage M & Titze IR (1994) Evidence Level IIa
■ Chan RW (1994) Evidence Level IIa

### Direct Treatment Approaches (A)

As part of the goal for more effective and efficient voice production, direct voice therapy approaches may aim to:

- Alter vocal fold adduction
- Alter respiratory patterns
- Modify pitch
- Reduce supraglottic activity
- Alter resonance
- Adjust articulatory tension

Patients must then learn to generalise these vocal behaviours. Techniques may be combined within a specific treatment scheme, eg, The Accent Method or Estill Method of Compulsory Voice Figures. Appropriate techniques will be selected on the basis of the full assessment findings.

*Rationale*
Changes in vocal behaviour maximise vocal effectiveness and reduce the handicapping effect of the voice problem.

*Evidence*
- Carding PN, Horsley IA & Dochery GJ (1998) Evidence Level Ib
- Ramig L, Countryman S, Thompson L & Horii Y (1995) Evidence Level Ib
- MacKenzie K, Millar A, Wilson JA, Sellars C & Deary I (2001) Evidence Level Ib
- Bassiouny S (1998) Evidence Level Ib
- Stemple J, Lee L, D'Amico B & Pickup B (1994) Evidence Level Ib
- Verdolini-Marston K, Burke M, Lessac A, Glaze L & Caldwell E (1995) Evidence Level IIa
- Murray T & Woodson G (1992) Evidence Level III
- Bloch CS, Gould WJ & Hirano M (1981) Evidence Level III
- Drudge M & Philips B (1976) Evidence Level III

## Indirect Treatment Approaches (A)

Additional indirect approaches, eg, relaxation strategies and psychological counselling, will be used where psychological or social factors are contributing to the development or maintenance of a voice problem. Their application may involve other members of the multidisciplinary team such as a psychologist.

*Rationale*
Some patients require help in addition to direct voice therapy approaches to resolve associated factors. The Speech &

Language Therapist is often best placed to identify and treat those patients who require this type of intervention. The Speech and Language Therapist may also instigate onward referral to other agencies.

*Evidence*
- Carding PN, Horsley IA & Docherty GJ (1998) Evidence Level Ib

## Themes Identified from the Consultation with Service Users

This was a significant aspect of the project. There were three main approaches to consulting with the users:

- Inviting representatives from voluntary organisations to attend meetings of the expert groups
- Expert groups with service users or their parents/carers
- Postal questionnaire

The following themes are based upon a sample of individuals' experiences and their perception of what a speech and language therapy service should offer. Full details of the process undertaken are outlined in the 'Consultation with Service Users' section.

- Provision of information
  - Voice production.
  - Specific strategies that form part of the therapeutic programme.
- Process of service delivery
  - Treatment should commence after diagnosis.
  - Regular reviews, as appropriate.

# 5.7 Deafness/Hearing Loss

## Introduction

This guideline refers to children and adults with congenital or acquired deafness which leads to a significant communication impairment that has educational and/or social consequences. It is acknowledged that some individuals may prefer alternative terms, eg, partially hearing, hard of hearing, hearing impaired or deaf, but for the sake of uniformity 'deaf' has been used throughout this guideline.

The population to which this guideline refers is:

- Children and adults with permanent congenital deafness.
- Children and adults with permanent acquired deafness of sudden or progressive onset.
- Children with temporary conductive deafness of chronic or fluctuating nature.

The aetiology of deafness is often difficult to ascertain. There is still a high incidence of deafness of unknown cause. Deafness may be associated with:

- Genetic causes, including syndromes
- Pre-, peri- or post-natal conditions

(Categorisation based on the MRC's Institute of Hearing Research.)[1]

Speech & Language Therapists should to be aware of ongoing changes in audiological criteria for cochlear implant candidates.

Permanent deafness may have lifelong consequences. It may impact on different aspects of everyday communication, including languages (spoken or sign), speech perception and production. It may also impact upon the social and emotional well-being of the deaf person and their relationships within their family, with hearing peers and their chosen linguistic community.

## Using the Guideline

This guideline describes the content of care being offered to deaf children and adults, and not the knowledge and skills needed by the speech and language therapy working with this client population. Such skills are outlined in the parallel 'Underpinning knowledge and skills framework' – a product of the Competencies Project – and should be read in conjunction with this and with *Communicating Quality*.

This guideline should be read alongside the 'Core Guideline' and in combination with any of the following that may be relevant:

- Aphasia
- Autistic Spectrum Disorders
- Cleft Palate & Velopharyngeal Abnormalities
- Clinical Voice Disorders
- Disorders of Feeding, Eating, Drinking & Swallowing (Dysphagia)
- Disorders of Fluency
- Disorders of Mental Health & Dementia
- Dysarthria
- Head & Neck Cancer
- Pre-school Children with Communication, Language & Speech Needs
- School-aged Children with Speech, Language & Communication Difficulties

## ASSESSMENT

When determining the consequences of deafness on communication skills, a Speech & Language Therapist needs to be aware that differential diagnosis requires a comparison between an individual's chronological age, hearing age and developmental age. The duration of deafness and age of onset may affect the nature of the assessment and intervention programme with deaf adults.

---

1  MRC's Institute of Hearing Research: http://www.ihr.mrc.ac.uk/

## Clinical History Checklist (C)

In addition to the usual case-history taking, consideration should be given to the following:

■ Aetiological information
■ Age at diagnosis: type and nature of hearing loss
■ Audiological information: eg, objective hearing tests; Evoked Response Audiometry (ERA); Computerised Tomography (CT); Magnetic Resonance Imaging (MRI scan); tympanometry; pure tone audiogram; speech audiometry; free field aided thresholds
■ Age when hearing aid fitted
■ Type of amplification: acoustic/digital hearing aids, cochlear implant
■ Age at intervention
■ Recommended settings of the prescribed hearing aids
■ Additional environmental devices (eg, tactile aid)
■ First language, includes British Sign Language(BSL)
■ Preferred mode of communication, eg, speech; manually coded English systems; cued speech; gesture; sign bilingualism (BSL)
■ Languages and range of modalities used within the home and elsewhere

Additional information required for adults:

■ Level of speech reading competency (related to onset of deafness)
■ Tinnitus
■ Balance
■ Type of amplification and consistency of use
■ Need for interpreter
■ Links with deaf community

*Rationale*
Information gathering and listening to the individual, their parents or primary caregivers are essential aspects of developing a comprehensive picture of the deaf individual's communication abilities and difficulties. Information should be gathered from a range of available sources in order to help the Speech & Language Therapist obtain a comprehensive baseline assessment and to consider the most appropriate treatment or support options.

*Evidence*
■ McCormick B (1993) Evidence Level IV
■ Boothroyd A (1992) Evidence Level IV

## Checking of Auditory Device (C)

At the beginning of each session the S&LT will:

■ Visually inspect the hearing aid/cochlear implant or other assistive listening device, referring to the recommended settings.
■ Check the quality of the signal of hearing aids, using stetaclips.

Liaison with the teacher of the deaf, educational audiologist or audiological scientist will occur as appropriate.

*Rationale*
It is essential to check the functioning of the device prior to any intervention, as any temporary or persistent problems with the device will adversely affect spoken language at speech perception functional listening and speech production levels during speech and language therapy sessions.

*Evidence*
■ McCormick B (1993) Evidence Level IV
■ Bench RJ (1992) Evidence Level IV
■ Boothroyd A (1992) Evidence Level IV
■ Boothroyd A, Geers AE & Moog JS (1991) Evidence Level IV

## Functional Use of Aided Hearing (C)

The individual's ability to use their aided hearing for functional listening in everyday home, school or work environments should be assessed.

*Rationale*
This will help a Speech & Language Therapist to distinguish between technical problems with the listening device or its current settings, and temporary or more permanent intrinsic factors affecting the audiological status of the deaf adult/child, for example, an ear infection or a deterioration in previously established hearing levels. If the auditory device is not

working effectively it will have a negative effect upon the rate of development of spoken language or maintenance of established spoken language skills.

NB With a small group of individuals, eg, those with mild to moderate losses, it may be useful to compare aided with unaided auditory perception abilities in either closed-set tests or functional listening in everyday situations in order to demonstrate benefit of the listening device.

### Evidence

- Archbold S, Lutman M & Nikolopoulos TP (1998) Evidence Level III
- Estabrooks WI (2000) Evidence Level IV

## Video Analysis (B)

**Assessments may be audio- or video-recorded, as appropriate and with the individual's consent.**

### Rationale

Deaf children and some deaf adults communicate in a very sophisticated way and it is not always possible for the clinician to transcribe simultaneously the range of potentially significant features of communication across a continuum of speech-sign modalities. For this reason audio or video recordings of an assessment may be appropriate, especially in instances where later evaluation is required, eg, parent–child interaction; bimodal communication; or transcribing the developmental features of speech production.

### Evidence

- Tait DM (1993) Evidence Level III
- Tait M, Lutman ME & Nikolopoulos TP (2001) Evidence Level III

## Sign Bilingualism (C)

**Assessment of the individual's use of multi-modal communication, for example gesture, spoken language, speech and sign will be undertaken. Assessment of the individual's sign language competence will require close collaboration with fluent BSL users. The Speech & Language Therapist needs to be aware of the unique needs of deaf children from multi-lingual backgrounds.**

### Rationale

Many deaf individuals will use different modes of communication and the clinician needs to ascertain the individual's preferred and most effective mode of communication. This information will then be used as a baseline for management decisions and, where appropriate, advice and therapy/support programmes.

### Evidence

- Gregory S & Pickersgill M (1998) Evidence Level IV

## Assessment of Preverbal Communication Skills (B)

**An assessment will be made of the child's preverbal communication skills with particular reference to symbolic play, eye contact, turn-taking and autonomy in spontaneous interaction and communicative contexts.**

### Rationale

Assessment of preverbal communication skills is necessary in order to:

- Establish a baseline of a deaf child's current communication skills.
- Inform parents and professionals regarding development of language and speech skills in the context of the child's overall rate of development.
- Ascertain the child's preferred mode of communication in different home/school environments.

### Evidence

- Tait ME, Lutman ME & Nikolopoulos TP (2001) Evidence Level III
- Paganga S, Tucker E, Harrigan S & Lutman M (2001) Evidence Level IV

## Communication Ability (Social & Interaction Skills)

An assessment of social and interaction skills should be made. This may include an assessment of the client's use and understanding of gesture, facial expression, social communicative behaviour and discourse skills in relation to both spoken and sign languages. The strategies that an individual uses to compensate for any communicative difficulties should also be observed. The communicative and linguistic competencies of an individual should be observed, where possible, across a range of contexts, eg, with deaf/hearing people, familiar/unfamiliar people.

*Rationale*
Deaf individuals can experience difficulties in interpreting and producing appropriate paralinguistic features in spoken language. Lack of exposure to deaf sign-language users may also result in difficulties with this aspect of communication in sign language.

*Evidence*
- Harris M (2000) Evidence Level IV

## Assessment of Understanding and Use of Language (Spoken, Written and Signed)

An evaluation will be carried out of the individual's understanding and use of spoken, signed (SSE/BSL) or written language. For sign language, close collaboration with a fluent BSL signer will be required. This will require analysis of the individual's understanding and use of both semantics and grammar.

*Rationale*
Deaf individuals may acquire understanding through different language modalities along a vision alone → vision + audition → audition alone continuum. It is important to assess understanding of mother tongue and/or English/BSL to provide a baseline for therapy and management decisions. For some people who have been deaf from birth, sign will be the first language and spoken and written English will be the second language. It is important to know which language is used by the client, family, caregivers and support professionals as this will influence post-speech and language therapy assessment priorities and goals.

*Evidence*
- Pickersgill M & Gregory S (1998) Evidence Level IV
- Herman R, Holmes S & Woll B (1999) Evidence Level IV

## Auditory Perception: Aided and Unaided (C)

The individual's ability to use their aided hearing for auditory perception should be assessed in order to ascertain their ability to detect, discriminate and identify both environmental and linguistic sounds.

Post-lingually deafened adults and some, but not all, school-aged deaf children may require assessment with closed-set speech perception materials.

*Rationale*
There may be a discrepancy between the sound signal delivered by an auditory device and the individual's ability to make full use of that signal. The information gained from a routine assessment of the deaf adult or child's auditory perception provides a baseline for auditory training as well as providing useful clinical information about functional listening.

*Evidence*
- Bench J (1992) Evidence Level IV
- Bamford J & Saunders E (1991) Evidence Level IV
- Hind S (1998) Evidence Level IV
- Klein S & Rapin I (1993) Evidence Level IV
- Barrett K (1994) Evidence Level IV
- Kirk KI, Diefendorf AO, Pisoni DB & Robbins AM (1997) Evidence Level IV

## Assessment of Speech Reading (C)

An assessment will be made of the individual's speech-reading skills and consideration given to strategies used: visual or auditory-visual. The assessment of speech-reading should extend from single words to connected discourse.

*Rationale*
To understand how the individual is accessing and participating in auditory-visual communication. This information will influence the means by which therapy will be delivered.

*Evidence*
- Plant G & Spens KE (1995) Evidence Level IV
- Plant G & McCrae J (1997) Evidence Level IV

## Assessment of Speech Production and Speech and/or Sign Intelligibility

A formal assessment and/or skilled observation of the individual's phonetic and phonological repertoire may be appropriate, and a profile of their speech and/or sign intelligibility in a range of communicative contexts should be drawn up. This should include both their use of segmental and supra-segmental features in spoken language.

*Rationale*

The phonetic and phonological systems of deaf and deafened individuals are often restricted and assessment and analysis are necessary prerequisites for planning therapy.

Deaf children who are functioning at the prelexical stage of speech production may benefit from phonetic awareness training and modified articulation therapy – within a developmental phonology framework. Children who are not spontaneously developing their sound system may benefit from phonetic knowledge and limited articulation therapy. Caution is needed with articulation therapy as inappropriate intervention may result in abnormal speech patterns.

Intelligibility amongst deaf individuals is variable and may be linked with competency at other linguistic levels. Perceptions of intelligibility vary from naïve to experienced interactors, so it is important to seek a variety of opinions.

*Evidence*
- Parker A & Irlam S (1994) Evidence Level IV
- Fisher J, King A, Parker A & Wright R (1983) Evidence Level IV
- Parker A & Kersner M (1997) Evidence Level IV

## Speech Intelligibility (C)

A profile of the individuals' speech and/or sign intelligibility in a range of communication settings may be appropriate. This should include both the segmental and non-segmental features of the language(s). This is likely to occur through formal assessment and/or skilled observation and discussion with others.

*Rationale*

Intelligibility amongst deaf individuals is variable and may be linked with competency at other linguistic levels. Perceptions of intelligibility vary from naïve to experienced interactors, so it is important to seek a variety of opinions.

*Evidence*
- Allen MC, Nikolopoulos TP & O'Donoghue GM (1998) Evidence Level III
- Parker A & Irlam S (1994) Evidence Level IV

## Assessment of Vocal Characteristics (Prosody) (C)

An assessment should be made of the individual's functional vocal characteristics such as quality, pitch, range, voice, resonance and volume in more than one communicative context. Assessment outcomes may indicate the need for a further audiological assessment or review of hearing aid recommended settings and/or referral to an ENT Surgeon.

*Rationale*

For adults or children with a post-lingual onset of deafness, changes in voice or prosodic features may be an early significant indicator of hearing loss. For those with congenital deafness, unusual vocal characteristics are also likely and therefore an assessment will be required as a precursor to therapy. A deterioration in vocal characteristics may influence the decision-making process with regard to audiological management.

*Evidence*
- House D (1995) Evidence Level IV

## Role of the Interdisciplinary Team (C)

The assessment findings and management plan should be discussed with all members of the interdisciplinary team. In the case of children, this should include the referrer, the school and the educational psychologist. The parents/carers should also be considered as members of this team.

*Rationale*

Effective interdisciplinary team work has been demonstrated to promote a better outcome for the individual involved. There are many different forms of team-working, and they may differ depending on the situational context.

*Evidence*
- Bray M (2001) Evidence Level IV

## MANAGEMENT

### Early Communication Skills (C)

The S&LT will explain the relationship between hearing and communication, and will be available for discussion and support. Intervention should seek to facilitate the development of early communication skills, particularly appropriate eye contact, initiation, communicative intent and turn-taking skills.

*Rationale*
Early intervention aims to monitor and influence developing communication, language(s) and speech production abilities in the context of a deaf child's overall development. Working with parents/carers will ensure communication is accessible. In the case of sign bilingualism or multilingualism users, a Speech & Language Therapist should consult/liaise with a fluent co-worker when interpreting assessment findings and planning/implementing therapy.

*Evidence*
- Bench J, McNeil-Brown D, Backhouse R & Heine C (1995) Evidence Level III
- Caissie R & Gibson CL (1997) Evidence Level III
- Galloway C & Woll (1994) Evidence Level IV
- Galloway C (1999) Evidence Level IV
- Woll B (1999) Evidence Level IV

### Communication Ability (Social and Interaction Skills) (C)

Direct and/or indirect approaches might be undertaken to facilitate the individual's development of:

- Non-verbal communication
- Conversational and discourse skills
- The social rules of communication
- The strategies used to compensate for linguistic or communicative difficulties.

This intervention may involve discussion of cultural differences and differences in modes of communication. It will usually be carried out in groups in conjunction with teachers.

*Rationale*
Deaf individuals can experience difficulties in interpreting and producing appropriate paralinguistic features. It is important to ensure the application of knowledge and skills in meaningful social exchanges.

*Evidence*
- Bench RJ (1992) Evidence Level IV

### Linguistic Competence (C)

Direct or indirect approaches might be undertaken to facilitate the individual's development in both the receptive and expressive aspects of semantic, grammatical and phonological competencies in sign and/or spoken language, as appropriate. Where spoken language is deemed inaccessible, written language may be the mode used to help the individual to access English.

*Rationale*
Deaf individuals may have difficulties with all aspects of language as each of these linguistic competencies impacts upon others.

- Semantics: difficulties with semantics are frequent at the level of lexis and with semantic relations.
- Grammar: difficulties with grammar are manifest. Particular attention often needs to be given to noun and verb phrases and complex sentences as well as word-level features which are dependent upon morphophonological aspects such as tense indicators, plurality and comparatives.
- Story grammars and narrative.
- Phonology.

In general, intervention should establish the individual's understanding of new concepts, vocabulary and grammatical structures before or in conjunction with work on production. Many aspects of grammatical features of English are not easily accessible to deaf people. Therefore some alternative means of developing an understanding of these features may need to be used, such as the use of written language or other visual markers such as fingerspelling.

*Evidence*
- Mogford K (1998) Evidence Level IV

## Modification of the Environment (C)

The Speech & Language Therapist will collaborate with others to adapt the physical, social, sensory and linguistic components of the environment in order to make language and communication more accessible to the individual.

*Rationale*
This approach ensures the removal or reduction of barriers to communication.

*Evidence*
- Beazley S & Moore M (1995) Evidence Level IV
- Berg FS (1997) Evidence Level IV
- Flexer C (1999) Evidence Level IV

## Auditory Training (B)

Auditory training will form an essential part of the management of speech intelligibility for those deaf children for whom spoken language will be the primary mode of communication. This extends from closed-set activities to functional listening. Functional listening may include auditory/speech-reading activities. It is therefore a prerequisite to any speech production work.

*Rationale*
The purpose of auditory training is to optimise the individual's listening and/or speech-reading skills in a variety of settings. This will allow for improved auditory feedback and therefore development of the individual's self-monitoring skills as well as shifting their phonological representations.

*Evidence*
- Abberton E, Hazan V & Fourcin A (1990) Evidence Level III
- Plant G & Spens KE (1995) Evidence Level IV

## Intelligibility: Phonology and Articulation (B)

Direct therapy may be needed to improve the individual's speech or sign intelligibility. In the latter case, this should be in conjunction with a competent sign language user.

Speech intelligibility therapy might take place at the phonological and/or phonetic level and may include both segmental and supra-segmental features. Therapy at this level should be proceeded by the development of speech perception skills

*Rationale*
Deaf individuals may need to access new articulatory movements in order to facilitate kinaesthetic awareness and motor speech patterning. This may be relevant to conserving intelligibility in deafened individuals or those with deteriorating hearing. A phonological approach is then appropriate in order to establish the new sound/s in the individual's phonological system. Deaf children often have inadequate phonological representations which influence spoken language development, vocabulary retention and literacy skills.

*Evidence*
- Gulian E, Fallside F, Hinds P & Keiller C (1983) Evidence Level IIa
- Brentari DK & Wolk S (1986) Evidence Level IIb
- Maassen B (1986) Evidence Level IIb
- Parker A & Rose H (1990) Evidence Level IV

## Speech-reading (C)

Speech-reading may be the focus of therapy and used as a prerequisite for auditory training. This will enable the client to become more aware of some of the visual patterns of speech and to identify some set phrases in certain contexts. Training may also facilitate recognition of lip shapes, anticipation and the use of context from very basic lip patterns to single words to running speech.

*Rationale*
Speech-reading is not a skill that is necessarily learnt automatically, although it is a skill that, when acquired, can help to facilitate better 'listening' in impoverished listening conditions.

*Evidence*
- Dodd B, McIntosh B & Woodhouse L (1998) Evidence Level IV
- Erber NP (1983) Evidence Level IV

In addition, the following aspects need to be considered for school-aged children. However, close collaboration with the teachers of the deaf needs to be considered throughout.

## Classroom Management (B)

The Speech & Language Therapist can advise on appropriate strategies for classroom management to enable pupils to access the curriculum. Language within the classroom should be interactive and the correct questioning will develop thinking skills. The classroom environment can be modified and strategies used to enable the pupils with speech, language and communication needs to access the curriculum and to reach their potential.

*Modification of methods of presentation of information*

- Practical experience of handling equipment to provide kinaesthetic information.
- Visual support.
- Mind maps to highlight vocabulary, establish semantic links within topics and aid organisation of information.
- Modifying the language of instruction, eg, simplifying vocabulary or rephrasing.
- Asking questions at varying levels (Bloom's Taxonomy of Thinking Skills).

*Development of range of tools to aid organisation*

- Writing frameworks for report writing.
- Use of ICT.
- Symbol systems.

*Different methods of delivery*

- The teacher and Speech & Language Therapist will work collaboratively and plan lessons which may include whole class delivery, small group, paired and individual work.
- The Therapist will provide a consultation service for school staff, which may include the provision of language programmes.
- The Speech & Language Therapist should advise on appropriate strategies for classroom management to enable pupils to access the curriculum. Language within

the classroom should be interactive and the correct questioning will develop thinking skills. The classroom environment can be modified and strategies used to enable the pupils with speech, language and communication needs to access the curriculum and to reach their potential.

*Training of staff*
Training sessions for school staff, including support assistants, to enable them to:
- Understand the pupils' difficulties.
- Meet the needs of the pupils though modification of classroom delivery.
- Carry out language programmes under the direction of the therapist.

*Rationale*
*The Code of Practice for Special Educational Needs* (DfES 2001) states 'since communication is so fundamental in learning and progression, addressing speech and language impairment should normally be recorded as educational provision unless there are *exceptional* reasons for not doing so. This statement confirms that speech and language therapy should be embedded within the curriculum and take the child's educational context and environment into consideration. It is important for teachers and speech and language therapists to develop models of best practice.'

*Evidence*
- Law J, Lindsay G, Peacey N, Gascoigne M, Soloff N, Radford J, Band S with Fitzgerald L (2000) Evidence Level III
- McCartney E (ed) (1999) Evidence Level IV
- Wright JA & Kersner M (1998) Evidence Level IV
- Martin D & Miller C (1999) Evidence Level IV

## Themes Identified from the Consultation with Service Users

This was a significant aspect of the project. There were three main approaches to consulting with the users:

- Inviting representatives from voluntary organisations to attend meetings of the expert groups
- Focus groups with service users or their parents/carers
- Postal questionnaire

The following themes are based upon a sample of individuals' experiences and their perception of what a speech and language therapy service should offer. Full details of the process undertaken are outlined in the 'Consultation with Service Users' section.

- Collaborative working
  - Required between all the disciplines involved, and in particular, between the Speech & Language Therapist and the class teacher.
- Working in partnership with parents
- Provision of information
  - The normal process of speech and language development.
  - General strategies that enhance communication.
  - Specific strategies which form part of the therapeutic programme.
- Training courses
  - For parents regarding the normal process of speech and language development and general strategies which enhance communication.
- Provision of group and individual therapy
- Service provision
  - School as well as clinic.

# 5.8 Disorders of Feeding, Eating, Drinking & Swallowing (Dysphagia)

## Introduction

This guideline refers to children and adults who have difficulty with feeding, eating, drinking and/or swallowing. The term 'dysphagia' is used within this guideline to refer to the total process of feeding, eating, drinking and swallowing. When a single aspect of the swallowing process needs to be identified, then the appropriate term will be employed, eg, feeding. The Speech & Language Therapist will plan intervention for children within the context of the developmental sequence of eating and drinking skills. Of paramount consideration will be safety, nutrition and hydration, balanced against the desire for developmental progress.

## Using the Guideline

This guideline addresses the speech and language therapy management practice for children and adults who have difficulty with feeding, eating, drinking and/or swallowing and not the knowledge and skills needed by the Speech & Language Therapist working with this client population. Such skills are outlined in the parallel 'Underpinning knowledge and skills framework' – a product of the Competencies Project – and should be read in conjunction with this and with *Communicating Quality*.

This guideline should be read alongside the 'Core Guideline' and in combination with any of the following that may be relevant.

- Aphasia
- Autistic Spectrum Disorders
- Cleft Palate & Velopharyngeal Abnormalities
- Clinical Voice Disorders
- Deafness/Hearing Loss
- Disorders of Fluency
- Disorders of Mental Health & Dementia
- Dysarthria
- Head & Neck Cancer
- Pre-school Children with Communication, Language & Speech Needs
- School-aged Children with Speech, Language & Communication Difficulties

## Multidisciplinary Team Working (B)

**The Speech & Language Therapist will work as a core member of the multi- or interdisciplinary team. The composition of the team may vary depending upon the setting.**

### Rationale
The multidisciplinary management of individuals with dysphagia ensures a timely, efficient, integrated and holistic period of care.

### Evidence
- Bach DB, Pouget S, Belle K, Kilfoil M, Alfieri M, McEvoy J & Jackson G (1989) Evidence Level III
- Logemann JA (1994) Evidence Level IV
- Siktberg LL & Bantz DL (1999) Evidence Level IV
- Goldsmith T (2000) Evidence Level IV

## ASSESSMENT

### Pre-clinical Evaluation (C)

**An assessment will always commence with the gathering of information from appropriate sources to inform further assessment methods, and to determine whether assessment and/or intervention is appropriate. An assessment of the individual's ability to eat, drink and swallow will be carried out in order to determine the safety and efficiency of this process.**

### Rationale
It is essential that information gathering is carried out as:

- It enables a preliminary assessment of risk to be undertaken.
- It informs the timing, methodology and scope of further assessment.

*Evidence*
- Arvedson JC & Brodsky L (1992) Evidence Level IV
- Groher ME (1997) Evidence Level IV

**Clinical Evaluation**

**Clinical Evaluation 1 (C)**

In addition to case history taking, the Speech & Language Therapist will consider the following aspects of assessment:

- An oro-facial examination
- Vocal tract function
- General motor skills/posture and tone
- Nutrition and hydration
- Respiratory status
- Presence of gastro-oesophageal reflux
- Management of secretions
- Tracheostomy status
- Cognitive levels
- Level of alertness
- Medication
- Oral hygiene
- Dental health
- Dietary preferences
- The individual's ability to participate
- Information on current feeding pattern
- Effects of emotional state, mood and behaviour

*Rationale*
Consideration of the different features enables the clinician to predict how the individual will cope with eating and drinking and determines the ongoing assessment procedure. It also enables the clinician to:

- Undertake a risk assessment in relation to current eating and drinking
- Determine the impact of disorder
- Prioritise further assessment
- Determine the safety of food trials
- Select methods and safety of further swallow assessment

*Evidence*
- Castell DO & Donner MW (1987) Evidence Level IV
- Hendrix TR (1993) Evidence Level IV

- Ekberg O (2000) Evidence Level IV
- Davies P (1994) Evidence Level IV

**Clinical Evaluation 2 (B)**

The Speech & Language Therapist will observe and consider the ability of the person(s) supporting the individual to eat and drink, paying particular attention to:

- Mealtime interaction
- Positioning
- Bolus size
- Pacing and presentation
- Utensils
- The environment

*Rationale*
The level of the carer's awareness, knowledge and skill in the eating and drinking experience is essential to successful implementation of the eating and drinking plan. The environment has a significant influence on the mealtime experience. At its best, it promotes socialisation, enhances awareness, and increases appetite and quality of life.

*Evidence*
- Kayser-Jones J & Schell E (1997) Evidence Level III
- Hall GR (1994) Evidence Level IV
- Hotaling DL (1990) Evidence Level IV

**Clinical Evaluation 3 (C)**

Subsequent to information gathering, the Speech & Language Therapist will make a clinical judgement with regard to whether they proceed in assessing the individual with food and liquid.

*Rationale*
To determine the safety and efficiency of eating, drinking and swallowing, or feeding in relation to developmental levels.

*Evidence*
Clinical consensus

## Clinical Evaluation 4 (B)

To date, there is inconsistent evidence that the use of pulse oximetry and cervical auscultation can assist in reliably determining the occurrence of aspiration. Clinical decisions should not be based solely upon information gained from these procedures. Instrumental tools may assist in evaluating swallow function when used in conjunction with clinical swallow evaluation.

*Rationale*
Pulse oximetry and cervical auscultation may provide additional information relevant to swallowing function, informing clinical decisions.

Instrumental tools should not form the *sole* basis of clinical decisions regarding oral intake and dysphagia management.

*Evidence*
- Smith HA, Lee SH, O'Neill PA & Connolly MJ (2000) Evidence Level IIb
- Sellars C, Dunnet C & Carter R (1998) Evidence Level III
- Colodny N (2000) Evidence Level III
- Zenner PM, Losinski DS & Mills RH (1995) Evidence Level III
- Cichero JA & Murdoch BE (1998) Evidence Level IV

## Clinical Evaluation 5 (A)

When the following information is required to supplement clinical decision-making, a Videofluoroscopic Evaluation of Swallowing (VFES) and/or Fibre-optic Endoscopic Evaluation of Swallowing (FEES) will be carried out:

- To further visualise the structure and function, and to gain a dynamic view of the upper aerodigestive tract.
- To assess presence and cause of aspiration and residue.
- To facilitate techniques which alleviate aspiration and residue and improve swallow efficiency.
- To compare baseline and post treatment function.
- Identify and direct specific therapeutic strategies and regimes.
- To further assist in diagnosis unless there are clear clinical contraindications. These may include medical conditions, social, environmental, psychological and safety factors.

Research has demonstrated poor inter-rater reliability in the interpretation of VFES, and the Speech & Language Therapist should therefore exercise caution.

This information will inform the management of the individual.

*Rationale*
The use of VFES/FEES informs:

- A decision regarding oral and non-oral intake.
- Specific recommendation of food and fluid textures and bolus size assessed as safe under direct visualisation.
- Delineation of swallow manoeuvres and postures which effect decreased aspiration and residue.
- Tailoring of therapy to the individual's physiological impairments, aiming to reduce aspiration risk and optimise swallowing efficiency.
- It should not form the *sole* basis of clinical decisions regarding oral intake and dysphagia management.

*Evidence*
- Leder SB & Karas DE (2000) Evidence Level Ib
- Logemann JA, Pauloski B, Roa B, Rademaker A, Cook B, Graner D, Milianti F, Beery Q, Stein D, Bowman J & Lazarus C (1992) Evidence Level IIa
- Splaingard MD, Hutchins B, Sulton LD & Chaudhuri G (1988) Evidence Level IIb
- Leder SB, Sasaki CT & Burrell MI (1998) Evidence Level IIb
- Langmore SE, Schatz K & Olson N (1991) Evidence Level III
- Mann G, Hankey GJ & Cameron D (1999) Evidence Level III
- Mirrett PL, Riski JE, Glascott J & Johnson V (1994) Evidence Level III

## Clinical Evaluation 6 (B)

Ultrasound, scintigraphy, manometry and EMG: each of these tools evaluates discrete components of swallowing function, and it is therefore inappropriate to use any of these as a stand-alone evaluation technique.

*Rationale*
Each of these tools evaluates discrete components of swallowing function or provides additional clinical information.

This information may contribute to building up a full clinical picture of the swallow. It is therefore inappropriate to use these as stand-alone evaluations technique. Clinical decisions should not be based solely upon information gained from these procedures.

*Evidence*
- Perie S, Laccourreye L, Flahault A, Hazebroucq V, Chaussade S & St Guily JL (1998) Evidence Level IIb

## Clinical Evaluation 7 (B)

For an individual who has a tracheostomy, it is physiologically contraindicated to assess or feed with the cuff inflated. However, in rare circumstances, a team decision may be taken to feed with the cuff inflated. Where a tracheostomy is sited, the individual should have a swallow assessment following the same principles as discussed above, having the adjunct of:

- Blue dye added to secretion and food and liquid
- Cuff deflation

The individual swallow will be assessed using a speaking valve to determine if there is an improvement in safety and efficiency.

*Rationale*
The speaking valve has not been shown to exclusively eliminate or reduce the risk of aspiration.

The use of blue dye can yield false negatives and so is only to be used as a screening adjunct to the bedside test.

It is widely considered that cuff deflation allows for improved laryngeal excursion during the swallow. Furthermore, it is known that a cuffed tracheostomy does not eliminate aspiration.

*Evidence*
- Peruzzi WT, Logemann JA, Currie D & Moen SG (2001) Evidence Level IIb
- Dettelbach MA, Gross RD, Mahlmann J & Eibling DE (1995) Evidence Level III
- Elpern EH, Okonek M, Borkgren M, Bacon M, Gerstung C & Skrzynski M (2000) Evidence Level III

- Logemann JA, Pauloski BR & Colangelo IA (1998) Evidence Level III
- Stachler RJ, Hamlet SL, Choi J & Fleming S (1996) Evidence Level III
- Conlan A & Kopec S (2000) Evidence Level IV

## MANAGEMENT

All the following management strategies must be systematically and regularly reviewed by the Speech & Language Therapist to ensure that the programme of intervention continues to be appropriate and valid.

### Timing of Intervention (C)

The Speech & Language Therapist will place the eating and feeding disorder within the context of the individual's overall:

- Development
- Emotional, psychological and behavioural well-being
- Medical and surgical status
- Respiratory and nutritional status
- Prognosis
- Physical environment and social setting

The Speech & Language Therapist will inform the individual (where possible), the multi-disciplinary team, carers and significant others of the nature of their intervention. The timing of intervention will be discussed and agreed with the individual (where possible), the multidisciplinary team, carers and significant others.

After consideration of the above factors, it may become apparent that further Speech & Language Therapy intervention for dysphagia is not appropriate.

*Rationale*
It is essential that all decisions regarding the individual's management are agreed within the multidisciplinary team and with the family/carers and significant others in order to:

- Identify and agree which interventions receive priority at any stage in time.
- Identify any factors that may negatively impact upon the individual's health status and well-being.

*Evidence*

■ Arvedson JC & Brodsky I (1992) Evidence Level IV

## Working Directly with the Individual – Individual's Readiness to Participate in Treatment (B)

The Speech & Language Therapist will aim to ensure that the individual is at their optimum level of alertness, calmness and receptiveness prior to oral trials. Hypo- and hypersensitivity will also be considered and managed.

*Rationale*

Distortions in the manner in which sensory input is organised and interpreted interferes with eating and drinking, including skilled oral motor patterns. Reduced ability to swallow safely and efficiently can be caused by:

■ Agitation and level of distress
■ Poor arousal/alertness
■ Facial and intra-oral hypo- or hypersensitivity
■ Impaired cognition or comprehension

*Evidence*

■ Frazier JB & Friedman B (1996) Evidence Level III
■ Brown GE, Nordloh S & Donowitz AJ (1992) Evidence Level IV
■ Anderson J (1986) Evidence Level IV
■ Davies P (1994) Evidence Level IV

## Preparation for Oral Intake (B)

The Speech & Language Therapist will consider and potentially modify the following aspects of eating and drinking as part of the initial intervention:

■ Presentation of food
■ Environment
■ Interest in food/appetite
■ Posture/position
■ Oral motor skills to include organisation of non-nutritive suck in infants
■ Oral stimulation
■ Reducing oral aversions and hypersensitivity

*Rationale*

Adequate preparation is essential for successful intervention using oral trials or specific techniques or manoeuvres.

*Evidence*

■ Pickler RH, Higgins KE & Crummette BD (1993) Evidence Level IIa
■ Gisel EG, Applegate-Ferrante T, Benson J & Bosma JF (1996) Evidence Level IIa
■ Avery-Smith W (1997) Evidence Level IV
■ Davies P (1994) Evidence Level IV
■ Palmer MM & Heyman MB (1993) Evidence Level IV

## Presentation of Food and Drink (Bolus) (B)

The Speech & Language Therapist will assess the effect of modified presentation of the bolus upon swallow function, in order to identify the method that facilitates the safest and most efficient swallowing. Such intervention may involve:

■ **Bolus placement into a specific part of the oral cavity**
■ **Bolus size**
■ **Bolus characteristics (eg, temperature, texture, taste, viscosity)**
■ **Pacing**
■ **Utensil**
■ **Frequency, timing and size of meals and alternative nutrition**

*Rationale*

Modifying any of the above factors can affect bolus preparation and swallow performance, thereby optimising swallow safety and efficient transit through the mouth and pharynx, to compensate for deficits. Frequency and size of meals can be manipulated to minimise effects of muscular fatigue, poor concentration, altered appetite and effects of non-oral feeding.

*Evidence*

■ Khulemeier KV, Palmer JB & Rosenberg D (2001) Evidence Level IIb
■ Robbins JA, Sufit R, Rosenbek J, Levine R & Hyland J (1987) Evidence Level III

## Type of Food or Liquid Given (B)

The Speech & Language Therapist will consider modifying food and liquid consistency, temperature, taste and texture to achieve improved swallow safety and efficiency. Any modifications will be systematically assessed to determine effectiveness.

### Rationale
The function of various components of the swallow mechanism alters in response to modifications of food and liquid characteristics, such as their taste, temperature, density, ability to flow and need for chewing. To some degree, these changes are predictable and can be utilised therapeutically to increase swallow safety (airway protection) and swallow efficiency (protection), time and effort taken to transport bolus to the oesophagus.

### Evidence
- Bisch EM, Logemann JA, Rademaker AW, Kahrilas PJ & Lazarus CL (1994) Evidence Level IIa
- Logemann JA, Pauloski BR, Colangelo L, Lazarus C, Fujui M & Karhilas PJ (1995) Evidence Level IIb

## Biofeedback (C)

Some instrumental procedures (eg, Surface EMG, ultrasound, videoendoscopy) can be used to provide biofeedback to patients undergoing swallowing therapy.

### Rationale
Visual and/or instrumental biofeedback helps the patient to understand a specific manoeuvre and augments the individual's proprioception. It may indicate when/if the target swallowing behaviour has been achieved.

### Evidence
- Huckabee ML & Cannito MP (1999) Evidence Level III
- Bryant M (1991) Evidence Level III
- Crary MA (1995) Evidence Level III

## Behavioural Strategies (A)

The Speech & Language Therapist will identify which behavioural strategies facilitate the eating and drinking

process and communicate these to the relevant carers. These may include:

- Situational strategies prior to, during and after mealtime
- Verbal cues
- Written cues and/or symbols
- Physical cues
- Visual cues

### Rationale
The above strategies aim to maximise the effectiveness of the individual's eating and drinking. It may also have a positive impact on the individual and carers' psychosocial experience of mealtimes.

### Evidence
- Coyne ML & Hoskins L (1997) Evidence Level Ib
- Rasnake LK & Linscheid TR (1987) Evidence Level III
- Kayser-Jones J & Schell E (1997) Evidence Level III
- Osborn CL & Marshall MJ (1993) Evidence Level III
- Babbitt RL, Hoch TA, Coe DA, Cataldo MF, Kelly KJ, Stackhouse C & Perman JA (1994) Evidence Level IV
- Morris SE (1989) Evidence Level IV

## Intra-oral Prosthetics (C)

In specific cases, the Speech & Language Therapist will liaise with the maxillo-facial prosthodontist in recommending and designing intra-oral palatal shaping, lifting and obturating prostheses to improve swallowing function.

### Rationale
Intra-oral prosthetics can improve velopharyngeal closure and tongue-to-palate contact, and obdurate post-surgical palatal and oral defects. This can improve efficiency and speed of oral and pharyngeal transit and reduce nasal penetration and regurgitation.

### Evidence
- Logemann JA, Kahrilas PJ, Hurst P, Davis J & Krugler C (1989) Evidence Level III
- Wheeler RL, Logemann JA & Rosen MS (1980) Evidence Level III

## Compensatory Strategies (B)

As part of clinical decision-making, compensatory strategies such as postural changes and manoeuvres will be implemented to improve swallowing function. The effectiveness of such strategies will be evaluated with the individual prior to implementation.

### Rationale

Postural changes and the use of swallowing manoeuvres alter aspects of swallowing physiology. This can improve swallowing function and reduce or eliminate symptoms of dysphagia.

### Evidence

- Logemann JA, Pauloski BR, Rademaker AW & Colangelo IA (1997) Evidence Level III
- Lazarus C, Logemann JA & Gibbons P (1993) Evidence Level III
- Larnert G & Ekberg O (1995) Evidence Level III
- Rasley A, Logemann JA, Kahrilas PJ, Rademaker AW, Pauloski BR & Dodds WJ (1993) Evidence Level III
- Veis S, Logemann JA & Colangelo I (2000) Evidence Level III
- Shanahan TK, Logemann JA, Rademaker AW, Pauloski BR & Kahrilas PJ (1993) Evidence Level III
- Logemann JA & Kahrilas PJ (1990) Evidence Level III
- Crary MA (1995) Evidence Level III

## Body Position during Swallowing (C)

The Speech & Language Therapist will identify the body position that enables optimum swallow function for each individual. This involves attaining a comfortable position in which trunk, limbs, shoulders and head are supported. Specialised seating equipment or physical facilitation may be required, and physiotherapy and occupational therapy input is essential in this process.

### Rationale

Abnormal head, body and trunk position can adversely affect swallowing performance. Underlying postural stability and mobility are the essential foundation for synchronised oral movements for swallowing. Achieving aligned body position, with normalised muscle tone, minimises effort of swallowing while increasing airway protection and pharyngeal clearance.

### Evidence

- Davies P (1994) Evidence Level IV
- Morris SE (2000) Evidence Level IV
- Avery-Smith W (1997) Evidence Level IV

## Stimulation and Range of Movement Exercises (B)

The Speech & Language Therapist will provide therapy to maintain and/or improve oromotor function, which will be within agreed optimal time frames. This may include range of motion, chewing and swallowing exercises, and thermal and tactile stimulation. This may be contraindicated for cardiac and certain degenerating conditions.

### Rationale

A range of motion exercises and stimulation are recognised as a way to maintain and/or improve muscle function.

### Evidence

- Rosenbek JC, Roecker EB, Wood JL & Robbins J (1996) Evidence Level IIb
- Helfrich-Miller KR, Rector KL & Straka JA (1986) Evidence Level III
- Logemann JA, Pauloski BR, Rademaker AW & Colangelo IA (1997) Evidence Level IV

## Modification of the Environment (B)

The Speech & Language Therapist will optimise the individual's environment in order to provide the most pleasurable, safe and positive mealtime experience. This can be achieved by the adjustment of:

- Distractions
- Level of lighting
- Level of noise
- Factors facilitating/enabling social interaction

### Rationale

The level of the carer's awareness, knowledge and skill in the eating and drinking experience is essential to the successful implementation of the eating and drinking plan. The environment has a significant influence on the mealtime experience. At its best, it promotes socialisation, enhances awareness and increases appetite and quality of life.

*Evidence*
■ Denny A (1997) Evidence Level IIb

## Education and Training for Caregivers (B)

The Speech & Language Therapist will instigate training for carers and care staff to whom the responsibility for supporting eating and drinking has been delegated, in order to increase their awareness and understanding of eating and drinking difficulties including behavioural problems. Strategies to address the problem will also be provided.

*Rationale*
Eating and drinking is an integral part of the daily care given to individuals with dysphagia. Caregivers need to be able to facilitate optimally safe, efficient and pleasurable eating and drinking. They need to have skills to accurately identify when input is required from Speech & Language Therapist for evaluation or review of a potential or actual problem with the eating and drinking process.

*Evidence*
■ Melin & Gotestrom KG (1981) Evidence Level Ib
■ Littlewood *et al* (1997) Evidence Level III

## Education of the Individual or Individual's Caregiver (C)

The Speech & Language Therapist will provide information related to an individual's swallowing difficulties, how to support the individual safely, how to implement the eating and drinking plan, and when to refer back to the Speech & Language Therapist.

*Rationale*
It is essential that caregivers have adequate understanding and are competent to carry out the eating and drinking plan effectively, to ensure the safety of the individual and to maintain personal dignity.

*Evidence*
Clinical consensus.

## Non-oral Nutrition (C)

The Speech & Language Therapist will contribute to the multi-disciplinary decision regarding the potential need for non-oral nutrition and hydration.

*Rationale*
Partial or total provision of nutrition and hydration by a non-oral route may be necessary where the daily intake requirements are not being met safely by the oral route. This decision is arrived at by the multidisciplinary team, including the dysphagic individual and their significant carers. The Speech & Language Therapist's role in this decision will be to contribute information regarding safety and efficiency of oral intake and the prognostic indicators for improvement.

*Evidence*
Clinical consensus.

## Oral Stimulation

The Speech & Language Therapist should offer non-oral fed children some oral stimulation (if deemed safe) in order to normalise sensation and maintain and promote skills.

*Rationale*
A child who is non-orally fed may become orally hypersensitive and unable to accept oral intake.

*Evidence*
■ Morris SE (1989) Evidence Level IV

## Long-term Review of Swallowing Ability

The evidence suggests that for some individuals their swallow function may continue to improve over time. Triggers for re-assessment of swallow function may include:

■ Changed level of alertness or medical status
■ Alteration in motivation or cognitive function and mealtime behaviour

Swallow re-evaluation will include formal oromotor examination and objective swallow assessment.

### *Rationale*

The swallow function may improve with time, allowing for some guided return to oral feeding or, in some patients, removal of the feeding tube.

### *Evidence*

- Wijdicks EF & McMahon MM (1999) Evidence Level IV
- Harper JR, Mcmurdo ME & Robinson A (2001) Evidence Level IV

## Themes Identified from the Consultation with Service Users

This was a significant aspect of the project. There were three main approaches to consulting with the users:

- Inviting representatives from voluntary organisations to attend meetings of the expert groups
- Focus groups with service users or their parents/carers
- Postal questionnaire

The following themes are based upon a sample of individuals' experiences and their perception of what a Speech & Language Therapy Service should offer. Full details of the process undertaken are outlined in the 'Consultation with Service Users' section.

- Meeting other individuals who have difficulty with eating, feeding and/or swallowing.
- Provision of information
  - The normal swallowing process.
  - Specific strategies that form part of the therapeutic programme.

# 5.9  Disorders of Fluency

## Introduction

This guideline addresses children and adults who present with a disorder of fluency which may be of sudden or gradual onset, have varying degrees of severity and include overt and covert features. Disorders of fluency occasionally arise as a part of, or as a result of, physical or psychological illness, disease or injury affecting the brain. In these cases remediation is driven by the theoretical knowledge and clinical experience relevant to the main diagnosis. When fluency problems persist, then collaboration between the fluency therapist and other therapists would be recommended. Throughout this guideline the terms 'developmental', 'acquired stammering' and the disorder of 'cluttering' have been used as defined below. Apraxia of speech is not addressed in this guideline.

NB 'Stammering' is used throughout the text, however, 'stuttering' occurs in some of the references. The terms are synonymous.

*Developmental Stammering* occurs initially during childhood. The overt speech symptoms will include some or all of the following: part word repetitions; prolongations; and/or blocking. Coping strategies, for example changing difficult words, situation avoidance, or changes in nonverbal behaviour, may occur early or develop over time. In addition, fear of stammering may cause psychological or emotional distress.

*Acquired Stammering* usually occurs in adult life but can start in childhood. Onset may be associated with a significant event, ie, it may be neurogenic, physiological, eg, post-viral fatigue syndrome, pharmacological, psychogenic, or may be of idiopathic origin.

*Cluttering* is usually characterised by perceptually fast or irregular speech rate; poor intelligibility; repetition or cessation of sounds; dysrhythmia; omission or elision of syllables. It may or may not include stammering. Cluttering may coexist with stammering, language, literacy and/or motoric difficulties.

## Using the Guideline

This guideline addresses the speech and language therapy management practice for children and adults who present with a disorder of fluency and not the knowledge and skills needed by the Speech & Language Therapist working with this client population. Such skills are outlined in the parallel 'Underpinning knowledge and skills framework' – a product of the Competencies Project which should be read in conjunction with these guidelines and with Communicating Quality.

At the beginning of the guidance section, recommendations are made that are applicable to all disorders of fluency. Thereafter, the document is subdivided into five categories providing detailed and specific guidance in each of the following areas:

1   Developmental stammering in children
2   Developmental stammering in young people
3   Developmental stammering in adults
4   Acquired/late-onset stammering
5   Cluttering

This guideline should be read alongside the 'Core Guideline' and in combination with any of the following that may be relevant.

- Aphasia
- Autistic Spectrum Disorders
- Cleft Palate & Velopharyngeal Abnormalities
- Clinical Voice Disorders
- Deafness/Hearing Loss
- Disorders of Mental Health & Dementia
- Disorders of Feeding, Eating, Drinking & Swallowing (Dysphagia)
- Dysarthria
- Head & Neck Cancer
- Pre-School Children with Communication, Language & Speech Needs
- School-Aged Children with Speech, Language & Communication Difficulties

# RECOMMENDATIONS FOR ALL DISORDERS OF FLUENCY

Stammering and, to a lesser extent, cluttering tend to become more complex over time. Coping strategies used by the individual can complicate the problem, and may manifest as increased tension and struggle, and/or the development of covert features. The impact on an individual's life is very variable and can range from being a limited impact on a few specific situations, to the fluency problem becoming a central feature of the individual's entire lifestyle. Specific therapy aims need to take account of the stage and nature of the person's stammering difficulties with speaking and should be discussed individually with the client or carer.

The impact of cluttering and the way it changes over time is variable. Therapists will need to assess for each individual the applicability of these general guidelines to individual clients with a cluttering speech pattern.

Clients or carers may come with information and beliefs regarding stammering or cluttering and with varied experiences of therapy, which may influence their current expectations.

Some clients retain a life-long vulnerability to fluency disruption and so may require repeated episodes of care at different stages in their lives.

## Information gathering and assessment (C)

1 Communication abilities in a range of contexts should always be considered.

2 A fluency disorder can be a part of a wider communication difficulty, therefore it is necessary to consider speech, language, social and communication skills.

3 A case history should include details of the problem, eg, onset details; family history of fluency problems; variability; speech behaviours; coping strategies; social environment; emotional responses and psychosocial impact.

4 An evaluation should include quantifiable measures including frequency; severity of dysfluency; speech rate and associated behaviours. The use of published measures is recommended.

5 The dysfluencies observed in the clinic may not be representative of all situations and so self/carer reports should be included.

6 Assessment also aims to investigate the effect of the difficulties with speaking on the individual's lifestyle, and the strengths and resources of the individual or carer that may impact on the therapy process.

7 Evaluation should include details of the client's previous therapy experiences, along with a description of their current expectations of therapy and desired outcomes.

### Rationale
A disorder of fluency may vary over time and therapy needs may alter as a result of changes in developmental, environmental, medical or other factors. It can be a complex problem, affecting people in different ways, and so a holistic view is required.

### Evidence
- Manning WH (2000) *Evidence Level IV*
- Guitar B (2000) *Evidence Level IV*

## Management (B)

1 The Speech & Language Therapist will:
- Provide the individual/carer with written and/or verbal information on communication difficulties pertinent to their needs.
- Outline the management options available to the individual/carer in relation to assessment results, including the individual's perception of the problem and his/her needs.
- explain the process of therapy to the individual/carer at the onset and at key stages of intervention. This should include information regarding the content of therapy sessions and the role of the individual/carer in continuing clinic work in everyday speaking contexts.
- Discuss the process of change, probable effects and therapeutic prognosis with the individual/carer in

order to give him/her a realistic expectation of outcomes.

2  The client should be involved in the decision-making process and in the identification of therapy goals.

3  Collaborative working should, as far as possible, reflect a shared perspective and, wherever applicable, build mutual understanding and appropriate support, eg, school, workplace, family.

4  This client group benefits from a range of service delivery options, eg, individual therapy, group therapy, intensive therapy. Parents/carers may also benefit from participating in a group setting to share experiences and acquire skills to support the individual during the course of therapy and in the longer term.

*Rationale*
Communication takes place within the social environment and the individual's communicative partners are therefore an integral part of the therapy process.

*Evidence*
- Hayhow R, Cray AM & Enderby P (2002) *Evidence Level III*
- Mallard AR (1998) *Evidence Level III*
- Rustin L & Cook F (1995) *Evidence Level IV*

## DEVELOPMENTAL STAMMERING IN CHILDREN

Developmental stammering occurs initially during childhood. The overt speech symptoms will include some or all of the following: part word repetition; prolongations and/or blocking. Coping strategies may occur early or develop over time, for example changing words, situation avoidance, or changes in nonverbal behaviour. In addition, fear of stammering may cause psychological or emotional distress.

Developmental stammering may be transient or persistent. Current research suggests that of the 5 percent of children who stammer, the problem will resolve in one third of cases within 18 months. An additional third will resolve by three years post-onset.

The following factors are thought to be related to persistence of stammering:

- Gender (females are more likely to recover).
- Family history of persistent stammering.
- Additional speech and language problems.
- Length of time since onset (greater risk if the stammering has persisted for more than a year).
- Stammering that is episodic is more likely to resolve.

Persistence is not related to the type or severity of stammering at onset. Early referral is encouraged in order that the Speech & Language Therapist can assess a child's risk for persistent stammering and thereby make case by case decisions regarding when and how to intervene.

### Assessment (B)

All points in the information gathering and assessment section apply. In addition, the following are particularly relevant to the assessment of children who stammer.

1  The assessment procedure should be adjusted for the stage and nature of the developmental stammering and the age or maturity of the child.

2  Syllables stammered and a detailed description of the stammering behaviours should be gained.

3  Published scales or questionnaires should be used to evaluate the child's perceptions, attitudes and sequelae of stammering.

4  Standardised speech and language assessments should be used as a screening procedure or in more depth as required. Coexisting speech and language difficulties may be present in half of the children who stammer.

5  Patterns of communication within a family influence a child's developing speech, language and fluency skills. Observations of the child interacting with significant others may be documented in order to ascertain whether changes in interaction styles would be beneficial to the child's fluency.

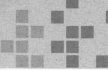
**6** With parental/carer permission, verbal or written reports should be obtained from the nursery or educational setting to provide a comprehensive picture of the child's communication skills. This will also provide an opportunity to learn about the strategies that others are using to help the child.

*Rationale*
Stammering is a complex disorder that requires a thorough investigation.

*Evidence*
- Yairi E, Ambrose NG, Paden EP & Throneburg RN (1996) *Evidence Level IIa*
- Yairi E & Ambrose NG (1999) *Evidence Level III*
- Hill DG (1995) *Evidence Level IV*
- Christie E (1999) *Evidence Level IV*

## MANAGEMENT

Management is guided by assessment results. These will influence decisions regarding the need for monitoring versus therapy, and whether the focus will be primarily on the child's communication environment or on the child's speaking. The aim is to facilitate the process of natural recovery and prevent a longer term problem.

### Therapy Approaches

Therapy options can be divided into those that focus on the child's communicative environment and those with a focus on the child's speech. These approaches are not necessarily mutually exclusive.

The choice of therapeutic approach is guided by the maturity of the child, the length of time the child has been stammering, the parents' opinion and their ability to participate in therapy, as well as the child's previous experiences of therapy.

When parents require information and advice, rather than therapy, then discussion regarding why the child is a relatively low risk for persistent stammering would provide a framework for giving relevant information about early stammering. This may include information about what is thought to facilitate fluency development and reassurance concerning the parents'

role in the development of stammering.

Collaborative practices with parents will ensure that they become key partners in the process. Active parental involvement in therapy is fundamental in most therapy programmes.

### 1) Demands and Capacities Model (B)

These therapy programmes are based on the principle that a child's capacity for fluency can be enhanced naturally by reducing the internal and external demands that may be being placed on a vulnerable system. Learning two languages does not necessarily increase a child's risk of stammering.

*Rationale*
Stammering is a highly variable, context-sensitive disorder. Most children who stammer have the capacity to be more fluent at certain times according to a range of internal and external factors, within differing communicative environments.

*Evidence*
- Matthews S, Williams R & Pring T (1997) *Evidence Level III*
- Guitar B, Schaefer HK, Donahue-Kilburg G & Bond L (1992) *Evidence Level III*
- Weiss AL & Zebrowski PM (1992) *Evidence Level III*
- Gottwald SR (1999) *Evidence Level IV*
- Yairi E (1997) *Evidence Level IV*

### 2) Child (fluency) focused therapy (A)

These therapies aim at direct modification of the child's stammering, usually involving a behavioural methodology and, in some cases, involving parents/carers. In the Lidcombe Program the therapist's role is to teach the parents how to carry out the therapy at home.

*Rationale*
Early stammering is viewed as a maladaptive response that can be replaced by more adaptive behaviours through the use of appropriate and timely feedback. Such therapies need to be carefully structured.

*Evidence*
- Harris V, Onslow M, Packman A, Harrison E & Menzies R

(2002) *Evidence Level Ib*
- Onslow M, Andrews C & Lincoln M (1994) *Evidence Level IIa*
- Kingston M, Huber A, Onslow M, Jones M & Packman A (2003) *Evidence Level IIa*
- Ryan BP & Van Kirk Ryan B (1995) *Evidence Level III*
- Onslow M, Costa L, Andrews C, Harrison E & Packman A (1996) *Evidence Level III*

### 3) Integrated approaches

Integrated approaches offer a personalised programme of therapy that accounts for the complexity of some children's stammering problem. Therapy will encompass the environmental factors that influence the child's stammering as well as addressing the cognitive, affective and behavioural aspects of stammering.

*Rationale*
Stammering in childhood may be seen as the result of the complex interaction between developing physiological, cognitive, affective, environmental and linguistic factors. Each child who stammers will need an approach that accounts for his or her particular needs.

*Evidence*
- Yaruss JS & Reardon N (2003) *Evidence Level IV*

### Coexisting Speech & Language Problems

Children with additional speech, language or oro-motor difficulties should be offered therapy that addresses these problems either in parallel or sequentially to their stammering therapy. The nature of the coexisting problems will determine the primary need of the child. Therapy for speech and language problems will focus initially on 'input', eg, phonological, word-finding strategies, rather than 'output' strategies.

*Rationale*
Speech, language and oro-motor problems may coexist with stammering. While the difficulties may not always achieve clinical significance, they could contribute to the risk of persistence and need to be included as part of the therapy programme.

*Evidence*
- Wolk L, Edwards ML & Conture EG (1993) *Evidence Level III*
- Ratner NB & Silverman SU (2000) *Evidence Level III*
- Logan K & LaSalle L (2003) *Evidence Level IV*
- Wolk L (1998) *Evidence Level IV*
- Nippold M (1990) *Evidence Level IV*

## THE YOUNG PERSON WHO STAMMERS

### Impact

Stammering can have a significant impact on a young person's emotional well-being. It can be a serious problem affecting participation in many aspects of daily life.

### Therapy (B)

Therapy may be drawn from aspects of the child and adult therapies, but special consideration should be given to this stage of life and the impact that physiological, psychological, social and educational changes will be having on an individual's stammering problem. The timing and type of therapy will need to be adjusted according to the needs and motivation of the individual.

*Rationale*
Adolescence can be a challenging life stage for many young people without the additional stress of stammering.

*Evidence:*
- Hancock K, Craig A, McCready C, McCaul A, Costello D, Campbell K & Gilmore G (1998) *Evidence Level IIa*
- Craig A, Hancock K, Chang E, McCready C, Shepley A, McCaul A, Costello D, Harding S, Kehren R, Masel C & Reilly K (1996) *Evidence Level IIa*
- Blood G, Blood I, Tellis G & Gabel R (2001) *Evidence Level IIa*
- Boberg E & Kully D (1994) *Evidence Level III*
- Cooper EB & Cooper CS (1995) *Evidence Level IV*
- Kully D & Langevin M (1999) *Evidence Level IV*
- Rustin L, Spence R & Cook F (1995) *Evidence Level IV*
- Botterill W & Cook F (1987) *Evidence Level IV*

## DEVELOPMENTAL STAMMERING IN ADULTS

Developmental stammering in adults can be defined as stammering that developed during childhood.

All points in the information gathering and assessment section apply. In addition, the following are particularly relevant to the assessment of adults who stammer.

### Assessment

Communication abilities in a range of contexts should always be considered. A fluency disorder should be considered in the context of the client's broader communication skills (eg, non-verbal, language, articulation/phonology, pragmatic skills). A case history should include:

- **Onset and developmental history of the stammer.**
- **Speech behaviours (including variability).**
- **Psychosocial impact (emotional responses).**
- **Avoidance behaviours (eg, words, situations).**
- **An estimate of the client's readiness to change.**

*Rationale*
In an adult, the interplay between the stammering behaviours (overt features), and the thoughts and feelings (covert features) related to stammering and the individual's environment, is likely to be well established.

*Evidence*
- Wright L & Ayre A (2000) *Evidence Level IV*
- Manning W (1999) *Evidence Level IV*
- Turnbull J (2000) *Evidence Level IV*

### Management

Therapy approaches include fluency shaping (eg, rate control), stammer-more-fluently approaches (eg, block modification), and psychological therapies, eg, cognitive therapies, PCP, counselling skills and communication skills training. These are not mutually exclusive.

The therapy approaches used are determined by the assessment findings, the agreed goals and time-scale for therapy. If the overt stammering features appear more significant than the covert features, fluency-shaping therapy may be the most appropriate first therapy approach. If the covert stammering features, eg, avoidance, appear more significant, therapy will address these features first, eg, avoidance reduction therapy.

*Rationale*
It is important to recognise both overt and covert aspects of stammering and the relative impact each has on the individual. Stammering in adults presents in a highly variable way, both intra- and inter-personally, so therapy approaches need to take this variability into account.

*Evidence*
- Evesham M & Fransella F (1985) *Evidence Level Ib*
- Stewart T (1996) *Evidence Level III*
- Stewart T & Grantham C (1993) *Evidence Level III*
- Hayhow R, Cray AM & Enderby P (2002) *Evidence Level III*

### Therapy Approaches

Therapy approaches can be focused on speech fluency, or the psychosocial aspects of stammering.

### 1) Speak more fluently (fluency shaping) (B)

**This approach advocates that therapy should aim to replace stammered speech with fluent speech. These strategies may include slower speech rate, easy phrase initiation (gentle voice onset), soft contacts and deliberate flow between words and/or breath-stream management. Traditionally, there is little attention given to changing feelings and attitudes during the therapy process.**

*Rationale*
Stammering is seen as a sensory-motor processing deficit with an overlay of learned behaviours. Developing skills that enable clients to cope with this deficit is the primary goal of therapy. Negative feelings and attitudes to speaking are assumed to change as a result of changes in speech behaviour.

*Evidence*
- Onslow M, Costa L, Andrews C, Harrison E & Packman A (1996) *Evidence Level III*
- Howie PM, Tanner S & Andrews G (1981) *Evidence Level III*

## 2) Stammer more fluently (stammering modification) (B)

These therapy approaches are based on the principle that increased fluency can be facilitated through developing the client's skills in modifying stammering as it occurs.

*Rationale*
Proponents of this approach view stammering as a momentary disruption in the timing and sequencing of the muscle movements for speech, which may be compounded by struggle behaviours. This approach therefore develops the client's ability to modify hard, tense moments of stammering into slow, easy and effortless ones. The development of a more open and accepting attitude towards stammering is seen as a prerequisite for this approach.

*Evidence*
- Blood G, Blood I, Tellis G & Gabel R (2001) *Evidence Level IIa*
- Manning W, Burlison A & Thaxton D (1999) *Evidence Level IIa*

## 3) Avoidance Reduction (B)

Management of stammering needs to consider the avoidance behaviours arising from the cognitive and emotional components that are part of the individual's beliefs about stammering. Therapy aims to reduce avoidance in a systematic, hierarchical way, at any or all of the following levels: word, situation, feelings and relationships.

*Rationale*
It is thought that the individual's inability to accept themselves as a person who stammers leads to avoidance of stammering at a variety of levels.

*Evidence*
Professional consensus

## 4) Communication Skills

A comprehensive approach to the management of stammering can include training in social skills, problem-solving and assertiveness skills.

*Rationale*
Facilitating the individual's understanding and experience of interpersonal and assertiveness skills can significantly enhance effective communication, and help to reduce the perceived negative impact of stammering.

*Evidence*
- Rustin L & Khur A (1998) *Evidence Level IV*

## 5) Psychological Therapies (A)

There are a number of psychological/counselling approaches that can be used to address the cognitive and/or affective aspects of stammering. Many of these approaches require additional postgraduate training, eg, personal construct therapy, cognitive-behavioural therapy.

*Rationale*
For some individuals the emotional and/or cognitive aspects of stammering may be the most significant components. They may compound the behavioural aspects of the stammer. It is therefore important to address the affective and/or cognitive aspects of stammering to facilitate long-term change.

*Evidence*
- Evesham M & Fransella F (1985) *Evidence Level Ib*
- DiLollo A, Manning WH & Neimeyer RA (2003) *Evidence Level IIa*

## 6) Other Approaches (C)

Although clinical evidence is accumulating for other approaches, such as solution-focused brief therapy and neuro-linguistuic programming, as yet research evidence is not available to guide the Speech & Language Therapist in the selection of such approaches. These approaches may be helpful as adjuncts to therapy previously mentioned.

*Rationale*
The highly individual nature of stammering and an individual's therapy needs and preferences require a range of therapies to facilitate long-term change.

*Evidence*
- Stewart T (1996) *Evidence Level IV*

## Maintenance (B)

Any management programme for dysfluent individuals must include strategies to promote change over the long term. The Speech & Language Therapist will include, where practicable, follow-up at 3, 6 and 12 months and 2 years post-therapy in order to determine effectiveness.

An intervention programme for adults who stammer should include consideration of strategies to manage relapse.

### Rationale
Speech fluency often relapses without the client using active behavioural and cognitive/emotional strategies to maintain the fluency skills and/or attitudinal changes. Life changes can affect speaking, and the communication demands placed upon the individual can require further episodes of therapy.

### Evidence
- Stewart T (1996) *Evidence Level III*
- Craig A (1998) *Evidence Level III*
- Stewart T (1996) *Evidence Level III*

## ACQUIRED / LATE ONSET IN ADULTS

### Assessment

Assessment for adults with late onset of stammering would not differ in essence from the assessments outlined for all disorders of fluency. However, a number of additional factors would need to be considered:

- Specific details of the onset of the symptoms (ie, sudden or gradual onset, progression or development of symptoms and events associated with the time of onset).
- Neurological investigations.
- Details of medication.
- Psychological status.
- Previous history of disorders of fluency.

This would include assessment of language and motor speech, as well as quantity and quality of the dysfluency.

### Rationale
Acquired dysfluency may be associated with a neurological condition (ie, trauma, progressive disease), may be induced by some types of drug/medication, or may also be a reoccurrence of dysfluency present at a younger age. It can also be of psychogenic origin.

### Evidence
- Van Borstel J, Van Lierde K, Van Cauwenberger P, Guldemont I & Orshoven M (1998) *Evidence Level III*
- Tippett D & Siebens A (1991) *Evidence Level III*
- Van Borsel J, Van Lierde K, Oostra K & Eeckhaut C (1997) *Evidence Level IV*
- Mahr G & Leith W (1992) *Evidence Level IV*
- Helm-Estabrooks N (1999) *Evidence Level IV*
- Baumgartner J (1999) *Evidence Level IV*

## Management (B)

The management of late-onset/acquired stammering disorders is based primarily on a hypothesis testing approach. In this approach, the therapist and the individual jointly agree on a proposed intervention strategy, based on the evidence available to them at that time. A review of progress at intervals of increasing duration is scheduled as part of the therapy approach. In this way, the desired outcome (eg, fluency enhancement, psychological readjustment) can be carefully monitored and, where it is not being achieved, the intervention strategy can be reconsidered and adapted as appropriate.

In order to facilitate this approach, it is incumbent on the Speech & Language Therapist to monitor the individual regularly, and record significant changes in response to the intervention agreed.

The Speech & Language Therapist will work collaboratively with other agencies/health professionals as appropriate.

### Rationale
Late-onset stammering is associated with a range of possible influencing factors, and occurs far less frequently than developmental stammering. There have been insufficient documented cases for profiles or subgroups to emerge.

*Evidence*
- Stewart T & Grantham C (1993) *Evidence Level III*
- Stewart T (1997) *Evidence Level III*

## Therapy Approaches (B)

Therapy approaches can focus on speech fluency and psychosocial aspects of stammering as they develop over time.

*Rationale*
Specific fluency shaping techniques and stammering modification techniques have been shown to be effective in managing late onset of stammering in adults. In addition, the individual with late-onset stammering can develop psychosocial issues as the symptoms persist.

*Evidence*
- Market KE, Montague JC, Buffalo MD & Drummond SS (1990) *Evidence Level III*
- Stewart T & Rowley D (1996) *Evidence Level III*
- Stewart, T (1997) *Evidence Level III*

# CLUTTERING

Cluttering is often described as a disorder of speech and language processing. It is almost always characterised by impairment in the formulation of language, and is likely to affect all channels of communication, eg, speech, reading and writing, in varying combinations and to varying degrees of severity.

Cluttering often results in rapid, dysrhythmic, sporadic, unintelligible speech, with frequent omission or elision of syllables.

There can often be a lack of awareness of symptoms in the individual who may or may not demonstrate poor concentration skills and a short attention span.

Cluttering can coexist with a range of other disorders that may include stammering, attention deficit hyperactivity disorder, language/learning difficulties and/or motor-speech impairments.

## Assessment (B)

1  The following should be considered in addition to the information obtained from a full case history:
   - The individual's awareness of difficulties, attitude towards therapy and intention to change.
   - Presence of associated difficulties, eg, in reading, writing, and how these have affected, and may continue to affect, functional as well as academic performance.

2  Evaluation of overt behaviour

*Speech and Language*
- Assessment of speech rate (ie, syllables per minute). This may be carried out by:
   a  spontaneous speaking (tape-recorded 5 minutes SPM)
   b  reading out loud (SPM tape-recorded, 500 words)
- Analysis of speech
- Voice, eg, monotone speech, initial loud voice that trails off to a murmur.
- Analysis of the reading out loud task, using the same evaluation as for the spontaneous speaking task, in order to make accurate comparison of the different speaking activities.
- Evaluation should include standardised/non-standardised measures of language, including word-finding skills, sequencing and narrative ability and appropriate use of syntax and grammar.
- Assessment also aims to include information on the individual's spelling, organisation of written language and reading skills.
- Assessment of pragmatic language
- To determine if cluttering coexists with stuttering, analyse speech samples for stuttering behaviours.
- The following should be observed and discussed with the individual as appropriate. Video evaluation can be helpful for discussion.
   - Attention/distractability, presence of heightened activity levels, prosody, reading and writing, rhythm/musicality, articulation and avoidance of polysyllabic words
   - It should also be noted whether the client shows improved speech when concentrating.

■ An evaluation should take into account the individual's level of awareness and insight concerning his/her communication difficulties.

*Non-verbal behaviours*
■ An assessment of motor skills:
  ● General coordination
  ● Dexterity and hand-writing accuracy
  ● Oral speech mechanism examination
  ● Organisational abilities

*Other behaviours*
■ It is to be noted that associated problems may be identified with a diagnosis of cluttering, eg, learning disability, dyslexia, behavioural problems, attention deficit disorder, auditory processing difficulties. This information may be obtained through either the interview process or referral and consultation with other professionals for diagnosis.

3 Covert evaluation
■ Awareness of fluency or intelligibility problems and insight in relation to speaking – the interview process and video feedback can facilitate this evaluation.
■ Report of confusion or frustration with regard to speaking and the responses of others.
■ Individual's attitude towards therapy and intention to change.

*Rationale*
Cluttering is a complex impairment affecting a range of speech output behaviours and higher order language functioning. The client's lack of insight concerning their communication behaviour is a diagnostic marker of this condition. Differentiating cluttering from other disorders can be difficult. Assessment therefore needs to be comprehensive and include behavioural, emotional, neuro-psychological and language components.

*Evidence*
■ Tiegland A (1996) *Evidence Level IIa*
■ St Louis KO & Myers FL (1995) *Evidence Level IV*
■ Ward D (2003) *Evidence Level IV*

**Management**

Following assessment, the Speech & Language Therapist will consider the impact that the reduced intelligibility has upon the individual's communication and life overall and their commitment to therapy.

**Therapy**

Cluttering is a complex and variable disorder and so individual planning is essential and hypotheses concerning the best approach to take with an individual need regular testing and modification as required. Therapy needs to be highly structured, and would usually focus on just one or two aspects of the condition during any one phase of therapy. Such intervention may include work on:

■ Developing rate-control strategies.
■ Increasing awareness and self-monitoring skills.
■ Developing attention and listening skills to enhance communication skills.
■ Consolidating and expanding semantic, syntactic and lexical abilities.
■ Extending speech production and articulatory accuracy, prosody and rhythm skills.
■ Enhancing language planning and formulation abilities.
■ Developing strategies to reduce the number of dysfluencies experienced.

When stammering is also present, this may become more apparent as the cluttering improves, and would need to be addressed.

*Rationale*
It has been shown that intervention on rate of speech and self-monitoring behaviours produces change.

*Evidence*
■ Thacker RC & De Nil LF (1996) *Evidence Level III*
■ Craig A (1996) *Evidence Level III*
■ Daly DA & Burnett ML (1996) *Evidence Level III*
■ Daly DA & Burnett ML (1999) *Evidence Level IV*
■ St Louis KO & Myers FL (1997) *Evidence Level IV*

# 5.10 Disorders of Mental Health & Dementia

## Introduction

This guideline refers to children, adolescents and adults who present with difficulty in communication. There is a complex interrelationship between mental health and communication disorders with a wide variety of communication disorders coexisting with mental health disorders. The field of the Child and Adolescent Mental Health Service covers emotional, behavioural and family relationship issues as well as psychiatric disorders.

This guideline has three distinct, yet interrelated strands. For the sake of clarity, the guideline has been divided into:

- Children and Adolescent Mental Health Disorders
- Adult Mental Health Disorders excluding Dementia
- Adult Organic Mental Health Disorders: Dementia

## Using the Guideline

This guideline addresses the speech and language therapy management practice for children, adolescents and adults who present with difficulty in communication and not the knowledge and skills needed by the Speech & Language Therapist working with this client population. Such skills are outlined in the parallel 'Underpinning knowledge and skills framework' – a product of the Competencies Project – and should be read in conjunction with this and with *Communicating Quality*.

This guideline should be read alongside the 'Core Guideline' and in combination with any of the following that may be relevant.

- Aphasia
- Autistic Spectrum Disorders
- Cleft Palate & Velopharyngeal Abnormalities
- Clinical Voice Disorders
- Deafness/Hearing Loss
- Disorders of Fluency
- Disorders of Feeding, Eating, Drinking & Swallowing (Dysphagia)
- Dysarthria
- Head & Neck Cancer
- Pre-school Children with Communication, Language & Speech Needs
- School-aged Children with Speech, Language and Communication Difficulties

## ASSESSMENT FOR CHILD AND ADOLESCENT MENTAL HEALTH DISORDERS

### Core Speech & Language Skills (C)

The individual's core speech and language levels will be assessed, ie, their verbal and non-verbal, receptive and expressive language skills. It is important to include evaluation of the following:

- **Use of language and pragmatics**
- **Verbal reasoning**
- **Attention and concentration**
- **Auditory and visual processing and short-term memory**
- **Prosodic features**
- **Fluency**
- **Idiosyncratic communication including neologisms**
- **Socially unacceptable means of communication**
- **Eating, drinking and swallowing**
- **Variability in performance**

*Rationale*
The profile may be used for differential diagnosis. It may identify previously undiagnosed communication difficulties.

*Evidence*
- Baker L & Cantwell DP (1987) Evidence Level III
- Giddon J, Milling I & Campbell NB (1996) Evidence Level III

### Variability in Performance (C)

Owing to the nature of emotional and behavioural disorders in mental health disorders:

- **Assessment will be carried out in a range of settings.**

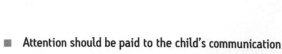

- Attention should be paid to the child's communication with a range of people.
- Medication must be taken into account.
- A variety of strategies should be used for collecting information including direct assessment, questionnaire and checklists, observation and interviewing significant others.

*Rationale*
Owing to the nature of emotional, behavioural and mental health disorders, there is likely to be significant variability in the individual's performance.

*Evidence*
- Greenspan SI (1992) Evidence Level IV
- Lund N (1993) Evidence Level IV
- Tankersley M & Balan C (1999) Evidence Level IV

## MANAGEMENT FOR CHILD AND ADOLESCENT MENTAL HEALTH DISORDERS

### General Principles (C)

The Speech & Language Therapist will place the communication disorder within the context of the overall emotional, behavioural or psychiatric disorder. The intervention will be discussed and agreed with the multi-disciplinary team, in collaboration with the parents and carers, the individual, educational staff and significant others.

*Rationale*
It is essential that all decisions regarding the individual's management are agreed with those involved in order to:

- Identify and agree which interventions receive priority at any stage in time.
- Identify any factors that may negatively impact upon speech and language management.
- Minimise any resistance which may be counterproductive.

*Evidence*
- Roth FP (1999) Evidence Level IV

### Type and Method of Intervention (C)

The Speech & Language Therapist may:

- Advise on the nature of the communication difficulty.
- Recommend appropriate strategies to enhance the individual's communication.
- Take on a wider role with the mental health team either individually or as a co-worker.

The Speech & Language Therapist should refer to the other relevant guidelines.

*Rationale*
Individuals may present with any form of communication disorder but the priorities for, and type of, intervention may not follow an expected route due to the impact of the disorder.

*Evidence*
- Jones J (1995) Evidence Level IV
- Wintgens A (2001) Evidence Level IV

## ASSESSMENT FOR ADULT MENTAL HEALTH DISORDERS (EXCLUDING DEMENTIA)

### Information Prior to First Appointment (C)

Prior to the first appointment, the Speech & Language Therapist will, if possible, liaise with other professionals involved in the client's care. This is not only to gather information on the client's communication but also on their interventions, both form and content.

*Rationale*
This will provide information on general compliance, presentation and behaviour which will help the therapist to be fully prepared.

*Evidence*
Professional consensus

## Clinical History Taking (C)

Included in the case-history for these clients should be a detailed psychiatric history:

- Psychiatric diagnosis (DSM or ICD)
- Past and present medication
- Past in-patient admissions
- Any forensic history
- Legal status
- Care Programme Approach information

*Rationale*
Information on medication is essential due to possible side effects, both long- and short-term. Admission information gives an indication of the severity and course of the illness. Forensic history and legal status give:

- Indications of possible risk factors, essential for safe patient management.
- A framework for the information the patient is giving.
- An indication of possible patterns of compliance.

*Evidence*
Professional consensus.

## Assessment of Factors Contributing to Communication

In order to form a diagnosis a clinical evaluation of the individual will consider:

- Attention and concentration
- Mood, motivation and behaviour
- Insight
- Memory – immediate, recent and long-term
- Orientation – time, place and person
- Medication – types, levels and side effects
- Effects of sensory impairment
- Psychotic symptoms, including for example, auditory hallucinations, visual hallucinations, lack of motivation, poverty of thought.
- Incidence or patterns of verbal or physical aggression.
- Implications of diagnosis of personality disorder, depending on type.

- Possibility of dual diagnosis. The presenting problem may be developmental, linked to the mental health problem or a combination of both.

*Rationale*
Different mental health diagnoses are associated with particular patterns of cognitive functioning, behaviour and psychological symptoms. It is therefore important to assess or gather information regarding all these aspects.

*Evidence*
Professional consensus.

## Assessment of Communication Skills (B)

The individual's core speech and language levels will be assessed, ie, their verbal and non-verbal, receptive and expressive language skills, placing particular emphasis on the following:

- Use of language and pragmatics – could be looking for delay in acquisition or disordered use of skills.
- Specific language features such as paraphasias, neologisms.
- Pressure or poverty of speech.
- Discourse analysis to ascertain presence of features such as derailment and circumlocution.
- Amount and relevance of content.
- Auditory processing – presence of skills or disruption of skills.
- Prosodic features of speech.
- Intelligibility.
- Topic.
- Sequencing – particularly when client is experiencing acute episodes of mental illness.
- Environment.
- Sensory motor evaluation.

Consideration will be given to whether the individual's communication profile is in line with their overall level of functioning.

*Rationale*

A comprehensive evaluation of communication is required in order to:

- Identify developmental delay and/or pervasive difficulties. Language disorder is under-diagnosed in this population.
- Establish a baseline against which to monitor change.
- Contribute to multidisciplinary assessment, care plans and management.
- Inform and advise carers.
- Facilitate opportunities for verbal and non-verbal communication.

A comprehensive evaluation of sensory-motor skills is required in order to establish if there is persistent or transient sensory-motor deficit which may be due to:

- Medication effects
- A degenerative condition
- A deterioration of existing skills

*Evidence*

- Faber R, Abrams R, Taylor MA, Kasprison A, Morris C & Weisz R (1983) Evidence Level III

**Variability in Performance (C)**

Assessment of communication and/or swallowing will be carried out in a range of settings. A variety of strategies should be used for collecting information including direct assessment, observation and interviewing significant others.

*Rationale*

Due to the nature of mental health disorders there is likely to be significant variability in the individual's performance. This variability can be seen over short periods of time. Deterioration over longer periods is also a possibility that must be considered depending on the course of the illness, response to medication, etc.

*Evidence*

Professional consensus.

## MANAGEMENT OF COMMUNICATION FOR ADULT MENTAL HEALTH DISORDERS

### Timing of Intervention (C)

The Speech & Language Therapist will place the communication disorder within the context of the overall emotional, behavioural or psychiatric disorder. The timing and content of intervention will be discussed and agreed with the multidisciplinary team, carers and significant others.

*Rationale*

It is essential that all decisions regarding the individual's management are agreed within the multidisciplinary team, family, carers and significant others in order to:

- Identify and agree which interventions receive priority at any stage in time.
- Identify any factors which may negatively impact upon speech and language therapy management, eg, course of the illness, changes in medication.
- Minimise any resistance to therapy/recommendations, whether from the patient, team or carers.

*Evidence*

Professional consensus.

### Communication Interventions (A)

The Speech & Language Therapist will remediate and/or facilitate communication in the areas that are difficult for the individual. Management of such must be within the context of the overall emotional, psychiatric and/or behavioural disorder. The Speech & Language Therapist should refer to the relevant RCSLT clinical guideline for additional guidance.

Variations seen in this client group in terms of management include:

- The likelihood that episodes of care will be longer and may need to be more flexible in their delivery.
- Awareness that breaks in treatment may result from fluctuations in the client's mental health and this has to be accommodated.

- The need for a strong motivational component in the therapy programme as a result of the negative symptoms of mental illness.
- The need to work closely with the whole multidisciplinary team and significant others in order to maximise the effectiveness of any intervention.
- A need to recognise the need to respond flexibly to fluctuations in the individual's mental health which result in changes in presentation and ability, even within a session.
- The communication environment can have a strong influence, either positive or negative, on the outcome of an episode of care. It may be that this is addressed prior to/or in place of direct work with the client.
- High levels of stress and distress are common in this client group. Interventions to assist the client's understanding and management of this, as well as ongoing support, are essential.

*Rationale*

Individuals may present with any form of communication disorder but the priorities for intervention or the hierarchy of intervention may not follow an expected route due to the impact of the disorder.

*Evidence*

- Atkinson JM, Coia DA, Gilmour WH & Harper JP (1996) Evidence Level Ib
- Wong SE & Woolsey JE (1989) Evidence Level III
- Hoffman RE & Satal S (1993) Evidence Level III

### Training (B)

Training for other members of the team, carers and significant others should be designed to have a positive effect on the individual's communication environment by:

- Raising staff and others' awareness of communication in general.
- Highlighting communication problems that may be present with this client group.
- Introducing strategies that other members of the team, carers or significant others can utilise to improve their communication with this client group.

*Rationale*

Training can benefit both the individual and the team, carers and significant others. The use of appropriate communication strategies can facilitate client management, reduce the intensity and frequency of behavioural problems and distress related to the illness.

Successful communication is also essential in enhancing the well-being of the individual.

*Evidence*

- Shulman MD & Mandel E (1988) Evidence Level III

## ASSESSMENT OF EATING AND SWALLOWING ASSOCIATED WITH MENTAL HEALTH DISORDERS

### Assessment of Eating and Swallowing (C)

The Speech & Language Therapist will take a detailed history in addition to carrying out structured observation at mealtimes. Particular attention should be paid to:

- Effects of mental health and mood on eating and swallowing.
- Effects of posture and general social skills on swallowing during the eating and drinking experience.
- Effects of medication on eating and swallowing.
- Effects of the environment on eating and swallowing.
- Case history including gradual versus sudden onset of problem and history of weight loss.

There may be limited awareness of the need for other investigations of swallowing, eg, videofluoroscopy, and it is essential that the Speech & Language Therapist highlight the possible usefulness of such investigations. In view of the nature of the disorders, patients are often unable/unwilling to cooperate with standardised dysphagia assessments and a functional approach needs to be taken.

*Rationale*

Eating and swallowing problems are common within this client group due to the side effects of medication. Differential diagnosis of the nature of the problem, eg, iatrogenic (due to drug therapy) versus psychological, is essential for effective management.

*Evidence*
- Bach DB, Pouget S, Belle K, Kilfoil M, Alfieri M, McEvoy J & Jackson G (1989)

## ASSESSMENT FOR ORGANIC MENTAL HEALTH DISORDERS: DEMENTIA

## ASSESSMENT OF COMMUNICATION

### Assessment of Factors Contributing to Communication (B)

In order to form a differential diagnosis a clinical evaluation of the individual will consider:

- Attention and concentration
- Effects of sensory impairment
- Mood, motivation and behaviour
- Insight
- Memory
  - Immediate
  - Recent and new learning
  - Long-term
- Registration, recall and recognition
- Orientation
- Perceptual and spatial disturbance
- Praxis
- Frontal lobe executive skills and reasoning
- The environment, eg, opportunity to communicate
- The communication skills of others
- Attitude or philosophy of caregivers

*Rationale*
Different dementing diseases are associated with particular patterns of cognitive impairment, behaviour and psychological symptoms. It is therefore important to assess or gather information regarding all these aspects. Cognition, behaviour and psychological factors all impact on communication skills and are also therefore important when considering advice and management.

*Evidence*
- Powell AL, Cummings JL, Hill MA & Benson DF (1988) Evidence Level III
- Azuma T & Bayles KA (1997) Evidence Level IV
- Purandare N, Allen NHP & Burns A (2000) Evidence Level IV

### Assessment of Communication Skills (B)

An evaluation of the individual's core communication skills will be undertaken. In addition, the following aspects will be considered:

- Case history, including gradual versus sudden onset and progression of problem
- Pragmatics and discourse
- Inadequate use of referents
- Repetition of topic or questions
- Paucity of speech
- Problems with turn-taking
- Non-verbal skills (particularly relevant for those with advanced dementia)
- Inappropriate topic change or maintenance
- Confabulation or evidence of memory disturbance
- Verbal fluency versus visual confrontation naming
- Intelligibility, eg, presence of dysarthria or apraxia
- Sequencing
- Verbal reasoning
- Environment
- Family situation
- Sentence and single word comprehension
- Reading aloud versus reading for meaning

*Rationale*
A comprehensive evaluation of communication is required in order to:

- Make an input to the contribution of differential diagnosis, eg, normal versus abnormal aging; different dementia types; dementia versus depression.
- Create a baseline for monitoring change.
- Contribute to multidisciplinary assessment, care plans and management.
- Inform and advise carers.
- Facilitate opportunities for verbal and non-verbal communication.

*Evidence*
- Monsch AU, Bondi MW, Butters N & Salmon DP (1992) Evidence Level III
- Ripich DN, Carpenter BD & Ziol EW (2000) Evidence Level III

## Variability of Performance (B)

A battery of assessments should be carried out across a range of settings, at different times of day, over a period of time and with a variety of speakers, as there may be significant variability in the individual's performance.

### Rationale
The progressive nature of dementia means that assessment must be an on-going dynamic part of intervention. Comprehension and ongoing language assessment may also be a more sensitive indicator of change in performance following drug treatment.

### Evidence
- McKeith IG, Perry RH, Fairbairn AF, Jabeen S & Perry EK (1992) Evidence Level III

# MANAGEMENT OF COMMUNICATION

## Communication Interventions in Early Dementia (B)

Interventions in early stage dementias will be based on the communication and cognitive strengths and weaknesses of the individual and assessment of the emotional impact these have on the individual and carer. Communication can be enhanced through specific work on conversation.

### Rationale
Dementia is not necessarily a global decline in all functions. In the early stages, some areas of cognition may be relatively spared and can compensate for those areas affected. This means that some individuals may be able to learn and retain strategies taught to them to increase communicative effectiveness.

### Evidence
- Acton GJ, Mayhew PA, Hopkins BA & Yauk S (1999) Evidence Level III
- Azuma T & Bayles KA (1997) Evidence Level IV
- Lubinski (1995) Evidence Level IV
- Erber NP (1994) Evidence Level IV

## Communication Interventions in Later Dementia (B)

Interventions in moderate to advanced dementia should focus on appropriate facilitation of verbal and non-verbal skills. A variety of techniques and activities may be used, including life-history books, memory aids and groupwork such as reminiscence and SONAS and use of sensory stimulation.

### Rationale
Communication, both verbal and non-verbal, is a fundamental human need. Meeting this need by facilitating and enhancing communication in any form can be vital to patients' well-being. This will include all those in the individual's communication environment.

### Evidence
- Pietro MJS & Boczko F (1998) Evidence Level IIa

## Partnership with Carer (B)

The main focus of intervention may be with the carer(s) rather than the individual. This may be on an individual basis or within a group, eg, a relatives' support group. The purpose of such intervention is to:

- Establish the carer's perception, expectation and response to communication impairment.
- Explain the patient's communication strengths and weaknesses and how this relates to their dementia.
- Discuss and agree communication strategies.
- Refer to appropriate agencies for further support and advice.

### Rationale
There is a great deal of evidence that carers of people with dementia experience high levels of stress. Communication difficulties are found to be particularly stressful. The individual is unlikely to be able to alter their behaviour, so changes should be made by those around them or to the environment.

### Evidence
- Ripich DN, Ziol E, Fritsch T & Durand EJ (1999) Evidence Level IIa
- Shulman MD & Mandel E (1988) Evidence Level III
- Greene VL & Monahan DJ (1989) Evidence Level III

■ Cavanaugh JC, Dunn NJ, Mowery D, Feller C, Niederehe G, Fruge E & Volpendesta D (1989) Evidence Level III

## Training (C)

Training should be designed to facilitate communication between the person with dementia and those people offering the care or support. It can be offered on a one-to-one basis or in groups, and can be in the form of workshops, role-play, information-giving or formal education.

### Rationale

Training can benefit both the individual and the caregivers. The use of appropriate communication strategies can facilitate patient care management during activities of daily living and can reduce the intensity and frequency of behavioural problems related to the illness.

Successful communication also enhances the well-being of the sufferer.

### Evidence

■ Bayles KA, Kaszniak Aw, Tomoeda CK (1987) Evidence Level IV

## Environment (C)

The Speech & Language Therapist will make a comprehensive assessment of the communication environment and will advise on environmental enhancement. Enhancement of the communication environment should include passive environmental enrichment and improvement of active interaction between dementia patients and their physical and social surroundings.

### Rationale

The environment is not a passive backdrop but an active contributor to how well older people will function. The 'total environment' comprises the physical background, the individual and the relationship of the individual to others.

The environment of those with dementia is a crucial determinant of their well-being.

### Evidence

■ Lubinski R (1995) Evidence Level IV

## Group language stimulation (C)

Group therapy may be used to stimulate use of language and communication. The focus of such sessions may be directly language based or involve other activities that encourage communication during the activity. Such sessions may be carried out jointly with other professionals.

### Rationale

Increased use of language may enable patients to maintain communication skills for longer or may have an impact on mood, confidence and general well-being.

### Evidence

■ Clark L (1995) Evidence Level IV

# ASSESSMENT OF SWALLOWING IN DEMENTIA

## Assessment of Swallowing (B)

The Speech & Language Therapist will take a detailed history in addition to carrying out structured observation at mealtimes. Particular attention should be paid to:

■ Case history, including gradual versus sudden onset of problem, and history of weight loss.
■ Effects of mood and behaviour on eating and swallowing.
■ Effects of environment on eating and swallowing.
■ Effects of medication on eating and swallowing.
■ Effects of skill and attitude of person feeding patient.
■ Effects of posture on swallowing.
■ The individual's capacity to consent to treatment.
■ The need for ongoing and timely intervention.

### Rationale

Swallowing problems are common in the advanced stages of dementia but can occur earlier in some dementing diseases. In view of the nature of the disorder, patients are often unable to cooperate with standard dysphagia assessments. Because dysphagia rarely occurs in isolation in this group, standard dysphagia assessments need to be enhanced with other clinical investigations. Information can most usefully be gathered by talking to significant others and through observation. The 'Food for Thought 2000' article from the Alzheimer's Society is a useful document.

*Evidence*
- Steele CM, Greenwood C, Robertson C, Sidmon-Carlson R (1997) Evidence Level III
- Feinberg MJ, Ekberg O, Segall L & Tully J (1992) Evidence Level III

## MANAGEMENT OF SWALLOWING IN DEMENTIA

### Management of Swallowing (B)

**The Speech & Language Therapist will contribute to the multidisciplinary team decision regarding the potential need for non-oral nutrition and hydration.**

*Rationale*
The Speech & Language Therapist's role in this decision will be to contribute information regarding safety and efficiency of oral intake and the prognostic indicators for change. For those with advanced dementia, ethical issues surround whether non-oral feeding prolongs life at a reasonable quality or prolongs suffering. The decision-making process is also complex, given that the patient is unlikely to be able to consent. Medically, questions remain as to whether those in the advanced stages of dementia will actually benefit from non-oral feeding or whether a palliative approach is more appropriate. The British Medical Association 1999 paper, 'Withholding and Withdrawing Life-prolonging Medical Treatment: Guidance for Decision-making' documents the factors that should be taken into account, the process which should be followed and the safeguards which should be in place when considering the withholding or withdrawal of life-prolonging treatment. It includes a section relating to adults who lack the capacity to make or communicate decisions (http://www.bma.org.uk).

*Evidence*
- Littlewood *et al* (1997) Evidence Level III
- Finucane TE, Christmas C & Travis K (1999) Evidence Level IV

### Behavioural strategies (A)

**The Speech & Language Therapist will identify which behavioural strategies facilitate the eating and drinking process and communicate these to the relevant carers. These may include:**

- Providing additional situational cues prior, during and after mealtime, to orient the individual to mealtime, eg, place setting, assisting in preparation of food.
- Reducing distractions, eg, clutter on the table, noise in the environment.
- Verbal cues, eg, ranging from constant prompting to chew, to reassurance.
- Visual cues or symbols, eg, place names, menu cards.

*Rationale*
The above strategies aim to maximise the effectiveness of the individual's eating and drinking. It may also have a positive impact on both the individual's and carer's psychosocial experience of mealtimes.

*Evidence*
- Coyne ML & Hoskins L (1997) Evidence Level Ib
- Kayser-Jones J & Schell E (1997) Evidence Level III
- Osborn CL & Marshall MJ (1993) Evidence Level III

# 5.11 Dysarthria

## Introduction

Dysarthria is the collective term given to a group of related speech disorders that are due to disturbances in muscular control of the speech mechanism arising from a variety of pathologies. Such disturbances arise from damage to the central and/or peripheral nervous system, or as a result of a structural abnormality. It can occur in both children and adults and may be developmental or acquired. All the systems which contribute to speech production may be affected, eg, respiration, resonance, phonation, articulation and prosody, in a uniform manner or be selectively impaired with varying degrees of severity. It can result in varying degrees of impairment and cause speech to be completely unintelligible. It can co-occur alongside other disorders such as aphasia, apraxia and dysphagia.

## Using the Guideline

This guideline addresses the speech and language therapy management practice for those with dysarthria and not the knowledge and skills needed by the Speech & Language Therapist working with this client population. Such skills are outlined in the parallel 'Underpinning knowledge and skills framework' – a product of the Competencies Project – and should be read in conjunction with this and with *Communicating Quality*.

This guideline should be read alongside the 'Core Guideline' and in combination with any of the following that may be relevant.

- Aphasia
- Autistic Spectrum Disorders
- Cleft Palate & Velopharyngeal Abnormalities
- Clinical Voice Disorders
- Deafness/Hearing Loss
- Disorders of Feeding, Eating, Drinking & Swallowing (Dysphagia)
- Disorders of Fluency
- Disorders of Mental Health & Dementia
- Head & Neck Cancer
- Pre-school Children with Communication, Language & Speech Needs
- School-aged Children with Speech, Language & Communication Difficulties

## ASSESSMENT

### Multidisciplinary Team Working (C)

**The Speech & Language Therapist will work as a core member of the multi-/interdisciplinary team. The composition of the team may vary depending upon the setting.**

*Rationale*
The multidisciplinary management of individuals with dysarthria ensures a timely, efficient, integrated and holistic period of care.

*Evidence*
- Mitchell PR & Mahoney G (1995) Evidence Level IV

### Perceptual Assessment (B)

**A perceptual assessment will be made in order to acquire an accurate profile for analysis. The following parameters should be assessed:**

- **Orofacial musculature**
- **Respiratory function for speech, in particular their control and coordination**
- **Phonation**
- **Resonance**
- **Articulation**
- **Prosody**
- **Intelligibility**
- **Rationale**

**The main aim of the perceptual assessment is to provide a description of the speech and the musculature on which to base therapy and measure change. It enables:**

■ An analysis of the interrelation between speech subsystems.

■ The highlighting of those parameters which are contributing to the dysarthria.

■ Evaluation of each speech subsystem and the potential for change.

■ Establishment of a baseline and a measure of overall severity.

*Evidence*

■ Netsell R & Daniel B (1979) Evidence Level III

■ Duffy JR (1998) Evidence Level III

## Instrumental Evaluation (C)

A good quality audio recording is beneficial. Access to additional instrumentation for the measurement of respiratory and vocal parameters such as aerodynamics, pitch, intensity resonance, vibratory cycle and/or other aspects of vocal quality is recommended.

*Rationale*

An audio recording provides a reproducible record of the patient's voice and speech, which can be used for the perceptual evaluation of change and as input to other instrumental tools. The complexity of the speech signal results in auditory confusions, which can be clarified through instrumental assessments.

*Evidence*

Professional consensus.

## Communication Skills Profile (C)

A full profile of each individual's communication skills should be carried out. This should include, at a minimum:

■ The communicative skills of the individual, their strengths and needs.

■ The use of communication by the individual, in their current and likely environments.

■ The communication partner's own skills and usage.

■ The impact of the environment upon their communication.

■ An identification of any disadvantageous or helpful factors within the environment.

*Rationale*

It is necessary to collate all pertinent information on skills or influences, which can help, or are disadvantageous to, the individual within their social contexts.

*Evidence*

■ Yorkston KM, Strand EA & Kennedy MRT (1996) Evidence Level IV

■ Berry W & Saunders S (1983) Evidence Level IV

## Perception of Dysarthria (B)

Information should be elicited from the individual and family regarding their understanding of dysarthria and what they consider the impact of dysarthria is likely to be.

*Rationale*

It is important to gain the perspective of the individual and family regarding how the dysarthria affects all aspects of their lives. This can help to direct intervention and enables the therapist to undertake a comprehensive approach to management. The individual's perceptions influence the management approaches adopted and specific joint goal-setting for therapy. They also provide a valid baseline from which to measure change in well-being. The level of impairment may be disproportionate to the level of handicap experienced.

*Evidence*

■ Fox CM & Ramig LO (1997) Evidence Level III

## Differential Diagnosis (C)

The assessment findings will be analysed in order for the clinician to formulate a differential diagnosis of the dysarthria.

*Rationale*

It is necessary to interpret all assessment findings in order to determine the causal and maintaining factors that constitute the dysarthria and so develop a working hypothesis on which to base management.

*Evidence*

■ Murdoch B (1998) Evidence Level IV

■ Yorkston KM, Beukelman DR & Bell KR (1987) Evidence Level IV

## Competing Environmental Stimuli

**The impact of any competing environmental stimuli should be assessed.**

*Rationale*
The performance of an individual with dysarthria may vary according to the environmental conditions, particularly if other cognitive processes are affected, eg, attention and concentration, or if there are concomitant problems such as hearing loss. These need to be evaluated to enable accurate and reliable assessment.

*Evidence*
■ Yorkston KM, Strand EA & Kennedy MRT (1996) Evidence Level IV

## Psychosocial Impact of Dysarthria (C)

**An evaluation of the emotional, psychological and psychosocial impact of the dysarthria should be made for both the individual and the family.**

*Rationale*
The psychosocial effects of dysarthria on both the individual and the family need to be considered to enable effective support and management to be offered in a timely manner. In order to promote psychological well-being, an assessment and monitoring of changes in lifestyle; experience of loss and adjustment; the effect on relationships; changes in behaviour; emotional responses; attitudes; perceptions and socialisation is required using a variety of tools and quality-of-life measures.

*Evidence*
■ Yorkston KM, Bombardier C & Hammen VL (1994) Evidence Level III

## Conversational Partners (B)

**Existing and potential conversational partners should be identified and an evaluation made of their skills and experience in communicative interaction. This may include** family members, friends, volunteers and health professionals.

*Rationale*
It enables conversational partners to communicate in more meaningful and helpful ways and to provide supported interactions for those with dysarthria.

Before commencing training, an assessment needs to be made of the effectiveness of naturally occurring strategies that facilitate communication and the interactive patterns being used with the person with dysarthria to enable these to be developed and enhanced. It also enables barriers to communication to be considered.

*Evidence*
■ King JM & Gallegos-Santillan P (1999) Evidence Level III

## MANAGEMENT

The choice of therapy approaches is determined by the assessment findings and may involve a physiological, compensatory and/or an augmentative approach. A physiological approach is one which works directly to change specific aspects of the function of the subsystems, ie, respiratory; resonatory; phonatory; articulatory; and prosody. The goals for therapy also differ depending on the assessment findings and may be preventative, facilitative, rehabilitative or supportive.

### Education & Explanation

**An explanation of the normal anatomy and physiology of the orofacial tract and speech production will be provided. In addition, an explanation of the causal and maintaining factors that make up the dysarthria will be discussed.**

*Rationale*
Improved understanding of the vocal mechanism and associated factors gives the individual a rationale for active participation in therapy.

*Evidence*
Professional consensus.

## Physiological Approaches (A)

Where the aim is to reduce the degree of impairment or increase the physiological support for speech, a physiological approach may be appropriate. This may occur separately or in combination with either or both a compensatory and/or augmentative approach.

*Rationale*
In some instances it may be appropriate to work directly on the strength, speed and or function of the impaired musculature. In such a case, a variety of physiological approaches can be used.

*Evidence*
- Katsikitis M & Pilowsky I (1996) Evidence Level Ib
- Ramig L, Countryman S, Thompson L & Horii Y (1995) Evidence Level Ib
- Robertson SJ & Thomson F (1984) Evidence Level IIb
- Le Dorze G, Dionne L, Ryalls J, Julien M & Ouellet L (1992) Evidence Level III
- Robertson S (2001) Evidence Level IV

## Compensatory Approaches (B)

Where the aim is to minimise the effect of the overall disability and promote intelligibility, various compensatory approaches should be used. These may occur separately or in combination with a compensatory and/or augmentative approach.

*Rationale*
Compensatory approaches, for example rate control and modification of the environment, can be extremely effective in enabling the individual to modify their speech and use strategies to enhance their intelligibility.

*Evidence*
- Yorkston KM, Hammen VL, Beukelman DR & Traynor CD (1990) Evidence Level IIa
- Workinger MS & Netsell R (1992) Evidence Level III
- Berry W & Saunders S (1983) Evidence Level IV

## Augmentative Approaches (B)

When speech alone is insufficient to meet the individual's communication needs, a variety of augmentative strategies should be used.

*Rationale*
In certain instances additional means of communication are necessary for the individual to communicate effectively. These are likely to range from low-tech aids such as pen and paper and gesturing, to high-tech aids such as speech synthesisers. A variety of aids can be used simultaneously.

*Evidence*
- Garcia JM & Dagenais PA (1998) Evidence Level III
- Garcia JM & Cannito MP (1996) Evidence Level III
- Beliveau C, Hodge MM & Hagler PH (1995) Evidence Level III
- Hustad KC & Beukelman DR (2002) Evidence Level III
- Garcia JM & Cobb DS (2000) Evidence Level III

# 5.11 Aphasia

## Introduction

This guideline refers to adults who have aphasia. For ease of reading, the term 'aphasia' will be used throughout the guideline to mean aphasia and dysphasia. These terms are often used interchangeably in the field, but recent literature tends to use aphasia as the main term. This is a multi-modal language disorder and may affect a person's ability to understand and produce spoken and written language, leaving other cognitive abilities intact. All languages are similarly affected, including the sign languages used by deaf people. In some individuals the ability to use non-linguistic communication, such as gesture and drawing, is also impaired.

Aphasia is not a unitary disorder and can co-occur with a number of other disorders, eg, apraxia of speech or cognitive communication disorders. These coexisting disorders must be taken into consideration in all aspects of management. However, this guideline only addresses aphasia of acute onset.

Aphasia is a long-term, life-changing condition, which affects both the individual and others around them. Living with aphasia involves individuals and those in their environment in a process of adaptation to change, in terms of communication style, lifestyle and sense of self. The influence of cultural factors on communication style and expectations should also be considered.

## Using the Guideline

This guideline primarily describes the content of care being offered to individuals who present with aphasia, and not the knowledge and skills needed by the Speech & Language Therapist working with this client population. Such skills are outlined in the parallel 'Underpinning knowledge and skills framework' – a product of the Competencies Project – and should be read in conjunction with it and with Communicating Quality.

This guideline should be read alongside the 'Core Guideline', and in combination with any of the following that may be relevant.

- Autistic Spectrum Disorders
- Cleft Palate & Velopharyngeal Abnormalities
- Clinical Voice Disorders
- Deafness/Hearing Loss
- Disorders of Fluency
- Disorders of Mental Health & Dementia
- Disorders of Feeding, Eating, Drinking & Swallowing (Dysphagia)
- Dysarthria
- Head & Neck Cancer
- Pre-School Children with Communication, Language and Speech Needs
- School Aged Children with Speech, Language and Communication Difficulties.

## Effectiveness of aphasia therapy

A Cochrane systematic review of randomised controlled trials in aphasia therapy has not produced conclusive evidence as to whether speech and language therapy works or does not work. Nevertheless, evidence from other experimental studies supports the conclusion that speech and language therapy for aphasia, particularly intensive therapy, is efficacious and effective. In particular:

- Outcomes for treated individuals are superior to those for untreated individuals in all stages of recovery. The difference in outcomes is greatest in the acute stage of recovery (less than 3 months post onset (MPO)) but continues to be appreciable even in the long term (more than 12 MPO).
- Outcomes are superior for people receiving treatment that is intensive, ie, more than two hours per week.

### Evidence
- Greener J, Enderby P & Whurr R (2004) Evidence Level I
- Robey RR (1998) Evidence Level II

## Key aims of intervention

The Royal College of Physicians' National Clinical Guidelines for Stroke identify the following as key aims of stroke

rehabilitation: to maximise the individuals' sense of well-being/quality of life and their social position/roles. Recent research in the UK has shown that the health-related quality of life of people with aphasia after stroke is significantly affected by their emotional distress, their activity level, the severity of their communication disability and their overall health. Speech and language therapists need to take these factors into consideration if they are to deliver interventions that address the key aims of stroke rehabilitation, and target the improvement of people's quality of life. Long-term services for people with aphasia should aim to minimise communication disability, address emotional health, and enable participation in an individual's social context and in the community and society more generally.

*Evidence*
- Hilari K, Wiggins RD, Roy P, Byng S & Smith SC (2003) Evidence Level II
- Royal College of Physicians (2000) Evidence Level IV
- Scottish Intercollegiate Guideline Network (SIGN) 64 (2002) Evidence Level IV

## Working in Partnership

In recent years patients have become increasingly involved in treatment decisions. The *Patient Partnership Strategy* aims to improve service delivery in the NHS by providing patients with information enabling then to make informed decisions about their health and healthcare. There is, also, general consensus that patients and carers are 'experts' in their own conditions. Patients are the best informants about symptoms, feelings and the ways in which illness affects what is important to them. For these reasons, measures of outcome from the patient's perspective (patient-based outcomes) are increasingly used in the evaluation of health care interventions.

*Evidence*
- NHS Executive (1999) Evidence Level IV
- Mayou R & Bryant B (1993) Evidence Level IV

## Recommendation 1 (C)

The individual and others in their environment should be involved in decisions about all aspects of intervention, including therapy goals.

*Rationale*
The person with aphasia and the relevant 'others' in his/her environment should be recognised as having unique experiences, knowledge and feelings with regard to the impact of aphasia on their own situation. This information should help to shape all aspects of therapy. Therapy should be client-driven, reflecting choice from a broad range of options, and responding to the diverse and changing nature of aphasia over time. This can be achieved by shifting the focus and/or context of therapy to meet the needs and priorities of an individual at any given time.

*Evidence*
- Pound C, Parr S, Lindsay J & Woolf C (2000) Evidence Level IV
- NHS Executive (1999) Evidence Level IV
- Professional Consensus

## Recommendation 2 (A)

**Training should be provided for those who come into contact with the person with aphasia to increase their understanding of aphasia and how best to communicate with the individual.**

*Rationale*
Those who have contact with the person with aphasia may have difficulty judging his/her level of ability. Training such persons enables the competence of the person with aphasia to be revealed. This facilitates the full involvement of the person with aphasia in decision-making.

*Evidence*
- Kagan A, Black S, Duchan J, Simmons-Mackie N & Square P (2001) Evidence Level I
- McClenahan R, Johnston M & Densham Y (1992) Evidence Level II

## Recommendation 3 (C)

**Intervention for the person with aphasia should take place within the context of the multidisciplinary team. The Speech & Language Therapist should work collaboratively within the multi-disciplinary/agency team, recognising the skills and contribution offered by other professions and agencies.**

*Rationale*

Working collaboratively will ensure that the person with aphasia's needs are being met in a holistic manner, and that communication is perceived as fundamental to the individual's well being.

*Evidence*
■ Professional Consensus

## ASSESSMENT

This section states general principles of assessment. More detailed assessment recommendations can be found in the individual sections of the guideline.

The choice and appropriateness of assessment will vary depending on the following factors which will need to be taken into consideration:

■ Timing and stage post-onset.
■ Cognition, including attention and memory.
■ Setting in which the individual is seen.
■ Social context.
■ Adjustment to disability.
■ Service delivery context.

### Recommendation 1 (C)

An assessment of the individual's communication strengths and weaknesses should be carried out.

*Rationale*

Assessment will enable the therapist to:

■ Identify the nature and extent of the communication deficit;
■ Negotiate therapy goals with the person with aphasia;
■ Design an individualised programme of therapy/intervention, specific to the needs of the individual;
■ Obtain a baseline from which to measure change;
■ Establish the most appropriate timing for therapy, review, ongoing referral and discharge.

*Evidence*
■ Kertesz A (1994) Evidence Level IV
■ Holland A (1998) Evidence Level IV

■ Professional Consensus

### Recommendation 2 (C)

Assessment should have a clear and immediate therapeutic reason for being undertaken and may occur at any stage of intervention. The assessment process may incorporate a range of approaches, including interview, conversation, observation and selective use of formal and informal assessment tools.

*Rationale*

Different methods of assessment will be appropriate for individuals at different times. During periods of rapid change, ie, during spontaneous recovery, it may not be appropriate to carry out formal, standardised assessments. Informal assessment will enable an early hypothesis to be made as to the nature of the communication impairments and their impacts. This will, when appropriate, drive the choice of further assessment and advice re communication. At different stages, formal and informal assessments can provide information to underpin the design and evaluation of specific therapy for individuals.

*Evidence*
■ Professional Consensus

### Recommendation 3 (B)

Types of assessment employed should include those focusing on:

■ The nature and extent of the speech and language impairment and level of preserved abilities;
■ Functional and pragmatic aspects of communication, including compensatory strategies;
■ Psychosocial well-being.

*Rationale*

It is important to take a holistic approach to assessment of the individual. All of the above areas interact with each other, and need to be addressed in subsequent goal-planning and intervention.

*Evidence*

■ Hilari K, Wiggins RD, Roy P, Byng S, & Smith SC (2003) Evidence Level II

■ Aftonomos LB, Steele RD, Appelbaum JS & Harris VM (2001) Evidence Level III

### Recommendation 4 (B)

The process of assessment should encompass the perception of the individual and relevant others with regard to the impact of the communication disability on their lives. This may include assessing the skills of the communication partner(s).

*Rationale*

The response of the individual and relevant others to aphasia may vary depending on several factors, eg, severity and type of communication disability, personality, age, employment and social context, including the attitudes of others. This response may impact on the intervention offered and its outcome.

*Evidence*

■ Aftonomos LB, Steele RD, Appelbaum JS & Harris VM (2001) Evidence Level III

■ Davidson B, Worrall L & Hickson L (2003) Evidence Level III

■ Parr S, Byng S & Gilpin S (1997) Evidence Level IV

## THERAPY

The term 'therapy' is used to encompass all aspects of speech and language therapy, at the levels of function, activity and participation. The approaches described below are not mutually exclusive, and may be mutually beneficial. Working on participation can improve communication, and working on communication skills can improve participation. A number of different approaches are usually required which often run concurrently. Whatever approach is used, therapies should have clearly specified hypotheses, aims, methods and expected outcomes that relate to a person's life.

## THERAPIES FOCUSING ON PARTICIPATION

'Participation Therapy' embodies treatment techniques aimed at supporting people with aphasia, and others affected by it, in achieving their immediate and longer-term life goals. These interventions can take place at any stage of living with aphasia and in any setting. They focus on facilitating autonomy, roles, and lifestyle. Therapies work at different levels, which may involve the person, the environment and the community, or all of these together. Many 'Participation Therapy' techniques overlap.

### Recommendation 1 (B)

Therapists should aim to:

■ Ensure individuals are given full information about their aphasia, and the management options available to them, in a form they can understand.

■ Provide accessible information in the individual's environment and daily life.

■ Refer individuals to other sources of relevant information and support.

### Recommendation 2 (B)

Therapists should aim to:

■ Facilitate access to goods and services, appropriate groups, leisure activities, education activities and, if relevant, employment.

■ Facilitate changes to the environment by, for example, altering room layout and reducing background noise.

### Recommendation 3 (B)

Therapists should aim to:

■ Raise interprofessional, local and public awareness of aphasia by means of educational and training packages for providers of care, employment and leisure.

■ Support individuals in making choices in legal or healthcare issues involving informed consent.

*Rationale*

There is a general consensus among experts that there is a need to actively generate and adapt practices that offer sustainable support and that complement impairment-focused work. This will allow re-engagement in life by strengthening daily participation in activities of choice.

*Evidence*

- Parr S (2001) Evidence Level III
- Chapey R, Duchan JF, Elman RJ, Garcia LJ, Kagan A, Lyon JG & Simmons-Mackie N (2001) Evidence Level IV
- Pound C, Parr S, Lindsay J & Woolf C (2000) Evidence Level IV
- RCP National Clinical Guidelines for Stroke (2004) Evidence Level IV

## THERAPIES FOCUSING ON IMPROVING LANGUAGE FUNCTIONING

This includes therapies that aim to directly modify aspects of the individual's impaired language. The aim of all impairment-based therapies should be to reduce the disability associated with aphasia and thereby promote increased participation. Impairment-based therapies should be grounded on an explicit theoretical foundation, with clearly specified hypotheses, aims, methods and expected outcomes that relate to a person's life. This section is not intended to be comprehensive – it covers the following areas:

- Single word auditory processing
- Spoken word production
- Single word reading
- Single word writing
- Sentence processing

Single word and sentence processing have been presented separately in this document to reflect the evidence. However, these levels of processing interact with each other and it is recommended that they should be considered jointly.

## 1 Single word auditory processing

Single word auditory processing includes the perception, recognition and understanding of spoken words. Difficulty in understanding speech can affect access to information; access to conversation and social participation; development and maintenance of relationships; autonomy; identity and self-esteem.

### Recommendation 1 (B)

Careful assessment is required to identify the presence, nature and severity of an auditory processing impairment, which may be difficult to detect in conversation or informal tasks.

*Rationale*

Auditory processing impairments have a negative impact on functional communication and quality of life, both for people with aphasia and for their families/communication partners. However, aphasic auditory processing difficulties are often undetected or underestimated unless specifically assessed.

*Evidence*

- McClenahan R, Johnston M & Densham Y (1992) Evidence Level II
- Le Dorze G, Brassard C, Larfeuil C & Allaire J (1996) Evidence Level III

### Recommendation 2 (B)

Assessment should separately consider abilities in speech sound discrimination, spoken word recognition and spoken word comprehension. Assessment should also consider the possible presence of coexisting hearing loss or central auditory processing disorder. Interpretation of assessment results should recognise that impairments and abilities at different levels of auditory processing may interact in a complex manner.

*Rationale*

Processing difficulties vary considerably in both nature and severity among individuals. Assessment of an individual's abilities in understanding spoken language should underpin therapy and can help to identify the best ways to present verbal information to the person with aphasia.

*Evidence*

- Behrmann M & Lieberthal T (1989) Evidence Level III
- Francis D R, Riddoch MJ & Humphreys GW (2001) Evidence Level III
- Franklin S (1989) Evidence Level III
- Grayson E, Hilton R & Franklin S (1997) Evidence Level III
- Morris J, Franklin S, Ellis AW & Turner JE (1996) Evidence Level III

### Recommendation 3 (B)

Assessment should consider the effects of both the linguistic context and the communication environment on auditory processing.

*Rationale*
A number of contextual factors may affect auditory processing, including background noise or other distractions, rate of speech, subtle topic changes, linguistic complexity and conversational context.

*Evidence*
- Grayson E, Hilton R & Franklin S (1997) Evidence Level III
- Maneta A, Marshall J & Lindsay J (2001) Evidence Level III

### Recommendation 4 (B)

Where impairments are primarily at the level of speech sound perception, therapy should aim to improve discrimination of speech sounds. Where impairments are primarily at the level of spoken word comprehension, therapy should aim to improve access to word meanings. Therapies should take account of factors affecting the individual's auditory processing, such as types of speech–sound contrast, word frequency and familiarity, and aspects of word meaning.

*Rationale*
Carefully targeted therapies can produce specific changes in both speech perception and spoken word comprehension. Therapies that do not directly target impaired aspects of auditory processing, or do not take account of preserved abilities, are less likely to be effective.

*Evidence*
- Behrmann M & Lieberthal T (1989) Evidence Level III
- Francis DR, Riddoch MJ & Humphreys GW (2001) Evidence Level III
- Grayson E, Hilton R & Franklin S (1997) Evidence Level III
- Morris J, Franklin S, Ellis AW & Turner JE (1996) Evidence Level III

### Recommendation 5 (B)

Therapies for auditory processing disorders should always aim to improve functional comprehension of speech. Therapies aimed at changing the communication environment to support auditory comprehension may be combined with, or used instead of, impairment-focused therapies.

*Rationale*
Training conversational partners to support the aphasic person's auditory processing, for instance by simplifying spoken language or using Total Communication strategies, can improve functional comprehension.

*Evidence*
- Maneta A, Marshall J & Lindsay J (2001) Evidence Level III

## 2 Spoken word production

Difficulty in producing spoken words is one of the most common features of aphasia. Such difficulties may arise from a number of different underlying impairments. These include difficulties in generating representations of word meanings, in accessing representations of spoken word-forms, and in assembling the sounds that make up word-forms. Therapy for spoken naming difficulties should be based on careful assessment of the individual, and may need to target more than one aspect of impaired processing. While some studies have shown beneficial effects of therapy after only a few sessions, others suggest that intensive practice is necessary. Therapy should take account of the individual's functional communication needs, for instance by selecting functionally useful words for treatment. Therapy should aim to achieve lasting improvements, and generalisation both to untreated words and to natural communication situations such as conversation.

### Recommendation 1 (B)

The therapist should identify the nature of the underlying deficit in order to plan appropriate therapy, using a range of tasks that test different aspects of spoken word production. These might include tests of semantic processing (such as word-to-picture matching and synonym judgement), tests of access to spoken word-forms (such as spoken picture naming, rhyme judgement and homophone judgement), and tests of word-form assembly (such as repeating words of different lengths). Results of these assessments should be considered in conjunction with tests of auditory processing, repetition, reading and writing in order to identify impaired and spared levels of processing.

*Rationale*
Detailed assessment of individuals with aphasia has revealed very different patterns of spoken word production impairment. Therapy that appropriately targets impaired processing in individuals is more likely to be effective. For many individuals a broad-based multimodality treatment that includes both semantic and phonological components is likely to be the most effective.

*Evidence*
- Hillis A & Caramazza A (1994) Evidence Level III

## Recommendation 2 (B)

For spoken output difficulties that involve difficulties in processing word-meanings, therapy should include tasks that focus on semantic processing. These might, for instance, include semantic cueing of spoken output, semantic judgements, categorisation and word-to-picture matching.

*Rationale*
Word-finding difficulties may result from difficulties in accessing semantic information. Such difficulties typically result in semantic errors, or failure to produce a word. Treatment aims to strengthen and/or improve access to semantic representations, and may also aim to strengthen links between word-meanings and word-forms. Since word comprehension and production systems are held to share common representations of word-meanings, treatment using comprehension tasks may also produce gains in spoken output.

*Evidence*
- Howard D, Patterson K, Franklin S, Orchard-Lisle V & Morton J (1985) Evidence Level II
- Hillis A (1989) Evidence Level III

- Marshall J, Pound C , White-Thompson M & Pring T (1990) Evidence Level III
- Coehlo CA, McHugh RE & Boyle M (2000) Evidence Level III
- Nickels L & Best W (1996) Evidence Level III

## Recommendation 3 (B)

For spoken output difficulties that are caused primarily by difficulties in accessing word-forms, therapy should include tasks that focus on producing spoken output or silently accessing phonological word-forms. These may include, for instance, phonemic cueing of spoken output, cueing spoken output with written letters, repetition, rhyme judgement and reading aloud. It may be beneficial to target the processing of word-meanings and of spoken word-forms together in therapy.

*Rationale*
Word-finding difficulties may be caused by impairments in the stored lexicon of spoken word-forms, or by difficulties in accessing word-forms from the semantic system. Treatment aims to improve access to word-forms, for instance by using unimpaired processes to bypass impaired processes, or by increasing the information available to the lexicon about the word. Therapies that require spoken production of word-forms have been shown to be more effective than therapies that only require a judgement about the word-form. Therapies that target word-forms and word-meanings together may result in greater generalisation to untreated words than therapies that focus only on word-forms.

*Evidence*
- Howard D, Patterson K, Franklin S, Orchard-Lisle V & Morton J (1985) Evidence Level II
- Bruce C & Howard D (1987) Evidence Level III
- Francis D, Clark N & Humphreys G (2002) Evidence Level III
- Hickin J, Best W, Herbert R, Howard D & Osbourne F (2002) Evidence Level III
- Hillis A (1989) Evidence Level III
- Le Dorze G, Boulay N , Gaudreau J & Brassard C (1994) Evidence Level III
- Miceli G, Amitrano A, Capasso R & Caramazza A (1996) Evidence Level III

- Nickels L (2002) Evidence Level III
- Spencer K, Doyle P, McNeil M, Wambaugh J, Park G & Carrol B (2000) Evidence Level III

## Recommendation 4 (B)

For spoken output difficulties that are caused primarily by difficulties in accessing and sequencing the sounds within words, therapy should include tasks that focus on the structure of spoken word-forms. These might include, for instance, listening to differences between spoken words, repeating words of increasing length, strengthening links between written spellings and spoken word-forms, and developing skills in self-monitoring of spoken output.

*Rationale*
Despite being able to access intact word-meanings and word-forms, people with aphasia may have difficulty saying words, due to problems in structuring and sequencing the sounds within words. This affects performance across a range of tasks requiring spoken responses, and may be particularly apparent on longer words. Treatment aims to improve the ability to assemble the sounds of spoken words, and may also aim to improve the ability to self-monitor for errors in spoken production.

*Evidence*
- Franklin S, Buerk F & Howard D (2002) Evidence Level III

## 3 Single word reading

Single word reading includes perception, recognition and understanding of written words. Reading difficulties can affect the aphasic person's access to information; social position and roles; autonomy; identity and self-esteem.

## Recommendation 1 (B)

Prior to assessing word reading, the following areas need to be considered:

- Pre-morbid literacy
- Visual acuity
- Visual neglect

*Rationale*
Literacy levels before stroke vary considerably between individuals. Therapy does not aim to treat pre-existing literacy problems. In order to determine the cause of a reading deficit, one must first ensure that the deficit is not perceptual in nature. Examination of the areas above can allow compensatory measures to be undertaken to maximise reading capacity. For example, alternative presentation of words and alerting devices may compensate for hemispatial neglect.

*Evidence*
- Ellis A, Flude B & Young A (1987) Evidence Level III

## Recommendation 2 (B)

A thorough assessment needs to consider how the individual uses reading in their everyday life. It also needs to incorporate analyses of orthographic, phonological and semantic processing of written words. These analyses will be hypothesis-driven, based on the individual's presentation. They may include a variety of tasks, including letter and word recognition, reading aloud and reading comprehension, using letters, non-words and words. Stimuli should be controlled for the variables known to affect reading performance, such as regularity, frequency, imageability and lexical status.

*Rationale*
Functional assessment of reading is needed to guide client-centred therapy goals and selection of relevant materials and tasks.

Detailed assessment of reading will reveal which of the underlying processes are affected. This will inform therapy, since different processing difficulties require different therapy approaches.

*Evidence*
- Coltheart M, Masterson J, Byng S, Prior M & Riddoch J (1983) Evidence Level III
- Funnell E (1983) Evidence Level III
- Patterson K & Kay J (1982) Evidence Level III
- Parr S (1995) Evidence Level IV
- Coltheart M, Patterson K E & Marshall J C (1980) Evidence Level IV

### Recommendation 3 (B)

Once the level of breakdown in reading processing has been established, therapy can focus on training the impaired component, or using intact mechanisms to compensate for the impairment. For example:

- When there is a letter recognition deficit, therapy should aim to improve the speed and efficiency of letter identification.
- When there is a deficit in recognising irregular written words, semantic approaches are helpful.
- When there is a deficit in recognising written words, semantic approaches are helpful.
- When there is a deficit in accessing phonology from orthography, retraining grapheme to phoneme correspondence can be helpful, in some cases in combination with a semantic component. If the client has difficulty blending phonemes into syllables, bigraph-phoneme correspondence should be considered.

*Rationale*
There is evidence that therapy programmes which take into account the underlying processing strengths and deficits can improve reading efficiency and/or reading comprehension of, at least, treated items.

*Evidence*
- Byng S & Coltheart M (1986) Evidence Level III
- De Partz MP (1986) Evidence Level III
- Friedman RB & Lott SN (2002) Evidence Level III
- Greenwald ML & Gonzalez–Rothi LJ (1998) Evidence Level III
- Lott SN, Friedman RB & Linebaugh CW (1994) Evidence Level III
- Maher LM, Clayton MC, Barrett AM, Schober-Peterson D & Gonzalez- Rothi LJ (1998) Evidence Level III
- Nickels L (1992) Evidence Level III
- Scott C & Byng S (1989) Evidence Level III

## 4 Single word writing

Deficits in writing depend on the location and degree of the language processing impairment and whether alternative routes can be used. Writing therapy may aim to directly restore the impaired process or module (reactivation strategies), or find ways of circumventing it (relay strategies). There are two main approaches – therapy targeting the lexical writing route and that targeting the sub-lexical writing route.

### Recommendation 1 (C)

A thorough assessment needs to consider how the individual uses writing in their everyday life. It also needs to incorporate analyses of semantic, orthographic and phonological processing of written words.

*Rationale*
Functional assessment of writing is needed to guide client-centred therapy goals and selection of relevant materials and tasks.

Detailed assessment of writing will reveal which underlying processes are affected. This will inform therapy, as different processing difficulties require different therapy approaches.

*Evidence*
- Parr S (1995) Evidence Level IV

### Recommendation 2 (B)

Once the level of breakdown in writing has been established, therapy can focus on training the impaired component or using intact mechanisms to compensate for the impairment. For example:

- Therapists can use anagrams or first letters of words for those clients who have both a) an impaired lexical route for writing and difficulty accessing written word-forms from meanings, and b) a well-preserved sub-lexical route to spelling. These strategies may improve copying or writing to dictation of target words. With repetitive practice, this may facilitate phoneme to grapheme conversion.
- Therapists can use oral spelling to aid written spelling for those with good auditory and written comprehension, but poor ability to store graphemic representations. Strategies may progress from writing words to dictation, to structured use of a dictionary, through to sentence-based writing tasks.
- Therapists can link a target word's spelling with a pictorial image where there is a deficit in accessing written word

forms. This may improve spelling of irregular words (the lexical route).

■ Therapists may consider using computer technology, for example an adaptive word processor, to optimise functional use of writing skills.

### Rationale

Reactivation therapy (for example, writing words via repetitive practice and use of anagrams and first letters of words) can promote item-specific learning. This may improve the ability to assemble written word-forms after assigning them meaning. Relay strategies, such as linking of spelling with a pictorial image, may improve lexical spelling.

### Evidence

■ Behrmann M (1987) Evidence Level III

■ Deloche G, Dordan M & Kremins H (1993) Evidence Level III

■ De Partz MP, Seron X & Van der Linden M (1992) Evidence Level III

■ Mortley J, Enderby P & Petheram B (2001) Evidence Level III

## 5 Sentence processing

Sentence processing impairments affect the comprehension and/or production of spoken and written language, and can arise even when single word processing is relatively intact. The impairments make it difficult to deal with language about events or complex ideas, since this typically requires the ability to understand and produce grammatical structure. Access to information and participation in conversation may be severely affected.

### Recommendation 1 (B)

Careful assessment is needed to identify the nature of the sentence processing impairment. This should be hypothesis driven, and may include tests of verb and sentence comprehension, and analyses of verb, sentence and narrative production.

### Rationale

People with sentence processing problems have different underlying impairments, and this may be the case even when

symptoms are superficially similar. No single assessment can identify the nature of the problem.

Different processing impairments require different therapy approaches.

### Evidence

■ Crerar MA, Ellis AW & Dean AC (1996) Evidence Level II

■ Byng S, Nickels L & Black M (1994) Evidence Level III

■ Schwartz MF, Saffran EM, Fink RB, Myers JL & Martin N (1994) Evidence Level III

■ Mitchum C, Greenwald M & Berndt R (2000) Evidence Level IV

### Recommendation 2 (B)

Assessment should explore verb comprehension and production, and the impact of any verb impairment on sentence processing abilities. Therapy aiming to improve verb processing should be considered when individuals have verb impairments.

### Rationale

Many people with sentence processing deficits have coexisting verb impairments, which may, in themselves, impede sentence generation. Therapy can improve access to treated verbs, and may improve sentence comprehension and production with those verbs.

### Evidence

■ Berndt R, Mitchum C, Haendiges A & Sandson J (1997a) Evidence Level III

■ Berndt R, Mitchum C, Haendiges A & Sandson J (1997b) Evidence Level III

■ Marshall J, Pring T & Chiat S (1998) Evidence Level III

■ Shapiro K & Caramazza A (2003) Evidence Level III

■ Raymer A & Ellsworth T (2002) Evidence Level III

### Recommendation 3 (B)

Assessment should explore mapping skills, ie, the ability to integrate syntactic form with meaning. When mapping skills are impaired, therapy aiming to improve these skills should be considered.

The use of dedicated computer-based therapy packages should be considered as a complement to linguistically-based therapies.

*Rationale*

Many people with aphasia show evidence of impaired mapping abilities. Different therapy approaches have been developed to improve mapping in aphasia, with evaluations showing benefits for sentence comprehension and production.

The combination of linguistically-based sentence processing therapies with computerised packages has lead to improvements in both comprehension and production of sentences, and this has generalised to non-computer usage.

*Evidence*

- Byng S, Nickels L & Black M (1994) Evidence Level III
- Schwartz MF, Saffran EM, Fink RB, Myers JL & Martin N (1994) Evidence Level III
- Mitchum C, Haendiges A & Berndt R (1996) Evidence Level III
- Crerar MA, Ellis AW & Dean AC (1996) Evidence Level II
- Marshall J, Chiat S & Pring T (1997) Evidence Level III
- Weinrich M, Shelton JR, Cox DM & McCall D (1997) Evidence Level III
- Linebarger MC, Schwartz MF, Romania JR, Kohn SE & Stephens DL (2000) Evidence Level III
- Beveridge MA & Crerar MA (2002) Evidence Level III

## Recommendation 4 (B)

Therapies may target the comprehension and production of complex, as well as simple, sentence forms.

*Rationale*

There is evidence that some individuals can improve processing of such sentences when given appropriate therapy, with generalisation to related, but less complex, sentences.

*Evidence*

- Schwartz MF, Saffran EM, Fink RB, Myers JL & Martin N (1994) Evidence Level III
- Ballard K & Thompson C (1999) Evidence Level III
- Jacobs B & Thompson C (2000) Evidence Level III

- Thompson C, Shapiro L, Kiran S & Sobecks J (2003) Evidence Level III

## Recommendation 5(B)

Pre and post therapy assessment should explore speech production in open conditions, such as narrative and conversation, as well as in constrained conditions, such as picture description.

*Rationale*

Although some studies demonstrate improvements in open speech following therapy, many do not. Therapists cannot assume that improved picture description signals improvements in other speaking conditions.

*Evidence*

- Thompson C (1998) Evidence Level III
- Marshall J (1999) Evidence Level III
- Weinrich M, Shelton JR, Cox DM & McCall D (1997) Evidence Level III

## THERAPIES FOCUSING ON COMPENSATORY STRATEGIES

This approach aims to develop strategies to find a way around the language impairments, by capitalising on the individual's communicative strengths in order to maximise communication potential. These may include drawing, gesture, writing key words, or using a communication book.

## Recommendation 1 (CB)

Assessment should aim to determine the individual's spared linguistic and non-verbal abilities. His/her ability to use these strategies in real-life settings to compensate for the impairments should also be assessed. The skills of relevant communication partners in interpreting and facilitating such strategies should be considered, as should cultural factors.

*Rationale*

People with aphasia often perform differently in their natural communication environments and with familiar partners.

Effectiveness and efficiency of communication may vary depending on environmental and interactant factors.

*Evidence*
- Holland A (1982) Evidence Level III
- Baker R (2000) Evidence Level IV
- Davidson B & Worrall L (2000) Evidence Level IV
- Worrall L, McCooey R, Davidson B, Larkins B & Hickson L (2002) Evidence Level IV
- Holland A (1998) Evidence Level IV

## Recommendation 2 (B)

Specific training in the development and/or refinement of non-verbal communication strategies is required for these to be used efficiently and effectively. Ideally these strategies should be used within a 'Total Communication' approach, that promotes the flexible use of multi-modality communication to improve communicative effectiveness.

*Rationale*
Therapy studies have shown that non-verbal communication modalities can be used as an alternative or adjunct to language, resulting in improved communicative effectiveness and efficiency.

*Evidence*
- Cubelli R, Trentini P, Montagna CG (1991) Evidence Level III
- Sacchett C, Byng S, Marshall J, Pound C (1999) Evidence Level III
- Carlomagno S et al (1991) Evidence Level III
- Pound C, Parr S, Lindsay J & Woolf C (2000) Evidence Level IV

## Recommendation 3 (B)

Spared linguistic capacities can be usefully exploited in specific tasks to improve communicative effectiveness and increase communicative opportunities. Examples are:

- The use of writing to bypass spoken production difficulties;
- The use of spoken output to compensate for difficulties in written production;
- The use of computer-based and other technologies, for example voice recognition software, and communication aids.

*Rationale*
The relative sparing of some linguistic and non-linguistic capacities, even in severe aphasia, can be exploited to compensate for more impaired or affected functions. Individuals, even those with chronic aphasia, are able to learn and retain strategies that will increase their overall communicative effectiveness in real-life situations.

*Evidence*
- Robson J, Marshall J, Chiat S & Pring T (2001) Evidence Level II
- Jackson-Waite K, Robson J & Pring T (2003) Evidence Level III
- Lustig AP & Tompkins CA (2002) Evidence Level III
- Mortley J, Enderby P & Petheram B (2001) Evidence Level III
- Bruce C, Edmundson A & Coleman M (2003) Evidence Level III

## Recommendation 4 (BC)

To promote generalisation of learned strategies, therapists should involve communication partners in therapy and conduct therapy within natural communication environments.

*Rationale*
Compensatory strategies typically do not generalise spontaneously. Specific steps should be taken to promote generalisation of learned strategies to functional, real-life situations.

*Evidence*
- Jackson-Waite K, Robson J & Pring T (2003) Evidence Level III
- Sacchett C, Byng S, Marshall J & Pound C (1999) Evidence Level III
- Lustig AP & Tompkins CA (2002) Evidence Level III

# THERAPIES FOCUSING ON THE SKILLS OF CONVERSATIONAL PARTNERS

These therapies aim to develop the use of appropriate and effective communication strategies by non-aphasic conversation partners to enable them to accommodate the changed communication of the individual with aphasia. They include working with family members/carers of people with aphasia and working with volunteers.

## 1 Working with family members/carers of people with aphasia

### Recommendation 1 (B)

The speech and language therapist should aim to:

- Assess the individual with aphasia's communication strengths and weaknesses;
- Assess the conversation/interaction patterns of the person with aphasia and their conversation partner. This may include conversation analysis (CA);
- Increase the conversation partner's awareness of their own skills and the communication strengths and needs of the person with aphasia;
- Train the conversation partner on verbal and non-verbal strategies to improve communication interactions and conversations.

### Evidence

- Booth S & Swabey D (1999) Evidence Level III
- Hopper T, Holland A & Rewega M (2002) Evidence Level III
- Maneta A, Marshall J & Lindsay J (2001) Evidence Level III
- Simmons N, Kearns K, & Potechin G (1987) Evidence Level IV

## 2 Working with volunteers

### Recommendation 2 (A)

In training volunteers, the speech and language therapist should aim to:

- Increase volunteers' understanding of aphasia
- Increase volunteers' knowledge of communication techniques to facilitate the communication of people with aphasia and support them in conversations
- Improve volunteers' conversation skills by direct training on the use of these communication techniques.

### Evidence

- Kagan A, Black S, Duchan J, Simmons-Mackie N & Square P (2001) Evidence Level I
- Rayner H & Marshall J (2003) Evidence Level III

### Rationale for Recommendations 1 & 2

The ultimate goal of most therapies for language and communication is to produce changes at the conversational level. It is often assumed that direct language therapy may result in better conversational fluency. In reality, conversational skills often do not emerge spontaneously. Also the very nature of communication as a two-way process means that both partners must adapt their communication skills for the conversation to work. Consequently, therapy directly at the level of conversation is necessary to improve the conversations of people with aphasia. In particular:

- Speaking partners may not alter their interaction patterns unless behaviours are directly trained and feedback is provided.
- Training speaking partners can improve not just their own communication, but also that of the person with aphasia.

## GROUP THERAPY

Group therapy refers to forms of intervention that bring together people with aphasia, thereby giving them the opportunity to interact with each other and to work together.

### Recommendation 1 (A)

There should be opportunities for individuals to participate in groups as well as in individual therapy.

### Rationale
There is a general clinical consensus that different forms of structured group therapy can lead to improvements in

linguistic function and functional communication, as well as providing opportunities for participation and autonomy. This is true for those with mild, moderate and severe forms of aphasia. Group therapy can provide participants with opportunities for generalising their skills to everyday contexts, and can help to reduce the negative psychosocial impact of aphasia. It can also have psychosocial benefits for the relatives/caregivers of individuals with aphasia.

*Evidence*
- Elman RJ & Berstein-Ellis E (1999a) Evidence Level I
- Mackenzie C (1991) Evidence Level II
- Avent JR (1997) Evidence Level III
- Bollinger RL, Musson ND & Holland AL (1993) Evidence Level III
- Elman RJ & Berstein-Ellis E (1999b) Evidence Level III

## COMPUTER SUPPORTED THERAPY

### Recommendation 1 (A)

Computer-based therapy offers the potential to provide intensive home-based therapy with minimal clinician input. Improvements in performance over a number of communicative modalities can occur.

*Rationale*
Computers can provide an additional method of delivering therapy, either during face-to-face therapy time, or with remote support from a therapist. This can provide greater access to therapy, particularly for individuals living in remote areas. With greater access to computers in society as a whole, computer-based therapy exploits the IT revolution and promotes an additional method of communication and accessing information.

*Evidence*
- Katz RC & Wertz RT (1997) Level of Evidence Ib
- Mortley J, Enderby P & Petheram B (2001) Evidence Level III

### Themes identified from the Consultation with Service Users

This was a significant aspect of the project. There were three main approaches to consulting with the users:

- Inviting representatives from voluntary organisations to attend meetings of the expert groups
- Focus groups with service users or their parents/carers
- Postal questionnaires.

The following themes are based upon a sample of the experiences of different individuals and their perception of what a speech & language therapy service should offer. Full details of the process undertaken are outlined in the 'Consultation with Service Users' section.

- Working in partnership
  - The therapy relationship should be viewed as a partnership

- Provision of information
  - Aphasia should be explained, as soon as possible, to the individual and the family.
  - The explanation should be repeated frequently to the individual and the family.
  - Such explanations should be accompanied by written information – however, this information should be aphasia- and user-friendly.

- Living with aphasia
  - There is a need for ongoing support once the individual has been discharged from therapy, therefore the therapist should provide information regarding support groups and opportunities to meet others with aphasia.

# 5.13 Head & Neck Cancer

## Introduction

The term 'head and neck cancer' encompasses a range of tumours. The commonest sites of head and neck cancers are, in descending order, larynx; oral cavity; pharynx; thyroid and salivary gland. These will occur mainly in adults, but there will be a small number of children with tumours, both benign and malignant.

The current treatments include one or a combination of radiotherapy, chemotherapy and surgery, and can produce physical, functional and psychosocial problems. The serious functional disabilities may result in voice, speech and swallowing difficulties.

This guideline applies to the speech, voice communication and swallowing disorders caused by head and neck cancer and its subsequent treatment and it is therefore essential that this guideline is read in conjunction with Clinical Voice Disorders and Disorders of Feeding, Eating, Drinking & Swallowing (Dysphagia).

## Using the Guideline

This guideline addresses the speech and language therapy management practice for those with head and neck cancer and not the knowledge and skills needed by the Speech & Language Therapist working with this client population. Such skills are outlined in the parallel 'Underpinning knowledge and skills framework' – a product of the Competencies Project – and should be read in conjunction with this and with *Communicating Quality*.

This guideline should be read alongside the 'Core Guideline' and in combination with any of the following which may be relevant.

- Aphasia
- Autistic Spectrum Disorders
- Cleft Palate & Velopharyngeal Abnormalities
- Clinical Voice Disorders
- Deafness/Hearing Loss
- Disorders of Feeding, Eating, Drinking & Swallowing (Dysphagia)
- Disorders of Fluency
- Disorders of Mental Health & Dementia
- Dysarthria
- Pre-school Children with Communication, Language & Speech Needs
- School-aged Children with Speech, Language & Communication Difficulties

## Membership of Multidisciplinary Team (C)

**The Speech & Language Therapist will be a core member of the head and neck multidisciplinary oncology team from time of presentation.**

### Rationale

The Speech & Language Therapist needs to be working within the multidisciplinary team in order to consider the impact and possible consequences of a communication and/or swallowing disorder. The Speech & Language Therapist has the skills to influence decision-making regarding treatment planning and consequences for rehabilitation of speech, voice and swallowing. Reference should be made to the 'Practice Care Guidelines for Clinicians Participating in the Management of Head and Neck Cancer Patients in the UK'.[1]

### Evidence

- British Association of Otorhinolaryngologists (BAO-HNS) (1998) Evidence Level IV
- British Association of Otorhinolaryngologists (BAO-HNS) (2000) Evidence Level IV
- Machin J & Shaw C (1998) Evidence Level IV
- Birchall M, Nettelfield P, Richardson A & Lee L (2000) Evidence Level IV

---

1 'Practice Care Guidelines for Clinicians Participating in the Management of Head and Neck Cancer Patients in the UK', *The European Journal of Surgical Oncology*, June 2001.

## ASSESSMENT

### Involvement Prior to Radiotherapy/Chemotherapy/Surgical Management (B)

Patients will ideally be seen for assessment as soon as possible after diagnosis and before treatment commences, where communication and/or swallowing problems are a foreseeable consequence.

*Rationale*

Pre-treatment assessment is an essential aspect of the overall management of the patient – it serves to:

- Provide the opportunity for the giving of information.
- Assess pre-treatment function levels.
- Identify and predict potential problem areas.
- Establish rapport and communication channels and identify areas of concern.
- Gather information which can contribute to joint goal planning.
- Feedback information to the appropriate team member for necessary action.

*Evidence*

- Dhillon R, Palmer B, Pittam M & Shaw H (1982) Evidence Level III
- Natvig K (1983) Evidence Level III
- Johnson AF, Jacobson BH & Benninger MS (1990) Evidence Level IV
- Doyle PC (1999) Evidence Level IV

### Pre- and Post-assessment (B)

Pre- and post-treatment assessment/management will incorporate the following areas:

- An evaluation of the patient's ability to adapt to their expected prognosis
- Patient and carer concerns and expectations
- Preferred communication/language
- Family support
- Psychosocial status
- Physical status and well-being
- Quality of life

- Hearing
- Manual dexterity
- Visual acuity
- Current medication
- General health and associated conditions
- Cognitive status
- Oromotor examination
- Vocal function
- Speech intelligibility
- Literacy skills
- General communication skills and need
- Swallowing function

*Rationale*

- To assess premorbid levels and determine areas that may be affected by the cancer and its treatment.
- To identify those factors likely to affect successful outcome that require appropriate and timely intervention.
- To facilitate the selection of appropriate treatment strategies.
- To ensure that appropriate support systems and alternative strategies are in place and accessible where indicated.

*Evidence*

- Kreuzer SH, Schima W, Schober E, Pokiese P, Kofler G, Lechner G & Denk DM (2000) Evidence Level III
- Panchal J, Potterton AJ, Scanlon E & McLean NR (1996) Evidence Level III
- De Leeuw JR, De Graeff A, Ros WJ, Hordijk GJ, Blijham GH & Winnubst JA (2000) Evidence Level III
- Doyle PC (1999) Evidence Level IV
- Edels Y (1983) Evidence Level IV
- Darley FL & Keith RL (1986) Evidence Level IV
- Salmon S (1979) Evidence Level IV

## MANAGEMENT

### Pre-treatment Counselling and Information Giving (B)

All patients will be offered the opportunity to discuss with the Speech & Language Therapist the probable effects of the proposed treatment on their voice, speech and swallowing and the options for post-treatment rehabilitation.

### Rationale

Pre-treatment counselling influences the ability to:

- Participate in post-treatment rehabilitation.
- Cope with the effects of treatment on functional abilities.
- Enable planned rehabilitation and timely intervention.
- Identify patients at risk of poor adjustment and psychological disturbance.

### Evidence

- Natvig K (1983) Evidence Level III
- Stam H, Koopmans J & Mathieson C (1991) Evidence Level III
- Annunziata M, Foladore S, Magni DM, Crivellari D, Feltrin A, Bidoli E & Veronesi A (1998) Evidence Level III
- Zeine L & Larson M (1999) Evidence Level III
- Dhillon RS, Palmer BV, Pittam MR & Shaw HJ (1982) Evidence Level III
- Doyle PC (1999) Evidence Level IV
- Mathieson CM, Henderikus J & Scott J (1990) Evidence Level IV
- McQuellon RP & Hurt GJ (1997) Evidence Level IV

## Meeting Others (C)

The Speech & Language Therapist will decide on the clinical appropriateness of offering an introduction to other patients and carers.

The Speech & Language Therapist should be involved in the selection of an appropriate patient to share information and offer support. The Speech & Language Therapist will also offer the opportunity to access other agencies for support, which should be tailored to the needs of the individual.

### Rationale

This will result in the patient receiving:

- Support.
- Information about the effect of the proposed treatment and its outcomes.

### Evidence

- Stam H, Koopmans J & Mathieson C (1991) Evidence Level III

- De Leeuw JR, De Graeff A, Ros WJ, Hordijk GJ, Blijham GH & Winnubst JA (2000) Evidence Level III
- Johnson AF, Jacobson BH & Benninger MS (1990) Evidence Level IV
- Doyle PC (1999) Evidence Level IV
- Birchall M, Nettelfield P, Richardson A & Lee L (2000) Evidence Level IV

## Selection of Communication Methods (B)

The Speech & Language Therapist will plan the most appropriate method for communication rehabilitation in consultation with other team members, the patient and their carer. Such plans will be tailored to meet the patient's needs and preferences as the aims, onset and speed of the rehabilitative method will be different for each patient.

### Rationale

Following pre-treatment counselling, the patients will be able to make an informed decision regarding post-treatment communication options. The overall outcome of rehabilitation will be greatly influenced by the effectiveness of the communication method achieved by the patient.

### Evidence

- Carr MM, Schmidbauer JA, Majaess L & Smith RL (2000) Evidence Level III
- Natvig K (1983) Evidence Level III
- Zeine L & Larson M (1999) Evidence Level III

## Provision and Planning of Alternative Communication (B)

Before treatment commences, anticipated loss of voice, speech and oromotor skills should be identified and alternative and supplementary methods of communication provided at the appropriate time according to patient need. These could include writing, gesture, mouthing or electronic aids, eg, artificial larynx and Lightwriter.

### Rationale

To enable the patient to continue to communicate as effectively as possible post-treatment.

*Evidence*

- Karnell LH, Funk GF & Hoffman HT (2000) Evidence Level III
- Carr MM, Schmidbauer JA, Majaess L & Smith RL (2000) Evidence Level III
- Edels Y (1983) Evidence Level IV

### Selection of Appropriate Treatment Strategies (B)

The Speech & Language Therapist will provide appropriate therapy to optimise function. Commencement of therapy will be following consultation with the multidisciplinary team. This will include the following:

- Oromotor therapy (range of motion exercises, strength and endurance exercises)
- Articulation therapy
- Advice on oral healthcare
- Swallowing therapy
- Voice care and hygiene
- Voice therapy
- Maximising intelligibility
- Teaching compensatory and substitution strategies
- Alaryngeal voice therapy including oesophageal and tracheo-oesophageal voice therapy and artificial larynx training
- Choice of humidification/filter systems

*Rationale*
To optimise the residual function in order to maximise communication and swallowing ability. When a return to normal is not possible, functional levels of ability should be the goal.

*Evidence*

- Pauloski BR, Rademake AW, Logemann JA & Colangelo LA (1998) Evidence Level III
- Sonies BC (1993) Evidence Level III
- Logemann JA, Pauloski BR, Rademaker AW & Colangelo LA (1997) Evidence Level IV

### Alaryngeal Voice Therapy: Oesophageal, Artificial Larynx, Surgical Voice Restoration (B)

The Speech & Language Therapist will select and teach the most appropriate method of laryngeal voice in consultation with the patient to achieve optimum functional voice. Detailed counselling will enable appropriate choice of communication method(s).

*Rationale*
Individualised tailoring is necessary due to individual patient abilities, needs and preferences.

*Evidence*

- Kalb MB & Carpenter MA (1981) Evidence Level III
- Carr MM, Schmidbauer JA, Majaess L & Smith RL (2000) Evidence Level III
- Finizia C, Hammerlid E, Westin T & Lindstrom J (1998) Evidence Level III
- St Guily JL, Angelard B, El-Bez M, Julien N, Debry C, Fichaux & Gondret R (1992) Evidence Level III

### Selection of Surgical Voice Restoration (SVR) with Laryngectomee (B)

It is recognised that surgical voice restoration offers the best opportunity for achieving the closest quality to laryngeal voice in the shortest time. It also offers the least communicative dysfunction. The Speech & Language Therapist will be involved in decision-making regarding the choice of prosthesis, sizing, fitting and ongoing management.

*Rationale*
The Speech & Language Therapist will have access to up-to-date information regarding the differences between various prostheses and their individual benefits and disadvantages.

*Evidence*

- Bertino GA, Bellomo C, Miani F, Ferrero F & Staffieri A (1996) Evidence Level IIb
- Robbins J, Fisher HB, Blom ED & Singer MI (1984) Evidence Level III
- Clements KS, Rassekh CH, Seikaly H, Hokanson JA & Calhoun KH (1997) Evidence Level III

■ RCSLT Tracheo-oesophageal puncture procedures (1999)
Evidence Level IV

## Long-term Management (C)

**When direct therapy is no longer indicated and the patient can be discharged, ongoing advice and support can be provided via the Speech & Language Therapist in the multidisciplinary clinic, in other teams, eg, palliative care or general departments.**

*Rationale*
A change in the status of the patient and/or the disease may require further input at a later stage prior to, or after, discharge from active intervention. Speech and swallowing changes may be indicative of further disease.

*Evidence*
Professional consensus.

## Themes Identified from the Consultation with Service Users

This was a significant aspect of the project. There were three main approaches to consulting with the users:

■ Inviting representatives from voluntary organisations to attend meetings of the expert groups
■ Focus groups with service users or their parents/carers
■ Postal questionnaire

The following themes are based upon a sample of individuals' experiences and their perception of what a Speech and Language Therapy Service should offer. Full details of the process undertaken are outlined in the 'Consultation with Service Users' section.

■ Working in partnership
■ Process of service delivery
  ■ Regular reviews, as appropriate.

# Appendix 1
# Tables of Evidence

## CORE CLINICAL GUIDELINE

### Assessment

| Author(s) & Title | Design | Sample | Objective of study | Conclusions | Evidence Level |
|---|---|---|---|---|---|
| Raaijmakers MF, Dekker J, Dejonckere PH & Zee J van der, 1995, 'Reliability of the assessment of impairments, disabilities and handicaps in survey research on speech therapy', *Folia Phoniatrica Logopedica* 47 (4):199–209. | Qualitative study | — | An important aspect to the practice of speech therapy is the diagnostic assessment. The International Classification of Impairments, Disabilities and Handicaps (ICIDH) is regarded as a good starting point for the classification of speech therapy assessments. Based on the ICIDH, a form was developed for the registration of impairments, disabilities and handicaps in survey research on speech therapy. The aim of this study was to evaluate the reliability of the assessment of impairments, disabilities and handicaps based on clinical observations and examinations by speech & language therapists. | On the basis of the percentage of agreement and kappa values, it is concluded that the reliability of the assessment of the impairments, disabilities and handicaps was satisfactory to excellent for most of the categories. | III |
| Raaijmakers MF, Dekker J & Dejonckere PH, 1998, 'Diagnostic assessment and treatment goals in logopedics: impairments, disabilities and handicaps', *Folia Phoniatrica Logopedica* 50 (2):71–79. | Qualitative study | 1,567 patients | This aim of this study was to investigate the extent to which impairments, disabilities and handicaps are used as diagnostic assessments and treatment goals in logopedics. A survey study was carried out on patients in logopedic practices in the Netherlands to provide an empirical quantitative description of diagnostic assessments and treatment goals, formulated in terms of impairments, disabilities and handicaps. | Results show that logopedists indeed often indicate impairments as diagnostic assessments and as treatment goals, particularly language development impairments and phonetic/phonological articulation impairments. Interestingly, large numbers of diagnostic assessments and treatment goals were also indicated at the level of disabilities and handicaps; the most important being disability in expressing communication and occupational handicap. These results demonstrate that disabilities and handicaps may serve an important function in logopedics, in that they may guide assessment as well as therapy. | III |

### Assessment and Bilingualism

| Author(s) & Title | Design | Sample | Objective of study | Conclusions | Evidence Level |
|---|---|---|---|---|---|
| Holm A, Dodd B, Stow C & Pert S, 1999, 'Identification and differential diagnosis of phonological disorder in bilingual children', *Language Testing* 16:271–92. | Qualitative study | Children aged 4.7 to 7.4 years old | Diagnosis of speech disorder in children acquiring two languages is problematic. There are few norms for bilingual language acquisition, and Speech & Language Therapist are unlikely to speak both languages of the bilingual populations they serve. Knowledge concerning the phonological structure of many languages is limited. This article describes the development of a phonological assessment for bilingual children. The assessment was administered to normally developing bilingual children and children suspected of speech disorder. The children were aged from 4.7 to 7.4 years. All children spoke either Mirpuri, Punjabi or Urdu at home but were exposed to English at nursery or school. The normal and atypical phonological development and error patterns of bilingual children in each language are described. | The error patterns are consistent with research evidence concerning subgroups of speech disorder in monolingual and bilingual children. The findings provide further support for the hypothesis that symptoms (surface error patterns) of speech disorder are language independent (ie, that a single deficit underlies the speech disorder across both languages). | III |
| De Houwer A, 1999, 'Implications from research on normally developing bilingual children for the assessment of bilingual children in the speech clinic', *Abstracts of the Second International Symposium on Bilingualism*, Department of Speech, University of Newcastle upon Tyne. | Conference proceedings | — | — | — | IV |

## CORE CLINICAL GUIDELINE

### Working in Partnership

| Author(s) & Title | Design | Sample | Objective of study | Conclusions | Evidence Level |
|---|---|---|---|---|---|
| Glogowska M, Campbell R, Peters TJ, Roulstone S & Enderby P, 2001, 'Developing a scale to measure parental attitudes towards preschool speech and language therapy services', *International Journal of Language and Communication Disorders* 36 (4):503–13. | Qualitative study | Parents of 16 pre-school children | Today, Speech & Language Therapists working with the pre-school population routinely involve parents in their children's treatment programmes. Also, there is increasing recognition of the importance of considering client and carer views in evaluating services. This paper reports an aspect of a study that investigated parents' views and perceptions of their pre-school children's speech and language difficulties and the speech and language therapy they received. The methodology of the study was qualitative and data were collected from the parents of 16 pre-school children, using in-depth interviews. The parents' perceptions could be characterised as a process with three phases. | On the whole, parents viewed their involvement in speech and language therapy positively but, crucially, the interviews highlighted discrepancies between therapists' and parents' perceptions of the therapy process. The study demonstrates that when parents' views are considered, a fuller understanding of the effectiveness and acceptability of treatment can emerge. | III |
| Langhorne P & Pollock A, 2002, 'What are the components of effective stroke unit care?', *Age Ageing* 31 (5):365–71. | Survey | — | The effectiveness of organised inpatient (stroke unit) care has been demonstrated in systematic reviews of clinical trials. However, the key components of stroke-unit care are poorly understood. This paper reports on a survey of recent trials (published 1985–2000) of a stroke unit/ward which had demonstrated a beneficial effect consistent with the stroke unit systematic review. | Eleven eligible stroke unit trials were identified, of which the majority described similar approaches to i) assessment procedures (medical, nursing and therapy assessment); ii) early management policies (eg, early mobilisation; avoidance of urinary catheterisation; treatment of hypoxia, hyperglycaemia and suspected infection); iii) ongoing rehabilitation policies (eg, co-ordinated multidisciplinary team care, early assessment for discharge). This survey provides a description of stroke unit care which can serve as a benchmark for general stroke patient care and future clinical research. | III |

| Author(s) & Title | Design | Sample | Objective of study | Conclusions | Evidence Level |
|---|---|---|---|---|---|
| Pollack MR & Disler PB, 2002, 'Rehabilitation of patients after stroke', *The Medical Journal of Australia* 77(8):452–56. | Expert opinion | — | Studies show clear advantages of treatment of patients in the acute phase of stroke in a dedicated stroke unit. Rehabilitation after stroke is a continuum, starting within days of stroke onset and ending only when it no longer produces any positive effect. More than half of the 75 percent of patients who survive the first month after a stroke will require specialised rehabilitation. Effective rehabilitation relies on a coordinated, multidisciplinary team approach. Regular team meetings, as well as meetings with the patient, his or her family and carers, are essential. | Evidence supporting rehabilitation programmes is based on evaluation of the multidisciplinary approach or on the effect of a particular discipline (eg, speech therapy), rather than on individual components of treatment. | IV |

### Management Planning and Goal Setting

| Author(s) & Title | Design | Sample | Objective of study | Conclusions | Evidence Level |
|---|---|---|---|---|---|
| John A, 1998, 'Measuring client and carer perspectives', *International Journal of Language and Communication Disorders* 33(Suppl):132–37. | Conference proceedings | — | — | — | IV |

## PRE-SCHOOL CHILDREN WITH COMMUNICATION, LANGUAGE & SPEECH NEEDS

| Author(s) & Title | Design | Sample | Objective of study | Conclusions | Evidence Level |
|---|---|---|---|---|---|
| **Assessment** | | | | | |
| Law J, Boyle J, Harris F, Harkness A & Nye C, 1998, 'Screening for speech and language delay: a systematic review of the literature', *Health Technology Assessment 2 (9).* | Systematic literature review | — | This report concerns the identification and treatment of children with primary speech and language delays, that is, delays which cannot be attributed to other conditions such as hearing loss or other more general developmental disabilities. Four domains (prevalence, natural history, intervention and screening) were identified as being key to a review of screening issues, with the following objectives being stated: 1) to undertake a systematic review of research into the value of screening and intervention for speech and language delays in children up to the age of 7 years; 2) to identify priority areas in need of further investigation; 3) to provide evidence-based direction for the future provision of services. | The review suggests that more attention might be shown to the role of parents in identifying children with speech and language delay. Primary-care workers should be involved in eliciting parental concerns and in making appropriate observations of children's communication behaviours. This would require formal training in delayed speech and language development and risk factors pertaining to it. Appropriate information would also have to be made available to parents to allow them to play an active role in judging need. Given the reported value of indirect approaches to intervention there is a case for widening the range of professionals able to promote good interactive practice in parents of young children. Speech & Language Therapists as a professional group are in a good position to play an active role in disseminating this information and coordinating such services. | IIa |

| Author(s) & Title | Design | Sample | Objective of study | Conclusions | Evidence Level |
|---|---|---|---|---|---|
| Gathercole SE, Willis CS, Emslie H & Baddeley AD, 1992, 'Phonological memory and vocabulary development during the early school years: A longitudinal study', *Developmental Psychology* 28 (5):887–98. | Longitudinal study | 118 children in the study; this article includes data on 80 | The nature of the developmental association between phonological memory and vocabulary knowledge was explored in a longitudinal study. At each of four waves (at ages 4, 5, 6 and 8 years), measures of vocabulary, phonological memory, non-verbal intelligence and reading were taken from 80 children. | Comparisons of cross-lagged partial correlations revealed a significant shift in the causal underpinnings of the relationship between phonological memory and vocabulary development before and after 5 years of age. Between 4 and 5 years, phonological memory skills appeared to exert a direct causal influence on vocabulary acquisition. Subsequently, though, vocabulary knowledge became the major pacemaker in the developmental relationship, with the earlier influence of phonological memory on vocabulary development subsiding to a non-significant level. | III |
| Gathercole SE & Adams AM, 1993, 'Phonological working memory in very young children', *Developmental Psychology* 29 (4): 770–77. | Clinical study | 111 children of 2 and 3 years old, article reports on the data for 54 children | This study was designed to establish whether phonological working memory skills could be assessed in children below 4 years of age. A group of 2– and 3–year-old children were tested on three phonological memory measures (digit span, non-word repetition, and word repetition) and were also given tasks that tapped other cognitive skills. Scores on the three phonological memory tasks were closely related. In addition, repetition performance was linked with both vocabulary knowledge and articulation rate. | Results indicate that phonological memory skills can be reliably assessed in very young children by using conventional serial span and repetition procedures. | III |

## PRE-SCHOOL CHILDREN WITH COMMUNICATION, LANGUAGE & SPEECH NEEDS

| Author(s) & Title | Design | Sample | Objective of study | Conclusions | Evidence Level |
|---|---|---|---|---|---|
| Dockrell JE, Messer D, George R & Wilson G, 1998, 'Children with word-finding difficulties – prevalence, presentation and naming problems', *International Journal of Language and Communication Disorders* 33 (44). | Survey | 123 practitioners who worked with children with language difficulties returned surveys | A questionnaire was designed to examine professionals' experiences of word-finding difficulties. It addressed prevalence, assessment, interventions and nature of word-find difficulties. A further section required the professionals to identify, from their clinical experience, the proportion of children with word-finding difficulties who experienced other language and learning problems. | Twenty-three percent of children in language support services were identified as having word-finding difficulties. Most subjects used a mixture of formal and informal assessments. It was reported that word-finding difficulties were associated with difficulties in grammatical production, word meaning and grammatical comprehension. Word-finding difficulties in addition were more likely to occur in situations with high processing demands. A variety of intervention strategies were identified. | III |
| Bloom L & Lahey M, 1978, *Language Development and Language Disorders*, John Wiley & Sons, London. | Expert opinion | — | — | — | IV |
| Goldin-Meadow S, 1998, 'The development of gesture and speech as an integrated system', in Iverson, JM (ed), Jossey Bass Inc, San Francisco. | Expert opinion | — | — | Notes that children produce gestures in communicative contexts early in their development. The relationship between gesture and speech during childhood is explored, focusing on the gestures that, in adults, typically co-occur with speech. Three questions are examined: 1) Do gesture and speech form an integrated system for speakers from the earliest stages of language development, and if not, when do the two modalities come together? 2) What is the relationship between gesture and speech for speakers during the school-age years, after language is well established? 3) Finally, do gesture and speech form an integrated system for listeners at the earliest stages of development and during the school-age years? | IV |

| Author(s) & Title | Design | Sample | Objective of study | Conclusions | Evidence Level |
|---|---|---|---|---|---|
| Parkinson A & Pate S, 2000, 'Speech and language assessment', in Law J, Parkinson A & Tamhne R (eds) *Communication Difficulties in Childhood*, Radcliffe Medical Press, Abingdon. | Expert opinion | — | — | — | IV |
| **Evenness of Development** | | | | | |
| Bloom L & Lahey M, 1978, *Language Development and Language Disorders*, John Wiley & Sons, London. | Expert opinion | — | — | — | IV |
| Sheridan MD, Frost M & Sharma A, 1997 *From Birth to Five Years: Children's Developmental Progress*, Taylor & Francis Ltd, London. | Expert opinion | — | — | — | IV |
| **Collaborative Working** | | | | | |
| Glogowska M & Campbell R, 2000, 'Notes and discussion. Investigating parental views of involvement in pre-school speech and language therapy', *International Journal of Language & Communication Disorders*, 35 (3):391–405. | Qualitative Study | Parents of 16 pre-school children | This paper reports an aspect of a study that investigated parents' views and perceptions of their pre-school children's speech and language difficulties and the speech and language therapy they received. Data were collected from the parents of 16 pre-school children, using in-depth interviews. | The parents' perceptions could be characterised as a process with three phases. On the whole, parents viewed their involvement in speech and language therapy positively but crucially, the interviews highlighted discrepancies between therapists' and parents' perceptions of the therapy process. The study demonstrates that when parents' views are considered, a fuller understanding of the effectiveness and acceptability of treatment can emerge. | III |

# PRE-SCHOOL CHILDREN WITH COMMUNICATION, LANGUAGE & SPEECH NEEDS

**Management Approaches**
**1 Health Promotion/Prevention of Future Difficulties**

| Author(s) & Title | Design | Sample | Objective of study | Conclusions | Evidence Level |
|---|---|---|---|---|---|
| Feldman MA, Sparks B & Case L, 1993, 'Effectiveness of home-based early intervention on the language development of children of mothers with mental retardation', *Research in Developmental Disabilities* 14 (5):387–408. | Randomised controlled trial | 28 mothers labelled mentally retarded with children under 28 months of age | The authors evaluated the effects of a home-based parent training programme for mothers with mental retardation on the language development of their children who were at risk for language delay. The participants, 28 mothers labelled mentally retarded with children under 28 months of age, initially showed significantly fewer positive mother-child interactions and child vocalisations and verbalisations than did a comparison group of 38 families with children of similar age, whose mothers were not mentally retarded. The 28 mothers with low IQ were then matched on child entry age and randomly assigned to either an interaction training or attention-control group. | After training, the training group scores were no longer lower than those of the comparison group of mothers without mental retardation and were also significantly higher than the scores of the attention-control group on all maternal positive interactions; child vocalisations; verbalisations; and language and social domains of the Bayley Scales of Infant Development. Speech emerged significantly sooner in the training group as compared to the control group. The training group parents and children maintained improvements up to 82 weeks following training, and the attention-control group, when subsequently trained, replicated the original training group results. Thus, home-based parent training increased positive maternal interactions of mothers with mental retardation, which facilitated language development in their young children. | Ib |
| Girolametto L, Pearce PS & Weitzman E, 1996, 'Interactive focused stimulation for toddlers with expressive vocabulary delays', *Journal of Speech & Hearing Research* 39 (6):1274–83. | Randomised controlled trial | 25 mothers and their toddlers | This study explored the effects of training 25 mothers to administer focused intervention to teach specific target words to their toddlers with expressive vocabulary delays. Twenty-five mothers and their late-talking toddlers were randomly assigned to treatment and delayed-treatment (control) groups. Vocabulary targets were individually selected for each toddler, based on the child's phonetic repertoire and parent report of vocabulary development. | Following treatment, mothers' language input was slower, less complex and more focused. The children used more target words, more words during play, and had larger vocabularies than the control group. | Ib |

| Author(s) & Title | Design | Sample | Objective of study | Conclusions | Evidence Level |
|---|---|---|---|---|---|
| Gibbard D, 1994, 'Parental-based intervention with pre-school language-delayed children', *European Journal of Disorders of Communication* 29 (2):131–50. | Randomised controlled study | — | Mothers of children randomly allocated to an experimental group attended fortnightly group parental language training sessions, over a six-month period. Mothers of children allocated to a matched no intervention control group received no special attention. A second experiment was designed to compare the parental involvement approach with direct, individual treatment and to clarify the role of non-specific 'Hawthorne-type' effects. The experimental group mothers attended parental language training sessions, as above. The parental control group mothers also attended training sessions, with the emphasis on general learning skills rather than language. A third group of children received individual, direct speech and language therapy. | The results showed significantly greater gains in the expressive language skills of the experimental group compared to the control group. Results showed significantly greater language gains in the parental language training group and in the individual group. The two former groups did not differ significantly, indicating that, for these groups and this methodology, parental language training is as effective as individual speech and language therapy. The results also indicate that the effectiveness of the parental involvement approach cannot be accounted for by non-specific factors. The research findings are discussed, together with the professional implications of the study and recommendations for further research. | Ib |
| Law J, Boyle J, Harris F, Harkness A & Nye C, 1998, 'Screening for speech and language delay: a systematic review of the literature', *Health Technology Assessment* 2 (9). | Systematic literature review | — | This report concerns the identification and treatment of children with primary speech and language delays, that is, delays which cannot be attributed to other conditions such as hearing loss or other more general developmental disabilities. Four domains (prevalence, natural history, intervention and screening) were identified as being key to a review of screening issues, with the following objectives being stated: 1) to undertake a systematic review of research into the value of screening and intervention for speech and language delays in children up to the age of 7 years; 2) to identify priority areas in need of further investigation; 3) to provide evidence-based direction for the future provision of services. | The review suggests that more attention might be shown to the role of parents in identifying children with speech and language delay. Primary-care workers should be involved in eliciting parental concerns and in making appropriate observations of children's communication behaviours. This would require formal training in delayed speech and language development and risk factors pertaining to it. Appropriate information would also have to be made available to parents to allow them to play an active role in judging need. Given the reported value of indirect approaches to intervention there is a case for widening the range of professionals able to promote good interactive practice in parents of young children. Speech & Language Therapists as a professional group are in a good position to play an active role in disseminating this information and coordinating such services. | IIa |

## PRE-SCHOOL CHILDREN WITH COMMUNICATION, LANGUAGE & SPEECH NEEDS

| Author(s) & Title | Design | Sample | Objective of study | Conclusions | Evidence Level |
|---|---|---|---|---|---|
| Barber M, Farrell P & Parkinson G, 2001, 'Evaluation of the Speech and Language Therapy Projects', *Sure Start*, DfES Publications. | Qualitative study | — | This report is an evaluation of the Speech and Language Therapy Projects supported by the 2000–2001 Standards Funding. | The main findings indicate that professionals have made progress in developing collaborative and flexible working strategies that enable best practice speech and language therapy to be delivered within educational contexts. | IV |
| **2 Maximising Communication Environment to Increase Potential for Participation and Activity** | | | | | |
| Peterson C, Jesso B & McCabe A, 1999, 'Encouraging narratives in preschoolers: an intervention study', *Journal of Child Language* 26 (1):49–67. | Randomised controlled trial | 20 children, mean age 3;7 years | Twenty economically disadvantaged pre-schoolers were randomly assigned to an intervention or a control group, and their mothers' styles of eliciting narratives from their children were assessed before and after intervention. Mothers of intervention children were encouraged to spend more time in narrative conversation, ask more open-ended and context-eliciting questions, and encourage longer narratives through back-channel responses. Children's narrative and vocabulary skills were assessed before and after the year-long intervention and 14 children participated in a follow-up assessment a year later. Narrative measures included the number and length of narratives as well as how decontextualised and informative they were. | Intervention children showed significant vocabulary improvement immediately after intervention terminated, and a year later they showed overall improvements in narrative skill. In particular, intervention children produced more context-setting descriptions about where and especially when the described events took place. Such decontextualised language has been emphasised as important for literacy acquisition. | Ib |
| Coulter L & Gallagher C, 2001, 'Evaluation of the Hanen Early Childhood Educators Programme', *International Journal of Language & Communication Disorders* 36 (Suppl):264–9. | Comparative study | — | The current study is an evaluation of the Hanen Early Childhood Educators Programme (Weitzman 1992). It explores outcomes for both staff and children following staff participation in the training programme. Using a comparative study design and pre- and post-training measures, the changes in staff and children were investigated. | Changes were observed in children's social interaction skills. This was reinforced by staff reports of changes in children's interaction. Staff changes included increased skills and confidence in identifying and supporting children with speech and language difficulties alongside positive changes in their interaction styles. | III |

## 4 Improve the child's level of functioning

| Author(s) & Title | Design | Sample | Objective of study | Conclusions | Evidence Level |
|---|---|---|---|---|---|
| Peterson C, Jesso B & McCabe A, 1999, 'Encouraging narratives in preschoolers: an intervention study', *Journal of Child Language* 26 (1):49–67. | Randomised controlled trial | 20 children, mean age 3;7 years | Twenty economically disadvantaged pre-schoolers were randomly assigned to an intervention or a control group, and their mothers' styles of eliciting narratives from their children were assessed before and after intervention. Mothers of intervention children were encouraged to spend more time in narrative conversation, ask more open-ended and context-eliciting questions, and encourage longer narratives through back-channel responses. Children's narrative and vocabulary skills were assessed before and after the year-long intervention and 14 children participated in a follow-up assessment a year later. Narrative measures included the number and length of narratives as well as how decontextualised and informative they were. | Intervention children showed significant vocabulary improvement immediately after intervention terminated, and a year later they showed overall improvements in narrative skill. In particular, intervention children produced more context-setting descriptions about where and especially when the described events took place. Such decontextualised language has been emphasised as important for literacy acquisition. | Ib |
| Robertson SB & Weismer SE, 1999, 'Effects of treatment on linguistic and social skills in toddlers with delayed language development', *Journal of Speech, Language & Hearing Research* 42 (5):1234–48. | Randomised controlled trial | 21 children | Investigated the effects of early language intervention on various linguistic and social skills of late-talking toddlers. The 21 children were randomly assigned to an experimental group (n = 11) or a control (delayed-treatment) group (n = 10). The experimental group participated in a twelve-week clinician-implemented language intervention programme. Groups were compared at pre-test and post-test on five linguistic variables: mean length of utterance; total number of words; number of different words; lexical repertoire; and percentage of intelligible utterances, as well as on socialisation and parental stress. | Significant group differences were found for each of the variables, indicating facilitative effects of the treatment. Notably, increases were observed in areas that were not specifically targeted by the intervention. Implications of these results are discussed with respect to considerations regarding clinical management decisions for toddlers with delayed language development. | Ib |

## PRE-SCHOOL CHILDREN WITH COMMUNICATION, LANGUAGE & SPEECH NEEDS

| Author(s) & Title | Design | Sample | Objective of study | Conclusions | Evidence Level |
|---|---|---|---|---|---|
| Glogowska M, Roulstone S, Enderby P & Peters TJ, 2000, 'Randomised controlled trial of community based speech and language therapy in preschool children', *BMJ* 321 (7266):923–6. | Randomised controlled trial | 159 pre-school children | To compare routine speech and language therapy in pre-school children with delayed speech and language against 12 months of 'watchful waiting' in 16 community clinics in Bristol. | Improvement in auditory comprehension was significant in favour of therapy. No significant differences were observed for expressive language phonology error rate, language development or improvement on entry criterion. At the end of the trial, 70 percent of all children still had substantial speech and language deficits. This study provides little evidence for the effectiveness of speech and language therapy compared with watchful waiting over 12 months. Providers of speech and language therapy should reconsider the appropriateness, timing, nature and intensity of such therapy in pre-school children. | Ib |
| Girolametto LE, 1988, 'Improving the social-conversational skills of developmentally delayed children: an intervention study', *Journal of Speech & Hearing Disorders* 53 (2):156–67. | Controlled study | 20 mothers and their pre-school children | Twenty mothers and their pre-school-aged, developmentally delayed children participated in this parent-focused intervention study. Nine mother-child dyads received an 11-week training programme that espoused a social-conversational approach, while 11 dyads served as controls | Pre- and post-test videotapes were transcribed and coded to yield measures of turn-taking, as well as indexes of responsiveness, topic control and uninvolvement. Following treatment, the mothers in the experimental group were more responsive to and less controlling of their children's behaviour than the mothers in the comparison group. The children initiated more topics, were more responsive to their mother's preceding turns, and used more verbal turns and a more diverse vocabulary than the control group children. No differences in language development, as measured by a standardised test, were found. | IIa |

| Author(s) & Title | Design | Sample | Objective of study | Conclusions | Evidence Level |
|---|---|---|---|---|---|
| Hesketh A, Adams C, Nightingale C & Hall R, 2000, 'Phonological awareness therapy and articulatory training approaches for children with phonological disorders: A comparative outcome study', *International Journal of Language & Communication Disorders* 35 (3): 337–54. | Comparative study | 61 children aged 3.5 to 5 years with developmental phonological disorders

59 normally speaking controls | 61 children (aged 3.5–5 years) with developmental phonological disorders (PD) participated in a study comparing the effects of metaphonologically (MET) or articulation-based (ART) therapy. Maturational effects were controlled by the inclusion of 59 normally speaking controls. Measures of phonological output and phonological awareness (PA) were taken before and after therapy for all children and at three months post-therapy for PD children. | Results showed that children with phonological disorders improved significantly in both phonological output and phonological awareness skills across the intervention period compared with control children, but that there was no significant difference on the phonological awareness measure between articulation-based therapy and metaphonologically-based therapy groups. Follow-up measures for both therapy groups showed that there was little difference between the groups in terms of phonological awareness change or speech development three months after intervention. However, there was a trend for metaphonologically based therapy children to continue to make more long-term change than the articulation-based therapy group on one output measure. There were generally few significant implications for outcome between phonologically disordered children with good initial phonological awareness skills and those who initially had poor phonological awareness skills. | III |

# SCHOOL-AGED CHILDREN WITH SPEECH, LANGUAGE & COMMUNICATION DIFFICULTIES

| Author(s) & Title | Design | Sample | Objective of study | Conclusions | Evidence Level |
|---|---|---|---|---|---|
| **Recommendations For All Children** | | | | | |
| **1 Collaboration** | | | | | |
| Law J, Lindsay G, Peacey N, Gascoigne M, Soloff N, Radford J, Band S & Fitzgerald L, 2000, *Provision for Children with Speech and Language Needs In England and Wales: Facilitating Communication Between Education and Health Services*, DfES Publications. http://www.dfes.gov.uk/research/ | Qualitative study | — | To report on existing provision across England and Wales and to help facilitate the process of collaboration between health and education services. | — | III |
| Reid J, Millar S, Tait L, Donaldson M, Dean EC, Thomson GOB & Grieve R, 1996, 'Pupils with special educational needs: The role of Speech & Language Therapists', *Interchange* (43). | Questionnaire interview | Variety of professionals involved with children | This report describes a research project that studied: the speech and language needs of Scottish children and young people with special educational needs; collaboration among parents and professionals; and the perceived effectiveness of different ways of providing speech and language therapy. Data were obtained from a series of mailed questionnaires, school visits, and interviews conducted between December 1993 and April 1995. | The project found that there is a pattern of ever-increasing demand for speech and language therapy which continuously outstrips increases in provision. Parents and professionals reported that pupils benefit when speech and language therapy is integrated into the curriculum. The study also showed evidence of collaborative practice among parents, Speech & Language Therapists, and other staff both in mainstream and special educational facilities. Parents' comments about the quality of their children's speech and language therapy were predominantly positive. | III |

| Author(s) & Title | Design | Sample | Objective of study | Conclusions | Evidence Level |
|---|---|---|---|---|---|
| **2 Assessment** | | | | | |
| Law J, Lindsay G, Peacey N, Gascoigne M, Soloff N, Radford J, Band S & Fitzgerald L, 2000, *Provision for Children with Speech and Language Needs In England and Wales: Facilitating Communication Between Education and Health Services*, DfES Publications. http://www.dfes.gov.uk/research/ | Qualitative study | — | To report on existing provision across England and Wales and to help facilitate the process of collaboration between health and education services. | — | III |
| **3 Management** | | | | | |
| Doherty KM & Masters RY, 1996, 'Collaborative consultation: a systemic activity', *Seminars in Speech and Language* 17 (2):123–8. | Single case study | 1 child | In a collaborative consultation model of speech-language service delivery, the treatment system is expanded beyond the traditional client-centred dyad. Further, services are provided in the context of the classroom, rather than in the non-contextual environment of a therapy room, and treatment goals relate to aspects of the school, such as curriculum, classroom behaviour, and social interactions with peers. The use of the model is illustrated with a child with a cognitive impairment. | — | III |
| **Assessment of Communication** | | | | | |
| **2 Environmental factors** | | | | | |
| Picard M & Bradley JS, 2001, 'Revisiting speech interference in classrooms', *Audiology* 40 (5):221–44. | Expert opinion | — | A review of the effects of ambient noise and reverberation on speech intelligibility in classrooms has been completed because of the long-standing lack of agreement on preferred acoustical criteria for unconstrained speech accessibility and communication in educational facilities. | An overwhelming body of evidence has been collected to suggest that noise levels, in particular, are usually far in excess of any reasonable prescription for optimal conditions for understanding speech in classrooms. | IV |

## SCHOOL-AGED CHILDREN WITH SPEECH, LANGUAGE & COMMUNICATION DIFFICULTIES

| Author(s) & Title | Design | Sample | Objective of study | Conclusions | Evidence Level |
|---|---|---|---|---|---|
| **Management of Communication** | | | | | |
| **2  Modification of the environment** | | | | | |
| Picard M & Bradley JS, 2001, 'Revisiting speech interference in classrooms', *Audiology* 40 (5):221–44. | Expert opinion | — | A review of the effects of ambient noise and reverberation on speech intelligibility in classrooms has been completed because of the long-standing lack of agreement on preferred acoustical criteria for unconstrained speech accessibility and communication in educational facilities. | An overwhelming body of evidence has been collected to suggest that noise levels, in particular, are usually far in excess of any reasonable prescription for optimal conditions for understanding speech in classrooms. | IV |
| **Management of Language** | | | | | |
| **Speech Perception** | | | | | |
| Tallal P, Stark RE & Mellits ED, 1985, 'Identification of language-impaired children on the basis of rapid perception and production skills', *Brain & Language* 25 (2):314–22. | Controlled study | 26 language impaired children aged 5 to 8 years and 33 matched controls | Discriminant function analysis was used to determine whether performance on temporal perception and production tasks alone could correctly classify 26 language-impaired children and 33 age, intelligence and matched normal control children, as either language impaired or normal. The children were administered a battery of non-verbal and speech perception and motor tests as well as a repetition test incorporating auditory, visual, and cross-modal non-verbal and verbal stimuli. | The analysis identified six variables, all of which assessed temporal, perceptual and production abilities, which, taken in combination, correctly classified 98 percent of the children. It is noted that none of these variables assessed the higher-level linguistic abilities (semantic, syntactic and pragmatic) that have classically been considered to be deficient in language-impaired children or that have been used to diagnose them clinically. Results suggest a possible biological basis for temporal perception/production mechanisms that may be associated with the development and maintenance of normal language function. | IIa |

| Author(s) & Title | Design | Sample | Objective of study | Conclusions | Evidence Level |
|---|---|---|---|---|---|
| **Vocabulary** | | | | | |
| Constable A.J, Stackhouse J & Wells B, 1997, 'Developmental word-finding difficulties and phonological processing: the case of the missing handcuffs', *Applied Psycholinguistics* 18:507–36. | Single case study | 7 year old | The case of a seven-year-old boy with severe word-finding difficulties is presented. In an attempt to investigate the cause of these difficulties, a series of theoretically motivated questions was used as a framework for psycholinguistic investigation. A range of tasks was administered, including word association; semantic knowledge; auditory discrimination; auditory lexical decision; naming; and real word and non-word repetition. | The child's performance of the tasks was compared with that of controls matched in terms of chronological and vocabulary age. Results reveal significant differences between the child's performance and that of the control groups. | III |
| Easton C, Sheach S & Easton S, 1997, 'Teaching vocabulary to children with word-finding difficulties using a combined semantic and phonological approach: an efficacy study', *Child Language Teaching & Therapy* 13 (2):125–42. | Single subject design | Four children aged ten years | This study evaluates a combined semantic and phonological approach to teaching vocabulary to children with word-finding difficulties. Four children were treated as single cases for the purpose of measuring their progress from pre-test maintenance. Target words were chosen according to age of acquisition. Naming ability on 80 words was tested pre- and post-intervention and at follow up. Forty of these words were presented over ten group teaching sessions in a five week period and the remaining 40 served as a control measure. | All children demonstrated improved naming ability on the 80-word test following the intervention and this was sustained at follow up. | III |
| Hyde Wright S, Gorrie B, Haynes C & Shipman A, 1993a, 'What's in a name? Comparative therapy for word-finding difficulties using semantic and phonological approaches', *Child Language Teaching and Therapy* 9 (3):214–29. | Comparative study | 30 children ranging in age from 8 to 14 years | The effect of two therapy methods in the treatment of word-finding problems during a confrontational picture-naming situation is compared in two groups of severely language-impaired children. A treatment technique that promotes the strengthening of the child's semantic networking is contrasted with an approach that fosters the child's phonological awareness. A course of 15 sessions of treatment over 5 weeks is undertaken by each subject. | The results are measured one week after the end of treatment. Those children receiving the semantic treatment indicate a highly significant improvement in naming untrained pictures, but the phonological treatment group makes no significant improvement. | III |

## SCHOOL-AGED CHILDREN WITH SPEECH, LANGUAGE & COMMUNICATION DIFFICULTIES

### Grammar

| Author(s) & Title | Design | Sample | Objective of study | Conclusions | Evidence Level |
|---|---|---|---|---|---|
| Hirschman M, 2000, 'Language repair via metalinguistic means', *International Journal of Language & Communication Disorders* 35 (2):251–68. | Controlled study | 2 experimental groups – children aged 9 and 10 years<br><br>2 control groups – children aged 9 and 10 years | Children with specific language impairment (SLI) have been shown to be deficient in the use of complex sentences. In an attempt to remediate this area of weakness, two groups of such children (mean ages 9;4 and 10;6) received about 55 half-hour sessions of metalinguistic training spread over 12 months. | Results showed that the use of complex sentences increased to at least normal levels in the experimental groups, and were significantly improved at both the written and oral levels, as compared with SLI control groups, which evidenced little change over the same period. Further analysis of the data revealed the striking finding that those children who had the poorest complex sentence usage tended to benefit the most from metalinguistic training. | IIa |
| Ebbels S & Lely H van der, 2001, 'Meta-syntactic therapy using visual coding for children with severe persistent SLI', *International Journal of Language & Communication Disorders* 36 (Suppl):345–50. | Single subject design | Four children aged 11 to 13 years old | The results of a pilot study into meta-syntactic therapy using visual coding for four children (age 11 to 13 years) with severe receptive and expressive specific language impairment (SLI) are presented. The coding system uses shapes, colours and a system of arrows to teach grammatical rules. A time-series design established baseline pre-therapy measures of comprehension and production of both passives and 'wh' questions. | All participants made progress with passives, and this was significant in three cases of the four. Comprehension and production of 'wh' questions also improved in all participants, although this did not always reach statistical significance. The results indicate that meta-syntactic therapy of grammatical rules, capitalising on visual strengths, can improve both comprehension and production in secondary-age children with severe persistent SLI. | III |
| Bryan A, 1997, 'Colourful Semantics', in Chiat S, Law J & Marshall J (eds) *Language Disorders in Children and Adults: Psycholinguistic Approaches to Therapy*, Whurr Publishers, London. | Expert opinion | — | — | — | IV |

| Author(s) & Title | Design | Sample | Objective of study | Conclusions | Evidence Level |
|---|---|---|---|---|---|
| **Narrative Structure** | | | | | |
| Camarata SM, Nelson K & Camarata M, 1994, 'Comparison of conversational-recasting and imitative procedures for training grammatical structures in children with specific language impairment', *Journal of Speech and Hearing Research* 37:1414–23. | Comparative study | 21 children ranging in age from 4 to 6 years | The purpose of this study was to compare the relative effectiveness of imitative intervention and conversational recast language intervention, applied to a wide range of grammatical morpheme and complex sentence targets in 21 children with specific language impairment. | The results indicated that although both kinds of treatments were effective in triggering acquisitions of most targets, consistently fewer presentations to first spontaneous use were required in conversational procedure. In addition, the transition from elicited production to generalised spontaneous production was more rapid under conversation-interactive treatment. Finally, although imitative treatment was more effective in generating elicited production, a significantly greater number of spontaneous productions occurred under the conversational training procedures. | III |
| Catts HW & Kamhi A, 1998, *Language and Reading Disabilities*, US Imports & PHIPEs. | Expert opinion | — | — | — | IV |
| Grove N, 1998, *Literature for All*, David Fulton Publishers, London. | Expert opinion | — | — | — | IV |

## SCHOOL-AGED CHILDREN WITH SPEECH, LANGUAGE & COMMUNICATION DIFFICULTIES

| Author(s) & Title | Design | Sample | Objective of study | Conclusions | Evidence Level |
|---|---|---|---|---|---|
| **Understanding of connected speech/narrative** | | | | | |
| Bishop DV & Adams C, 1992, 'Comprehension problems in children with specific language impairment: literal and inferential meaning', *Journal of Speech Hearing Research* 35 (1):119–29. | Controlled study | 61 children aged 8 to 12 years with specific language impairment (SLI)<br><br>Ten children aged 5, 6, 8, 10 & 12 acted as a control group | A group of 61 school children with specific language impairment (SLI) was compared with a control group on a comprehension task, in which the child was questioned about a story that had been presented either orally or as a series of pictures. Half the questions were literal, requiring the child to provide a detail that had been mentioned or shown explicitly in the story. The remainder required the child to make an inference about what had not been directly shown or stated. | SLI children were impaired on this task, even after taking into account 'comprehension age', as assessed on a multiple-choice test. However, the effects of mode of presentation and question type were similar for control and SLI groups. Children who fitted the clinical picture of semantic-pragmatic disorder had lower scores than other SLI children on this task. In addition, they were more prone to give answers that suggested they had not understood the question. However, as with the other SLI children, there was no indication that they had disproportionate difficulty with inferential questions. It is concluded that SLI children are impaired in constructing an integrated representation from a sequence of propositions, even when such propositions are presented non-verbally. | IIa |

| Author(s) & Title | Design | Sample | Objective of study | Conclusions | Evidence Level |
|---|---|---|---|---|---|
| McFadden TU & Gillam RB, 1996, 'An examination of the quality of narratives produced by children with language disorders', *Language, Speech & Hearing Services in the Schools* 27 (1):48–56. | Comparative study | | A team of regular and special educators used a holistic scoring procedure to rate the overall quality of spoken and written narratives produced by students with language disorders and their age, language, and reading-matched peers. | Students with language disorders earned significantly lower holistic scores than their age-matched peers. However, their holistic scores were similar to the scores earned by their language- and reading-matched peers. Correlations between holistic scores and structural measures of language revealed that quality judgements were moderately related to textual-level measures but were unrelated to sentence-level measures of form and content. Holistic scoring is shown to have clinical and research utility as a means for socially validating the effects of language disorders on storytelling. Clinicians who want to influence the overall quality of their students' stories may wish to focus their intervention on textual-level narrative features. | III |
| Hayward D & Schneider P, 2000, 'Effectiveness of teaching story grammar knowledge to pre-school children with language impairment: An exploratory study', *Child Language Teaching and Therapy*, pp255–84. | Comparative study | 13 children with language impairment, ranging in age from 4 to 6 years old | In this study, 13 children with language impairments participated in a narrative intervention programme. Narrative intervention activities explicitly taught story grammar components. Two measures of content were used to analyse children's story productions: story information and episode level. | As a group, the children included more story information and produced more structurally complex stories following intervention. Single subject data revealed that half the children showed statistically significant improvements for story information and episode level. | III |

## SCHOOL-AGED CHILDREN WITH SPEECH, LANGUAGE & COMMUNICATION DIFFICULTIES

### Understanding of Figurative Language

| Author(s) & Title | Design | Sample | Objective of study | Conclusions | Evidence Level |
|---|---|---|---|---|---|
| Kerbel D & Grunwell P, 1998, 'A study of idiom comprehension in children with semantic-pragmatic difficulties. Part I: task effects on the assessment of idiom comprehension in children', *International Journal of Language & Communication Disorders* 33 (1):1–22. | Controlled study | Twenty-six children (aged between 6 and 11 years), considered to have semantic-pragmatic difficulties, were compared with two groups of mainstream children (aged 6;6 to 7;6 and 10;6 to 11;6, respectively) and with a group of children (aged between 8 and 11 years) diagnosed with (other) language disorders not primarily of a semantic or pragmatic nature. | This study examined the relationship between a newly developed play task and a more conventional definition task. Four groups of children were included.

On the play task, children listened to a 1.5-minute, tape-recorded story into which were embedded 12 common idioms drawn from recordings of classroom teaching and children's television. As the story was then played again, sentence by sentence, the children were required to act it out using a play set and props. For each idiom, it was possible to act out either the idiomatic or literal meaning, but only the idiomatic meaning made sense in the context. The children's actions were video-taped and then played back to the child during the definition task. For this task, the video was stopped after each idiom occurred and the children were asked what they thought each idiom meant.

Using a play-based methodology and a symptom checklist, this study investigated idiom comprehension in 26 children aged between 6 and 11 years who were considered to have semantic-pragmatic difficulties. This group was compared with two groups of mainstream children and a group of children with (other) language disorders not primarily of a semantic or pragmatic nature. | The results indicate that the definition task underestimated common-idiom comprehension in normally developing children and, in particular, in children diagnosed with semantic-pragmatic difficulties or (other) language disorders. Furthermore, a significant difference in idiom comprehension between the two clinical groups evidenced in the play task was entirely masked in the definition task. It appeared that the expressive and metalinguistic demands of the definition task had a greater negative effect on the group of children with language disorders than on the children with semantic-pragmatic difficulties.

The results indicate that the children with semantic-pragmatic difficulties did, as a group, demonstrate significantly fewer appropriate idiomatic interpretations and significantly more inappropriate interpretations than did any of the other three groups. However, the higher level of inappropriate scores in the semantic-pragmatic difficulties group reflected a larger number of 'fuzzy' actions rather than significantly higher rates of literality. | IIa |

| Author(s) & Title | Design | Sample | Objective of study | Conclusions | Evidence Level |
|---|---|---|---|---|---|
| **Understanding of Social Aspects of Language** | | | | | |
| Rowe C, 1999, 'Do social stories benefit children with autism in mainstream primary schools', *British Journal of Special Education* 26 (1). | Case study | One boy with Asperger Syndrome in Year 2 of mainstream school | Outlines the case of a boy for whom a social story approach was implemented. | Observations and changes made over 12 months are detailed alongside the positive effect this approach. | III |
| **Classroom management** | | | | | |
| Law J, Lindsay G, Peacey N, Gascoigne M, Soloff N, Radford J, Band S & Fitzgerald L, 2000, *Provision for Children with Speech and Language Needs In England and Wales: Facilitating Communication Between Education and Health Services*, DfES Publications. http://www.dfee.gov.uk/research/ | Qualitative study | | To report on existing provision across England and Wales and to help facilitate the process of collaboration between health and education services. | — | III |
| McCartney E (ed), 1999, *Speech and Language Therapists and Teachers Working Together: a Systems Approach to Collaboration*, Whurr Publishers, London. | Expert opinion | — | — | — | IV |
| Martin D & Miller C, 1999, *Language and the Curriculum. Practitioner Research in Planning Differentiation*, David Fulton Publishers Ltd, London. | Expert opinion | — | — | — | IV |
| Wright JA & Kersner M, 1998, *Supporting children with Communication Problems: Sharing the Workload*, David Fulton Publishers, London. | Expert opinion | — | — | — | IV |

## SCHOOL-AGED CHILDREN WITH SPEECH, LANGUAGE & COMMUNICATION DIFFICULTIES

| Author(s) & Title | Design | Sample | Objective of study | Conclusions | Evidence Level |
|---|---|---|---|---|---|
| **Use of Signs and Symbols with Language Impaired Children** | | | | | |
| Hurd A, 1995, 'The influence of signing on adult/child interaction in a teaching context', *Child Language Teaching Therapy* 11(3). | Comparative study | Eight children aged between 3 and 6 years with severe learning difficulties who were divided into two groups | This study examines the influence of signing on an individual teaching session. The teaching of big and little was investigated in 8 children with severe learning difficulties. Each child was seen once individually and for 4 (group 1), the teacher used signing and verbal expression with the child as a tool to teach big/little. Only big/little was signed by the teacher. With group 2 only verbal expression was used and no gesture. | An observation schedule was designed that reflected the three most important areas that signalled a child's learning within a session. These were vocalisation, signing and eye contact. Results indicate that signing group produced more attempts at the spoken words, more signing and greater total amount of eye contact. | III |
| **Assessment of Phonology & Articulation** | | | | | |
| **Phonological Processing** | | | | | |
| Bird J, Bishop DVM & Freeman NH, 1995, 'Phonological awareness and literacy development in children with expressive phonological impairments', *Journal of Speech & Hearing Research* 38 (2):446–62. | Controlled study | 31 children aged 5 to 7 years with phonological impairment<br><br>31 age-matched controls | This study investigated the link between expressive phonological impairments, phonological awareness and literacy. Thirty-one children with expressive phonological impairments were compared with control children matched on age and non-verbal ability on three occasions, at mean ages of 70, 79 and 91 months. On each occasion they were given three tests of phonological awareness. | Children with phonological impairments scored well below their controls on phonological awareness and literacy, independent of whether or not they had other language problems. Results suggest that both speech impairment and literacy problems arise from failure to analyse syllables into smaller phonological units. | IIb |

| Author(s) & Title | Design | Sample | Objective of study | Conclusions | Evidence Level |
|---|---|---|---|---|---|
| Gillon G & Dodd BJ, 1994, 'A Prospective Study of the Relationship between Phonological, Semantic, and Syntactic Skills and Specific Reading Disability', *Reading & Writing: An Interdisciplinary Journal* 6 (4):321–45. | Comparative longitudinal study | 20 good readers<br><br>20 poor readers<br><br>17 younger average readers<br><br>Ages ranged from 8 to 10 years | Compares the performance of poor readers with that of matched good readers on a series of spoken and written language tasks on three assessment trials 12 months apart, and then to younger average readers. Five experimental tasks were used to measure the readers' phonological processing skills, and three subtests from the CELF-R were selected to measure the students' syntactic and semantic skills. | It was found that all poor readers performed poorly in all three linguistic areas concurrently, and these difficulties persisted; poor readers demonstrated a difference between their phonological processing skills and their semantic/syntactic skills; and poor readers' phonological processing skills were particularly impaired. | IIb |

### Discrete phonological difficulty

| Author(s) & Title | Design | Sample | Objective of study | Conclusions | Evidence Level |
|---|---|---|---|---|---|
| Stackhouse J, 1982, 'An investigation of reading and spelling performance in speech disordered children', *The British Journal of Disorders of Communication* 17 (2):53–60. | Comparative study | 10 developmental verbal dyspraxic and 10 cleft palate children<br><br>20 children acting as controls<br><br>Ages ranged from 7 to 11 years | The reading and spelling abilities of two groups of speech disordered children were compared with matched controls. Children with developmental verbal dyspraxia differed quantitatively from normal children and cleft palate children. | A specific problem with grampheme-phoneme conversion rules is postulated for dyspraxic children. | III |

## AUTISTIC SPECTRUM DISORDERS

### Multidisciplinary Team

| Author(s) & Title | Design | Sample | Objective of study | Conclusions | Evidence Level |
|---|---|---|---|---|---|
| The National Autistic Society, 2003, *National Initiative: Autism Screening and Assessment – National Autism Plan for Children.* | Expert opinion | — | To set national standards. | — | IV |
| Public Health Institute of Scotland, XXXX, *Needs Assessment Report* http://www.phis.org.uk | — | — | — | — | IV |
| Charman T & Baird G, 2002, 'Practitioner review: Diagnosis of autism spectrum disorder in 2- and 3- year-old children', *Journal of Child Psychology & Psychiatry* 43 (3):289–305. | Literature review | — | A selective review of recent research literature on the characteristic features of ASD in pre-school children. | Multidisciplinary diagnostic assessment should include detailed information on developmental history; parents' descriptions of the everyday behaviour and activities of the child; direct assessment of the child's social interaction style, including where possible with age peers; and formal assessment of communicative, intellectual and adaptive function. Clinical assessments need to concentrate on the identification of impairments in early non-verbal social communication behaviours that characterise children with ASD from the second year of life, including social orienting, joint attention, imitation, play and reciprocal affective behaviour. | IV |

| Author(s) & Title | Design | Sample | Objective of study | Conclusions | Evidence Level |
|---|---|---|---|---|---|
| **Collaboration** | | | | | |
| Reid J, Millar S, Tait L, Donaldson M, Dean EC, Thomson GOB & Grieve R, 1996, 'Pupils with special educational needs: The role of Speech & Language Therapists', *Interchange* (43). | Questionnaire interview | Variety of professionals involved with children | This report describes a research project that studied: the speech and language needs of Scottish children and young people with special educational needs; collaboration among parents and professionals; and the perceived effectiveness of different ways of providing speech and language therapy. Data were obtained from a series of mailed questionnaires, school visits, and interviews conducted between December 1993 and April 1995. | The project found that there is a pattern of ever-increasing demand for speech and language therapy which continuously outstrips increases in provision. Parents and professionals reported that pupils benefit when speech and language therapy is integrated into the curriculum. The study also showed evidence of collaborative practice among parents, Speech & Language Therapists, and other staff both in mainstream and special educational facilities. Parents' comments about the quality of their children's speech and language therapy were pre-dominantly positive. | III |
| Law J, Lindsay G, Peacey N, Gascoigne M, Soloff N, Radford J, Band S & Fitzgerald L, 2000, *Provision for Children with Speech and Language Needs in England and Wales: Facilitating Communication Between Education and Health Services*, DfES Publications. http://www.dfee.gov.uk/research/ | Qualitative study | — | To report on existing provision across England and Wales and to help facilitate the process of collaboration between health and education services. | — | III |
| Miller C, 1999, 'Teachers and Speech and Language Therapists: a shared framework', *British Journal of Special Education* 26(3):141–6. | Expert opinion | — | This paper identifies the different perspectives of Speech & Language Therapists and teachers in looking at language and language difficulties, and suggests that they can be combined to ensure a more collaborative language practice. | — | IV |
| Howlin P, 1998, 'Psychological and educational treatments for autism', *Journal of Child Psychology and Psychiatry* 39 (3):307–22. | Expert opinion | — | The review discusses various interventions that have been used in the treatment of children with autism. | It concludes that no single mode of treatment is ever likely to be effective for all children and all families. Instead, intervention will need to be adapted to individual needs, and the value of approaches that involve a functional analysis of problems is explored. | IV |

## AUTISTIC SPECTRUM DISORDERS

| Author(s) & Title | Design | Sample | Objective of study | Conclusions | Evidence Level |
|---|---|---|---|---|---|
| Hart C, 1995, 'Perspectives on autism: what parents want', in Quill KA (ed) *Teaching Children with Autism: Strategies to Enhance Communication*, Delmar Publishers, New York. | Expert opinion | — | — | — | IV |
| **Triad of Impairment** | | | | | |
| Wing L & Gould J, 1979, 'Severe impairments of social interaction and associated abnormalities in children: Epidemiology and classification', *Journal of Autism & Developmental Disorders* 9 (1):11–29. | Observation interviews | 914 children less than 15 years old screened<br><br>132 selected | Investigated the prevalence of severe impairments of social interaction, language abnormalities and repetitive stereotyped behaviours in under 15-years-old children. | A 'socially impaired' group (more than half of whom were severely disabled) and comparison group of 'sociable severely mentally disabled' were identified in 132 children. Mutism or echolalia, and repetitive stereotyped behaviours, were found in almost all the socially impaired children, but to a less marked extent in a minority of the sociable severely mentally disabled. Certain organic conditions were found more often in the socially impaired group. A system of classification based on quality of social interaction is considered. | III |
| Frith U, 1989, *Autism: Explaining the Enigma*, Blackwell Publishers, Oxford. | Expert opinion | — | — | — | IV |
| Baron-Cohen S, Tager-Flusberg H & Cohen D (eds), 1993, *Understanding Other Minds: Perspectives from Autism*, Oxford University Press, Oxford. | Expert opinion | — | — | — | IV |

## Joint Attention

| Author(s) & Title | Design | Sample | Objective of study | Conclusions | Evidence Level |
|---|---|---|---|---|---|
| Baron-Cohen S, Allen J & Gillberg C, 1992, 'Can autism be detected at 18 months? The needle, the haystack, and the CHAT', *British Journal of Psychiatry* 161:839–43. | Comparative study | 41 toddlers (aged 17–21 months), who were at high genetic risk for developing autism<br><br>50 randomly selected toddlers (aged 17–20 months) | 41 toddlers who were at high genetic risk for developing autism, and 50 randomly selected toddlers, were screened with the Checklist for Autism in Toddlers (CHAT). | More than 80 percent of the children passed on all items, and none failed on more than one of pretend play; protodeclarative pointing; joint attention; social interest; and social play. Four children in the high-risk group failed on two or more of these five key types of behaviour. At follow-up at 30 months of age, the four children who had failed on two or more of these key types of behaviour at 18 months had received a diagnosis of autism. | III |
| McArthur D & Adamson LB, 1996, 'Joint attention in preverbal children: Autism and developmental language disorder', *Journal of Autism & Developmental Disorders* 26 (5):481–96. | Comparative study | 15 pre-school children with autism and 15 pre-school children with developmental language disorder | The joint attentional processes of 15 pre-school children with autism and 15 pre-school children with developmental language disorder were compared during play sessions with unfamiliar adults. | It was found that the children with autism monitored the channel of communication with their adult play partners 37 percent less often than children in the comparison group. | III |
| Mundy P, Sigman M & Kasari C, 1990, 'A longitudinal study of joint attention and language development in autistic children', *Journal of Autism & Developmental Disorders* 20 (1):115–28. | Longitudinal study | 15 autistic children (mean age of 45 months)<br><br>15 children with learning disabilities, matched for language ability<br><br>15 children with learning disabilities, matched for mental age | Study designed to investigate joint attention and language development in autistic children. | Compared to age-matched and language-matched controls, 15 autistic children who were administered the Early Social-Communication Scales displayed deficits in gestural joint attention skills in two testing sessions 13 months apart. The measure of gestural non-verbal joint attention predicted language development in subjects. | III |

## AUTISTIC SPECTRUM DISORDERS

| Author(s) & Title | Design | Sample | Objective of study | Conclusions | Evidence Level |
|---|---|---|---|---|---|
| Charman T, 1998, 'Specifying the nature and course of the joint attention impairment in autism in the pre-school years: Implications for diagnosis and intervention', *Autism* 2 (1):61–79. | Literature review | — | The paper reviews recent experimental findings over ten years on the extent and specificity of the joint attention impairments shown by pre-school children with autism. | In contrast to the commonly held view that children with autism are impaired in declarative gestures but intact in requesting gestures, the pattern of intact and impaired joint attention abilities revealed by recent research is more complex. The lessons to be learned from this research for clinical diagnosis, and early intervention and education programmes, are considered. | IV |
| Trevarthen C & Aitken KJ, 2001, 'Infant intersubjectivity: research, theory, and clinical applications', *Journal of Child Psychology & Psychiatry* 42 (1):3–48. | Review of research | — | This paper reviews research evidence on the emergence and development of active 'self-and-other' awareness in infancy, and examines the importance of its motives and emotions to mental health practice with children. This relates to how communication begins and develops in infancy, how it influences the individual subject's movement, perception, and learning, and how the infant's biologically grounded self-regulation of internal state and self-conscious purposefulness is sustained through active engagement with sympathetic others. | It reviews recent findings on post-natal depression, prematurity, autism, ADHD, specific language impairments and central auditory processing deficits, and comments on the efficacy of interventions that aim to support intrinsic motives for intersubjective communication when these are not developing normally. | IV |

| Author(s) & Title | Design | Sample | Objective of study | Conclusions | Evidence Level |
|---|---|---|---|---|---|
| **Readiness to focus and shift attention** | | | | | |
| Pascualvaca DM, Fantie BD, Papageorgiou M & Mirsky AF, 1998, 'Attentional capacities in children with autism: Is there a general deficit in shifting focus?', *Journal of Autism and Developmental Disorders* 28 (6): 40–46. | Comparative study | 23 children with autism and two control groups | Twenty-three children with autism and two control groups completed an attention battery comprising three versions of the continuous performance test (CPT), a digit cancellation task, the Wisconsin Card Sorting Test (WCST) and two novel, computerised tests of shifting attention. | Children with autism could focus on a particular stimulus and sustain this focus as indicated by their performance on the digit cancellation task and the CPT. Their performance on the WCST suggested problems in some aspects of shifting attention (ie, disengaging attention). The autism group performed as well as controls on the Same–Different Computerised Task, however, that required successive comparisons between stimuli. This implies that they could, in fact, shift their attention continuously. In addition, they did not differ from controls on the Computerised Matching Task, an analogue of the WCST, suggesting that they do not have a general deficit in shifting attention. | III |
| Cooper J, Moodley M & Reynell J, 1978, *Helping Language Development*, E Arnold, London. | Expert opinion | — | — | — | IV |
| **Social Interaction** | | | | | |
| Dawson G, Meltzoff AN, Osterling J, Rinaldi J & Brown E, 1998, 'Children with autism fail to orient to naturally occurring social stimuli', *Journal of Autism & Developmental Disorders* 28 (6):479–85. | Comparative study | 20 children with autism<br><br>20 children with Down syndrome<br><br>20 'typical peer' children | Twenty children with autism were compared to children with Down syndrome (n=19) and typical peers (n=20) in visual orientation to two social and two non-social stimuli and in ability to share attention. | Children with autism frequently failed to orient to all stimuli, particularly social stimuli, and exhibited attention deficits. | III |

## AUTISTIC SPECTRUM DISORDERS

| Author(s) & Title | Design | Sample | Objective of study | Conclusions | Evidence Level |
|---|---|---|---|---|---|
| Wing L & Gould J, 1979, 'Severe impairments of social interaction and associated abnormalities in children: Epidemiology and classification', *Journal of Autism & Developmental Disorders* 9 (1):11–29. | Observation interviews | 914 children less than 15 years old were screened<br><br>132 selected | Investigated the prevalence of severe impairments of social interaction, language abnormalities and repetitive stereotyped behaviours in under-15-years-old children. | A 'socially impaired' group (more than half of whom were severely disabled) and comparison group of 'sociable severely mentally disabled' were identified in 132 children. Mutism or echolalia, and repetitive stereotyped behaviours, were found in almost all the socially impaired children, but to a less marked extent in a minority of the sociable severely disabled. Certain organic conditions were found more often in the socially impaired group. A system of classification based on quality of social interaction is considered. | III |
| Wimpory DC, Hobson RP, Williams JM & Nash S, 2000, 'Are infants with autism socially engaged? A study of recent retrospective parental reports', *Journal of Autism & Developmental Disorders* 30 (6):525–36. | Qualitative study | Ten parents of pre-school-aged children with autism and ten parents of pre-schoolers without autism | The purpose of this study was to identify the specific aspects of social engagement that distinguish infants with autism from infants of similar age and developmental level who do not have autism. Ten parents of pre-schoolers with autism and ten parents of matched children without autism were given a semi-structured interview, the Detection of Autism by Infant Sociability Interview (DAISI), which elicits reports on whether 19 aspects of social engagement characteristic of typically developing infants were present at some time during the child's first 24 months. | The reports of infants with autism differed from those of the control group on 16 items. Findings suggest that infants with autism have marked limitation in both person-to-person and person-person-object social engagement, in keeping with the theory that autism involves impairments in primary as well as secondary intersubjectivity. | III |
| Frith U, 1989, *Autism: Explaining the Enigma*, Blackwell Publishers, Oxford. | Expert opinion | — | — | | IV |

| Author(s) & Title | Design | Sample | Objective of study | Conclusions | Evidence Level |
|---|---|---|---|---|---|
| Happe F, 2001, 'Social and nonsocial development in autism: Where are the links?' in Burack JA, Charman T, Yirmiya N & Zelazo PR (eds) *The Development of Autism: Perspectives from Theory and Research*, Lawrence Erlbaum Associates, Mahwah, NJ. | Expert opinion | — | — | — | IV |
| Baron-Cohen S, Wheelwright S, Cox A, Baird G, Charman T, Swettenham J, Drew A & Doehring P, 2000, 'The early identification of autism: The checklist for autism in toddlers (CHAT)', *Journal of Royal Society of Medicine* 93 (10):521–5. | Expert opinion | — | — | — | IV |
| **Communicative Strategies** | | | | | |
| Brady NC & Halle JW, 1997, 'Functional analysis of communicative behaviours', *Focus on Autism & Other Developmental Disabilities* 12 (2):95–104. | Case study | 2 children with autism | Two case studies illustrate the implementation of the three components of functional analysis: interviews; direct observation and analogue probes. | Information gained contributes to the knowledge base regarding each individual's communicative strategies. It can then contribute to intervention plans. | III |
| **Play Skills and Interests** | | | | | |
| Libby S, Powell S, Messer D & Jordan R, 1998, 'Spontaneous play in children with autism: a reappraisal', *Journal of Autism & Developmental Disorders* 28 (6):487–97. | Controlled study | 27 children: 9 with autism 9 with Down syndrome 9 with typical development | Children with ASD, Down syndrome, and typical development with verbal mental ages of approximately two years, were assessed for play abilities. | It was possible to distinguish the pattern of play abilities of the ASD group from the others. | IIa |
| Charman T, 1997, 'Infants with autism: An investigation of empathy, pretend play, joint attention, and imitation', *Developmental Psychology* 33 (5):781–9. | Prospective study | 16,000 children who were 18 months old | 16,000 children who were 18 months old were screened using the CHAT. Subsequently 3 groups emerged: ■ autism risk group n=12 ■ developmental delay risk group n=44 ■ no risk group n=15,944 Performance of infants with autism, developmental delays and normal development were compared on a prospective screening instrument for autism. | It was found that 20-month-olds with autism lacked social gaze in empathy and joint attention tasks. Infants with autism or developmental delays demonstrated functional play. Few produced spontaneous pretend play. Infants with developmental delay but not autism showed pretend play with prompting. | III |

## AUTISTIC SPECTRUM DISORDERS

| Author(s) & Title | Design | Sample | Objective of study | Conclusions | Evidence Level |
|---|---|---|---|---|---|
| Jarrold C, Boucher J & Smith P, 1993, 'Symbolic play in autism: A review' *Journal of Autism & Developmental Disorders* 23 (2):281–307. | Review of research | — | Experimental research into the symbolic play of children with autism is reviewed in an attempt to outline the nature of their deficit in this area. | Evidence is found for an impairment in the spontaneous symbolic play of autistic children, but autistic children may have a capacity for symbolic play that they do not spontaneously exhibit. | IV |
| Williams E, Costall A & Reddy V, 1999, 'Children with autism experience problems with both objects and people', *Journal of Autism & Developmental Disorders* 29(5):367–78. | Expert opinion | — | This paper draws attention to evidence of widespread impairments in relating to objects, not only in interpersonal aspects of object use but also in early sensorimotor exploration and the functional and conventional uses of objects. | In stressing these problems with objects, the purpose is not to downplay the social dimension of autism, but rather to highlight the reciprocal nature of the interactions between the child, other people, and objects. Given the evidence that other people play an important role in introducing objects to children, it is proposed that an impairment in interpersonal relations should itself lead to expect corresponding disruption in the autistic child's use of objects. Conversely, an unusual use of objects is likely to manifest itself in disturbances in relating to other people, given the importance of a shared understanding and use of objects in facilitating interaction. | IV |

### Learning Potential and Preferred Learning Style

| Author(s) & Title | Design | Sample | Objective of study | Conclusions | Evidence Level |
|---|---|---|---|---|---|
| Howlin P, 1998, 'Psychological and educational treatments for autism', *Journal of Child Psychology and Psychiatry* 39 (3):307–22. | Expert opinion | — | The review discusses various interventions that have been used in the treatment of children with autism. | It concludes that no single mode of treatment is ever likely to be effective for all children and all families. Instead, intervention will need to be adapted to individual needs, and the value of approaches that involve a functional analysis of problems is explored. | IV |

| Author(s) & Title | Design | Sample | Objective of study | Conclusions | Evidence Level |
|---|---|---|---|---|---|
| Schopler E, 1998, 'Prevention and management of behavior problems: The TEACCH approach', in Sanavio E (ed) *Behavior and Cognitive Therapy Today: Essays in Honor of Hans J Eysenck*, Elsevier Science Ltd. | Expert opinion | — | — | — | IV |
| Powell S (ed), 2000, *Helping Children with Autism to Learn*, David Fulton Publishers, London. | Expert opinion | — | — | — | IV |
| **Mental Health** | | | | | |
| Bailey A, Phillips W & Rutter M, 1996, 'Autism: towards an integration of clinical, genetic, neuropsychological, and neurobiological perspectives', *Journal of Child Psychology & Psychiatry* 37 (1):89–126. | Clinical review | — | This paper states that 'autism constitutes one of the best validated child psychiatric disorders. Empirical research has succeeded in delineating the key clinical phenomena, in demonstrating strong genetic influences on the underlying liability, and in identifying basic cognitive deficits. A range of neurobiological abnormalities has also been found, although the replicability of specific findings has not been high.' | The research findings for each research perspective are critically reviewed in order to consider how to move towards an integration across levels. | IV |
| Wolff S, 1991, 'Childhood autism: its diagnosis, nature, and treatment', *Archives of Disease in Childhood* 66 (6):737–41. | Clinical review | — | This paper presents an overview of the various theories relating to the aetiology, nature and treatment of autism. | — | IV |
| **Early Intervention** | | | | | |
| Rogers SJ, 1996, 'Brief report: Early intervention in autism', *Journal of Autism and Developmental Disorders* 26 (2):143–6. | Meta-analysis | — | — | Meta-analysis examining six published studies showing positive outcomes with children with autism. | IIa |

## AUTISTIC SPECTRUM DISORDERS

| Author(s) & Title | Design | Sample | Objective of study | Conclusions | Evidence Level |
|---|---|---|---|---|---|
| Salt J, Shemilt J, Sellars V, Boyd S, Coulson T & McCool S, 2002, 'The Scottish Centre for Autism pre-school treatment programme. II: The results of a controlled treatment outcome study', *Autism* 6 (1):33–46. | Controlled study | 20 children and their families<br><br>14 children in the experimental group and 6 in the control group | This article evaluates the effectiveness of a developmentally based early intervention programme. Two groups of children were compared, a treatment group and a no-treatment control group. Standardised assessments were administered before and after the intervention period by an independent clinician. Pre-treatment comparisons revealed that the control group had a significantly higher pre-treatment IQ; but the two groups were comparable for age, mental age, socio-economic status and number of hours of non-experimental therapy. | Results demonstrated that children in the treatment group improved significantly more than those in the control group on measures of joint attention, social interaction, imitation, daily living skills, motor skills and an adaptive behaviour composite. A measure of requesting behaviour fell short of statistical significance. The total stress index reduced for treatment group parents and increased for the control group parents (but not significantly). The results of the study are considered to support the efficacy of this treatment approach. | IIa |
| Jordan R, Jones G & Murray D, 1998, *Educational Interventions for Children with Autism: A Literature Review of Recent and Current Research*, Department for Education and Employment. | Literature review | — | Expert review of educational interventions for children with an ASD indicating sufficient consistent evidence to suggest that early intervention is effective. | — | IV |
| Salt J, Sellars V, Shemilt J, Boyd S, Coulson T & McCool S, 2001, 'The Scottish Centre for Autism pre-school treatment programme. A developmental approach to early intervention', *Autism* 5 (4):362–73. | Review of intervention programme | — | Early intervention is an area of intense current interest for parents and professionals.<br><br>This article describes a mainstream National Health Service approach to early intervention, developed at the Scottish Centre for Autism. The aims of treatment are to improve the child's early social communication and social interaction skills, leading to the potential development of play and flexibility of behaviour. This is achieved by 1:1 intensive treatment by trained therapists, and a schedule of parent training. The treatment protocol incorporates a child led approach; the use of imitation as a therapeutic strategy; using language contingent on activities; and the introduction of flexibility into play and social exchanges | — | IV |

## Support and Training of Primary Carers

| Author(s) & Title | Design | Sample | Objective of study | Conclusions | Evidence Level |
|---|---|---|---|---|---|
| Klinger L & Dawson G, 1992, 'Facilitating early social and communicative development in children with autism', in Warren SF & Reiche J (eds) *Causes and Effects in Communication and Language Intervention*, Paul H Brookes, Baltimore, MD. | Expert opinion | — | — | — | IV |
| McDade A & McCartan P, 1998, 'Partnership with parents: a pilot project', *International Journal of Language and Communication Disorders* 33 (Suppl):556–61. | Controlled study | 11 families in experimental group<br><br>9 families in control group | This paper looks at a controlled study that aimed to measure the efficacy of a parent programme. The parents involved were all parents of pre-school children with specific expressive language delay (SELD). A number of measures were used to identify changes in mother-child interaction and language development. | Significant differences were noted in the experimental group, while the control group remained stable over time. The results indicate the potential effectiveness of this type of intervention for children identified as having SELD. | IV |
| Shields J, 2001, 'The NAS EarlyBird Programme: partnership with parents in early intervention. The National Autistic Society', *Autism* 5 (1):49–56. | Review of parent package | — | The National Autistic Society has developed an autism-specific three-month parent package, the NAS EarlyBird Programme that emphasises partnership with parents. Six families participate in each three-month programme, which combines weekly group training sessions for parents with individualised home visits. During the programme parents learn to understand autism, to build social communication, and to analyse and use structure, so as to prevent inappropriate behaviours. The use of video and the group dynamic amongst families are important components of the programme. An efficacy study evaluated the pilot programme and further monitoring is in progress. | Strengths and weaknesses of the programme are discussed. This short-term, affordable package, with supporting evidence of efficacy, offers a model of early intervention that is very popular with parents. | IV |

## AUTISTIC SPECTRUM DISORDERS

### Social Communication Programme

| Author(s) & Title | Design | Sample | Objective of study | Conclusions | Evidence Level |
|---|---|---|---|---|---|
| Kamps DM, Leonard BR, Vernon S, Dugan EP, Delquadri JC, Gershon B, Wade L & Folk L, 1992, 'Teaching social skills to students with autism to increase peer interactions in an integrated first-grade classroom', *Journal of Applied Behaviour Analysis* 25 (2):281–8. | Case series | 3 boys (aged 7 years) with autism and their non-disabled peers in an integrated classroom | Investigated the use of social skills groups to facilitate increased social interactions among 3 boys (aged 7 years) with autism and their non-disabled peers in an integrated classroom. Social skills groups consisted of training students and peers in initiating, responding and keeping interactions going; greeting others and conversing on a variety of topics; giving and accepting compliments; taking turns and sharing; asking for help and helping others; and including others in activities. Training occurred during the first ten minutes of 20-minute play groups, four times a week. | Using a multiple baseline across subjects design, results demonstrated increases in the frequency, time engaged in, and duration of social interactions, as well as the responsivity of students and peers to each other. Results were maintained when students were monitored and given feedback on social performance in play groups and during follow-up. | III |
| Hall L-J & Smith K-L, 1996, 'The generalisation of social skills by preferred peers with autism', *Journal of Intellectual and Developmental Disability* 21 (4):313–30. | Case series | 15 children with autism | The study used a replicated AB design to evaluate the generalisation to the playground of selected social skills taught in a brief programme conducted in an early intervention centre. Suggestions for future research based on the results from this study are discussed. | Results indicate that children with autism can identify preferred peers, and when mutually selected pairs of children with autism participate in a social skills program as an addition to their ongoing participation in early intervention, increases in skills can be observed in the generalisation setting. | III |
| Aarons M & Gittens T, 2003, *Social Skills Programmes: An Integrated Approach from Early Years to Adolescence*, Speechmark Publishing, Bicester. | Expert opinion | — | — | — | IV |

### Alternative and Augmentative communication

| Author(s) & Title | Design | Sample | Objective of study | Conclusions | Evidence Level |
|---|---|---|---|---|---|
| Schepis MM, Reid DH, Behrmann MM & Sutton KA, 1998, 'Increasing communicative interactions of young children with autism using a voice output communication aid and naturalistic teaching', *Journal of Applied Behaviour Analysis* 31 (4):561–78. | Comparative study | Four children aged 3 to 5 years with autism | A study evaluated the effects of a voice output communication aid (VOCA) and naturalistic teaching procedures on the communicative interactions of four children with autism. | Children showed increases in communicative interactions using VOCAs. There was no apparent reductive effect of VOCA use on other communicative behaviours. | III |
| Light JC, Roberts B, Dimarco R & Greiner N, 1998, 'Augmentative and alternative communication to support receptive and expressive communication for people with autism', *Journal of Communication Disorders* 31 (2):153–80. | Case study | 6-year-old boy with autism and severe expressive and receptive language impairments | Discusses the use of augmentative and alternative communication (AAC) to enhance comprehension and expression of people with autism. A theoretical model for AAC assessment and intervention is presented and illustrated with a case study of a 6-year-old boy with autism and severe expressive and receptive language impairments. | — | III |
| Bondy AS & Frost LA, 1994, 'The Delaware autistic program', in Harris SL & Handleman JS (eds) *Preschool Education Program for Children with Autism*, Pro-ed, Austin, Texas. | Expert opinion | Three case studies | Three case studies of pre-school children with autism. | — | IV |
| Jordan R, Jones G & Murray D, 1998, *Educational Interventions for Children with Autism: A Literature Review of Recent and Current Research*, Department for Education and Employment. | Literature review | — | Expert review of educational interventions for children with an ASD. | — | IV |
| Park K, 1997, 'How do objects become objects of reference? A review of the literature on objects of reference and a proposed model for the use of objects in communication', *British Journal of Special Education* 24 (3):108–14. | Literature review | — | A model of object use in communication is proposed. By using three categories of sign (index, icon and symbol) a method of providing a developmental framework for the use of objects of reference is developed. | — | IV |

## CLEFT PALATE & VELOPHARYNGEAL ABNORMALITIES

### Interdisciplinary Team Working

| Author(s) & Title | Design | Sample | Objective of study | Conclusions | Evidence Level |
|---|---|---|---|---|---|
| Bearn D, Mildinhall S, Murphy T, Murray JJ, Sell D, Shaw WC, Williams AC & Sandy JR, 2001, 'Cleft lip and palate care in the United Kingdom – the Clinical Standards Advisory Group (CSAG) Study. Part 4: outcome comparisons, training, and conclusions', *The Cleft Palate Craniofacial Journal* 38 (1):38–43. | Retrospective review | Children, 5 & 12-year-olds born with unilateral complete clefts of the lip and palate | A critical appraisal of cleft care in the United Kingdom. | This paper highlights the poor outcomes for the fragmented cleft care in the United Kingdom, compared with European centres. There is an urgent need for a review of structure, organisation and training. | III |
| Clinical Standards Advisory Group (CSAG) Report, 1998, *Cleft Lip and Palate*, HMSO, London. | Professional report | — | — | — | IV |

### Speech Outcomes of Primary Surgery,
### Timing of Speech & Language Therapy Intervention and Surgery

| Author(s) & Title | Design | Sample | Objective of study | Conclusions | Evidence Level |
|---|---|---|---|---|---|
| Bardach J, Morris HL & Olin WH, 1984, 'Late results of primary veloplasty: the Marburg Project', *Plastic and Reconstructive Surgery* 73 (2):207–18. | Clinical study | Forty-five randomly selected patients with unilateral cleft lip, alveolus and palate | All patients were evaluated by three US specialists to assess the validity of primary veloplasty. | Examination revealed an unusually high incidence of short palate and poor mobility of the soft palate. Facial growth was found to be highly acceptable in the majority of the patients. Unusually high incidence of velopharyngeal incompetence was found in these patients. | IIb |
| Shaw WC, Semb G, Nelson P, Brattstrom V, Molsted K & Prahl-Andersen B, 2000,*The Euroclett Project 1996–2000. Standards of Care for Cleft Lip and Palate in Europe*, European Commission Biochemical and Health Research, IOS Press, Amsterdam. | Comparative study | European Cleft Palate Centres | The study developed a preliminary methodology to compare practices and the potential for wider European collaboration, including opportunities for the promotion of clinical trials. Intercentre comparison was recognised by the European Commission. Therefore, the project: 'Standards of Care for Cleft Lip and Palate in Europe: Eurocleft' ran between 1996 and 2000 and aimed to promote a broad uplift in the quality of care and research in the area of cleft lip and palate. | The results of the 1996–2000 project include: a register of services in Europe, with details of professionals and teams involved in cleft care; service organisation; clinical protocols and special facilities for research; a set of common Policy Statements governing clinical practice for European cleft teams; Practice Guidelines describing minimum recommendations for care that all European children with clefts should be entitled to; and recommendations for documentation governing minimum records that cleft teams should maintain. It encourages initial efforts to compare outcomes (results) of care between centres. | III |

| Author(s) & Title | Design | Sample | Objective of study | Conclusions | Evidence Level |
|---|---|---|---|---|---|
| Lohmander-Agerskov A, Soderpalm E, Friede H & Lilja J, 1995, 'A longitudinal study of speech in 15 children with cleft lip and palate treated by late repair of the hard palate', *Scandinavian Journal of Plastic & Reconstructive Surgery and Hand Surgery* 29 (1):21–31. | Longitudinal study | 15 children | The present paper is a longitudinal study of 15 consecutive patients whose speech development was analysed at the mean ages of 5:3, 7:0, 8:5 and 9:7 years. | Hypernasality gradually decreased over the years whereas nasal escape almost completely ceased after closure of the residual cleft. There was no glottal articulation at any age. Despite the fact that retraction of apicodental consonants decreased in frequency with age and presumably with speech therapy, it was the main problem throughout the observation period. It was presumably caused by the residual cleft in the hard palate compensating for subnormal pressure in front of the opening to the nasal cavity. | III |
| Witzel MA, Salyer KE & Ross RB, 1984, 'Delayed hard palate closure: the philosophy revisited', *The Cleft Palate Journal* 21 (4):263–69. | Literature review | — | This essay is a review of the rationale and supporting evidence for this procedure, with emphasis on its effect on speech, particularly articulation and velopharyngeal function. | Concluded that the assumptions on which this method is based have never been proven, and that the deleterious effects on speech often noted have not received appropriate attention. | IV |
| **Early Monitoring** | | | | | |
| Chapman KL, 1993, 'Phonologic processes in children with cleft palate', *Cleft Palate-Craniofacial Journal* 30(1): 64–72. | Comparative study | 30 children with cleft palate (with or without cleft lip) and 30 non-cleft palate children | This study examined the phonologic process usage of 3-, 4- and 5-year-old children with cleft palate. The children's whole word productions were analyzed for frequency and type of phonologic process usage. | Results indicated that the three- and four-year-old children with cleft palate exhibited more instances of process usage, compared to their non-cleft peers. The five-year-old cleft and non-cleft groups were similar in total instances of process usage. Further, the children with cleft palate employed common phonologic processes; however, some processes were noted more frequently in the speech of the three-year-old children with cleft palate. | III |

## CLEFT PALATE & VELOPHARYNGEAL ABNORMALITIES

| Author(s) & Title | Design | Sample | Objective of study | Conclusions | Evidence Level |
|---|---|---|---|---|---|
| Harding A & Grunwell P, 1998, 'Active versus passive cleft-type speech characteristics', *International Journal of Language & Communication Disorders* 33:329–52. | Longitudinal study | 5 bilateral cleft lip and palate subjects (BCLP) aged 1;6–4;6<br><br>12 mixed unilateral cleft lip and palate and BCLP subjects aged 4;6–7;6<br><br>9 mixed unilateral cleft lip and palate and bilateral cleft lip and palate subjects aged 9;0–11;0<br><br>Reference is also made to data from 12 mixed cleft-type subjects aged 13;0 who had been treated with different surgical timing regimes | Passive and active patterns of articulation are described and defined in the context of three longitudinal studies of subjects who were at various stages of two different surgical regimes: five bilateral cleft lip and palate (BCLP) subjects aged 1;6–4;6, twelve mixed unilateral cleft lip and palate (UCLP) and BCLP subjects aged 4;6–7;6 and nine mixed UCLP and BCLP subjects aged 9;0–11;0. Reference is also made to data from 12 mixed cleft-type subjects aged 13;0 who had been treated with different surgical timing regimes. Comparison is made between the incidence of active versus passive processes in relation to oral structure. | A distinction between passive and active cleft-type speech characteristics whereby passive characteristics were thought to be the product of structural abnormality or dysfunction and active characteristics were specific articulatory gestures replacing intended consonants. Indications from this study are that active cleft-type characteristics require destabilisation in a course of speech and language therapy before the potential benefits of surgery can be properly assessed. An analytical protocol for the interpretation of speech samples is presented and some therapy strategies are proposed for active and passive processes. | III |
| Grundy K & Harding A, 1995, 'Disorders of Speech Production' in Grundy K (ed) *Linguistics in Clinical Practice*, Taylor & Francis. | Expert opinion | — | — | — | IV |

| Author(s) & Title | Design | Sample | Objective of study | Conclusions | Evidence Level |
|---|---|---|---|---|---|
| Harding A & Grunwell P, 1996, 'Characteristics of cleft palate speech', *European Journal of Disorders of Communication* 31:331–57. | Review of research | — | — | This overview of contemporary research reveals new perspectives on cleft palate speech development and the phonological consequences of early articulatory constraints. | IV |
| Russell J & Grunwell P, 1993, 'Speech development in children with cleft lip and palate', in Grunwell P (ed) *Analysing Cleft Palate Speech*, Whurr Publishers, London. | Expert opinion | — | — | — | IV |
| Golding-Kushner KJ, 2001, *Therapy Techniques for Cleft Palate Speech and Related Disorders*, Singular, London. | Expert opinion | — | — | — | IV |
| **Assessment of Speech** | | | | | |
| D'Antonio LL, Muntz HR, Province MA & Marsh JL, 1988, 'Laryngeal/voice findings in patients with velopharyngeal dysfunction', *Laryngoscope* 98 (4):432–8. | Clinical study | 85 patients referred for multi-method evaluation of velopharyngeal dysfunction | This paper describes the prevalence of laryngeal/voice findings in a group of 85 patients referred for multi-method evaluation of velopharyngeal dysfunction. | There was no clear relationship between laryngeal/voice findings and nasoendoscopic or aerodynamic assessments of velopharyngeal dysfunction. However, there was a significant relationship between laryngeal/voice findings and estimated subglottal pressure. Patients with laryngeal/voice findings (with or without nodules) had average estimated subglottal pressure values which were outside the normal range more often than patients without laryngeal/voice findings. | III |

## CLEFT PALATE & VELOPHARYNGEAL ABNORMALITIES

| Author(s) & Title | Design | Sample | Objective of study | Conclusions | Evidence Level |
|---|---|---|---|---|---|
| Harding A & Grunwell P, 1998, 'Active versus passive cleft-type speech characteristics', *International Journal of Language & Communication Disorders* 33:329–52. | Longitudinal study | 5 bilateral cleft lip and palate (BCLP) subjects aged 1;6–4;6<br><br>12 mixed unilateral cleft lip and palate and BCLP subjects aged 4;6–7;6<br><br>9 mixed unilateral cleft lip and palate and bilateral cleft lip and palate subjects aged 9;0–11;0<br><br>Reference is also made to data from 12 mixed cleft-type subjects aged 13;0 who had been treated with different surgical timing regimes | Passive and active patterns of articulation are described and defined in the context of three longitudinal studies of subjects who were at various stages of two different surgical regimes: five bilateral cleft lip and palate (BCLP) subjects aged 1;6–4;6, twelve mixed unilateral cleft lip and palate (UCLP) and BCLP subjects aged 4;6–7;6 and nine mixed UCLP and BCLP subjects aged 9;0–11;0. Reference is also made to data from 12 mixed cleft-type subjects aged 13;0 who had been treated with different surgical timing regimes. Comparison is made between the incidence of active versus passive processes in relation to oral structure. | A distinction between passive and active cleft-type speech characteristics whereby passive characteristics were thought to be the product of structural abnormality or dysfunction and active characteristics were specific articulatory gestures replacing intended consonants. Indications from this study are that active cleft-type characteristics require destabilisation in a course of speech and language therapy before the potential benefits of surgery can be properly assessed. An analytical protocol for the interpretation of speech samples is presented and some therapy strategies are proposed for active and passive processes. | III |

| Author(s) & Title | Design | Sample | Objective of study | Conclusions | Evidence Level |
|---|---|---|---|---|---|
| Sell D, Harding A & Grunwell P, 1999, 'GOS.SP.ASS.'98: an assessment for speech disorders associated with cleft palate and/or velopharyngeal dysfunction (revised)', *International Journal of Language & Communication Disorders* 34 (1):17–33. | Clinical study | — | In a recent survey undertaken to review the different speech assessment protocols used in six cleft palate centres in the UK, GOS.SP.ASS. was selected from six protocols as the optimal procedure for clinical and research purposes. This paper describes important revisions to the original GOS.SP.ASS. protocol in order to ensure comparable data from different clinicians. | This detailed speech assessment is now complemented by the Cleft Audit Protocol for Speech (CAPS), a tool recommended for clinical audit. As a result of close collaboration in their preparation, the results are directly comparable. | IV |
| Harding A & Grunwell P, 1996, 'Characteristics of cleft palate speech', *European Journal of Disorders of Communication* (31):331–57. | Review of research | — | — | This overview of contemporary research reveals new perspectives on cleft palate speech development and the phonological consequences of early articulatory constraints. | IV |
| Trost JE, 1981, 'Articulatory additions to the classical description of the speech of persons with cleft palate', *Cleft Palate Journal* 18 (3):193–203. | Clinical overview | — | — | Three types of compensatory articulation used by speakers with cleft palate and velopharyngeal inadequacy are described: the pharyngeal stop; the mid-dorsum palatal stop; and the posterior nasal fricative. These articulatory characteristics have not previously been reported in the literature. | IV |
| Kuehn DP, 1982, 'Assessment of resonance disorders', in Lass NJ, McReynolds LV, Northam JC & Yoder DE (eds) *Speech, Language and Hearing, Vol 11, Pathologies of Speech and Language,* WB Saunders Co, Philadelphia. | Expert opinion | — | — | — | IV |
| McWilliams BJ & Philips BJ, 1979, *Velopharyngeal Incompetence. An Audio Seminar,* BC Decker Inc, Hamilton. | Expert opinion | — | — | — | IV |

## CLEFT PALATE & VELOPHARYNGEAL ABNORMALITIES

### Hearing

| Author(s) & Title | Design | Sample | Objective of study | Conclusions | Evidence Level |
|---|---|---|---|---|---|
| Grant HR, Quiney RE, Mercer DM & Lodge S, 1988, 'Cleft palate and glue ear', *Archives of Disease in Childhood* 63:176–9. | Prospective trial | 116 children with cleft palate aged from 2 to 20 months | The purpose of this study was to ascertain the incidence of otitis media in children with cleft palate. In this trial, myringotomy was performed for all children irrespective of previous otological findings. | 113/116 (97.4 percent) of children had a high incidence of otitis media when confirmed by myringotomy. | IIb |
| Broen PA, Devers MC, Doyle SS, Prouty JM & Moller KT, 1998, 'Acquisition of linguistic and cognitive skills by children with cleft palate', *Journal of Speech, Language & Hearing Research* 41 (3): 676–87. | Comparative study | 28 children with cleft palate and 29 children with non-cleft. | This study compared the early cognitive and linguistic development of young children with cleft palate to that of non-cleft children. | Children with cleft palate, although well within the normal range, performed significantly below the children in the control group on the Mental Scale of the Bayley Scales of Infant Development, some subscales of the Minnesota Child Development Inventory, and words acquired by 24 months. Differences observed in the cognitive development of children with and without cleft palate were verbal as opposed to non-verbal (ie, linguistic in nature) and were related to hearing status at 12 months and velopharyngeal adequacy. | III |
| Rach GH, Zielhuis GA & Broek P van den, 1988, 'The influence of chronic persistent otitis media with effusion on language development of 2- to 4-year-olds', *International Journal of Pediatric Otorhinolaryngolgy* 15 (3):253–61. | Clinical study | 52 children with known history of bilateral otitis media and in 13 children without otitis media | As part of a large epidemiological study on otitis media in pre-school children, language development was measured in 52 children with known history of bilateral otitis media and in 13 children without otitis media. | Verbal comprehension scores were not or only slightly reduced in otitis media children. Expressive language, however, was significantly lower than the standard with the effect being larger when the otitis media had lasted for a longer period. This is one of the first prospective studies that confirms the hypothesis of an effect of persistent bilateral middle ear effusion on language development. | III |

| Author(s) & Title | Design | Sample | Objective of study | Conclusions | Evidence Level |
|---|---|---|---|---|---|
| Teele DW, Klein JO & Rosner BA, 1984, 'Otitis media with effusion during the first three years of life and development of speech and language', *Pediatrics* 74 (2):282–7. | Case series | 205 three-year-old children | To determine the association between time spent with middle ear effusion and development of speech and language, 205 three-year-old children were studied. Each child had been followed prospectively from birth to record the number of episodes of middle ear disease and to document time spent with middle ear effusion. Standardised tests of speech and language were administered at age 3 years to children who had spent much time with middle ear effusion and to children who had spent little or no time with middle ear effusion. | Children who had spent prolonged periods of time with middle ear effusion had significantly lower scores when compared with those who had spent little time with middle ear disease. The correlation was strongest in children from higher socio-economic strata. Time spent with middle ear effusion in the first 6 to 12 months of life was most strongly associated with poor scores. | III |

**Language**

| Author(s) & Title | Design | Sample | Objective of study | Conclusions | Evidence Level |
|---|---|---|---|---|---|
| Chapman KL, Graham KT, Gooch J & Visconti C, 1998, 'Conversational skills of pre-school and school-age children with cleft lip and palate', *Cleft Palate Craniofacial Journal* 35 (6): 503–16. | Comparative study | 20 children with unilateral cleft lip and palate (ten pre-schoolers and ten school-age children) | The purpose of this study was to examine the conversational skills of pre-school and school-age children with cleft lip and palate. | Paired t-tests revealed no significant differences between the pre-school and school-age children with cleft lip and palate and their non-cleft peers in level of conversational participation. However, individual child comparisons revealed less assertive profiles of conversational participation for 50 percent of the pre-school and 20 percent of the school-age children with cleft lip and palate. | III |

## CLEFT PALATE & VELOPHARYNGEAL ABNORMALITIES

| Author(s) & Title | Design | Sample | Objective of study | Conclusions | Evidence Level |
|---|---|---|---|---|---|
| Neiman GS & Savage HE, 1997, 'Development of infants and toddlers with clefts from birth to three years of age', *Cleft Palate Craniofacial Journal* 34 (3):218–25. | Qualitative study | 186 infants and toddlers with cleft lip (48); cleft palate (46); and cleft lip/palate (92); at one of the following age categories: 5 months (47); 13 months (46); 25 months (47); and 36 months (46) | The purpose of this study was to use care giver report measures to describe the developmental status of infants and toddlers with clefts. Developmental assessment data were obtained on 186 infants and toddlers. | At 5 months, lower motor and self-help developmental quotients were evident compared to the 13-month-old level. When compared to the normative sample, the 5-month-old infants exhibited 'at-risk/ delayed' development in the motor, self-help and cognitive domains, depending on the cleft type, and as reflected in their full-scale scores. Infants at 13 and 25 months were within normal limits in all developmental domains, with the exception of the 13-month-old infants with cleft palate who demonstrate 'at-risk' development in the motor domain. At 36 months of age, all toddlers demonstrated significantly lower developmental performance in the fine motor, gross motor and expressive language domains compared to the 25-month-old toddlers. Toddlers with cleft palate exhibit 'at-risk/delayed' development in the expressive language domain at 36 months. | III |
| Broen PA, Devers MC, Doyle SS, Prouty JM & Moller KT, 1998, 'Acquisition of linguistic and cognitive skills by children with cleft palate', *Journal of Speech, Language & Hearing Research* 41 (3): 676–87. | Comparative study | 28 children with cleft palate and 29 children with non-cleft | This study compared the early cognitive and linguistic development of young children with cleft palate to that of non-cleft children. | Children with cleft palate, although well within the normal range, performed significantly below the children in the control group on the Mental Scale of the Bayley Scales of Infant Development, some subscales of the Minnesota Child Development Inventory, and words acquired by 24 months. Differences observed in the cognitive development of children with and without cleft palate were verbal as opposed to non-verbal and were related to hearing status at 12 months and velopharyngeal adequacy. | III |

| Author(s) & Title | Design | Sample | Objective of study | Conclusions | Evidence Level |
|---|---|---|---|---|---|
| Golding-Kushner J, Weller G & Shprintzen RJ, 1985, 'Velo-cardio-facial syndrome: language and psychological profiles', *Journal of Craniofacial Genetics Developmental Biology* 5 (3):259–66. | Case series | 26 patients | The purpose of this report is to add to the phenotype of the velo-cardio-facial syndrome by providing a description of the language, and academic and psychological profiles of 26 patients. | A distinctive pattern of language disorders and personality characteristics that has not been previously described. | III |
| Scherer NJ & D'Antonio LL, 1995, 'Parent questionnaire for screening early language development in children with cleft palate', *Cleft Palate-Craniofacial Journal* 32:7–13. | Qualitative study | 30 non-syndromic children with cleft lip and palate and 30 children without clefts | This study investigated the efficacy of a parent questionnaire as a component for screening early language development of children 16–30 months of ages for cleft lip and palate. | — | III |

### Assessment of Velopharyngeal Dysfunction

| Author(s) & Title | Design | Sample | Objective of study | Conclusions | Evidence Level |
|---|---|---|---|---|---|
| Witt PD & D'Antonio LL, 1993, 'Velopharyngeal insufficiency and secondary palatal management. A new look at an old problem', *Clinics Plastic Surgery* 20 (4):707–21. | Expert opinion | — | This article focuses on the problem of VPI and emphasises the need for differential diagnosis at the most critical step in management planning. The challenge of the future is to implement the team approach, integrating the expertise of speech scientists and plastic surgeons, so that differential diagnosis can and will lead to differential management. | — | IV |
| Kuehn DP & Moller KT, 2000, 'The state of the art: speech and language issues in the cleft palate population', *Cleft Palate Craniofacial Journal* 37:348. | Expert opinion | — | This article reviews the development and progression of our knowledge base over the last several decades in the area of speech, language, anatomy and physiology of the velopharynx; assessment of velopharyngeal function; and treatment, both behavioural and physical, for velopharyngeal problems. | Early and aggressive management for speech and language disorders should be conducted. | IV |
| Clinical Standards Advisory Group (CSAG) Report, 1998, *Cleft Lip and Palate*, HMSO, London. | Expert opinion | — | — | — | IV |

## CLEFT PALATE & VELOPHARYNGEAL ABNORMALITIES

### Evaluation of Velopharyngeal Dysfunction

| Author(s) & Title | Design | Sample | Objective of study | Conclusions | Evidence Level |
|---|---|---|---|---|---|
| Hemmingsson GE & Isberg AM, 1986, 'Velopharyngeal movement patterns in patients alternating between oral and glottal articulation: a clinical and cineradiographical study', *Cleft Palate Journal* 23 (1):1–9. | Comparative study | Eight patients who presented velopharyngeal incompetence | Eight patients who presented velopharyngeal incompetence and who spontaneously alternated between oral and glottal stop articulation were cineradiographically examined in lateral and frontal projections to compare their oral stops and glottal stop substitutions. | A cineradiographic frame-by-frame analysis of the movements of the velum and the lateral and posterior pharyngeal walls was performed. During glottal stop substitutions, and coarticulation involving glottal stops and oral lingual or bilabial stop gestures, all patients demonstrated either no velopharyngeal movement or impaired movement, mostly affecting the lateral pharyngeal walls. In contrast, during oral stops, moderate-to-good velopharyngeal movements were produced. Poor quality or absence of velopharyngeal movement associated with glottal stop substitutions may be misinterpreted as weakness or inability to perform motor activity. Presurgical cineradiographic or fluoroscopic analysis of a patient's speech with regard to velopharyngeal movements should therefore be based on speech sequences free from glottal stop substitutions. A careful speech analysis should also precede pre-surgical cineradiography. | III |
| Dalston RM, Warren D & Dalston E, 1991a, 'A Preliminary Investigation Concerning Use of Nasometry in Identifying Patients with Hyponasality and/or Nasal Airway Impairment', *Journal of Speech and Hearing Research* 34:11–18. | Clinical study | Series of 76 patients, children and adults | A series of 76 patients referred for evaluation in an attempt to determine the extent to which acoustic assessments of speech corresponded with clinical judgements of hyponasality and aerodynamic measurements of nasal cross-sectional area. | The sensitivity and specificity of nasometry in correctly identifying the presence or absence of hyponasality were 0.48 and 0.79 respectively. However, when patients with audible nasal emission were eliminated form the analysis, the sensitivity rose to 1.0 and the specificity rose to 0.85. | III |

| Author(s) & Title | Design | Sample | Objective of study | Conclusions | Evidence Level |
|---|---|---|---|---|---|
| Dalston RM, Warren D & Dalston E, 1991b, 'Use of nasometry as a diagnostic tool for identifying patients with velopharyngeal impairment', *The Cleft Palate-Craniofacial Journal* 28:1184–8. | Comparative study | 117 patients | 117 patients were studied in an attempt to determine the extent to which acoustic assessments of speech made with a Kay Elemetrics Nasometer corresponded with aerodynamic estimates of velopharyngeal area and clinical judgements of hypernasality. Nasometer data and listener judgements were made. | The results suggest that the Nasometer is an appropriate instrument that can be of value in assessing patients suspected of having velopharyngeal impairment. | III |
| Dalston R & Warren D, 1986, 'Comparison of Tonar II, pressure-flow, and listener judgements of hypernasality in assessment of velopharyngeal function', *Cleft Palate Journal* 23:108–15. | Comparative study | 124 adults and children | The purpose of the present investigation was to study the interrelationships among Tonar 11, pressure flow and listener judgements of hypernasality in a consecutive series of patients. | The results indicated that nasalance scores and clinical ratings of hypernasality change systematically among patients as a function of their pressure-flow categorisation. | III |
| Witt PD & D'Antonio LL, 1993, 'Velopharyngeal insufficiency and secondary palatal management. A new look at an old problem', *Clinical Plastic Surgery* 20 (4):707–21. | Expert opinion | — | This article focuses on the problem of VPI and emphasises the need for differential diagnosis at the most critical step in management planning. The challenge of the future is to implement the team approach, integrating the expertise of speech scientists and plastic surgeons, so that differential diagnosis can and will lead to differential management. | — | IV |
| **Early Advisory Role** | | | | | |
| Golding-Kushner KJ, Weller G & Shprintzen RJ, 1985, 'Velo-cardio-facial syndrome: language and psychological profiles', *Journal of Craniofacial Genetics & Developmental Biology* 5 (3):259–66. | Case series | 26 patients | The purpose of this report is to add to the phenotype of the velo-cardio-facial syndrome by providing a description of the language, and academic and psychological profiles of 26 patients. | A distinctive pattern of language disorders and personality characteristics that has not been previously described. | III |
| Russell J & Harding A, 2001, 'Speech development and early intervention', in Watson ACH, Grunwell P & Sell D (eds) *Management of Cleft Lip and Palate*, Whurr Publishers, London. | Expert opinion | — | — | — | IV |

## CLEFT PALATE & VELOPHARYNGEAL ABNORMALITIES

| Author(s) & Title | Design | Sample | Objective of study | Conclusions | Evidence Level |
|---|---|---|---|---|---|
| Golding-Kushner KJ, 2001, *Therapy Techniques for Cleft Palate Speech and Related Disorders*, Singular, London. | Expert opinion | — | — | — | IV |
| Hahn E, 1989, 'Directed home training programme for infants with cleft lip and palate', in Bzoch K (ed) *Communicative Disorders Related to Cleft Lip and Palate*, Little Brown, Boston. | Expert opinion | — | — | — | IV |
| **Partnership with Parents** | | | | | |
| Pamplona MC, Ysunza A & Jimenez-Murat Y, 2001, 'Mothers of children with cleft palate undergoing speech intervention change communicative interaction', *International Journal of Pediatric Otorhinolaryngology* 59 (3):173–9. | Randomised control trial | Fifty-nine children with cleft palate and their mothers | To find out if including the mother as an active participant during speech therapy sessions would improve the communicative style and mode of the interaction of the mothers with their cleft-palate children. | Eighty-nine percent of the mothers of the experimental group modified their patterns of interaction. In contrast, only 19 percent of the mothers of the control group modified their style and mode of interaction. | Ib |
| Pamplona MC, Ysunza A & Uriostegui C, 1996, 'Linguistic interaction: The active role of parents in speech therapy for cleft palate patients', *International Journal of Pediatric Otorhinolaryngology* 37:17–27. | Randomised control trial | 21 children ranging in age 3;0 to 4;8 years | This paper compares two different speech and language therapy groups of cleft-palate children. Children included in the first group received therapy without the mother (10) whereas those from the second group were accompanied by their mother (11). The purpose was to evaluate, and provide the mothers with, interaction modes for facilitating communication. | The children accompanied by their mothers showed a significantly higher linguistic advance as compared to those receiving therapy without their mothers. | Ib |
| Pamplona MC & Ysunza A, 2000, 'Active participation of mothers during speech therapy improved language development of children with cleft palate', *Scandinavian Journal of Plastic and Reconstructive Surgery & Hand Surgery* 34 (3):231–6. | Controlled Study | — | This paper compares the outcome of speech therapy given in different settings to two groups of children with cleft palate. Those in the first group were treated by the Speech & Language Therapist alone (control group), whereas those in the second group were treated by the Speech & Language Therapist but were also accompanied by their mothers (experimental group). The purpose of this study was to find out if including the mother as an active participant in speech therapy sessions would improve the language development of children with cleft palate who also had additional language delays. | Both groups were evaluated before and after treatment to evaluate the advance of each group. The patients accompanied by their mothers had significantly better language skills compared to patients treated without their mothers. The results support the statement that language development is related to the mother-child mode of daily life interaction in children with cleft palate. | IIa |

| Author(s) & Title | Design | Sample | Objective of study | Conclusions | Evidence Level |
|---|---|---|---|---|---|
| Golding-Kushner KJ, 2001, *Therapy Techniques for Cleft Palate Speech and Related Disorders*, Singular, London. | Expert opinion | — | — | — | IV |
| **Feeding Support** | | | | | |
| Brine EA, Rickard KA, Brady MS, Liechty EA, Manatunga A, Sadove M & Bull MJ, 1994, 'Effectiveness of two feeding methods in improving energy intake and growth of infants with cleft palate: a randomised study', *Journal of the American Dietetic Association* 94 (7):732–8. | Randomised control trial | Thirty-one infants (median age = 15 days) were randomised to one of two feeding methods (18 infants, squeezable cleft lip/palate nurser; 13 infants, crosscut nipple) within sex (21 boys, 10 girls) and palatal defect (22 cleft lip and palate, 9 isolated cleft palate) categories | To compare two feeding methods advocated for infants with cleft palate: (a) a squeezable plastic container with a narrow, long crosscut nipple; and (b) a standard nipple with a crosscut. The effectiveness of a nutrition intervention protocol for these infants was also documented. | Both feeding methods were effective in supporting normal growth. These data support the need for feeding and nutrition education and early nutrition intervention. | Ib |
| Shaw WC, Bannister RP & Roberts CT, 1999, 'Assisted feeding is more reliable for infants with clefts – a randomised trial', *Cleft Palate Craniofacial Journal* 36 (3):262–8. | Randomised control trial | 101 consecutively born children with cleft lip and/or palate who were otherwise healthy | To compare the effectiveness of squeezable and rigid feeding bottles for infants with clefts. | There were statistically significant differences between the two groups in weight at 12 months, and in head circumference, indicating increased growth in the squeezable bottle group. | Ib |
| Clarren SK, Anderson B & Wolf LS, 1987, 'Feeding infants with cleft lip, cleft palate, or cleft lip and palate', *Cleft Palate Journal* 24 (3):244–9. | Clinical study | 143 infants with cleft lip and palate | To describe the clinical parameters of feeding deficit in terms of the anatomic lesion and then attach the deficits to specific, successful feeding devices or techniques. | In assessing 143 infants with cleft lip and palate, feeding problems were found to vary with the patients' anatomic lesion. Effective feeding techniques were identified by first assessing the infant's ability to generate negative intraoral pressure and to move the tongue against the nipple, and then by matching these deficits to appropriate feeding devices. | III |

## CLEFT PALATE & VELOPHARYNGEAL ABNORMALITIES

| Author(s) & Title | Design | Sample | Objective of study | Conclusions | Evidence Level |
|---|---|---|---|---|---|
| Choi BH, Kleinheinz J, Joos U & Komposch G, 1991, 'Sucking efficiency of early orthopaedic plate and teats in infants with cleft lip and palate', *International Journal of Oral and Maxillofacial Surgery* 20 (3):167–9. | Comparative study | Seven infants with cleft lip and palate, eight infants with cleft lip; two infants with cleft palate, two infants with cleft lip, four infants with operated cleft lip and palate and seven normal infants | Intraoral negative pressure during bottle feeding with two kinds of teats was measured in 7 infants with cleft lip and palate; 8 infants with cleft lip; 2 infants with cleft lip; 4 infants with operated cleft lip and palate; and 7 normal infants. | Infants with cleft lip and palate or cleft palate were unable to generate negative pressure before cleft lip and palate closure. In infants with unoperated cleft lip and with operated cleft lip and palate, peak negative pressure during feeding differed little from that of normal infants. | III |
| **Phonology and Articulation** | | | | | |
| Alberg L & Enderby P, 1984, 'Intensive speech therapy for cleft palate children', *British Journal of Disorders of Communication* 19 (2): 115–24. | Randomised controlled trial | 46 children with deviant articulation secondary to cleft palate or other velopharyngeal disorders | 46 children with deviant articulation secondary to cleft palate or other velopharyngeal disorders were selected to gauge the efficacy of intensive speech therapy. Subjects were randomly allocated to either attend a six week intensive course or to continue with their conventional weekly therapy. | Results indicate a significant improvement in articulation for those children receiving intensive help immediately post-course as compared with a very slight improvement seen in the speech of the control group. This improvement achieved by children on the course and was maintained throughout the two year follow up. | Ib |
| Grunwell P & Dive D, 1988, 'Treating "cleft palate speech"; combining phonological techniques with traditional articulation therapy', *Child Language Teaching & Therapy* 193–210. | Case study | Two children with cleft palate | It is suggested that contrary to clinical practice, phonological therapy is an appropriate and in some instances essential procedure. | These two studies have demonstrated that a combination of articulatory and phonological treatment strategies facilitates the reorganisation and expansion of previously static phonological systems. | III |
| Golding-Kushner KJ, 2001 'Treatment of articulation and resonance disorders associated with cleft palate and VPI', in Shprintzen RJ (ed) *Cleft Palate Speech Management: a Multidisciplinary Approach*, Mosby, London. | Expert opinion | — | — | — | IV |

| Author(s) & Title | Design | Sample | Objective of study | Conclusions | Evidence Level |
|---|---|---|---|---|---|
| Golding-Kushner KJ, 2001, *Therapy Techniques for Cleft Palate Speech and Related Disorders*, Singular, London. | Expert opinion | — | — | — | IV |
| Russell J & Harding A, 2001, 'Speech Development and early intervention', in Watson ACH, Grunwell P, Sell D (eds) *Management of Cleft Lip and Palate*, Whurr Publishers, London. | Expert opinion | — | — | — | IV |
| **Electropalatography Intervention** | | | | | |
| Michi K, Suzuki N, Yamashita Y & Imai S, 1986, 'Visual training and correction of articulation disorders by use of dynamic palatography: serial observation in a case of cleft palate', *Journal of Speech and Hearing Disorders* 51:226–38. | Case study | Six-year-old with cleft lip and palate | Describes the use of the dynamic palatograph (an electrical apparatus that generates a visual display of constantly changing palatolingual contact as a function of time via an artificial plate with affixed electrodes) in the speech therapy treatment of a 6-year-old Japanese female with a repaired unilateral cleft lip and palate. | Findings indicate that after therapy with the dynamic palatograph, the subjects palatolingual contact was normal in comparison with average speakers, suggesting that constant visual indication of tongue posture to the clinician and patient, during corrective speech therapy using dynamic palatography, may expedite improvement of cleft palate patients when implemented in a carefully structured treatment plan. | III |
| Gibbon F, Crampin L, Hardcastle B, Nairn M, Razzell R, Harvey L & Reynolds B, 1998, 'Cleft Net (Scotland): A network for the treatment of cleft palate speech using EPG', *International Journal of Language and Communication 33* (Suppl). Proceedings of the conference of the Royal College of Speech and Language Therapists. | Conference proceedings | Case Studies | In order to improve access to EPG therapy, a network has been established that electronically links cleft palate centres throughout Scotland with EPG specialists based at Queen Margaret College, Edinburgh. The network was set up through a collaborative project entitled 'CleftNet Scotland', funded by the Scottish Office Department of Health. | In this paper, the rationale and overarching aims of CleftNet Scotland are described and the efficacy of this form of EPG therapy illustrated by two cases. | IV |

## CLEFT PALATE & VELOPHARYNGEAL ABNORMALITIES

| Author(s) & Title | Design | Sample | Objective of study | Conclusions | Evidence Level |
|---|---|---|---|---|---|
| Dent H, Gibbon F & Hardcastle B, 1995, 'The application of electropalatography (EPG) to the remediation of speech disorders in school-aged children and young adults. Papers from the European Seminar on ELG and EPG, Edinburgh, July 1994', *European Journal of Disorders of Communication* 30 (2): 264–77. | Conference proceedings | — | This paper briefly examines the function of biofeedback systems within the remediation process and looks in particular at the features of the EPG system which render it a useful therapeutic tool. | Details are summarised of a project initiated to evaluate the use of EPG in the management of a large group of speech-disordered children and young adults. Successful applications of the technique are presented by examining the different types of motor-speech skill which subjects acquired during intervention. These are summarised as the establishment of completely new articulatory patterns, the inhibition of abnormal lingual patterns, and the modification of temporal or spatial aspects of one or several existing patterns. Possible reasons for the success of EPG as a therapeutic technique, and issues concerning subject selection, are discussed. | IV |

### Management of the Speech Consequences of Velopharyngeal Dysfunction: Surgery

| Author(s) & Title | Design | Sample | Objective of study | Conclusions | Evidence Level |
|---|---|---|---|---|---|
| Sommerlad BC, Henley M, Birch M, Harland K, Moiemen N & Boorman JG, 1994, 'Cleft palate re-repair – a clinical and radiographic study of 32 consecutive cases', *British Journal of Plastic Surgery* 47 (6):406–10. | Comparative study | 32 patients | The results of clinical and radiographic assessment of palate re-repair (by a single operator) are presented. | This has shown that radical muscle correction as a secondary procedure (following limited or no muscle correction in primary repair) has produced measurable improvement in velar function and should be considered as the first option in many patients with velopharyngeal incompetence. | III |
| Witt PD & D'Antonio LL, 1993, 'Velopharyngeal insufficiency and secondary palatal management. A new look at an old problem', *Clinical Plastic Surgery* 20 (4):707–21. | Clinical opinion | — | This article focuses on the problem of VPI and emphasises the need for differential diagnosis at the most critical step in management planning. The challenge of the future is to implement the team approach, integrating the expertise of speech scientists and plastic surgeons, so that differential diagnosis can and will lead to differential management | — | IV |

| Author(s) & Title | Design | Sample | Objective of study | Conclusions | Evidence Level |
|---|---|---|---|---|---|
| Sommerlad BC, Mehendale FV, Birch MJ, Sell DA, Hattee C, Harland K, 2002, 'Palate re-repair revisited', *Cleft Palate – Craniofacial Journal* | | | | | |
| **Management of the Speech Consequences of Velopharyngeal Dysfunction: Therapy aimed at muscle activities** | | | | | |
| Ruscello DMA, 1982, 'Selected review of palatal training procedures', *Cleft Palate Journal* 19 (3):181–93. | Review of research | — | This paper reviews the various palatal training procedures and discusses variables that may deserve consideration in future research. | — | IV |
| Starr CD, 1990, 'Treatment by Therapeutic Exercises', in Bardach J & Morris HL (eds) *Multidisciplinary Management of Cleft Lip and Palate*, Saunders, Philadelphia. | Expert opinion | — | — | — | IV |
| **Management of the Speech Consequences of Velopharyngeal Dysfunction: Therapy aimed at Speech Production Modification techniques** | | | | | |
| D'Antonio LL, 1992, 'Evaluation and management of velopharyngeal dysfunction', *Problems in Plastic & Reconstructive Surgery* 2 (1):86–111. | Clinical opinion | — | — | An overview of the evaluation and management of velopharyngeal dysfunction from a Speech & Language Therapist's perspective. | IV |
| Sell D & Grunwell P, 2001, 'Speech assessment and therapy', in Watson ACH, Grunwell P & Sell D (eds) *Management of Cleft Lip and Palate*, Whurr Publishers, London. | Expert opinion | — | — | — | IV |
| **Management of the Speech Consequences of Velopharyngeal Dysfunction using Visual Biofeedback** | | | | | |
| Ysunza A, Pamplona M, Femat T, Mayer L & Garcia-Velasco M, 1997, 'Videonasopharyngoscopy as an instrument for visual biofeedback during speech in cleft palate patients', *International Journal of Pediatric Otorhinolaryngology* 41 (3):291–8. | Randomised clinical trial | Seventeen cleft palate patients were randomly selected for the study | All patients showed velopharyngeal insufficiency (VPI), compensatory articulation (CA) and negative movement of lateral pharyngeal walls (NMLPW) during speech. Nine patients received speech therapy for correcting CA. Eight patients received speech therapy and underwent videonasopharyngoscopy as an instrument for visual biofeedback of the velopharyngeal sphincter. | After 12 weeks, NMLPW was modified in the patients receiving speech therapy and visual biofeedback. In contrast, NMLPW was still present in eight out of nine patients receiving only speech therapy. These patients received visual biofeedback and NMLPW was corrected in all cases. After six months, all 17 patients had corrected CA during isolated speech. All patients received a tailor-made pharyngeal flap. VPI was completely corrected in 15 cases. | Ib |

## CLEFT PALATE & VELOPHARYNGEAL ABNORMALITIES

| Author(s) & Title | Design | Sample | Objective of study | Conclusions | Evidence Level |
|---|---|---|---|---|---|
| Kawano M, Isshiki N, Honjo I, Kojima H, Kurata K, Tanokuchi F, Kido N & Isobe M, 1997, 'Recent progress in treating patients with cleft palate', *Folia Phoniatrica et Logopaedica* 49 (3–4): 117–38. | Clinical Study | — | This paper describes the advantages of the combined use of nasopharyngofiberscopy and fluorovideoradiography in assessing slight velopharyngeal incompetence and the mechanisms of faulty articulation. | This paper deals with two problems: (1) Slight velopharyngeal incompetence: The combined use of fiberscopy and fluorovideoscopy can provide useful information as to: a) the exact place of the faulty articulation; b) the detailed pattern of inconsistent velopharyngeal function; c) changes in articulation induced by speech therapy; and d) the relation between velopharyngeal function and faulty articulation. (2) Analysis of faulty articulation. It was revealed that faulty articulations such as laryngeal fricative and affricates; pharyngeal stop; and glottal stop in cleft palate speech, secondary to velopharyngeal incompetence, were produced by articulation in the larynx at various sites such as the epiglottis, arytenoids, aryepiglottic folds and vocal folds. These faulty articulation points were located lower than supposed on the basis of auditory perception. | III |
| Siegel-Sadewitz VL & Shprintzen RJ, 1982, 'Nasopharyngoscopy of the normal velopharyngeal sphincter: an experiment of biofeedback', *Cleft Palate Journal* 19 (3):194–200. | Single case study | One subject | The goal of the experiment was for the subject, utilising nasopharyngoscopy, to alter the velopharyngeal valving pattern observed during spontaneous speech by manipulating the relative contributions of the velum and pharyngeal walls. | After six sessions, each lasting twenty minutes, the subject was able to change velopharyngeal valving pattern at will during short samples of connected speech. | III |
| Witzel MA & Posnick JC, 1989, 'Patterns and location of velopharyngeal valving problems: atypical findings on video nasopharyngoscopy', *Cleft Palate Journal* 26 (1):63–67. | Prospective clinical study | 246 patients | Patterns of velopharyngeal (VP) valving and the location of velopharyngeal gaps were investigated in 246 consecutive nasopharyngoscopy studies. | The predominant pattern of closure was coronal (68 percent); followed by the circular (23 percent); circular with a Passavant's ridge (5 percent); and sagittal (4 percent) patterns. Atypical findings occurred primarily in patients with a coronal pattern of valving. | III |

| Author(s) & Title | Design | Sample | Objective of study | Conclusions | Evidence Level |
|---|---|---|---|---|---|
| Golding-Kushner KJ, 1994, 'Treatment of articulation and resonance disorders associated with cleft palate and VPI', in Shprintzen RJ (ed) *Cleft Palate Speech Management: A Multidisciplinary Approach* Mosby, London. | Expert opinion | — | — | — | IV |

## Management of Velopharyngeal Dysfunction: Speech Therapy for Consonant Production

| Author(s) & Title | Design | Sample | Objective of study | Conclusions | Evidence Level |
|---|---|---|---|---|---|
| Harding A & Grunwell P, 1998, 'Active versus passive cleft-type speech characteristics', *International Journal of Language & Communication Disorders* 33:329–52. | Longitudinal study | 5 bilateral cleft lip and palate subjects aged 1;6–4;6<br><br>12 mixed unilateral cleft lip and palate and BCLP subjects aged 4;6–7;6<br><br>9 mixed unilateral cleft lip and palate and bilateral cleft lip and palate subjects aged 9;0–11;0<br><br>Reference is also made to data from 12 mixed cleft-type subjects aged 13;0 who had been treated with different surgical timing regimes | Passive and active patterns of articulation are described and defined in the context of three longitudinal studies of subjects who were at various stages of two different surgical regimes: five bilateral cleft lip and palate (BCLP) subjects aged 1;6–4;6; twelve mixed unilateral cleft lip and palate (UCLP) and BCLP subjects aged 4;6–7;6; and nine mixed UCLP and BCLP subjects aged 9;0–11;0. Reference is also made to data from 12 mixed cleft-type subjects aged 13;0 who had been treated with different surgical timing regimes. Comparison is made between the incidence of active versus passive processes in relation to oral structure. | A distinction between passive and active cleft-type speech characteristics whereby passive characteristics were thought to be the product of structural abnormality or dysfunction and active characteristics were specific articulatory gestures replacing intended consonants. Indications from this study are that active cleft-type characteristics require destabilisation in a course of speech and language therapy before the potential benefits of surgery can be properly assessed. An analytical protocol for the interpretation of speech samples is presented and some therapy strategies are proposed for active and passive processes. | III |

## CLEFT PALATE & VELOPHARYNGEAL ABNORMALITIES

| Author(s) & Title | Design | Sample | Objective of study | Conclusions | Evidence Level |
|---|---|---|---|---|---|
| Peterson-Falzone S & Graham MS, 1990, 'Phoneme-specific nasal emission in children with and without physical anomalies of the velopharyngeal mechanism', *Journal of Speech and Hearing Disorders* 55:132–9. | Clinical study | 36 children | Phoneme-specific nasal emission was identified in 36 children ranging in age from 3 years, 3 months to 16 years, 5 months; 19 children had no physical anomalies of the orofacial mechanism, whereas 17 had findings ranging from minor to severe. | Five patterns of phoneme-specific nasal emission were exhibited by two or more children. An additional eight patterns were exhibited by one child each. Sibilants were clearly the most frequently affected phonemes. There was no significant correlation between the number of phonemes affected by nasal emission and the number of phonologic processes exhibited by the children in either subject group. The two subject groups were more alike than different in the speech behaviours observed, underscoring a fundamental homogeneity among speakers who exhibit phoneme-specific nasal emission. | III |
| Hoch L, Golding-Kushner K, Siegel-Sadewitz VL & Shprintzen RJ, 1986, 'Speech Therapy', in McWilliams BJ (ed) *Seminars in Speech and Language: Current Methods of Assessing and Treating Children with Cleft Palates*, Thieme, New York. | Expert opinion | — | — | — | IV |

## Management of Velopharyngeal Dysfunction: Prosthetics

| Author(s) & Title | Design | Sample | Objective of study | Conclusions | Evidence Level |
|---|---|---|---|---|---|
| Witt PD, Rozelle AA, Marsh JL, Marty-Grames L, Muntz HR, Gay WD & Pilgram TK, 1995, 'Do palatal lift prostheses stimulate velopharyngeal neuromuscular activity?', *The Cleft Palate Craniofacial Journal* 32 (6):469–75. | Clinical trial | 25 patients | The purpose of this investigation was to evaluate the ability of palatal lift prostheses to stimulate the neuromuscular activity of the velopharynx. Nasoendoscopic evaluations were audio-videotaped, pre-prosthetic and post-prosthetic management, for 25 patients who underwent placement of a palatal lift prosthesis for velopharyngeal dysfunction. These audio-videotapes were presented in blinded fashion and random order to three Speech & Language Therapists experienced in assessment of patients with velopharyngeal dysfunction. They rated the tapes on the following parameters: VP gap size; closure pattern; orifice estimate; direction and magnitude of change; and qualitative descriptions of the adequacy of VP closure during speech. VP closure for speech was unchanged in 69 percent of patients and the number of patients rated as improved or deteriorated was nearly identical at about 15 percent. | Post-intervention gap shape remained unchanged in 70 percent of patients. The extent of VP orifice closure during speech remained unchanged in 57 percent of patients. Articulations that could impair VP function improved in 30 percent of patients, deteriorating in only 4 percent. Results of this study neither support the concept that palatal lift prostheses alter the neuromuscular patterning of the velopharynx, nor provide objective documentation of the feasibility of prosthetic reduction for weaning. | IIb |
| Golding-Kushner KJ, Cisneros G & LeBlanc E, 1995, 'Speech Bulbs', in Shprintzen RJ & Bardach J (eds) *Cleft Palate Speech Management: A Multidisciplinary Approach*. | Expert opinion | — | — | — | IV |
| Sell D & Grunwell P, 2001, 'Speech assessment and therapy', in Watson ACH, Grunwell P & Sell D (eds) *Management of Cleft Lip and Palate*, Whurr Publishers, London. | Expert opinion | — | — | — | IV |

## CLINICAL VOICE DISORDERS

| Author(s) & Title | Design | Sample | Objective of study | Conclusions | Evidence Level |
|---|---|---|---|---|---|
| **Voice Clinic** | | | | | |
| Casiano RR, Zaveri V & Lundy DS, 1992, 'Efficacy of videostroboscopy in the diagnosis of voice disorders', *Otolaryngology and Head and Neck Surgery* 107 (1):95–100. | Case series | 292 dysphonic patients who were categorised into 4 broad groups. Ages 5–85 136 men 156 women | 292 dysphonic patients were identified who underwent indirect laryngoscopy as well as videolaryngoscopy with and without stroboscopic examination. | Videostrobolaryngoscopy was found to alter the diagnosis and treatment outcome in 14 percent of the patients. It is most useful in patients with a diagnosis of functional dysphonia and vocal-fold paralysis by indirect laryngoscopy. The increased illumination and magnification afforded by rigid fibre-optic telescopes during videolaryngoscopy, combined with the detailed assessment of glottic closure, mucosal wave and amplitude characteristics provided by stroboscopic examination, allowed detection of subtle vocal-fold pathology otherwise missed by indirect laryngoscopy. | III |
| Woo P, Colton R, Casper J & Brewer D, 1992, 'Analysis of spasmodic dysphonia by aerodynamic and laryngostroboscopic measurements', *Journal of Voice*, 6 (4):344–51. | Comparative study | 18 patients with spasmodic dysphonia | This study compared acoustic, aerodynamic and laryngostroboscopy findings in 18 patients before treatment; after unilateral recurrent laryngeal nerve block; after bilateral injections of Botox; and prior to Botox reinjection. | Of all the treatments assessed, bilateral partial denervation by Botox appeared to be the most physiologic in restoring normal vocal-fold vibratory function and airflow. | III |
| **Perceptual Assessment** | | | | | |
| Dejonckere PH, Remacle M, Fresnel-Elbaz E, Woisard V, Crevier L & Millet B, 1998, 'Reliability and clinical relevance of perceptual evaluation of pathological voices', *Revue de Laryngology – Atologie – Rhinology (Bord)* 119 (4):247–48. | Clinical study | 943 individuals | The perceptual GRBAS scale for deviant voice quality was tested in 5 different institutes on 943 voice patients. Each voice was evaluated separately by two professionals. One of the aims of this study was to provide information about reliability of perceptual rating with the GIRBAS scale. | The interrater and intrarater correlation is satisfactory for G, R and B. The GIRBAS scale seems to be a valuable instrument for clinical practice. | III |

| Author(s) & Title | Design | Sample | Objective of study | Conclusions | Evidence Level |
|---|---|---|---|---|---|
| Carding P, Carlson E, Epstein R, Mathieson L & Shewell C, 2000, 'Formal perceptual evaluation of voice quality in the United Kingdom', *Logopedics, Phoniatrics, Vocology* 25 (3):133–8. | Expert opinion | — | This document is a position statement on the formal perceptual evaluation of voice quality in the United Kingdom (UK). | The conclusion is that the GRBAS scheme should be recommended as the absolute minimum standard for practising UK voice clinicians. However, there is a clear need to develop a more satisfactory perceptual rating scheme that is clinically realistic, theoretically sound, internationally acceptable and has proven reliability. | IV |
| **Instrumental Evaluation** | | | | | |
| Baken R & Orlikoff R, 2000, *Clinical measurement of Speech and Voice*, 2nd edn, Singular Press, San Diego. | Expert opinion | — | — | — | IV |
| **Client Self-assessment** | | | | | |
| MacKenzie K, Millar A, Wilson JA, Sellars C & Deary I, 2001, 'Is voice therapy an effective treatment for dysphonia? A randomised controlled trial', *BMJ* 323:658–61. | Single blind random controlled trial | 204 dysphonic outpatients | To assess the overall efficacy of voice therapy for dysphonia. | Voice therapy improved voice quality as assessed by patients themselves and by observers. | Ib |
| Benninger MS, Ahuja AS, Gardner G & Grywalski C, 1998, 'Assessing outcomes for dysphonic patients', *Journal of Voice* 12 (4):540–50. | Observational study | 260 individuals evaluated for alterations of voice | This study was designed to evaluate a disease-specific outcome measure for patients with selected voice disorders and to relate this instrument to a standardised quality of life measurement. In addition, the study attempts to document the degree of handicap for dysphonia patients globally, between different vocal pathologies, and in comparison to other chronic diseases. | The SF-36 correlates with the Voice Handicap Index (VHI) domains of social functioning, mental health and role functioning emotional. The baseline handicap for voice disorders represents a significant disability even in comparison to conditions such as angina pectoris, sciatica and chronic sinusitis. | III |
| Jacobson BH, Johnson A, Grywalski C, Silbergleit A, Jacobson G, Benninger MS & Newman CW, 1997, 'The Voice Handicap Index: development and validation', *American Journal of Speech – Language Pathology* 6 (3):66–70. | Qualitative | 65 patients seen in voice clinic | The aim of this study was the development of a statistically robust Voice Handicap Index (VHI). An 85 item version was administered to 65 consecutive patients seen in a voice clinic. This version was subsequently reduced to a 30 item final version which was administered to 63 consecutive patients on two occasions. | The findings of the second trial demonstrated that a change between administrations of 18 points represents a significant shift in psychosocial function. | III |

## CLINICAL VOICE DISORDERS

| Author(s) & Title | Design | Sample | Objective of study | Conclusions | Evidence Level |
|---|---|---|---|---|---|
| Smith E, Verdolini K, Gray S, Nichols S, Lemke J, Barkmeier J, Dove H & Hoffman H,1996, 'Effect of voice disorders on quality of life', *Journal of Medical Speech-Language Pathology* 4 (4):223–44. | Comparative study | 174 voice patients<br><br>173 controls | 174 voice patients and 173 controls were asked to complete a questionnaire designed to elicit information about the frequency and effects of voice impairments on quality of life. | The findings indicated that the voice patient group was significantly more likely to report a higher frequency of ten specific voice symptoms and adverse quality of life effects. | III |

### Palpation of the Extrinsic Laryngeal Musculature

| Author(s) & Title | Design | Sample | Objective of study | Conclusions | Evidence Level |
|---|---|---|---|---|---|
| Lieberman J, 1998, 'Principles and techniques of manual therapy: applications in management of dysphonia', in Harris T, Harris S, Rubin J & Howard D (eds), *The Voice Clinic Handbook*, Whurr Publishers, London. | Expert opinion | — | — | — | IV |
| Roy N, Ford C & Bless D, 1996, 'The role of manual laryngeal tension reduction in diagnosis and management', paper presented at the meeting of the American Laryngological Association Florida, 4–5 May 1996.<br>http://www.stic.net/users/ta2man/dystonia.html> | Expert opinion | — | — | — | IV |

### Education and Explanation

| Author(s) & Title | Design | Sample | Objective of study | Conclusions | Evidence Level |
|---|---|---|---|---|---|
| Chan RW, 1994, 'Does the voice improve with vocal hygiene education? A study of some instrumental voice measures in a group of kindergarten teachers', *Journal of Voice* 8 (3):279–91. | Controlled study | 12 female teachers<br><br>13 controls | This study investigated the efficacy of a programme of vocal hygiene education, in kindergarten teachers. Twelve female teachers explored concepts and knowledge of vocal abuse and vocal hygiene in a workshop session and attempted to practice vocal hygiene for two months. | The results demonstrated significant voice improvement as assessed instrumentally in terms of three acoustic and electroglottographic parameters. There was no significant change of voice in a control group of 13 teachers. | IIa |

| Author(s) & Title | Design | Sample | Objective of study | Conclusions | Evidence Level |
|---|---|---|---|---|---|
| Drudge M & Philips B, 1976, 'Shaping behaviour in voice therapy', *Journal of Speech & Hearing Disorders* XLI:398–411. | Case series | 3 patients with vocal nodules | This study demonstrates the process of learning and shaping of behaviour which occurs during a programme of therapy for individuals with hyperfunctional hoarse voice quality. First a therapy programme delineating the techniques and criteria to be used was written. The programme was presented during 16 individual half-hour sessions over an eight-week period to three clients known to have vocal nodules. The clients' responses were charted at various points from audiotape recordings of each therapy session, to obtain data to demonstrate the learning processes. | It was concluded that: 1) the clients' behaviours in this vocal rehabilitation program reflected a learning process; 2) facilitating techniques were used to modify or shape behaviour through successive approximations to the terminal goal; 3) self-evaluation is an important factor needed to bring about successful changes in behaviour; 4) analysis of clients' behaviours in relation to the learning process can aid in evaluating the effectiveness of the facilitating techniques; and 5) from such evaluation intraclient and interclient programme changes are derived, hopefully resulting in a greater success rate and maximum benefits from time spent in therapy. | III |

### Vocal Tract Care and Voice Conservation

| Author(s) & Title | Design | Sample | Objective of study | Conclusions | Evidence Level |
|---|---|---|---|---|---|
| Verdolini-Marston K, Sandage M & Titze IR, 1994, 'Effect of hydration treatments on laryngeal nodules and polyps and related voice measures', *Journal of Voice* 8 (1):30–47. | Controlled study | 6 adult female patients with laryngeal nodules or polyps | In this study the effectiveness of hydration treatments in the clinical management of selected voice disorders was determined. Six adult female patients with laryngeal nodules or polyps each received 5 consecutive days of hydration treatment and 5 consecutive days of placebo/control treatment. | The combined results indicated improvements in voice and in laryngeal appearance following both placebo/control and hydration treatments as compared with baseline. However, the greatest improvements were obtained following the hydration treatment. | IIa |
| Chan RW, 1994, 'Does the voice improve with vocal hygiene education? A study of some instrumental voice measures in a group of kindergarten teachers', *Journal of Voice* 8 (3):279–91. | Controlled study | 12 female teachers 13 controls (teachers) | This study investigated the efficacy of a programme of vocal hygiene education in kindergarten teachers. Twelve female teachers explored concepts and knowledge of vocal abuse and vocal hygiene in a workshop session and attempted to practice vocal hygiene for two months. | The results demonstrated significant voice improvement as assessed instrumentally in terms of three acoustic and electroglottographic parameters. There was no significant change of voice in a control group of 13 teachers. | IIa |

## CLINICAL VOICE DISORDERS

### Direct Treatment Approaches

| Author(s) & Title | Design | Sample | Objective of study | Conclusions | Evidence Level |
|---|---|---|---|---|---|
| Carding PN, Horsley IA & Docherty GJ, 1999, 'A study of the effectiveness of voice therapy in the treatment of 45 patients with non-organic dysphonia', *Journal of Voice* 13 (1):72–104. | Randomised controlled trial | 45 patients diagnosed as having non-organic dysphonia | Forty-five patients diagnosed as having non-organic dysphonia were assigned in rotation to one of three groups. Patients in group 1 received no treatment and acted as a control group. Patients in groups 2 and 3 received a programme of indirect therapy and direct with indirect therapy, respectively. A range of qualitative and quantitative measures were carried out on all patients before and after treatment to evaluate change in voice quality over time. | Most of the patients (86 percent) in group 1 showed no significant change on any of the measures. Some patients in treatment group 2 (46 percent) showed significant change in voice quality. Fourteen out of 15 patients (93 percent) in treatment group 3 showed significant changes in voice quality. | Ib |
| Ramig L, Countryman S, Thompson L & Horii Y, 1995, 'Comparison of two forms of intensive speech treatment for Parkinson Disease', *Journal of Speech & Hearing Research* 38:1232–51 | Randomised controlled trial | 45 individuals with idiopathic Parkinson's Disease | This study investigated the effects of two forms of intensive speech treatment:<br>■ Respiration (R)<br>■ Voice and respiration (LSVT)<br>On the speech and voice deficits associated with idiopathic Parkinson Disease (IPD), forty-five individuals completed 16 sessions of intensive speech treatment, 4 times per week for one month. A range of variables were assessed pre- and post-treatment. | Significant pre-post treatment improvements were observed for more variables, and were of greater magnitude, for the individuals who received the LSVT. Only those who received the LSVT rated a significant decrease post-treatment on the impact of IPD on their communication. | Ib |
| MacKenzie K, Millar A, Wilson JA, Sellars C, Deary I, 2001, 'Is voice therapy an effective treatment for dysphonia? A randomised controlled trial', *BMJ* 323:658–61. | Single blind randomised controlled trial | 204 dysphonic outpatients | To assess the overall efficacy of voice therapy for dysphonia. | Voice therapy improved voice quality as assessed by rating by patients themselves and by observers. | Ib |

| Author(s) & Title | Design | Sample | Objective of study | Conclusions | Evidence Level |
|---|---|---|---|---|---|
| Bassiouny S, 1998, 'Efficacy of the accent method of voice therapy', *Folia Phoniatrica et Logopaedia* 50 (3):46–64. | Randomised control study | 42 patients with a variety of vocal pathologies | This study was conducted in order to evaluate the efficacy of the accent method of voice therapy. Group 1 is given the full aspect of the accent method, plus the accent exercises to correct the faulty vocal technique. Group 2 received only voice hygiene advice. | The difference in improvement between Group 1 and Group 2 at the end of the observation was generally significant in favour of Group 1. There were significant improvements in Group 1 in certain items specific for the various aetiologic categories. The improvement from pre-test to mid-test to post-test values followed a linear tendency. | Ib |
| Stemple J, Lee L, D'Amico B & Pickup B, 1994, 'Efficacy of vocal function exercise as a method of improving voice production', *Journal of Voice* 8(3):271–8. | Randomised controlled trial | 35 women | Objective voice analysis including acoustic; aerodynamic; and laryngeal videostroboscopic measures; demonstrated normal voice in 35 adult women. The subjects were then randomly divided into experimental, placebo and control groups. The experimental group engaged in vocal function exercises. The placebo group engaged in a placebo exercise programme. | Objective measures taken after four weeks of exercise demonstrated significant changes in phonation volume; flow rate; maximum phonation time; and frequency range for the experimental group. No significant changes were noted in the measurements of the control and placebo groups. | Ib |
| Verdolini-Marston K, Burke M, Lessac A, Glaze L & Caldwell E, 1995, 'Preliminary study of two methods of treatment for laryngeal nodules', *Journal of Voice* 9(1):74–85. | Controlled study | 13 women | Thirteen women with nodules participated as paid subjects. Some subjects received 'confidential voice therapy', some received 'resonant voice therapy' and some received no therapy (control condition) over a period of approximately two weeks. | Pre- and post-therapy measures of phonatory effort, auditory-perceptual status of voice, and laryngeal appearance provided evidence of a benefit from therapy. Baseline measures were then repeated two weeks after therapy was terminated. The final results indicated that, for auditory-perceptual and phonatory effort measures, the likelihood of benefiting from therapy directly covaried with compliance scores (reflecting the reported extraclinical utilisation of the therapy technique), but not with therapy type (confidential versus resonant voice therapy). At this level, the results point to the importance of assessing not only therapy type but also compliance in future, larger studies. | IIa |

## CLINICAL VOICE DISORDERS

| Author(s) & Title | Design | Sample | Objective of study | Conclusions | Evidence Level |
|---|---|---|---|---|---|
| Murry T & Woodson G, 1992, 'A comparison of three methods for the management of vocal fold nodules', *Journal of Voice* 6(3):271–6. | Comparative study | 59 patients with diagnosis of vocal fold nodules | The improvement of the voices of 59 patients following the diagnosis of vocal fold nodules was evaluated according to the type of treatment:<br>■ Voice therapy<br>■ Voice therapy following surgery<br>■ Combined voice therapy and management by an otolaryngologist | Results indicate that satisfactory improvement can be obtained using any of the three approaches. | III |
| Bloch CS, Gould WJ & Hirano M, 1981, 'Effect of voice therapy on contact granuloma of the vocal fold', *The Annals of Otology, Rhinology and Laryngology* 90 (1):48–52. | Case series | 17 patients with contact granuloma | This paper describes 17 patients in whom treatment of the contact granuloma was approached through voice therapy. Treatment consisted of a comprehensive history and voice evaluation; stress reduction; relaxation methods; auditory and kinesthetic feedback; pitch change, and elimination of voice abuse. | As a result of voice therapy, the granuloma disappeared in 9 patients, was reduced in size in 4 and remained unchanged in 1. For the remaining three patients, post-therapeutic laryngoscopic findings were not available. The Speech & Language Therapist found voice and manner of phonation returned to normal in 4 patients, improved in 7 and remained unchanged in 6. | III |
| Drudge M & Philips B, 1976, 'Shaping behaviour in voice therapy', *Journal of Speech & Hearing Disorders* XLI:398–411. | Case series | 3 patients with vocal nodules | This study demonstrates the process of learning and shaping of behaviour which occurs during a programme of therapy for individuals with hyperfunctional hoarse voice quality. First a therapy programme delineating the techniques and criteria to be used was written. The programme was presented during 16 individual half-hour sessions over an eight-week period to three clients known to have vocal nodules. The clients' responses were charted at various points from audiotape recordings of each therapy session using a modification of the Boone-Prescott analysis system, to obtain data to demonstrate the learning processes. | It was concluded that: 1) the clients' behaviours in this vocal rehabilitation program reflected a learning process; 2) facilitating techniques were used to modify or shape behaviour through successive approximations to the terminal goal; 3) self-evaluation is an important factor needed to bring about successful changes in behaviour; 4) analysis of clients' behaviours in relation to the learning process can aid in evaluating the effectiveness of the facilitating techniques; and 5) from such evaluation intraclient and interclient programme changes are derived, hopefully resulting in a greater success rate and maximum benefits from time spent in therapy. | III |

## Indirect Treatment Approaches

| Author(s) & Title | Design | Sample | Objective of study | Conclusions | Evidence Level |
|---|---|---|---|---|---|
| Carding PN, Horsley IA & Docherty GJ, 1999, 'A study of the effectiveness of voice therapy in the treatment of 45 patients with non-organic dysphonia', *Journal of Voice* 13 (1):72–104. | Randomised controlled trial | 45 patients diagnosed as having non-organic dysphonia | Forty-five patients diagnosed as having non-organic dysphonia were assigned in rotation to one of three groups. Patients in group 1 received no treatment and acted as a control group. Patients in groups 2 and 3 received a programme of indirect therapy and direct with indirect therapy, respectively. A range of qualitative and quantitative measures were carried out on all patients before and after treatment to evaluate change in voice quality over time. | Most of the patients (86 percent) in group 1 showed no significant change on any of the measures. Some patients in treatment group 2 (46 percent) showed significant change in voice quality. Fourteen out of 15 patients (93 percent) in treatment group 3 showed significant changes in voice quality. | Ib |

## DEAFNESS/HEARING LOSS

| Author(s) & Title | Design | Sample | Objective of study | Conclusions | Evidence Level |
|---|---|---|---|---|---|
| **Clinical History Checklist** | | | | | |
| McCormick B, 1993, *Paediatric Audiology: 0–5 Years*, Whurr Publishers, London. | Expert opinion | — | — | — | IV |
| Boothroyd A, 1992, 'Profound Deafness', in Tyler RS (ed) *Cochlear Implants Audiological Foundations*, Whurr Publishers, London. | Expert opinion | — | — | — | IV |
| **Checking of Auditory Device** | | | | | |
| McCormick B, 1993, *Paediatric Audiology: 0–5 Years*, Whurr Publishers, London. | Expert opinion | — | — | — | IV |
| Bench RJ,1992, *Communication Skills in Hearing Impaired Children*, Whurr Publishers, London. | Expert opinion | — | — | — | IV |
| Boothroyd A, 1992, 'Profound Deafness', in Tyler RS (ed) *Cochlear Implants Audiological Foundations*, Whurr Publishers, London. | Expert opinion | — | — | — | IV |
| Boothroyd AE, Geers AE & Moog JS, 1991, 'Practical implications of cochlear implants in children', *Ear and Hearing* 12 (4 Suppl):81S–89S. | Expert opinion | — | The purpose of this paper is to discuss the practical implications of cochlear implants in children, and five questions are addressed which relate to the auditory capacity of implanted children. | — | IV |
| **Functional Use of Aided Hearing** | | | | | |
| Archbold S, Lutman M & Nikolopoulos TP, 1998, 'Categories of Auditory Performance: Inter-User Reliability', *British Journal of Audiology* 32:7–11. | Comparative study | 23 children | Categories of Auditory Performance (CAP) describes a scale used to rate outcomes from paediatric cochlear implantation in everyday life. Being based on subjective assessments, there is a need to establish whether ratings by different persons are comparable. Therefore, an analysis of inter-user reliability was undertaken using ratings from 23 children followed up at various intervals after implantation. | Analysis relating scores by local teachers of the deaf and the teachers of the deaf at the implant centre revealed very high inter-user reliability (correlation coefficient 0.97). This result establishes the reliability of CAP as an outcome measure for use in cochlear implant programmes. | III |

| Author(s) & Title | Design | Sample | Objective of study | Conclusions | Evidence Level |
|---|---|---|---|---|---|
| Hind S, 1998, 'Implications of otitis media for development', in Gregory S, Knight P, McCracken W & Watson L (eds) *Issues in Deaf Education*, David Fulton Publishers Ltd, London. | Expert opinion | — | — | — | IV |
| Klein S & Rapin I, 1993, 'Intermittent conductive hearing loss and language development' in Bishop D & Mogford K (eds) *Language Development in Exceptional Circumstances*, Lawrence Erlbaum Associates, Mahwah, NJ. | Expert opinion | — | — | — | IV |
| Barrett K, 1994, 'Hearing and middle ear screening of school age children', in Katz J (ed) *Handbook of Clinical Audiology*, Lippincott Williams & Wilkins, Philadelphia. | Expert opinion | — | — | — | IV |
| Kirk KI, Diefendorf AO, Pisoni DB & Robbins AM, 1997, 'Assessing Speech perception in children' in Mendel LL & Danhauer JL (eds) *Audiological Evaluation and Management and Speech Perception Assessment*, Singular Publishing, London. | Expert opinion | — | — | — | IV |
| **Assessment of Speech Reading** | | | | | |
| Plant G & Spens KE, 1995, *Profound Deafness and Speech Communication*, Whurr Publishers, London. | Expert opinion | — | — | — | IV |
| Plant G & McCrae J, 1997, 'Testing visual and auditory perception', in Martin M (ed), *Speech Audiometry*, Delmar Publishers, Albany, NY. | Expert opinion | — | — | — | IV |
| **Assessment of Speech Production and Speech and/or Sign Intelligibility** | | | | | |
| Parker A & Irlam S, 1994, 'Speech intelligibility and deafness: the skills of the listener and speaker', in Wirz S (ed) *Perceptual Approaches to Communication Disorders*, Whurr Publishers, London. | Expert opinion | — | — | — | IV |

## DEAFNESS/HEARING LOSS

| Author(s) & Title | Design | Sample | Objective of study | Conclusions | Evidence Level |
|---|---|---|---|---|---|
| Fisher J, King A, Parker A & Wright R, 1983, 'Assessment of speech production and speech perception as a basis for therapy', in Hochberg I, Levitt H & Osberger MJ (eds) *Speech of the Hearing Impaired*, University Park Press, Baltimore. | Expert opinion | — | — | — | IV |
| Parker A & Kersner M, 1997, 'How you look is what you find: observing the phonology of deaf speakers', *Journal of Clinical Speech and Language Studies* 7:115. | Expert opinion | — | This paper discusses the phonological patterns which are found in the speech of deaf people and advocates such patterns need to be taken into account when assessing speech. The *PETAL Speech Assessment* is outlined. | — | IV |
| **Speech Intelligibility** | | | | | |
| Allen MC, Nikolopoulos TP & O'Donoghue GM, 1998, 'Speech intelligibility in children after cochlear implantation', *American Journal of Otology* 19 (6):742–6. | Prospective study | All children in the study were congenitally deaf or deafened before three years of age. They each received a Nucleus multi-channel cochlear implant before the age of seven years. Eighty-four subjects were evaluated up to five years after cochlear implantation. | The study design was a prospective study following a large group of consecutively implanted deaf children with up to five years cochlear implant use. A speech intelligibility rating scale evaluated the spontaneous speech of each child before, and at yearly intervals for five years after, implantation. This study aimed to evaluate the long-term speech intelligibility of young deaf children after cochlear implantation. | After cochlear implantation, the difference between the speech intelligibility ratings increased significantly each year for four years. Congenital and prelingually deaf children gradually develop intelligible speech that does not plateau five years after implantation. | III |

| Author(s) & Title | Design | Sample | Objective of study | Conclusions | Evidence Level |
|---|---|---|---|---|---|
| Parker A & Irlam S, 1994, 'Speech intelligibility and deafness: the skills of the listener and speaker', in Wirz S (ed) *Perceptual Approaches to Communication Disorders*, Whurr Publishers, London. | Expert opinion | — | — | — | IV |
| **Assessment of Vocal Characteristics (Prosody)** | | | | | |
| Wirz S (ed), 1995, *Perceptual Approaches to Communication Disorders*, Whurr Publishers, London. | Expert opinion | — | — | — | IV |
| **Role of the Interdisciplinary Team** | | | | | |
| Bray M, 2001, 'Working with parents', in Kersner M & Wright JA (eds) *Speech & Language Therapy: The Decision-Making Process when Working with Children*, David Fulton Publishers, London. | Expert opinion | — | — | — | IV |
| **Early Communication Skills** | | | | | |
| Bench J, McNeill-Brown D, Backhouse R & Heine C, 1995, 'Speech therapy with a group of hearing-impaired adolescents I: a sociolinguistic analysis of therapy sessions', *Child Language Teaching & Therapy* 11:289–307. | Qualitative study | 5 hearing university students and 5 hearing-impaired adolescents | Speech therapy conversations between five dyads, comprising senior speech pathology students and hearing-impaired adolescents enrolled in a Total Communication Programme, were video-recorded for five weekly sessions. Samples over one-minute intervals at the start, middle and end of the sessions were analysed for topic initiations and initiators, conversational turns and responses to questions according to the communication modes: speech; sign or gesture; and speech combined with sign or gesture. | Statistical analyses explored differences between dyads; conversational partners; sessions; and intervals; and their interactions, in relation to mode. The results are discussed with reference to changes in conversational competence with therapy. | III |

## DEAFNESS/HEARING LOSS

| Author(s) & Title | Design | Sample | Objective of study | Conclusions | Evidence Level |
|---|---|---|---|---|---|
| Caissie R & Gibson CL, 1997, 'The effectiveness of repair strategies used by people with hearing losses and their conversational partners', *Volta-Review* 99 (4):203–18. | Qualitative study | 25 adults with acquired sensorineural hearing losses were videotaped while conversing with normally hearing partners | This study investigated the effectiveness of requests for clarification by adults who are deaf or hard of hearing and of partner responses to these requests in overcoming communication breakdowns in everyday conversations. Twenty-five adults with acquired sensorineural hearing losses were videotaped while conversing with normally hearing partners. The conversation samples were analysed for the occurrence of three types of clarification requests and eight types of partner repair strategies, and for the frequency with which the repair strategies successfully solved misperceptions. | Overall, non-specific clarification requests; requests for the repetition of a specific constituent; and requests for confirmation by the participants with hearing losses were all similarly effective in managing communication breakdowns. In contrast, some partner repair strategies were more effective than others: paraphrase and confirmation of the message were the most effective strategies, while message elaboration was the least effective. Partial repetition of the message was highly effective following a request that the partner repeat a specific constituent, but not following a non-specific request for clarification. The effectiveness of full repetition of the message was unaffected by the preceding clarification-request type. Except for requests for confirmation, which nearly always elicited confirmation responses, the type of clarification request used did not consistently elicit the most effective repair strategy from partners. Partners had more control over the facility with which communication breakdowns were repaired, because they could select particular repair strategies, than did the adults who are deaf or hard of hearing through their selection of clarification-request types. This emphasises the essential role conversational partners play in effective management of communication breakdowns. | III |
| Galloway C & Woll B, 1994, 'Interaction and childhood deafness', in Gallaway C & Richards BJ (eds), *Input and Interaction in Language Acquisition*, Cambridge University Press, Cambridge. | Expert opinion | — | — | — | IV |

| Author(s) & Title | Design | Sample | Objective of study | Conclusions | Evidence Level |
|---|---|---|---|---|---|
| Galloway C, 1999, 'Early interaction', in Gregory S, Powers S, Watson L, Knight P & McCracken W (eds), *Issues in deaf education*, David Fulton Publishers, London. | Expert opinion | — | — | — | IV |
| Woll B, 1999, 'Development of signed and spoken languages', in Gregory S, Powers S, Watson L, Knight P & McCracken W (eds) *Issues in Deaf Education*, David Fulton Publishers, London. | Expert opinion | — | — | — | IV |
| **Communication Ability (Social and Interaction Skills)** | | | | | |
| Bench RJ, 1992, *Communication Skills in Hearing Impaired Children*, Whurr Publishers. | Expert opinion | — | — | — | IV |
| **Linguistic Competence** | | | | | |
| Mogford K, 1998, 'Oral language acquisition in the pre-linguistically deaf', in Bishop DVM & Mogford K (eds) *Language Development in Exceptional Circumstances*, Churchill Livingstone, Edinburgh. | Expert opinion | — | — | — | IV |
| **Modification of the Environment** | | | | | |
| Beazley S & Moore M, 1995, *Deaf Children, Their Families and Professionals: Dismantling Barriers*, David Fulton Publishers, London. | Expert opinion | — | — | — | IV |
| Berg FS, 1997, 'Optimum listening and learning environments', in McCracken W & Laiode-Kemp S (eds) *Audiology in Education*, Whurr Publishers, London. | Expert opinion | — | — | — | IV |
| Flexer C, 1999, *Facilitating Hearing and Listening in Young Children*, 2nd edn, Singular Publishing Group, San Diego. | Expert opinion | — | — | — | IV |

## DEAFNESS/HEARING LOSS

| Author(s) & Title | Design | Sample | Objective of study | Conclusions | Evidence Level |
|---|---|---|---|---|---|
| **Auditory training** | | | | | |
| Abberton E, Hazan V & Fourcin A, 1990, 'The development of contrastiveness in profoundly deaf children's speech', *Clinical Linguistics and Phonetics* 4 (3): 209–20. | Case series | 16 severely–profoundly deaf children | This paper presents some of the results from a study of certain perceptual and productive characteristics of the speech of a group of severely–profoundly deaf children over a period of four years. Under consideration is the development of two segmental phonemic contrasts – one for vowels and one for consonants. | In general the results show that there is a strong relationship between perception and production. There is some evidence to show that perceptual ability precedes production. | III |
| Plant G & Spens KE, 1995, *Profound Deafness and Speech Communication*, Whurr Publishers, London. | Expert opinion | — | — | — | IV |
| **Intelligibility: Phonology and Articulation** | | | | | |
| Gulian E, Fallside F, Hinds P & Keiller C, 1983, 'Acquisition of frication by severely hearing-impaired children', *British Journal of Audiology* 17 (4):219–31. | Controlled study | 9 hearing impaired children aged between 10 and 17 years old. Divided into 3 groups: ■ Experimental group ■ Control group 1 ■ Control group 2 | The ability of severely deaf school children to master fricative production and the fricative-affricate distinction was studied over a period of six months. The children were given daily speech therapy and half of them received, in addition, visual feedback from a microprocessor-based speech training aid – the 'Fricative and Timing Aid'. The speech of a third group of children, who received no training, was also monitored. | Results were analysed in terms of the acquisition of fricatives and affricates, and of their position in a word. Results yielded by perceptual tests showed a substantial increase in the intelligibility of all trained children for almost all phonemes at the end of the training programme. Retention scores, ie, intelligibility scores obtained by re-testing the children after a two-month period of non-practice, showed that practically no forgetting of articulatory skills occurred during this interval. Comparisons between children trained with or without visual feedback in general showed no difference between them; however, the former were more intelligible when producing affricates. No improvement in intelligibility was found when no systematic speech training was available. It was concluded that while frication may not be acquired spontaneously, it is a task within the reach of severely deaf children when adequately trained. | IIa |

| Author(s) & Title | Design | Sample | Objective of study | Conclusions | Evidence Level |
|---|---|---|---|---|---|
| Brentari DK & Wolk S, 1986, 'The relative effects of three expressive methods upon the speech intelligibility of profoundly deaf speakers', *Journal of Communication Disorders* 19 (3):209–18. | Experimental study | 5 profoundly deaf undergraduates who were receiving continuous speech training | Two experiments were conducted over a nine-month interval to evaluate the relative effects of three expressive methods (speech alone, speech and signs, and speech with cues) on speech intelligibility. Five profoundly deaf undergraduates who were receiving continuous speech training were recorded while reading lists of individual words under all three expressive modes. Listeners were required to identify through a multiple-choice format the target stimuli from auditory presentations only. | Results from Experiment I indicate that speech with cues produced the highest level of intelligibility, while speech and signs produced the lowest level. Findings from Experiment II, with an expanded set of word stimuli, reveal that speech alone produced a 65 percent rate of correct identification by listeners; speech and signs again produced the lowest rate of correct identifications. | IIb |
| Maassen B, 1986, 'Marking word boundaries to improve the intelligibility of the speech of the deaf', *Journal of Speech & Hearing Research* 29 (2):227–30. | Experimental study | 10 deaf children ranging in age from 10 to 12 years | Speech of deaf talkers has often been characterised as staccato, leading to the perception of improper grouping of syllables. In an attempt to compensate for this syllabication, word boundaries of 30 sentences spoken by 10 deaf children were acoustically marked by means of silent pauses with a duration of 160 ms inserted between words. | Subsequent tests with normal-hearing listeners demonstrated that after insertion of pauses the intelligibility of the sentences increased significantly from 27 percent to 31 percent. A control measure showed that this increase was not merely due to a general deceleration of speech rate. When all phonemes were lengthened until the same sentence duration was obtained as after insertion of pauses, a (non-significant) decrease in intelligibility resulted. The results are compared to earlier studies of speech of the deaf in which segmental and suprasegmental aspects were manipulated. | IIb |

## DEAFNESS/HEARING LOSS

| Author(s) & Title | Design | Sample | Objective of study | Conclusions | Evidence Level |
|---|---|---|---|---|---|
| Parker A & Rose H, 1990, 'Deaf children's phonological development', in Grunwell P (ed), *Developmental Speech Disorders*, Churchill Livingstone, Edinburgh. | Expert opinion | — | — | — | IV |
| **Speech-reading** | | | | | |
| Dodd B, McIntosh B & Woodhouse L, 1998, 'Early lip-reading ability and speech and language development of hearing-impaired pre-schoolers' in Campbell R, Dodd B & Burnham D (eds) *Hearing by Eye (II): The Psychology of Speechreading and Auditory-Visual Speech*, Psychology Press, Hove. | Expert opinion | — | — | — | IV |
| Erber NP, 1983, 'Speech perception and speech development in the hearing-impaired child', in Hochberg I, Levitt H & Osberger MJ (eds), *Speech of the Hearing-Impaired*, University Park Press, Baltimore. | Expert opinion | — | — | — | IV |
| **Classroom Management** | | | | | |
| Law J, Lindsay G, Peacey N, Gascoigne M, Soloff N, Radford J, Band S & Fitzgerald L, 2000, *Provision for Children with Speech and Language Needs In England and Wales Facilitating Communication Between Education and Health Services*, DfES Publications. Also http://www.dfes.gov.uk/research/ | Qualitative study | — | To report on existing provision across England and Wales and to help facilitate the process of collaboration between health and education services | — | III |

| Author(s) & Title | Design | Sample | Objective of study | Conclusions | Evidence Level |
|---|---|---|---|---|---|
| McCartney E (ed), 1999, *Speech and Language Therapists and Teachers Working Together: a Systems Approach to Collaboration*, Whurr Publishers, London. | Expert opinion | — | — | — | IV |
| Martin D & Miller C, 1999, *Language and the Curriculum. Practitioner Research in Planning Differentiation*, David Fulton Publishers, London. | Expert opinion | — | — | — | IV |
| Wright JA & Kersner M, 1998, *Supporting Children with Communication Problems: Sharing the Workload*, David Fulton Publishers, London. | Expert opinion | — | — | — | IV |

# DISORDERS OF FEEDING, EATING, DRINKING & SWALLOWING (DYSPHAGIA)

| Author(s) & Title | Design | Sample | Objective of study | Conclusions | Evidence Level |
|---|---|---|---|---|---|
| **Multidisciplinary Team Working** | | | | | |
| Bach DB, Pouget S, Belle K, Kilfoil M, Alfieri M, McAvoy J & Jackson G, 1989, 'An integrated team approach to the management of patients with oropharyngeal dysphagia', *Journal of Allied Health* 18 (5):459–68. | Case study | 65 year-old female post-CVA | Describes a team approach to the assessment and management of a patient with dysphagia. Discusses the value of a team approach for those with dysphagia. | The team's major focus was to determine the need for adjustments to the patient's diet to maintain or restore the safety of oral feeding. This involved the development of a detailed radiographic examination and a series of dysphagia diets, in addition to comprehensive evaluations by an occupational therapist, physiotherapist and Speech & Language Therapist. The effects of deteriorating swallowing ability on the physical, cognitive and emotional status of the patient are discussed in the context of a multidisciplinary approach. | III |
| Logemann JA, 1994, 'Multidisciplinary management of dysphagia', *Acta Oto-Rhinio-Laryngologica Belgica* 48 (2):235–38. | Expert opinion | — | Expert opinion on value and need for multidisciplinary team. | Multidisciplinary management of dysphagia ensures that the dysphagic patient receives careful, in-depth assessment and treatment/rehabilitation of their swallowing disorders, and of their underlying aetiology. | IV |
| Siktberg IL & Bantz DL, 1999, 'Management of children with swallowing disorders', *Journal of Paediatric Health Care* 13 (5):223–9. | Expert opinion | — | — | Increased knowledge about the normal swallowing process, children at risk for feeding and swallowing disorders, and associated symptoms, enhances early diagnosis and treatment. The child's general health history and physical evaluation, along with additional diagnostic tests, provide the basis for the formulation of an individualised feeding programme by an interdisciplinary team. | IV |

| Author(s) & Title | Design | Sample | Objective of study | Conclusions | Evidence Level |
|---|---|---|---|---|---|
| Goldsmith T, 2000, 'Evaluation and treatment of swallowing disorders following endotracheal intubation and tracheostomy', *International Anaesthesiology Clinics* 38 (3):219–42. | Expert opinion | — | Presents a comprehensive account of the evaluation and treatment of swallowing disorders following endotracheal intubation and tracheostomy. | A multidisciplinary approach that reaches beyond the physiology of swallowing alone to examine a variety of important patient characteristics can prevent life-threatening pneumonia and improve patient outcome. | IV |
| **Pre-clinical Evaluation** | | | | | |
| Arvedson JC & Brodsky l, 1992, *Paediatric swallowing and feeding: assessment and management*, Thomson Learning. | Expert opinion | — | — | — | IV |
| Groher ME (ed), 1997, *Dysphagia: Diagnosis and Management*, Butterworth Heinemann. | Expert opinion | | | | IV |
| **Clinical Evaluation 1** | | | | | |
| Castell DO & Donner MW, 1987, 'Evaluation of dysphagia: a careful history is crucial', *Dysphagia* 2 (2):65–71. | Clinical opinion | — | Expert opinion regarding clinical evaluation. | The need for a detailed and careful clinical evaluation is emphasised, detailing questions for consideration. | IV |
| Hendrix TR, 1993, 'Art and science of history-taking in the patient with difficulty swallowing', *Dysphagia* 8 (2):69–73. | Expert opinion | — | Review of history taking defined by stage of swallow. | History-taking is the first step in the evaluation of a patient. An analysis of the information obtained provides the basis for the choice and order of diagnostic tests. In addition, it provides the clinician with the necessary information to determine the relevance of 'abnormal tests' to the patient's problem. | IV |
| Ekberg O, 2000, 'Diagnostic aspects of dysphagia', *Acta Oto-Laryngologica Supplementum* 543:225–28. | Expert opinion | — | Review of need for clinical examination for dysphagia. | Clinical work-up must start with a careful evaluation of the symptomatology, which should then lead to appropriate investigations. A crucial point in the evaluation of these patients is the comparison between the patient's symptoms and the findings during the examination. | IV |

## DISORDERS OF FEEDING, EATING, DRINKING & SWALLOWING (DYSPHAGIA)

| Author(s) & Title | Design | Sample | Objective of study | Conclusions | Evidence Level |
|---|---|---|---|---|---|
| Davies P, 1994, *Starting Again: Rehabilitation following Traumatic Brain Injury*, Springer Verlag, Berlin. | Expert opinion | — | — | — | IV |
| **Clinical Evaluation 2** | | | | | |
| Kayser-Jones J & Schell E, 1997, 'Clinical outlook. The mealtime experience of a cognitively impaired elder: ineffective and effective strategies', *Journal of Gerontological Nursing* 23 (7):33–39. | Case study | 86 year-old woman with Alzheimer's disease | 100 residents of nursing homes were observed for 6 months or longer by graduate students in nursing and sociology. Each resident was observed weekly at all three meals, noting how, when and what food was served, what the resident ate, and a variety of interactions. This paper presents a case study of one woman and reports on effective and ineffective mealtime strategies. | Recommendations for positive strategies are suggested. | III |
| Hall GR, 1994, 'Chronic dementia. Challenges in feeding a patient', *Journal of Gerontological Nursing* 20 (4):21–30. | Expert opinion | — | Presents an overview of feeding behaviours at various phases in dementia. | Clinicians must determine food preferences and ability to eat, meet nutritional needs, and have a basic understanding of what techniques might assist professional and family caregivers with appropriate feeding techniques. | IV |
| Hotaling DL, 1990, 'Adapting the mealtime environment: setting the stage for eating', *Dysphagia* 5 (2):77–83. | Expert opinion | — | This paper discusses the subtle but strong influence that the environment has in preparing residents for eating. | Providing residents with a home-like, pleasant dining atmosphere should promote socialisation, enhance awareness, and increase appetites, thereby improving the residents' quality of life. | IV |

| Author(s) & Title | Design | Sample | Objective of study | Conclusions | Evidence Level |
|---|---|---|---|---|---|
| **Clinical Evaluation 4** | | | | | |
| Smith HA, Lee SH, O'Neill PA & Connolly MJ, 2000, 'The combination of bedside swallowing assessment and oxygen saturation monitoring of swallowing in acute stroke: a safe and humane screening tool', *Age Ageing* 29 (6):495–9. | Double-blind observational study | 53 patients with CVA aged 51 to 90 | The study examined the predictive values of pulse oximetry, and speech and language therapy bedside swallowing assessment in the detection of aspiration compared with videofluoroscopy. | 15/53 patients aspirated. Bedside swallowing assessment and saturation assessment gave good sensitivity (80 percent and 87 percent respectively) but low predictive values (50 percent and 36 percent respectively). They conclude that screening by saturation assessments detects 86 per cent of aspirators/penetrators, and should be followed immediately by bedside swallowing assessment, as the combination of the two assessments gives the best positive predictive value. | IIb |
| Sellars C, Dunnet C & Carter R, 1998, 'A preliminary comparison of videofluoroscopy of swallow and pulse oximetry in the identification of aspiration in dysphagic patients', *Dysphagia* 13 (2):82–86. | Comparative study | 6 patients with neurogenic dysphagia 5 normal controls | The present study was devised to examine whether pulse oximetry could be exploited to determine episodes of aspiration in patients with known dysphagia of neurologic origin. To this end, pulse oximetry was undertaken in six patients undergoing videofluoroscopic study of swallow. Normal controls also underwent pulse oximetry during feeding. | The results indicate that there is no clear-cut relationship between changes in arterial oxygenation and aspiration. However, some support is found for the association between altered arterial oxygenation and oral feeding in dysphagic individuals. Further research in both normal and compromised individuals is needed. | III |
| Colodny N, 2000, 'Comparison of dysphagics and non-dysphagics on pulse oximetry during oral feeding', *Dysphagia* 15 (2):68–73. | Comparative study | 181 adults 104 of whom were dysphagic: ages ranged from 62 to 102 77 non-dysphagic: ages ranged from 23 to 93 | Study was designed to determine whether significant differences in SpO$_2$ levels existed among elderly individuals with dysphagia and, more specifically, whether pulse oximetry can discriminate dysphagic from non-dysphagic individuals. | This study showed no dramatic changes in SpO$_2$ during or after swallowing or during episodes of aspiration. These data were consistent with previous findings that dysphagics have compromised pulmonary systems, but at variance with studies that indicated changes in pulse oximetry during aspiration. | III |

## DISORDERS OF FEEDING, EATING, DRINKING & SWALLOWING (DYSPHAGIA)

| Author(s) & Title | Design | Sample | Objective of study | Conclusions | Evidence Level |
|---|---|---|---|---|---|
| Zenner PM, Losinski DS & Mills RH, 1995, 'Using cervical auscultation in the clinical dysphagia examination in long-term care', *Dysphagia* 10 (1):27–31. | Comparative study | 50 adults with suspected oro-pharyngeal dysphagia ranging in age from 23–103 years old | Cervical auscultation with stethoscope was incorporated into the clinical examination for dysphagia in an attempt to enhance the clinical examination's ability to detect aspiration and to determine specialised diet management in long-term care. Each patient also had a videofluoroscopic assessment. | Comparison of the clinical examination's results with results from videofluoroscopy revealed significant agreement in both areas. Results support the use of cervical auscultation as a highly sensitive and specific method of dysphagia assessment in long-term care. | III |
| Cichero JA & Murdoch BE, 1998, 'The physiologic cause of swallowing sounds: answers from heart sounds and vocal tract acoustics', *Dysphagia* 13 (1):39–52. | Expert opinion | — | It is suggested that the pharynx contains a number of valves and pumps that produce reverberations within it to generate swallowing sounds. As heart sounds are propagated via vibration of muscles and valves, it is further suggested that an analogy exists between the generation of heart sounds and swallowing sounds. | The inability of the current literature to explain the cause of swallowing sounds is seen to limit the diagnostic potential of cervical auscultation for dysphagia assessment. | IV |
| **Clinical Evaluation 5** | | | | | |
| Leder SB & Karas DE, 2000, 'Fiberoptic endoscopic evaluation of swallowing in the pediatric population', *Laryngoscope* 110 (7):1132–6. | Randomised controlled trial | 30 in-patients, their ages ranging from 11 days to 20 years (mean, 10 years and 4 months) | In a random fashion, seven subjects were assessed with both VFES and FEES, and 23 subjects were assessed solely with FEES. Diagnosis of dysphagia was determined by spillage, residue, laryngeal penetration, and aspiration. Rehabilitative strategies, eg, positioning and modification of bolus consistencies, were based on diagnostic findings. | There was 100 percent agreement between the blinded diagnostic results for the 7 subjects randomly assigned to both VFES and FEES, and also for the 23 subjects randomly assigned to FEES. Feeding recommendations were also in 100 percent agreement. | Ib |

| Author(s) & Title | Design | Sample | Objective of study | Conclusions | Evidence Level |
|---|---|---|---|---|---|
| Logemann JA, Roa Pauloski B, Rademaker A, Cook B, Graner D, Milianti F, Beery Q, Stein D, Bowman J & Lazarus C, 1992, 'Impact of the diagnostic procedure on outcome measures of swallowing rehabilitation in head and neck cancer patients', *Dysphagia* 7 (4):179–86. | Controlled trial | 10 institutions participated in this study, enrolling a total of 103 partial laryngectomised patients; 21 in the bedside arm and 82 in the videofluoroscopy arm. | Designed to determine whether swallow rehabilitation outcomes were affected by the type of evaluation procedure utilised by the clinician. The two evaluation techniques compared were the bedside examination and videofluoroscopy. | Overall swallow measures of transit times and swallow efficiencies after three months revealed significantly better function in the videofluoroscopy group. | IIa |
| Splaingard ML, Hutchins B, Sulton LD & Chaudhuri G, 1988, 'Aspiration in rehabilitation patients: videofluoroscopy vs bedside clinical assessment', *Archives of Physical Medicine & Rehabilitation* 69:637–40. | Blinded comparative study | 107 inpatients from a general rehabilitation hospital<br>■ 87 CVA (adult)<br>■ 16 brain injury (adult)<br>■ 10 children<br>■ 4 chronic neuromuscular disease (adult) | Over a 44 month period, 107 patients were assessed for possible dysphagia. All patients had a clinical assessment of swallowing followed by a videofluorscopic exam within 72 hours. | Of the total population, 40 percent aspirated at least on food consistency during videofluoroscopy. During clinical examination, less than half (42 percent) of these aspirators had been identified. | IIb |
| Leder SB, Sasaki CT & Burrell MI, 1998, 'Fiberoptic endoscopic evaluation of dysphagia to identify silent aspiration', *Dysphagia* 13 (1):19–21 | Comparative study | 400 consecutive, at-risk subjects ranging in age from 10 to 101 years | This study investigated the aspiration status of 400 consecutive, at-risk subjects by fibre-optic endoscopic evaluation of swallowing (FEES). There were two subgroups and the first subgroup was evaluated by VFES and FEES (57 subjects) and the second subgroup by FEES only. | Study demonstrated that 175 of 400 (44 percent) subjects were without aspiration, 115 of 400 (29 percent) exhibited aspiration with a cough reflex, and 110 of 400 (28 percent) aspirated silently. No significant differences were observed for age or gender and aspiration status. | IIb |
| Langmore SE, Schatz K & Olson N, 1991, 'Endoscopic and videofluoroscopic evaluations of swallowing and aspiration', *Annals of Otology, Rhinology & Laryngology* 100 (8):678–81. | Comparative study | 21 subjects | Results of the fibre-optic endoscopic evaluation of swallowing (FEES) and videofluoroscopy examinations were compared for presence or absence of abnormal events. | Good agreement was found, especially for the finding of aspiration (90 percent agreement). It was concluded that the FEES is a valid and valuable tool for evaluating oropharyngeal dysphagia. | III |

## DISORDERS OF FEEDING, EATING, DRINKING & SWALLOWING (DYSPHAGIA)

| Author(s) & Title | Design | Sample | Objective of study | Conclusions | Evidence Level |
|---|---|---|---|---|---|
| Mann G, Hankey GJ & Cameron D, 1999, 'Swallowing function after stroke: Prognosis and prognostic factors at 6 months', *Stroke* 30 (4):744–8. | Case series | 128 hospital-referred patients with acute first stroke | To prospectively study the prognosis of swallowing function over the first six months after acute stroke,e and to identify the important independent clinical and videofluoroscopic prognostic factors at baseline that are associated with an increased risk of swallowing dysfunction and complications. | Swallowing function should be assessed in all acute stroke patients because swallowing dysfunction is common, it persists in many patients, and complications frequently arise. The assessment of swallowing function should be both clinical and videofluoroscopic. The clinical and videofluoroscopic features at presentation that are important predictors of subsequent swallowing abnormalities and complications are videofluoroscopic evidence of delayed oral transit; a delayed or absent swallow reflex; and penetration. | III |
| Mirrett PL, Riski JE, Glascott J & Johnson V, 1994, 'Videofluoroscopic assessment of dysphagia in children with severe spastic cerebral palsy', *Dysphagia* 9 (3):174–9. | Case series | 22 patients with the primary diagnosis of severe spastic cerebral palsy. The ages of the subjects ranged from 7 months to 19 years. | This paper describes the histories and analyses the videofluorographic swallow studies of 22 patients with the primary diagnosis of severe spastic cerebral palsy. | 15 patients (68.2 percent) demonstrated significant silent aspiration during their swallow study. The data suggest that early diagnostic work-up, including baseline and comparative videofluoroscopic swallow studies, could be helpful in managing the feeding difficulties in these children and preventing chronic aspiration, malnutrition and unpleasant, lengthy mealtimes. | III |
| **Clinical Evaluation 6** | | | | | |
| Perie S, Laccourreye L, Flahault A, Hazebroucq V, Chaussade S & St Guily JL, 1998, 'Role of videoendoscopy in assessment of pharyngeal function in oropharyngeal dysphagia: Comparison with videofluoroscopy and manometry', *Laryngoscope* 108 (11, pt1):1712–16. | Comparative study | 34 patients with oropharyngeal dysphagia | The purpose of the current report is to evaluate the ability of videoendoscopic swallowing study in assessing pharyngeal propulsion and aspiration episodes when compared with videofluoroscopy and manometry. | Total agreement between videoendoscopy and videofluoroscopy was found in 76.4 percent of cases for pharyngeal propulsion and in 82.3 percent for aspiration. | IIb |

| Author(s) & Title | Design | Sample | Objective of study | Conclusions | Evidence Level |
|---|---|---|---|---|---|
| **Clinical Evaluation 7** | | | | | |
| Peruzzi WT, Logemann JA, Currie D & Moen SG, 2001, 'Assessment of aspiration in patients with tracheostomies: comparison of the bedside coloured dye assessment with videofluoroscopic examination', *Respiratory Care* 46 (3):243–7. | Comparative study | 20 patients with tracheostomy | The purpose of this study was to determine the reliability of a bedside coloured-dye assessment of aspiration in tracheostomised patients and to determine its comparability to a more sophisticated videofluoroscopic study. The sample was twenty consecutive patients who underwent tracheostomy for bronchial hygiene needs and who were referred for videofluorographicevaluation for suspected oropharyngeal dysphagia and possible aspiration. A nurse, blinded to the results of videofluorographic swallow study, performed coloured-dye assessments for aspiration. Speech & Language Therapists, blinded to the results of the coloured-dye assessments, interpreted simultaneous (preliminary) and subsequent complete (final) videofluorographic evaluations of swallow. | The coloured-dye aspiration assessments and the videofluoroscopic studies were compared for the frequency of aspiration detection. Sensitivity and specificity were determined using standard methods. Seven patients showed no aspiration on either the coloured-dye test or videofluoroscopic examination. Eight patients were judged to aspirate by videofluorography but not by the coloured-dye test. Five patients were judged to aspirate by both the coloured-dye test and videofluorography. The data indicate that the coloured-dye test for aspiration carries a low sensitivity of 38 percent, but a high specificity of 100 percent. The videofluoroscopic study detected a significantly greater frequency of aspiration than did the coloured-dye test. It is concluded that the coloured-dye test for aspiration can provide useful information when positive, but because there is a significant false negative rate, decisions made on the basis of a negative test must be made with caution. | IIb |
| Dettelbach MA, Gross RD, Mahlmann J & Eibling DE, 1995, 'Effect of the Passy-Muir valve on aspiration in patients with tracheostomy', *Head Neck* 17 (4):297–302. | Case series | 11 alert patients with a tracheostomy and clinical evidence of aspiration were eligible for study | To assess the potential benefit of a Passy-Muir Speaking Valve (PMV) in decreasing aspiration in patients with a tracheostomy. | Aspiration was reduced (or eliminated) during swallowing in all 11 patients when they wore a PMV, when compared to swallowing with an open (unvalved) tube. This improvement was achieved with liquids, semisolids, and pureed consistencies. | III |

## DISORDERS OF FEEDING, EATING, DRINKING & SWALLOWING (DYSPHAGIA)

| Author(s) & Title | Design | Sample | Objective of study | Conclusions | Evidence Level |
|---|---|---|---|---|---|
| Elpern EH, Okonek M, Borkgren M, Bacon M, Gerstung C & Skrzynski M, 2000, 'Effect of the Passy-Muir tracheostomy speaking valve on pulmonary aspiration in adults', *Heart Lung* 29 (4):287–93. | Case series | 15 adults with tracheostomies scheduled for videofluoroscopic swallowing examinations who met inclusion criteria were enrolled | Instances of aspiration were determined in adults with tracheostomies and the effect of the Passy-Muir tracheostomy speaking valve (PMV) on occurrences of aspiration was investigated. | Seven of 15 subjects aspirated material on one or more presentations of thin liquid. Five subjects aspirated material only with the PMV off, whereas two subjects aspirated material with and without the valve. No subject aspirated material exclusively while the valve was on. Aspiration was significantly less frequent with the PMV on than with it off. | III |
| Logemann JA, Pauloski BR & Colangelo IA, 1988, 'Light digital occlusion of the tracheostomy tube: a pilot study of effects on aspiration and biomechanics of the swallow', *Head Neck* 20 (1): 52–57. | Comparative study | 8, treated, head & neck cancer patients, 6 of whom had undergone surgical treatment for oral or laryngeal cancer and 2 who had undergone high-dose chemotherapy and radiotherapy for laryngeal cancer | Eight, treated, head & neck cancer patients were studied, six of whom had undergone surgical treatment for oral or laryngeal cancer and two who had undergone high-dose chemotherapy and radiotherapy for laryngeal cancer. Videofluorographic studies of oropharyngeal swallowing were accomplished on 3-ml boluses of liquid in seven patients and 3-ml boluses of paste in three patients, first with the tracheostomy not occluded and then with it lightly digitally occluded by the patient. Videofluorographic studies of swallow were examined for observations of aspiration and residue. Biomechanical analysis of each liquid swallow was also completed. | Four of the seven patients aspirated on thin liquids with the tube unoccluded. Aspiration was eliminated with the tracheostomy digitally occluded in two of these four patients. One of the patients also aspirated on paste with the tube unoccluded, and the aspiration was eliminated with the tube occluded. A third patient who aspirated on thin liquid had no change when the tube was occluded, and one patient's swallow worsened with the tube occluded on liquid. There were significant changes in five measures of swallow biomechanics on liquids with the tube occluded: 1) duration of base of tongue contact to the posterior pharyngeal wall was reduced; 2) maximal laryngeal elevation increased; 3) laryngeal and 4) hyoid elevation at the time of initial cricopharyngeal opening increased; and 5) onset of anterior movement of the posterior pharyngeal wall relative to the onset of cricopharyngeal opening began later. | III |

| Author(s) & Title | Design | Sample | Objective of study | Conclusions | Evidence Level |
|---|---|---|---|---|---|
| Stachler RJ, Hamlet SL, Choi J & Fleming S, 1996, 'Scintigraphic quantification of aspiration reduction with the Passy-Muir valve', *Laryngoscope* 106 (2, pt 1):231–4. | Comparative study | 11 patients who had a tracheostomy in place and were either known to aspirate or were suspected of aspirating | In this study, scintigraphy was used to quantify the amount of material aspirated. Eleven patients were studied who currently had a tracheostomy in place and were either known to aspirate or were suspected of aspirating. Most were post-treatment head and neck cancer patients who were tumour free at the time of testing. Swallowing was evaluated using videofluoroscopy and scintigraphy. Videofluoroscopy was performed to assess anatomy and determine whether aspiration had occurred. Scintigraphic testing was then performed when the patient had the one-way valve on, and again with it off and tracheostomy open. | Following a swallow, the amount (percent) of aspirate with the valve in place was found to be significantly less than with the tracheostomy open. A one-way valve can be helpful in reducing aspiration in patients who are at risk for aspiration and who require that their tracheostomy be open. | III |
| Conlan A & Kopec S, 2000, 'Tracheostomy in the ICU', *Journal of Intensive Care Medicine* 15 (1). | Expert opinion | — | This article provides a comprehensive review regarding tracheostomies in the intensive care setting. Specifically reviewed are indications; timing; surgical options including percutaneous dilation tracheostomy; complications; decannulation; oral feeding; speaking devices; stomal stents; and routine tracheostomy care. | — | IV |

### Timing of Intervention

| | | | | | |
|---|---|---|---|---|---|
| Arvedson JC & Brodsky I, 1992, *Paediatric Swallowing and Feeding: Assessment and Mangement*, Thomson Learning, London. | Expert opinion | — | — | — | IV |

### Working Directly with the Individual – Individual's Readiness to Participate in Treatment

| | | | | | |
|---|---|---|---|---|---|
| Frazier JB & Friedman B, 1996, 'Swallow function in children with Down's Syndrome: A retrospective study', *Developmental Medicine & Child Neurology* 38 (8);695–703. | Case series | 19 children with Down syndrome | The swallow behaviour of 19 children with Down syndrome was reviewed. | Findings suggest their oral, phase may be impacted by oral hypersensitivity, which can interfere with their acceptance of textured foods. | III |

## DISORDERS OF FEEDING, EATING, DRINKING & SWALLOWING (DYSPHAGIA)

| Author(s) & Title | Design | Sample | Objective of study | Conclusions | Evidence Level |
|---|---|---|---|---|---|
| Brown GE, Nordloh S & Donowitz AJ, 1992, 'Systematic desensitisation of oral hypersensitivity in a patient with a closed head injury', *Dysphagia* 7 (3):138–141. | Case study | 36-year-old man who had sustained a closed head injury | The patient's fear increased his muscle tone and hypersensitivity in the facial and oral area, thereby preventing assessment of his dysphagia. | Systematic desensitisation is used to alleviate the patient's fear, thus allowing successful completion of a videofluoroscopic barium swallow examination. | IV |
| Anderson J, 1986, 'Sensory intervention with the pre-term infant in the neonatal intensive care unit', *American Journal of Occupational Therapy* 40 (1):19–26. | Expert opinion | — | Normal deviations in the healthy pre-term baby's development at the equivalent age of the full-term baby are identified as a basis for sensory intervention. Environmental factors affecting the pre-term infant's interactions and therapeutic needs, such as the NICU environment and medical intervention, are reviewed. | These approaches primarily focus on visual; tactile; proprioceptive; vestibular; and, to a lesser degree, auditory stimulation. | IV |
| Davies P, 1994, *Starting again: Rehabilitation Following Traumatic Brain Injury,* Springer Verlag, Berlin. | Expert opinion | — | — | — | IV |

### Preparation for oral intake

| Author(s) & Title | Design | Sample | Objective of study | Conclusions | Evidence Level |
|---|---|---|---|---|---|
| Pickler RH, Higgins KE & Crummette BD, 1993, 'The effect of non-nutritive sucking on bottle-feeding stress in pre-term infants', *Journal of Obstetric, Gynecologic & Neonatal Nursing* 22 (3):230–4. | Controlled study | 20 pre-term infants whose gestational ages at birth ranged from 26 to 34 weeks. Divided into two groups of 10 | To examine the effects of non-nutritive sucking on the physiologic and behavioural stress reactions of pre-term infants at early bottle-feedings and to examine the effect of non-nutritive sucking on the feeding performance of pre-term infants at early bottle-feedings. Ten infants were provided non-nutritive sucking for 5 minutes before and 5 minutes after an early bottle-feeding. Ten infants served as controls. | Infants who received non-nutritive sucking before and after bottle feedings were more likely to be in a quiescent behaviour state 5 minutes after the feeding and had higher feeding performance scores than infants who did not receive non-nutritive sucking. | IIa |

| Author(s) & Title | Design | Sample | Objective of study | Conclusions | Evidence Level |
|---|---|---|---|---|---|
| Gisel EG, Applegate-Ferrante T, Benson J & Bosma JF, 1996, 'Oral-motor skills following sensorimotor therapy in two groups of moderately dysphagic children with cerebral palsy: aspiration vs nonaspiration', *Dysphagia* 11 (1):59–71. | Controlled study | 27 children aged 2.5 to 10.0 years participated in this study (aspiration: n=7, non-aspiration: n=20). | To determine the effect of oral sensorimotor treatment on oral-motor skills and measures of growth in moderately eating-impaired children with cerebral palsy who were stratified by state of aspiration/non-aspiration. Children were observed at lunch time and six domains of feeding were examined: spoon feeding; biting; chewing; cup drinking; straw drinking; swallowing; and drooling. Children underwent 10 weeks of control and 10 weeks of sensorimotor treatment, 5–7 minutes per day, 5 days per week. | Children who aspirated had significantly poorer oral-motor skills in spoon feeding; biting; chewing; and swallowing than children who did not aspirate. There was significant improvement in eating: spoon feeding; chewing; and swallowing. There were no significant changes in drinking skills. | IIa |
| Avery-Smith W, 1997, 'Management of neurologic disorders: the first feeding session', in Groher ME (ed) *Dysphagia: Diagnosis and Management*, Butterworth Heinemann, Oxford. | Expert opinion | — | — | — | IV |
| Davies P, 1994, *Starting Again: Rehabilitation Following Traumatic Brain Injury*, Springer Verlag, Berlin. | Expert opinion | — | — | — | IV |
| Palmer MM & Heyman MB, 1993, 'Assessment and treatment of sensory- versus motor-based feeding problems in very young children', *Infants & Young Children* 6 (2):67–73. | Expert opinion | — | This article discussed the assessment and treatment of sensory-based oral feeding disorders. | — | IV |

## Presentation of Food and Drink (Bolus)

| Author(s) & Title | Design | Sample | Objective of study | Conclusions | Evidence Level |
|---|---|---|---|---|---|
| Khulemeier KV, Palmer JB & Rosenberg D, 2001, 'Effect of liquid bolus consistency and delivery method on aspiration and pharyngeal retention in dysphagic patients', *Dysphagia* 16:19–22. | Clinical trial | 190 patients with dysphagia | This study examines the rates of aspiration and pharyngeal retention in 190 dysphagic patients given thin and thick liquids delivered by teaspoon and cup, and ultra-thick liquid delivered by teaspoon. Each patient was tested with each of the bolus/delivery method combinations. | These results suggest that utilising thin, thick and ultra-thick liquids and delivery by cup and spoon during a VFES of a patient with mild or moderate dysphagia can increase the chances of identifying a consistency that the patient can swallow without aspirating and without pharyngeal retention after swallowing. | IIb |

## DISORDERS OF FEEDING, EATING, DRINKING & SWALLOWING (DYSPHAGIA)

| Author(s) & Title | Design | Sample | Objective of study | Conclusions | Evidence Level |
|---|---|---|---|---|---|
| Robbins JA, Sufit R, Rosenbek J, Levine R & Hyland J, 1987, 'A modification of the modified barium swallow', *Dysphagia* 2:83–86. | Case series | 64 patients with dysphagia 7 normal adults | The ability of 64 patients and 7 normal adult subjects to swallow 2 cc and 30 cc amounts of radiopaque liquid was tested. | Bolus size had no influence on the swallowing ability of the normal subjects. However, six of the patients aspirated on the 30 cc but not on the 5 cc, and three patients aspirated on the 5 cc but not on the 30 cc. | III |

### Type of Food or Liquid Given

| Author(s) & Title | Design | Sample | Objective of study | Conclusions | Evidence Level |
|---|---|---|---|---|---|
| Bisch EM, Logemann JA, Rademaker AW, Kahrilas PJ & Lazarus CL, 1994, 'Pharyngeal effects of bolus volume, viscosity, and temperature in patients with dysphagia resulting from neurologic impairment and in normal subjects', *Journal of Speech & Hearing Research* 37 (5): 1041–59. | Controlled study | 10 CVA patients 10 normal subjects 8 neurologically impaired subjects | The oropharyngeal swallow was studied videofluorographically to examine the effects of two bolus temperatures (room temperature and 33 °F); two volumes; and two viscosities on the durations of pharyngeal stage swallow events, and the frequency and nature of oropharyngeal swallowing problems and bolus transit. Results are discussed in terms of the potentially therapeutic effects of bolus volume and viscosity. | Normal subjects exhibited significantly longer pharyngeal response times and longer laryngeal elevation only for 1ml cold liquid. The stroke patients and the eight significantly dysphagic neurologically impaired patients exhibited very few significant effects of temperature on swallowing disorders or swallow measures. Increases in bolus volume and viscosity decreased pharyngeal delay times in both neurologically impaired patient groups. Stroke patients exhibited significantly longer pharyngeal delay times but shorter pharyngeal response times; laryngeal closure; crico-pharyngeal opening; and laryngeal elevation than normal subjects on some bolus volumes and viscosities. | IIa |
| Logemann JA, Pauloski BR, Colangelo L, Lazarus C, Fujui M & Kahrilas PJ, 1995, 'Effects of a sour bolus on oropharyngeal swallowing measures in patients with neurogenic dysphagia', *Journal of Speech & Hearing Research* 38 (3):556–63. | Comparative study | Group 1: 19 patients who had suffered at least one stroke. Group 2: 8 patients with dysphagia related to other neurogenic aetiologies. | This study examines the effects of a sour bolus (50 percent lemon juice, 50 percent barium liquid) on pharyngeal swallow measures in two groups of patients with neurogenic dysphagia. All patients were selected because they exhibited delays in the onset of the oral swallow and delays in triggering the pharyngeal swallow on boluses of 1 ml and 3 ml liquid barium during videofluoroscopy. | Results showed significant improvement in oral onset of the swallow in both groups of patients and a significant reduction in pharyngeal swallow delay in Group 1 patients, and in frequency of aspiration in Group 2 patients with the sour, as compared to the non-sour boluses. Other selected swallow measures in both subject groups also improved with the sour bolus. | IIb |

| Author(s) & Title | Design | Sample | Objective of study | Conclusions | Evidence Level |
|---|---|---|---|---|---|
| **Biofeedback** | | | | | |
| Huckabee ML & Cannito MP, 1999, 'Outcomes of swallowing rehabilitation in chronic brainstem dysphagia: a retrospective evaluation', *Dysphagia* 14 (2):93–109. | Case series | 10 patients with chronic dysphagia subsequent to a single brainstem injury | This study examines the functional and physiological outcomes of treatment in a group of 10 patients with chronic dysphagia subsequent to a single brainstem injury. All patients participated in a structured swallowing treatment programme at a metropolitan teaching hospital. This programme included surface electromyography biofeedback as a treatment modality and the completion of 10 hours of direct treatment in the first week of intervention. | Physiological change in swallowing treatment, as measured by severity ratings of videofluoroscopic swallowing studies, was demonstrated in 9 of 10 patients after one week or 10 sessions of treatment. Functional change was measured by diet level tolerance after one week of treatment, at six months, and again at one year post treatment. Eight of the ten patients were able to return to full oral intake with termination of gastrostomy tube feedings, whereas two demonstrated no long-term change in functional swallowing. | III |
| Bryant M, 1991, 'Biofeedback in the treatment of a selected dysphagic patient', *Dysphagia* 6 (3):140-4. | Case study | Single dysphagic subject | This report documents the application of biofeedback techniques to the treatment of swallowing dysfunction in a selected dysphagic patient. | — | III |
| Crary MA, 1995, 'A direct intervention program for chronic neurogenic dysphagia secondary to brainstem stroke', *Dysphagia* 10:6–18. | Case series | 6 patients with chronic dysphagia secondary to brainstem CVA – time post-onset ranging from 5 to 54 months and all on gastrostomy tube feeding | This study describes a direct therapy programme for chronic neurogenic dysphagia resulting from brainstem stroke. The aim was to increase the duration and strength of pharyngeal aspects of swallowing and to improve swallowing coordination using postural changes and SEMG. | Over a variable time period (3 weeks to 7 months) 5/6 patients were able to resume total oral feeding and have their gastrostomies removed. At follow up, 18–24 months later, all five continued with total oral nutrition. | III |

# DISORDERS OF FEEDING, EATING, DRINKING & SWALLOWING (DYSPHAGIA)

| Author(s) & Title | Design | Sample | Objective of study | Conclusions | Evidence Level |
|---|---|---|---|---|---|
| **Behavioural Strategies** | | | | | |
| Coyne ML & Hoskins L, 1997, 'Improving eating behaviours in dementia using behavioural strategies', *Clinical Nursing Research* 6 (3):275–90. | Randomised controlled trial | 24 subjects from a dementia unit were randomly selected and randomly assigned to three experimental groups and three | The purpose of this experimental pilot study was to determine the short- and long-term efficacy of directed verbal prompts and positive reinforcement on the level of eating independence (LEI) of elderly nursing home patients with dementia. | Short-term effects were assessed on two consecutive days following treatment (t2) and long-term effects on two consecutive days, seven days following treatment. Significant differences were found in eating performance but not in frequency. Experimental groups retained treatment at both post-tests. The dementia diagnosis should not preclude the control groups possibility that eating skills may be reacquired. | Ib |
| Rasnake LK & Linscheid TR, 1987, 'A behavioural approach to the treatment of pediatric feeding problems', *Journal of Paediatric & Perinatal Nutrition* 1 (2):75–82. | Case study | 2.5-year-old boy who ate only strained foods | This paper presents a rationale for using a behavioural approach to remediate feeding problems. Describes the basic elements and structure of a behavioural treatment programme. | — | III |
| Kayser-Jones J & Schell E, 1997, 'Clinical outlook. The mealtime experience of a cognitively impaired elder: ineffective and effective strategies', *Journal of Gerontological Nursing* 23 (7):33–39. | Case study | 86-year-old woman with Alzheimer's disease | 100 residents of nursing homes were observed for six months or longer by graduate students in nursing and sociology. Each resident was observed weekly at all three meals noting how, when and what food was served, what the resident ate and a variety of interactions. This paper presents a case study of one woman and reports on effective and ineffective mealtime strategies. | Recommendations for positive strategies are suggested. | III |
| Osborn CL & Marshall MJ, 1993, 'Self-feeding performance in nursing home residents', *Journal of Gerontological Nursing* 19 (3):7–14. | Qualitative study | 23 residents in a nursing home who were identified as partially dependent in feeding and had moderate to severe cognitive impairment | The study involved observations of the residents' self-feeding behaviours during two meals. Each resident was assessed individually at one meal for capability and at another meal for performance. Resident–staff interaction was also observed. Excess disability was found in the specific mealtime task of drinking liquids and among those eating a pureed diet. | Nursing home staff tended to rely on spoon feeding, a process in which the resident is a passive recipient of care rather than an active participant in it, as an intervention among residents who were partially able to feed themselves. Feeding techniques other than spoon feeding – including verbal and non-verbal prompts, and physical guiding – can support residents' participation in feeding even when independence is no longer possible. | III |

| Author(s) & Title | Design | Sample | Objective of study | Conclusions | Evidence Level |
|---|---|---|---|---|---|
| Babbitt RL, Hoch TA, Coe DA, Cataldo MF, Kelly KJ, Stackhouse C & Perman JA, 1994, 'Behavioural assessment and treatment of paediatric feeding disorders', *Journal of Developmental & Behavioral Paediatrics* 15 (4):278–91. | Expert opinion | — | The systematic use of Behaviour Analysis in conjunction with other approaches (medical, nutrition, occupational therapy, physical therapy, and so forth) is being carried out in an in-patient treatment unit at the Kennedy Krieger Institute. Key aspects are described here, including direct observation behaviour assessment; approaches for increasing and decreasing feeding behaviour; skill acquisition; transfer of treatment gains; and parent training. | The results based on case studies and overall programme evaluation indicate that medically complicated, severe feeding disorders can be treated successfully in a few months with a multidisciplinary approach which incorporates behavioural procedures. | IV |
| Morris SE, 1989, 'Development of oral-motor skills in the neurologically impaired child receiving non-oral feedings', *Dysphagia* 3 (3):135–54. | Expert opinion | — | Treatment of children with swallowing dysfunction requires a holistic approach based on a global view of their problems and needs. The connection of the swallowing mechanism with the sensorimotor organisation of postural tone and movement throughout the body is a critical factor in the evaluation and treatment of children whose dysphagia is rooted in a neurologic disorder. An appropriate programme includes work with the development of movement skills, sensory processing, learning, social skills and communication. | — | IV |

**Intra-oral Prosthetics**

| Author(s) & Title | Design | Sample | Objective of study | Conclusions | Evidence Level |
|---|---|---|---|---|---|
| Logemann JA, Kahrilas J, Hurst P, Davis J & Krugler C, 1989, 'Effects of intraoral prosthetics on swallowing in patients with oral cancer', *Dysphagia* 4 (2):118–20. | Comparative study | Four patients with oral cancer with intraoral palate reshaping/ lowering prostheses | The swallowing patterns of four patients with oral cancer with intra-oral palate reshaping/ lowering prostheses were studied with and without their prostheses three months postoperatively. | The prostheses resulted in improved swallow efficiency, increased duration of tongue contact to the pharyngeal wall, and improved speed of movement of the bolus from the valleculae to the pyriform sinus. These results emphasise the effects of the tongue on the pharyngeal, as well as oral, stage of the swallow. | III |

## DISORDERS OF FEEDING, EATING, DRINKING & SWALLOWING (DYSPHAGIA)

| Author(s) & Title | Design | Sample | Objective of study | Conclusions | Evidence Level |
|---|---|---|---|---|---|
| Wheeler RL, Logemann JA & Rosen MS, 1980, 'Maxillary reshaping prostheses: Effectiveness in improving speech and swallowing of post surgical oral cancer patients', *Journal of Prosthetic Dentistry* 43 (3):313–19. | Case series | 10 patients ranging in age from 46 to 74 years. All had been surgically treated for intraoral carcinoma. | The following questions were asked: ■ Will a custom designed maxillary prostheses with the palatal vault shaped to match the patient's range of tongue function increase the intelligibility of their speech? ■ Will the prostheses reduce the patient's oral and pharyngeal swallowing times, thus bringing them closer to normal? | Oral transit times decreased with all materials when they were wearing the prostheses. Thin paste transit appeared to be most positively affected. | III |

### Compensatory strategies

| Author(s) & Title | Design | Sample | Objective of study | Conclusions | Evidence Level |
|---|---|---|---|---|---|
| Logemann JA, Pauloski BR, Rademaker AW & Colangelo IA, 1997, 'Super-supraglottic swallow in irradiated head and neck cancer patients', *Head Neck* 19 (6):535–40. | Case series | 9 patients who suffered from dysphagia after radiation to the head and neck | Lateral videofluoroscopic studies examined oro-pharyngeal swallowing status. Each patient completed two swallows each of 1 ml or 3 ml liquid barium without a voluntary swallow manoeuvre and with the super-supraglottic swallow. | The super-supraglottic swallow resulted in changes in airway entrance closure and hyolaryngeal movement. Fewer swallowing disorders were observed with the manoeuvre. | III |
| Lazarus C, Logemann JA & Gibbons P, 1993, 'Effects of manoeuvres on swallowing function in a dysphagic oral cancer patient', *Head Neck* 15 (5):419–24. | Single subject | 47–year-old | This study examined the effects of three swallow manoeuvres: 1) the supraglottic swallow; 2) the super-supraglottic swallow; 3) the Mendelssohn manoeuvre; on swallow functioning in a 47-year-old patient with oral cancer. All manoeuvres were employed during the same videofluorographic swallow study conducted six months after the patient's surgery. | The Mendelssohn manoeuvre compensated for anatomic and physiologic changes in the oropharyngeal swallow, and enabled reinstatement of safe oral intake in this surgically treated head and neck cancer patient who was previously unable to take nutrition orally. | III |
| Larnert G & Ekberg O, 1995, 'Positioning improves the oral and pharyngeal swallowing function in children with cerebral palsy', *Acta Paediatr* 84 (6):689–92. | Case series | 5 children with feeding problem, aged 3 to10 years, with cerebral palsy | The aim of this study was to investigate if trunk and neck positioning influenced oral and pharyngeal swallow. All children were examined using videofluoroscopy and all had tetraplegia with dystonia. All children had gross aspiration and posterior oral leak. The pharyngeal phase was delayed in relation to the oral phase. | The aim of this study was to investigate if trunk and neck positioning influenced oral and pharyngeal swallow. Five children with feeding problems aged 3 to 10 years with cerebral palsy were examined using videofluoroscopy. All children had tetraplegia with dystonia, ie, poor head control and poor trunk stability. All children had gross aspiration and posterior oral leak. The pharyngeal phase was delayed in relation to the oral phase. | III |

| Author(s) & Title | Design | Sample | Objective of study | Conclusions | Evidence Level |
|---|---|---|---|---|---|
| Rasley A, Logemann JA, Kahrilas PJ, Rademaker AW, Pauloski BR & Dodds WJ, 1993, 'Prevention of barium aspiration during videofluoroscopic swallowing studies: Value of change in posture', *American Journal of Roentgenology* 160 (5):1005–9. | Comparative study | The study group comprised 165 patients consecutively referred for videofluoroscopic examination of the oropharyngeal stages of swallowing | This study investigated the frequency with which changes in the position of a patient's head or body eliminated aspiration of liquid barium during videofluoroscopic swallowing studies in patients with oropharyngeal dysphagia. It also studied factors that influenced the effect of posture on aspiration. | Changes in head or body position eliminated aspiration of at least one bolus of barium in 127 (77 percent) of the 165 patients, and of all four boluses plus drinking barium from a cup in 41 patients (25 percent). Postural changes were less beneficial in preventing aspiration in patients with substantial language or cognitive defects or restricted head movement. | III |
| Veis S, Logemann JA & Colangelo I, 2000, 'Effects of three techniques on maximum posterior movement of the tongue base', *Dysphagia* 15 (3): 142–5. | Comparative study | 20 subjects | Effects of three techniques designed to improve maximum range of posterior movement of the base of tongue were investigated under videofluoroscopy in 20 subjects. Retraction of the tongue base during 3 ml pudding swallows; tongue pull-back; yawn; and gargle tasks was measured in millimetres, with the second cervical vertebra as a reference point, and was also judged subjectively. | The gargle task was the most successful in eliciting most tongue base retraction for the group of subjects, although not in every subject. Gargle also resulted in greater tongue base movement than swallow more often than the other two voluntary tasks. | III |
| Shanahan TK, Logemann JA, Rademaker AW, Pauloski BR & Kahrilas PJ, 1993, 'Chin-down posture effect on aspiration in dysphagic patients', *Archives of Physical Medicine Rehabilitation* 74 (7):736–9. | Comparative study | 30 neurologically impaired patients | This study measured four pharyngeal dimensions in 30 neurologically impaired patients who aspirated before the swallow because of a delay in triggering the pharyngeal swallow. | For 15, the posture eliminated aspiration, and 15 also aspirated despite the chin-down position. Patients who did not benefit from the posture were significantly younger and aspirated material from the pyriform sinus rather than the valleculae when the pharyngeal swallow was triggered. | III |
| Logemann JA & Kahrilas JK, 1990, 'Re-learning to swallow after stroke: Application of manoeuvres and indirect biofeedback: a case study', *Neurology* 40 (7):1136–8. | Single case study | 45-year-old patient | A patient with medullary infarct recovered swallowing at 45 months after stroke by using a series of pharyngeal swallow manoeuvres, including head rotation, supraglottic swallow and the Mendelssohn manoeuvre. | Each manoeuvre effected quantifiable changes in specific elements of the pharyngeal swallow. At 50 months post-onset, full oral nutrition was resumed and gastrostomy feeding discontinued. | III |

## DISORDERS OF FEEDING, EATING, DRINKING & SWALLOWING (DYSPHAGIA)

| Author(s) & Title | Design | Sample | Objective of study | Conclusions | Evidence Level |
|---|---|---|---|---|---|
| Crary MA, 1995, 'A direct intervention program for chronic neurogenic dysphagia secondary to brainstem stroke', *Dysphagia* 10:6–18. | Case series | 6 patients with chronic dysphagia secondary to brainstem CVA, time post-onset ranging from 5 to 54 months, and all on gastrostomy tube feeding | This study describes a direct therapy programme for chronic neurogenic dysphagia resulting from brainstem stroke. Aim was to increase the duration and strength of pharyngeal aspects of swallowing and to improve swallowing coordination using postural changes and SEMG. | Over a variable time period (3 weeks to 7 months) 5/6 patients were able to resume total oral feeding and have their gastrostomies removed. At follow up, 18 to 24 months later, all five continued with total oral nutrition. | III |
| **Body Position During Swallowing** | | | | | |
| Davies P, 1994, *Starting Again: Rehabilitation Following Traumatic Brain Injury*, Springer Verlag, Berlin. | Expert opinion | — | — | — | IV |
| Morris SE, 1989, 'Development of oral-motor skills in the neurologically impaired child receiving non-oral feedings', *Dysphagia* 3 (3):135–54. | Expert opinion | — | Treatment of children with swallowing dysfunction requires a holistic approach based on a global view of their problems and needs. The connection of the swallowing mechanism with the sensorimotor organisation of postural tone, and movement throughout the body, is a critical factor in the evaluation and treatment of children whose dysphagia is rooted in a neurologic disorder. An appropriate programme includes work with the development of movement skills, sensory processing, learning, social skills and communication. | — | IV |
| Avery-Smith W, 1997, 'Management of neurologic disorders: the first feeding session', in Groher ME (ed) *Dysphagia Diagnosis & Management*, Butterworth Heinemann, Oxford. | Expert opinion | — | — | — | IV |

## Stimulation and Range of Movement Exercises

| Author(s) & Title | Design | Sample | Objective of study | Conclusions | Evidence Level |
|---|---|---|---|---|---|
| Rosenbek JC, Roecker EB, Wood JL & Robbins J, 1996, 'Thermal application reduces the duration of stage transition in dysphagia after stroke', *Dysphagia* 11 (4):225–33. | Experimental cross-over study | 22 dysphagia stroke patients | This study provided variability data on objectively measured durational parameters of swallowing as accomplished by dysphagic patients secondary to stroke. It also examined the short-term effects of thermal application on these same durational measures. The study employed a cross-over design, with each dysphagic stroke subject swallowing ten times in both untreated and treated conditions. | Two findings emerged: 1) swallowing durations in the 22 dysphagic stroke subjects were highly variable within and across subjects, and have distributions that were non-normal with non-homogeneous variances; 2) thermal application reduced duration of stage transition and total swallow duration. | IIb |
| Helfrich-Miller KR, Rector KL & Straka JA, 1986, 'Dysphagia: its treatment in the profoundly retarded patient with cerebral palsy', *Archives of Physical Medicine Rehabilitation* 67 (8):520–5. | Case series | 6 patients with cerebral palsy | Oral motor and swallowing patterns of six profoundly retarded cerebral-palsied patients were examined with videofluoroscopy. All subjects had delayed swallow reflexes and lingual dysfunction. Two subjects aspirated 10 percent or more of the bolus. Therapy consisted of dietary modifications; oral motor treatment; and thermal stimulation. | Results showed significant gains in pharyngeal transit times; amount of material aspirated; amount of residue in the valleculae and pyriform sinuses; and number of swallows required to clear the oropharynx. | III |
| Logemann JA, Pauloski BR, Rademaker AW & Colangelo IA, 1997, 'Speech and swallowing rehabilitation for head and neck cancer patients', *Oncology (huntingt)* 11 (5):651–6; 659. | Literature review | — | This paper reviews the literature on speech and swallowing problems in various types of treated head and neck cancer patients. | Pilot data support the use of range of motion (ROM) exercises for the jaw, tongue, lips and larynx in the first three months after oral or oropharyngeal ablative surgical procedures, as patients who perform ROM exercises on a regular basis exhibit significantly greater improvement in global measures of both speech and swallowing, as compared with patients who do not do these exercises. | IV |

## DISORDERS OF FEEDING, EATING, DRINKING & SWALLOWING (DYSPHAGIA)

| Author(s) & Title | Design | Sample | Objective of study | Conclusions | Evidence Level |
|---|---|---|---|---|---|
| **Modification of the Environment** | | | | | |
| Denney A, 1997, 'Quiet music. An intervention for mealtime agitation?', *Journal of Gerontological Nursing* 23 (7):16–23. | Controlled clinical trial | 10 adults suffering from Alzheimer's disease, ranging in age from 65 to 84 years. These adults also acted as their own control. | A time series with baseline incidence scoring, followed by introduction, withdrawal and restitution of treatment. The selected music was played at mealtimes every day during the specified period of the study. | The results indicate a reduction in the incidence of agitated behaviour when quiet music was played at lunchtime. | IIb |
| **Education and Training for Caregivers** | | | | | |
| Melin L & Gotestrom KG, 1981, 'The effects of rearranging ward routines on communication and eating behaviour of psychogeriatric patients', *Journal of Applied Behaviour Analysis* 14 (1):47–51. | Randomised controlled trial | 21 patients participated; 15 had senile dementia; 2 multiple infarct dementia; 2 presenile dementia; and 2 chronic schizophrenia. They were randomly assigned to either experimental or control group. | Several aspects of ward routine were changed to study the effects of environment manipulation on the behaviour of 21 psychogeriatric patients. Patients were divided into experimental and control groups, and data were collected on the frequency of verbal and tactile communication and degree of skills in eating behaviour. | Results show that the frequency of communication increased for the experimental group, as compared to the baseline and the control group. Eating behaviours also improved in the experimental group. | Ib |

| Author(s) & Title | Design | Sample | Objective of study | Conclusions | Evidence Level |
|---|---|---|---|---|---|
| Littlewood *et al*, 1997, 'Meal times: a missed opportunity?', *Journal of Dementia Care* July/Aug 18–20. | Qualitative study | 23 adults with dementia 21 staff | A questionnaire and an observation form were compiled to assess the following: ■ Patient's choices at mealtimes ■ Mealtime environment ■ Interactions between patients and with nursing staff ■ General mealtime atmosphere Data was collected by two observers over a five week period. | 15 out of 23 (65 percent) of patients participated in the questionnaire survey. 18/21 (85 percent) of staff completed the questionnaire. Changes have been made to the organisation of the ward subsequent to the study. | III |
| **Oral Stimulation** | | | | | |
| Morris SE, 1989, 'Development of oral-motor skills in the neurologically impaired child receiving non-oral feedings', *Dysphagia* 3 (3):135–54. | Expert opinion | — | Treatment of children with swallowing dysfunction requires a holistic approach based on a global view of their problems and needs. The connection of the swallowing mechanism with the sensorimotor organisation of postural tone and movement throughout the body is a critical factor in the evaluation and treatment of children whose dysphagia is rooted in a neurologic disorder. An appropriate programme includes work with the development of movement skills, sensory processing, learning, social skills and communication. | — | IV |
| **Long-term Review of Swallowing Ability** | | | | | |
| Wijdicks EF & McMahon MM, 1999, 'Percutaneous endoscopic gastrostomy after acute stroke: Complications and outcome', *Cerebrovascular Disease* 9 (2):109–11. | Qualitative study | Medical record review and follow-up of 74 patients with acute stroke admitted to a referral centre | To review the complications and outcome of percutaneous endoscopic gastrostomy placement (PEG) in 74 patients with acute stroke. | In 18 patients (28 percent), PEG could be subsequently removed due to improvement in swallowing. | IV |
| Harper JR, McMurdo ME & Robinson A, 2001, 'Rediscovering the joy of food: the need for long-term review of swallowing ability in stroke patients', *Scottish Medical Journal* 46 (2):54–55. | Expert opinion | Three cases of patients with dysphagia following stroke | — | Three cases of patients with dysphagia following stroke benefited from long-term review of swallowing ability. The benefits of such follow-up, and how it might best be achieved in the community are discussed. | IV |

## DISORDERS OF FLUENCY

| Author(s) & Title | Design | Sample | Objective of study | Conclusions | Evidence Level |
|---|---|---|---|---|---|
| **RECOMMENDATIONS FOR ALL DISORDERS OF FLUENCY** | | | | | |
| **Information gathering and assessment** | | | | | |
| Manning WH, 2000, *Clinical Decision Making in Fluency Disorders*, Singular Press, Baltimore. | Expert opinion | — | — | — | IV |
| Guitar B, 2000, *Stuttering: an Integrated Approach to Its Nature and Treatment*, Lippincott Williams and Wilkins, Baltimore. | Expert opinion | — | — | — | IV |
| **Management** | | | | | |
| Hayhow R, Cray AM & Enderby P, 2002, 'Stammering and therapy views of people who stammer', *Journal of Fluency Disorders*, 27 (1):1–16. | Questionnaire | 1058 questionnaires sent to members of the British Stammering Association; 180 sent to Speech & Language Therapists with an interest in adult stammering with a request to distribute to clients. | This study used a postal questionnaire to seek the views of adults who stammer concerning the effect of stammering on their lives, the speech and language therapy and other remedies they have tried, and their hopes for speech and language therapy in the future. | The 332 returned questionnaires indicated that stammering had the greatest adverse effect on school life and occupation. Speech and language therapy had been helpful to many, but the nature of the benefits and specific therapies used were not cited in many responses. An emergent theme in unhelpful therapy was the dissatisfaction that arises when individual needs are not met. In the future, people want help in controlling stammering and in developing coping strategies. The desire for timely and effective therapy for children, ongoing help and group or intensive work has implications for service organisation and therapist's skills. The survey highlights the need for therapists and clients to negotiate therapy aims and procedures that are clearly defined, appropriate to individual needs, achievable, and, if possible, recorded and measured. | III |

| Author(s) & Title | Design | Sample | Objective of study | Conclusions | Evidence Level |
|---|---|---|---|---|---|
| Mallard AR, 1998, 'Using problem-solving procedures in family management of stammering', *Journal of Fluency Disorders*, 23 (2):127–35. | Descriptive study | 28 families with 5 to 12-year-old children | Presents the results of a family-oriented therapy programme for elementary-age children who stammer. A two-week therapy programme, based on the work of Rustin (1987a, 1987b), was developed in which speech therapy, social skills, and transfer activities were integrated from a problem-solving perspective. | Results indicate that 82 percent of the children did not need further professional help for stammering for at least one year after therapy. Transfer and social skills activities were the most frequently used procedures by the family to manage stammering. The use of social skills training in speech therapy may provide the proper foundation for stammering children to become more efficient communicators. | III |
| Rustin L & Cook F, 1995, 'Parental Involvement in the Treatment of Stammering', *Language Speech and Hearing Services in School*, 26 (2):127–38. | Expert opinion | — | Three approaches to speech therapy for children who stammer are proposed, reflecting differences in the type and degree of parent involvement required for different age groups. The first approach considers parent-child interaction skills as a basis for facilitating development of fluency skills in young children. Intensive group therapy programmes are suggested for older age groups. | — | IV |

### DEVELOPMENTAL STAMMERING IN CHILDREN

### Assessment

| Author(s) & Title | Design | Sample | Objective of study | Conclusions | Evidence Level |
|---|---|---|---|---|---|
| Yairi E, Ambrose NG, Paden EP & Throneburg RN, 1996, 'Predictive factors of persistence and recovery: Pathways of childhood stammering', *Journal of Communication Disorders*, . 29 (1):51–77 | Controlled study | 100+ pre-school children who stammer 45 non-stammering children served as controls | This article presents broad preliminary findings from a longitudinal study of stammering pertaining to differentiation of developmental paths of childhood stammering, as well as possible early prediction of High Risk, Low Risk and No Risk for chronic stammering. More than 100 pre-school children who stammer have been followed closely for several years from near the onset of stammering using a multiple data collection system, with 45 non-stammering children serving as controls. | Thirty-two stammering and 32 control subjects who have progressed through several stages of the investigation were identified for the present in-depth analyses. They represent four subgroups: I Persistent Stammering; II Late Recovery; III Early Recovery; IV Control. Comparative data for the groups with special reference to differences in frequency of disfluency; acoustic features; phonological skills; language development, non-verbal skills; and genetics are presented. The results suggest several promising predictors of recovery and chronicity. | IIa |

## DISORDERS OF FLUENCY

| Author(s) & Title | Design | Sample | Objective of study | Conclusions | Evidence Level |
|---|---|---|---|---|---|
| Yairi E & Ambrose NG, 1999, 'Early childhood stuttering 1: Persistence and recovery rates', *Journal of Speech, Language and Hearing Research*, 42:1097–112. | Longitudinal study | 147 pre-school children | The purpose of this investigation is to study the pathognomonic course of stammering during its first several years in early childhood, with special reference to the occurrence of persistent and spontaneously recovered forms of the disorder. Employing longitudinal methodology with thorough, frequent periodic follow-up observations, multiple testing and recording of extensive speech samples, 147 pre-school children who stammer have been closely followed for several years from near the onset of stammering. | Findings regarding the current stammering status of 84 of these children, who have been followed for a minimum of four years after their onset of stammering, are presented. The data indicate continuous diminution in the frequency and severity of stammering over time as many children progressed toward recovery. Our findings lead to conservative estimates of 74 percent overall recovery and 26 percent persistency rates. The process of reaching complete recovery varied in length among the children and was distributed over a period of four years after onset. | III |
| Hill DG, 1995, 'Assessing the language of children who stammer', *Topics in Language Disorder*, 15:60–79. | Expert opinion | — | Research and clinical data regarding concomitant speech and language problems in children who stammer are reviewed, along with theoretical models explaining this interrelationship. A framework is presented for the differential evaluation of children who stammer, involving four areas of assessment: case history, fluency assessment, language skills assessment, and parent-child interaction. | — | IV |
| Christie E, 1999, The Primary Healthcare Workers Project – A four year investigation into changing referral patterns to ensure the early identification and referral of dysfluent preschoolers in the UK Primary Project Healthcare Workers *A Report by the British Stammering Association* | Qualitative | 225 NHS Community Trusts | The overall objective of the Primary Healthcare Workers Project was to change dysfluency referral patterns across the UK to ensure all young dysfluent children are identified and referred to Speech and Language Therapy as soon as possible after stammering onset. If achieved this would create greater opportunities for Speech & Language Therapists to deliver effective therapy at the optimum time period when it can be most cost- and time-effective and has long-term benefits for the child and his/her parents. | 123 NHS Community Trusts provided baseline data on UK-wide referral trends on over 3500 stammering children (aged 0 to 16 years). In the current study, 32 Trusts completed all three phases of the project within the timescale. This provided comparative referral information based on 2648 dysfluent children. | IV |

| Author(s) & Title | Design | Sample | Objective of study | Conclusions | Evidence Level |
|---|---|---|---|---|---|
| **Demands and Capacities Model** | | | | | |
| Matthews S, Williams R & Pring T, 1997, 'Parent-child interaction therapy and dysfluency: A single-case study', *European Journal of Disorders of Communication*. 32:346–57. | Single case study | Four-year-old boy | The hypothesis that the modification of parent-child interaction would reduce the dysfluency of a pre-school child was tested in an experimental single-case study. The subject, a four-year-old boy with a moderate to severe stutter, and his parents, attended their local clinic for a total of 17 weeks. On each visit, 20-minute play periods with each parent were recorded and measures of fluency taken. No advice was offered in the first six weeks and these measures were used as a baseline for subsequent therapy. Therapy was given over the next six weeks. The parents were advised to make changes in their style of interaction and were asked to practise these at home each day. During the final five weeks, which served as consolidation, the parents continued to practise their skills at home but no new advice was offered. | The analysis found no significant trend in the child's dysfluency during the baseline period, with a significant improvement during therapy and stabilisation of the lower rate of dysfluencies during the maintenance period. | III |
| Guitar B, Schaefer HK, Donahue-Kilburg G & Bond L, 1992, 'Parent Verbal Interactions and Speech Rate: A Case Study in Stammering', *Journal of Speech & Hearing Research*, 35 (4):742–54. | Case study | Five-year-old girl | This single-case study of indirect stammering treatment is intended to identify variables for further research. The study used post-hoc analyses of changes in parent speech variables and changes in the child's stammering. The analysis was conducted in two parts. Study I examined the relationships between the child's percentage syllables stammered and the parents' speech rates and percentages of non-accepting statements, interruptions, questions, non-accepting questions, and talk time. The only parent variable significantly correlated with the child's stammering was the mother's speech rate. In Study II the child's percentage syllables stammered were subdivided into primary (effortless) and secondary (tense) stammering. Each category was then correlated with the parent variables examined previously. | Results suggested that the parent variables that were significantly related to the child's primary stammering were not the same as those significantly related to her secondary stammering. Specific parent variables are suggested for further study. | III |

## DISORDERS OF FLUENCY

| Author(s) & Title | Design | Sample | Objective of study | Conclusions | Evidence Level |
|---|---|---|---|---|---|
| Weiss AL & Zebrowski PM, 1992, 'Disfluencies in the conversations of young children who stammer: some answers about questions', *Journal of Speech and Hearing Research*, 35 (6): 1230–38. | Case series | Eight parent–child pairs | This study assessed parent-child conversational speech for eight parent-child pairs to determine the relative amounts of disfluency in the child's responses to questions versus making assertions. Length and complexity of the children's utterances and the frequency of the parents' requests by level of demand were also evaluated. | Results suggested that the responses made by the children to their parents' requests were significantly less likely to contain disfluencies than were their assertions. Also, longer and more complex utterances were more likely to contain disfluencies, regardless of their designation as assertions or responses. Parents were shown to favour request types of lower levels of demand in conversations. Requests posed with greater levels of demand were somewhat more likely to yield dysfluent responses than were those at a lower demand level. | III |
| Gottwald SR, 1999, 'Family Communication Patterns and Stammering Development: An Analysis of the Research Literature in Stammering Research and Practice', in Ratner NB & Healey EC (eds), *Bridging the Gap*, Lawrence Erlbaum Associates, Mahawh, NJ. | Expert opinion | — | — | — | IV |
| Yairi E, 1997, 'Home environment and parent–child interaction in Childhood Stammering', in Curlee R & Siegel G (eds), *Nature and Treatment of Stammering: New Directions*, Allyn & Bacon, Needham Heights, MA. | Expert opinion | — | — | — | IV |

### Child (fluency) focused therapy

| Author(s) & Title | Design | Sample | Objective of study | Conclusions | Evidence Level |
|---|---|---|---|---|---|
| Harris V, Onslow M, Packman A, Harrison E & Menzies R, 2002, 'An experimental investigation of the impact of the Lidcombe Program on early stammering', *Journal of Fluency Disorders*, 27 (3):203–13. | Randomised controlled study | 23 pre-school children | Participants in this study were 23 pre-school children who were randomly assigned to either a control group or a treatment group that received the Lidcombe Program for 12 weeks. It addresses short-term treatment effects. | A repeated measures ANOVA showed no main effect on stammering for the group (control/treatment), a significant main effect for the measurement occasion (at the start and at the end of the treatment period), and a significant interaction between group and measurement occasion. Stammering in the treatment group reduced twice as much as in the control group. These results are interpreted to mean that the introduction of the Lidcombe Program has a positive impact on stammering rate, which exceeds that attributable to natural recovery. | Ib |
| Onslow M, Andrews C & Lincoln M, 1994, 'A Control/Experimental Trial of an Operant Treatment for Early Stammering', *Journal of Speech & Hearing Research*, 37 (6):1244–59. | Controlled study | | This study was designed to expand preliminary findings which suggested that a parent-conducted programme of verbal response-contingent stimulation would be an effective treatment for stammering children younger than five years. This study used a larger group of children than the aforementioned study (preliminary findings) and compared them to a control group of children. | Twelve children in the experimental group achieved median percentage syllables stammered (%SS) scores below 1.0 for a 12-month post-treatment period. The children's treatments were completed in a median of 10.5 one-hour clinic sessions and a median of 84.5 days from the start of treatment. The majority of parents of the control children withdrew from the study and elected to have treatment begin for their child. These results suggest that the programme may be a cost-effective method for managing a clinical caseload of stammering children younger than five years. | IIa |

## DISORDERS OF FLUENCY

| Author(s) & Title | Design | Sample | Objective of study | Conclusions | Evidence Level |
|---|---|---|---|---|---|
| Kingston M, Huber A, Onslow M, Jones M & Packman A, 2003, 'Predicting treatment time with the Lidcombe Program: replication and meta-analysis', *International Journal of Language and Communication Disorder*, 38 (2):165–77. | Controlled study | 66 children who began treatment before six years old | The study included 66 children who began treatment before six years of age. They were treated with the Lidcombe Program at a specialist stammering clinic. Logistic regression analyses were conducted on the data. The present study, conducted independently in the UK, was designed to replicate the Australian study. (Jones M, Onslow M, Harrison E & Pachman A, 2000, 'Treating stuttering in young children: Predicting treatment time in the Lidcombe Program', *Journal of Speech, Language & Hearing Research*, 43, 1440–50.) Direct replication enabled pooling of the data from the two studies in a meta-analysis. The data from both the British and Australian cohorts were pooled in a meta-analysis. | Results indicated that Stage 1 of the Lidcombe Program was completed in a median of 11 clinic visits, which is in line with the findings of the Australian study. Stammering rate at first clinic visit was again found to be a significant predictor of treatment time. The remaining data trends were similar to those in the Australian data. In the meta-analysis, stammering rate was once more found to be a predictor of treatment time. Of particular interest, however, was that the increased power provided by the meta-analysis identified an additional predictor, namely onset-to-treatment interval. Contrary to what is known about the responsiveness of children to the Starkweather and Gottwald treatment, and contrary to what might be expected given what we know about natural recovery, children who had been stammering for more than 12 months took less time to progress through the programme than children who had been stammering for less than 12 months. These findings indicate that delaying intervention with the Lidcombe Program for one year after onset, within the pre-school years, is unlikely to jeopardise responsiveness to treatment. | IIa |
| Ryan BP & Van Kirk Ryan B, 1995, 'Programmed stammering treatment for children: comparison of two establishment programs through transfer, maintenance, and follow-up', *Journal of Speech & Hearing Research*, 38 (1):61–75. | Comparative study | 24 students | Two different establishment programmes were compared: Delayed Auditory Feedback (DAF) and Gradual Increase in Length and Complexity of Utterance (GILCU), for improving the fluency of school-age children who stammer. The programmes were carried out by 12 clinicians under supervision, with 24 clients (12 elementary and 12 junior/senior high school) in the schools. | Both programmes produced important improvement in fluency in a reasonable time period and resulted in similar levels of transfer and maintenance. | III |

| Author(s) & Title | Design | Sample | Objective of study | Conclusions | Evidence Level |
|---|---|---|---|---|---|
| Onslow M, Costa L, Andrews C, Harrison E & Packman A, 1996, 'Speech outcomes of a prolonged-speech treatment for stammering', *Journal of Speech & Hearing Research*, 39 (4):734–49. | Case series | 12 adults | This study used extensive speech outcome measures across a variety of situations in evaluating the outcome of an intensive prolonged speech treatment. The speech of 12 clients in this treatment was assessed on three occasions prior to treatment and frequently on eight occasions after discharge from the residential setting. For seven clients, a further assessment occurred at three years post-treatment. Concurrent dependent measures were percentage syllables stammered, syllables per minute, and speech naturalness. The dependent measures were collected in many speaking situations within and beyond the clinic. Dependent measures were based on speech samples of substantive duration, and covert assessments were included in the study. | Detailed data were presented for individual subjects. Results showed that 12 subjects who remained with the entire two- to three-year program achieved zero or near-zero stammering. The majority of subjects did not show a regression trend in percentage syllables stammered or speech naturalness scores during the post-treatment period, either within or beyond the clinic. Some subjects showed higher post-treatment percentage syllables stammered scores during covert assessment than during overt assessment. Results also showed that stammering was eliminated without using unusually slow and unnatural speech patterns. This treatment programme does not specify a target speech rate range, and many clients maintained stammer-free speech using speech rates that were higher than the range typically specified in intensive prolonged speech programmes. A significant correlation was found between speech rate and perceived post-treatment speech naturalness. | III |

# DISORDERS OF FLUENCY

## Integrated Approaches

| Author(s) & Title | Design | Sample | Objective of study | Conclusions | Evidence Level |
|---|---|---|---|---|---|
| Yaruss JS & Reardon N, 2003, 'Fostering Generalization and Maintenance in School Settings', *Seminars in Speech and Language*, 24(1):33–40, C1–9. | Expert opinion | – | This article reviews common roadblocks to generalisation and maintenance, including the goals of therapy; the nature of the treatment strategies that require generalisation; the scheduling and implementation of generalisation activities within the overall therapy process; and the child's understanding of the treatment goals. Specific strategies for overcoming these roadblocks include: desensitising children to both stammering and treatment strategies designed to improve fluency; using hierarchies as a way of structuring treatment and moving children toward success in their daily activities; integrating the child's real world and clinical settings; and using structured practice activities to help children solidify all of the lessons they learn in treatment. | This article highlights the importance of taking a broad-based view of stammering to help children improve their overall communication across a variety of settings and over time. | IV |

## Coexisting Speech & Language Problems

| Author(s) & Title | Design | Sample | Objective of study | Conclusions | Evidence Level |
|---|---|---|---|---|---|
| Wolk L, Edwards ML & Conture EG, 1993, 'Coexistence of stammering and disordered phonology in young children', *Journal of Speech & Hearing Research*, 36 (5):906–17. | Comparative | Subjects were 21 boys representing three groups of seven children each: (a) stammering and normal phonological abilities; (b) stammering and disordered phonology; productions. (c) normal fluency and disordered phonology. | The purpose of the study was to assess differences in stammering, phonological and diadochokinetic behaviours in young children who exhibit both stammering and disordered phonology and children who exhibit only one of the disorders. Stammering behaviour was assessed during a 30-minute conversational speech task; phonological behaviour was assessed during a 162 item picture-naming task; and diadochokinetic abilities were assessed during bi- and multisyllable | Results indicated that the stammering and disordered phonology group produced significantly more sound prolongations and significantly fewer iterations per whole-word repetition than the stammering and normal phonological abilities group. However, there were no differences between the two groups in other stammering indices. Moreover, no differences were noted between the stammering and disordered phonology and normal fluency and disordered phonology groups in phonological behaviour. Diadochokinetic rates did not differ among the three groups. The possibility of two types of stammering, one occurring with and one without disordered phonology, is discussed. | III |

| Author(s) & Title | Design | Sample | Objective of study | Conclusions | Evidence Level |
|---|---|---|---|---|---|
| Ratner NB & Silverman SU, 2000, 'Parental perceptions of children's communicative development at stammering onset', *Journal of Speech Language & Hearing Research*, 43(5):1252–63. | Comparative study | 15 children, aged 2.3–3.9 years, close to the onset of stammering symptoms<br><br>15 matched fluent children | The authors appraised the language abilities of 15 children close to the onset of stammering symptoms and 15 matched fluent children using an array of standardised tests and spontaneous language sample measures. Parents concurrently completed two parent-report measures of the children's communicative development. | Results indicated generally depressed performance on all child speech and language measures by the children who stammer. Parent report was closely attuned to child performance for the stammering children; parents of non-stammering children were less accurate in their predictions of children's communicative performance. Implications for clinical advisement to parents of stammering children are discussed. | III |
| Logan K & LaSalle L, 2003, 'Developing Intervention Programs for Children with Stammering and Concomitant Impairments', *Seminars in Speech and Language*, 24(1):13–9, C1–9. | Expert opinion | — | School-aged children who stammer often present concomitant impairments in articulation and language that can complicate treatment. In this article, a framework is offered for designing intervention programmes for such children. It is stressed that clinicians must first identify clinical priorities by determining the severity of the impairments; their impact on daily activities; others' reactions to the impairments; and the likelihood of unassisted recovery. | Several potential treatment models are presented, as are general treatment principles and specific treatment strategies for three profiles of children who stammer. Suggestions are also provided for including parents and teachers in the intervention plan. | IV |
| Wolk L, 1998, 'Intervention strategies for children who exhibit coexisting phonological and fluency disorders: A clinical note', *Child Language Teaching and Therapy*, 14(1):69–82. | Expert opinion | — | The purpose of this paper is to present suggestions for intervention strategies found to be useful for children exhibiting coexisting stammering and phonological disorders. Six guiding principles form the basis for clinical management: (1) the use of an indirect phonological approach; (2) employing a phonological process approach; (3) the use of direct fluency modification techniques; (4) the concurrent application of phonological and fluency principles; (5) parental involvement; and (6) the use of a group setting. Specific guidelines for selection of target processes and target sounds are discussed together with fluency modification techniques. | — | IV |

# DISORDERS OF FLUENCY

| Author(s) & Title | Design | Sample | Objective of study | Conclusions | Evidence Level |
|---|---|---|---|---|---|
| Nippold M, 1990, 'Concomitant speech and language disorders in stammering children: A critique of the literature', *Journal of Speech and Hearing Disorders*, 55:51–60. | Literature review | — | This article presents a critical review of the literature concerning concomitant speech and language disorders in stammering children. Studies published since the 1920s that examine language onset and disorders of articulation, syntax and morphology, semantics and word finding are analyzed. Collectively, the studies present a mixed impression of stammerers, not only because of methodological variations, but also because of the tremendous variability that exists among children who stammer. Although the evidence is not convincing that stammerers as a group are more likely than non-stammerers to have deficits in any of these areas, it is clear that some stammerers do have concomitant speech and language problems that may bear some relationship to their stammering. The message from this body of research is that individual differences among stammering children should not be ignored during clinical or research activities. | — | IV |

## THE YOUNG PERSON WHO STAMMERS

### Therapy

| | | | | | |
|---|---|---|---|---|---|
| Hancock K, Craig A, McCready C, McCaul A, Costello D, Campbell K & Gilmore G, 1998, 'Two-to six-year controlled-trial stammering outcomes for children and adolescents', *Journal of Speech Language & Hearing Research*, 41 (6):1242–52. | Controlled study | 62 children and adolescents | This research is a long-term follow-up of a previously published, controlled trial on the effectiveness of three stammering treatments (intensive smooth speech; parent-home smooth speech; and intensive electromyography feedback) for children and adolescents, aged 11 to 18 years, who stammer. The previous controlled trial showed all three treatments to be effective compared to no treatment after 12 months. This paper reports on the treatment effectiveness after an average of four years post-treatment. | Results demonstrate that treatment gains were maintained in the long term, with rates of stammering similar to the one-year post outcomes. There were no significant differences among the three treatments in long-term effectiveness. This controlled study substantiates the claim that the treatments investigated will more than likely have substantial long-term benefits for the fluency and personality of children and adolescents who stammer. | IIa |

| Author(s) & Title | Design | Sample | Objective of study | Conclusions | Evidence Level |
|---|---|---|---|---|---|
| Craig A, Hancock K, Chang E, McCready C, Shepley A, McCaul A, Costello D, Harding S, Kehren R, Masel C & Reilly K, 1996, 'A controlled clinical trial for stammering in persons aged 9 to 14 years', *Journal of Speech Hearing Research*, 39 (4):808–26. | Controlled study | — | This paper presents the results of a controlled trial of child stammering treatment. The aim of the study was, first, to compare the effectiveness of three viable treatments, and second, to compare these three treatments to a no-treatment control composed of children who stammered of a similar age and sex ratio, who were on treatment waiting lists. The three treatments investigated were intensive smooth speech; intensive electromyography feedback; and home-based smooth speech. The children/ adolescents were assessed across three speaking contexts on measures of percentage syllables stammered and syllables spoken per minute, and outcomes were assessed 12 months later. | Repeated measures analyses of variance demonstrated significant differences between the control group and all three treatment groups across time on conversations in the clinic, on the telephone, and at home (although home measures were not taken for the intensive smooth speech group). Although the controls' stammering did not change across time, the treatment groups' stammering was decreased to very low levels post treatment (less than one percentage syllables stammered on average), with mean improvement in stammering frequency of at least 85 percent to 90 percent across all assessment contexts. Stammering did not increase significantly up to three months and one year post-treatment in the experimental groups, although levels did rise across time (less than 3 percentage syllables stammered on average). Speech naturalness results showed increasing naturalness across time as rated by the clinician and parent. This was not the case for the controls. The children were also less anxious across time following treatment. The results suggest that all three treatments for children aged 9–14 who stammer were very successful in the long term for over 70 percent of the group, though the EMG feedback and home-based treatments were superior when percentages falling below a cut-off point were used to discriminate between groups. | IIa |

## DISORDERS OF FLUENCY

| Author(s) & Title | Design | Sample | Objective of study | Conclusions | Evidence Level |
|---|---|---|---|---|---|
| Blood G, Blood I, Tellis G & Gabel R, 2001, 'Communication apprehension and self perceived communication competence in adolescents who stammer', *Journal of Fluency Disorders*, 26 (3):161–78. | Controlled study | 39 adolescents who stammer and 39 adolescents who do not stammer | The purpose of this study was to examine the communication apprehension and self-perceived communication competence of 39 adolescents who stammer and 39 adolescents who do not stammer using two standardised communication measures. | Significantly higher levels of communication apprehension and poorer scores on self-perceived communication competence were found in adolescents who stammer when compared with adolescents who do not stammer. | IIa |
| Boberg E & Kully D, 1994, 'Long-Term Results of an Intensive Treatment Program for Adults and Adolescents Who Stammer', *Journal of Speech & Hearing Research*, 37 (5):1050–59. | Longitudinal | 17 adult and 25 adolescent stammerers | This study tested 17 adult and 25 adolescent stammerers during a 12- to 24-month post-intensive treatment phase. | It revealed that 69 percent of subjects maintained satisfactory fluency on surprise phone calls at home/work and 80 percent of subjects rated their speech fluency as good or fair on the Speech Performance Questionnaire | III |
| Cooper EB & Cooper CS, 1995, 'Treating fluency disordered adolescents', *Journal of Communication Disorders*, 28 (2):125–42. | Expert opinion | — | This paper presents fluency disorders in three types of stammering syndromes with etiological considerations. The syndromes consist of affective, behavioural and cognitive components useful for fluency assessment and establishment of therapy goals with adolescents who stammer. The ultimate goal of the treatment programme is a feeling of fluency control rather than actual fluency. A therapy process for fluency disordered adolescents is suggested which outlines four stages with goals and objectives for each stage. Behaviour techniques for eliciting a feeling of fluency control are also included. Finally, a case history illustrates the therapy process for an adolescent with a fluency disorder. | — | IV |
| Rustin L, Spence R & Cook F, 1995, *Management of Stammering in Adolescence: A Communication Skills Approach*, Whurr, London. | Expert opinion | — | — | - | IV |

| Author(s) & Title | Design | Sample | Objective of study | Conclusions | Evidence Level |
|---|---|---|---|---|---|
| Kully D & Langevin M, 1999, 'Intensive Treatment for Stammering Adolescents', in Curlee R (ed), *Stammering and Related Disorders of Fluency*, 2nd edn, Thieme Medical Publishers, New York. | Expert opinion | — | — | — | IV |
| Botterill W & Cook F, 1987, 'Personal Construct Theory and the Treatment of Adolescent Dysfluency', in Rustin L, Purser H & Rowley D (eds) *Progress in the Treatment of Fluency Disorders*, Taylor & Francis, London. | Expert opinion | — | — | — | IV |

## DEVELOPMENTAL STAMMERING IN ADULTS

### Assessment

| Author(s) & Title | Design | Sample | Objective of study | Conclusions | Evidence Level |
|---|---|---|---|---|---|
| Wright L & Ayre A, 2000, *WASSP: Wright & Ayre Stammering Self-Rating Profile*, Speechmark, Bicester. | Expert opinion | — | — | — | IV |
| Manning W, 1999, 'Management of Adult Stammering' in Curlee R (ed), *Stammering and Related Disorders of Fluency*, 2nd edn, Thieme Medical Publishers, New York. | Expert opinion | — | — | — | IV |
| Turnbull J, 2000, 'The transtheoretical model of change: examples from stammering', *Counselling Psychology Quarterly*, 31 (1):13–21. | Expert opinion | — | — | Procaska and DiClemente's model of intentional change was initially associated with the field of addiction but has been more recently used in the treatment of a broad range of difficulties. Examples in this article come mainly from therapy with adults who stammer. The model explores how people initiate and maintain change and is based on empirical evidence. It comprises three dimensions. Ten processes describe the 'how' of change. Five levels outline the 'what' of change, arranged hierarchically from symptom/situational to intrapersonal conflicts level. The five stages of change, the 'when' of change, are described here in some detail, together with ideas for the most suitable therapeutic approaches to be used at each. | IV |

## DISORDERS OF FLUENCY

| Author(s) & Title | Design | Sample | Objective of study | Conclusions | Evidence Level |
|---|---|---|---|---|---|
| **Management** | | | | | |
| Evesham M & Fransella F, 1985, 'Stammering relapse: the effect of a combined speech and psychological reconstruction programme', *British Journal of Disorders of Communication*, 20 (3):237–48. | Randomised controlled trial | 47 adult stammerers | This study tested the hypothesis that stammerers who achieved fluent speech during two weeks of intensive treatment would be less likely to relapse if they were also helped to reconstrue themselves as fluent speakers. Forty-seven adult stammerers were randomly allocated to a technique or a construct group. By means of a form of behaviour modification they were helped to speak fluently. The treatment of the technique group focused on the practice of fluent speech in many situations, while the construct group was helped to reconstrue this fluency along the lines of personal construct therapy. | The treatment proved to be effective in reducing stammering behaviour, and the relapse rate was low. A comparison of the groups showed that the construct group had a significantly lower relapse rate than the technique group. | Ib |
| Stewart T, 1996, 'A further application of the Fishbein and Ajzen model to therapy for adult stammerers', *European Journal of Disorders of Communication*, 31 (4):445–64. | Longitudinal study | 12 adults, aged between 18 and 38 | Examined the continuing problems of the maintenance of acquired fluent speech by stammerers and attempted to establish a link between successful maintenance and change in the attitude of stammerers to fluent speech. Twelve adults participated in the programme and assessments were made of five separate occasions: at the beginning of the study; following a programme of group therapy sessions that attempted to change the subjects' attitudes to fluent speech; following a programme of group therapy sessions that taught a fluency-controlling speech technique; after a period which developed the subjects' ability to use the speech technique outside the clinic environment; and two years after the beginning of the study. | The attitude change group sessions produced modifications in the physical concomitant movements associated with stammering behaviour, but did not result in specific quantitative changes. The technique group sessions resulted in significant changes across all three speaking situations, with reading and monologue showing the greatest amount of change. The attitude data results indicate that some change did take place during the programme. | III |

| Author(s) & Title | Design | Sample | Objective of study | Conclusions | Evidence Level |
|---|---|---|---|---|---|
| Stewart T & Grantham C, 1993, 'A case of acquired stammering: the pattern of recovery', *European Journal of Disorders of Communication*, 28 (4):395–403. | Case study | 21-year-old female student | A case is presented of a 21-year-old student who demonstrated sudden onset of severe stammering speech. | The findings of speech assessments over a one year period post-onset are described and discussed. In addition a comprehensive description of the client's own perceptions of her difficulties during the same time scale is recounted. The case demonstrates a possible pattern of recovery and the profound psychological implications in the event of acquired stammering in adulthood. | III |
| Hayhow R, Cray AM & Enderby P, 2002, 'Stammering and therapy views of people who stammer', *Journal of Fluency Disorders*, 27 (1):1–16. | Questionnaire | 1058 questionnaires sent to members of the British Stammering Association; 180 sent to speech & language therapists with an interest in adult stammering | This study used a postal questionnaire to seek the views of adults who stammer, concerning the effect of stammering on their lives, the speech and language therapy and other remedies they have tried, and their hopes for speech and language therapy in the future. | The 332 returned questionnaires indicated that stammering had the greatest adverse effect on school life and occupation. Speech and language therapy had been helpful to many, but the nature of the benefits and specific therapies used were not cited in many responses. An emergent theme in unhelpful therapy was the dissatisfaction that arises when individual needs are not met. In the future, people want help in controlling stammering and in developing coping strategies. The desire for timely and effective therapy for children, ongoing help and group or intensive work has implications for service organisation and therapists' skills. The survey highlights the need for therapists and clients to negotiate therapy aims and procedures that are clearly defined, appropriate to individual needs, achievable, and, if possible, recorded and measured. | III |

# DISORDERS OF FLUENCY

**Therapy Approaches**

*Speak more fluently (Fluency shaping)*

| Author(s) & Title | Design | Sample | Objective of study | Conclusions | Evidence Level |
|---|---|---|---|---|---|
| Onslow M, Costa L, Andrews C, Harrison E & Packman A, 1996, 'Speech outcomes of a prolonged-speech treatment for stammering', *Journal of Speech & Hearing Research*, 39 (4):734–49. | Case series | 12 adults | This study used extensive speech outcome measures across a variety of situations in evaluating the outcome of an intensive prolonged speech treatment. The speech of 12 clients in this treatment was assessed on three occasions prior to treatment and frequently on eight occasions after discharge from the residential setting. For seven clients, a further assessment occurred at three years post-treatment. Concurrent dependent measures were percentage syllables stammered; syllables per minute; and speech naturalness. The dependent measures were collected in many speaking situations within and beyond the clinic. Dependent measures were based on speech samples of substantive duration, and covert assessments were included in the study. | Detailed data were presented for individual subjects. Results showed that 12 subjects who remained with the entire two to three year programme achieved zero or near-zero stammering. The majority of subjects did not show a regression trend in percentage syllables stammered or speech naturalness scores during the post treatment period, either within or beyond the clinic. Some subjects showed higher post-treatment percentage syllables stammered scores during covert assessment than during overt assessment. Results also showed that stammering was eliminated without using unusually slow and unnatural speech patterns. This treatment programme does not specify a target speech rate range, and many clients maintained stammer-free speech using speech rates that were higher than the range typically specified in intensive prolonged speech programmes. A significant correlation was found between speech rate and perceived post-treatment speech naturalness. | III |

| Author(s) & Title | Design | Sample | Objective of study | Conclusions | Evidence Level |
|---|---|---|---|---|---|
| Howie PM, Tanner S & Andrews G, 1981, 'Short and long-term outcome in an intensive treatment program for adult stammerers', *Journal of Speech and Hearing Disorders*, 46:104–9 | Case series | | A three-week intensive treatment programme for adult stammerers is described. This treatment has evolved from an original programme developed by Ingham and Andrews (1973) using speech prolongation techniques, gradual shaping of speech rate to normal, and systematic transfer of skills acquired in the clinic to real-life situations. | Immediately after intensive treatment, stammering was virtually eliminated and speech rate and attitudes toward communication were normalised. There was no substantial deterioration in these treatment effects when clients were evaluated in the clinic after two months in the Maintenance Phase of treatment. Speech and attitude measures collected outside the clinic 12 to18 months after intensive treatment showed lasting overall improvement in most clients, although some deterioration in fluency from immediate post-intensive treatment levels had occurred in 40 percent of clients. Covertly collected data supported this finding. | III |

### Stammer more fluently (Stammering modification)

| Author(s) & Title | Design | Sample | Objective of study | Conclusions | Evidence Level |
|---|---|---|---|---|---|
| Blood G., Blood I, Tellis G & Gabel R, 2001, 'Communication apprehension and self perceived communication competence in adolescents who stammer', *Journal of Fluency Disorders*, 26 (3):161–78. | Controlled study | 39 adolescents who stammer and 39 adolescents who do not stammer | The purpose of this study was to examine the communication apprehension and self-perceived communication competence of 39 adolescents who stammer and 39 adolescents who do not stammer using two standardised communication measures. | Significantly higher levels of communication apprehension and poorer scores on self-perceived communication competence were found in adolescents who stammer when compared with adolescents who do not stammer. | IIa |

## DISORDERS OF FLUENCY

| Author(s) & Title | Design | Sample | Objective of study | Conclusions | Evidence Level |
|---|---|---|---|---|---|
| Manning W, Burlison A & Thaxton D, 1999, 'Listener response to stammering modification techniques', *Journal of Fluency Disorders*, 24 (4):267–80. | Controlled study | 24 adults (16–68) performed as listeners<br><br>50 adults (18–63) as volunteer listeners<br><br>Adult male who stammered | In two investigations, non-professional listeners used a 25-item bi-polar adjective scale to evaluate an adult male speaker who stammered. In investigation one, 24 listeners evaluated the speaker during a Stammering Only and a Stammering + Cancellation condition. In investigation two, 50 listeners evaluated the speaker in a Stammering Only and a Stammering + Pullout condition. | Listeners in the first investigation did not assign significantly different ratings to the Stammering Only and Stammering + Cancellation conditions. In the second investigation listeners rated the Stammering Only condition more positively than the Stammering + Pullout condition. Analysis of listener response to four open-ended questions indicated significantly more positive reaction to the Stammering Only condition than either of the Stammering + Modification conditions. Finally, listeners rated the speaker using the Cancellation and Pullout techniques as being significantly more handicapped than when he was stammering only. The findings provided preliminary evidence indicating that everyday listeners may react less favourably to an adult male speaker who is modifying his stammered speech than when this same speaker is simply stammering. | IIa |

### *Communication Skills*

| | | | | | |
|---|---|---|---|---|---|
| Rustin L & Kuhr A, 1998, *Social skills and the Speech Impaired*, Whurr, London. | Expert opinion | — | — | — | IV |

| Author(s) & Title | Design | Sample | Objective of study | Conclusions | Evidence Level |
|---|---|---|---|---|---|
| **Psychological Therapies** | | | | | |
| Evesham M & Fransella F, 1985, 'Stammering relapse: the effect of a combined speech and psychological reconstruction programme', *British Journal of Disorders of Communication*, 20 (3):237–48. | Randomised controlled trial | 47 adult stammerers | This study tested the hypothesis that stammerers who achieved fluent speech during two weeks of intensive treatment would be less likely to relapse if they were also helped to reconstrue themselves as fluent speakers. Forty-seven adult stammerers were randomly allocated to a technique or a construct group. By means of a form of behaviour modification they were helped to speak fluently. The treatment of the technique group focused on the practice of fluent speech in many situations, while the construct group was helped to reconstrue this fluency along the lines of personal construct therapy. | The treatment proved to be effective in reducing stammering behaviour, and the relapse rate was low. A comparison of the groups showed that the construct group had a significantly lower relapse rate than the technique group. | Ib |
| DiLollo A, Manning WH & Neimeyer RA, 2003, 'Cognitive anxiety as a function of speaker role for fluent speakers and persons who stammer', *Journal of Fluency Disorders*, 28 (3):167–86. | Controlled study | 29 adults who stammered<br><br>29 fluent speakers | This study investigated the 'meaningfulness' with which fluent and disfluent persons were able to construe themselves in stammering and non-stammering speaker roles. | Results indicated that persons who stammered displayed greater cognitive anxiety (difficulty integrating their experience meaningfully) in a fluent speaking role than in a stammering role, whereas the reverse was found for fluent speakers. These results suggest the relevance of assessing and addressing the meaningfulness of the 'dominant' disfluent speaker role in treating persons who stammer, insofar as a tendency to maintain the predictability of this familiar role may contribute to stammering maintenance and relapse. | IIa |
| **Other Approaches** | | | | | |
| Stewart T, 1996, 'A Solution Focused Brief Therapy Approach to working with dysfluent clients', *Oxford Dysfluency Conference Proceedings*, June. | Conference proceedings | — | — | — | IV |

## DISORDERS OF FLUENCY

### Maintenance

| Author(s) & Title | Design | Sample | Objective of study | Conclusions | Evidence Level |
|---|---|---|---|---|---|
| Stewart T, 1996, 'A further application of the Fishbein and Ajzen model to therapy for adult stammerers', *European Journal of Disorders of Communication*, 31 (4):445–64. | Longitudinal study | 12 adults, aged between 18 and 38 | Examined the continuing problems of the maintenance of acquired fluent speech by stammerers and attempted to establish a link between successful maintenance and change in the attitude of stammerers to fluent speech. Twelve adults participated in the programme and assessments were made of five separate occasions: at the beginning of the study; following a programme of group therapy sessions that attempted to change the subjects' attitudes to fluent speech; following a programme of group therapy sessions that taught a fluency-controlling speech technique; after a period which developed subjects' ability to use the speech technique outside the clinic environment; and two years after the beginning of the study. | The attitude change group sessions produced modifications in the physical concomitant movements associated with stammering behaviour, but did not result in specific quantitative changes. The technique group sessions resulted in significant changes across all three speaking situations, with reading and monologue showing the greatest amount of change. The attitude data results indicate that some change did take place during the programme. | III |
| Craig A, 1998, 'Relapse following treatment for stammering: a critical review and correlative data', *Journal of Fluency Disorders*, 23 (1):1–30. | Review | — | A critical review of data-based research revealed two methods of studying relapse. In one approach, attempts are made to isolate predictors of relapse; in the second, the effectiveness of strategies that reduce the risk of relapse are evaluated. In addition to the critical review, original data are presented to illustrate the relative and combined importance of several predictors of long-term fluency in four groups of adults who stammer. Independent variables included demographics; frequency of stammering; speech rate; personality; locus of control; speech attitudes; and participation in anti-relapse activities. | The data reveal few factors that could be considered reliable determinants of relapse, although the results are in agreement with findings reported elsewhere, namely, that several factors in combination may provide a reasonably valid prediction of relapse. | III |

| Author(s) & Title | Design | Sample | Objective of study | Conclusions | Evidence Level |
|---|---|---|---|---|---|
| Stewart T, 1996, 'Good maintainers and poor maintainers: a personal construct approach to an old problem', *Journal of Fluency Disorders*, 21 (1):33–48. | Case series | | This paper describes the application of personal construct theory to the treatment of stammering in adults. Attempts are made to link the acquisition and maintenance of a fluency-enhancing speech technique with construing of fluency. Two individual stammerers attending a group therapy programme of three phases were followed up at one-year and two-year intervals after therapy. | When the results of the initial and final assessments were compared, very different levels of maintenance of fluency were observed. It was hypothesised that their individual construing of fluency during the programme and follow-up phase affected the maintenance of fluent speech. Analysis and comparison of their repertory grids completed at each stage of the programme were carried out to establish the validity of this hypothesis. The data indicated different patterns of construing that linked with behaviour change. The 'good maintainer' had longer periods of loosening and different construing of self when compared with the 'poorer maintainer'. On the basis of these results, suggestions for future therapy with adult stammerers were made. | III |

## ACQUIRED / LATE ONSET IN ADULTS

### Assessment

| Author(s) & Title | Design | Sample | Objective of study | Conclusions | Evidence Level |
|---|---|---|---|---|---|
| Van Borstel J, Van Lierde K, Van Cauwenberger P, Guldemont I & Orshoven M, 1998, 'Severe acquired stammering following injury of the left supplementary motor region: a case report', *Journal of Fluency Disorders*, 23 (1):49–58. | Case study | 69-year-old man post-CVA | Stammering secondary to nervous system damage (neurogenic stammering) has been considered not to have any localising significance. Recently, it has been suggested, however, that stammering due to damage of the supplementary motor region might yet represent a specific constellation of dysfluencies. Ackermann (1996) put forward the suggestion that in stammering associated with supplementary motor region involvement, dysfluencies are restricted to word-initial position and are absent during sentence repetition and reading aloud. A case to the contrary is presented in this article. | — | III |

## DISORDERS OF FLUENCY

| Author(s) & Title | Design | Sample | Objective of study | Conclusions | Evidence Level |
|---|---|---|---|---|---|
| Tippett D & Siebens A, 1991, 'Distinguishing psychogenic from neurogenic dysfluency when neurologic and psychologic factors co-exist', *Journal of Fluency Disorders*,16:3–12. | Case study | 23-year-old man | This paper describes the onset of dysfluency in a 23-year-old man who had anoxic encephalopathy with diffuse weakness and spasticity, pseudoseizures and depression, following an episode of status epilepticus. Differential diagnosis was complicated by the presence of both objective neurologic abnormalities and psychologic factors. The history, physical examination and analysis of speech characteristics were insufficient to make the diagnosis; however, the effect of a therapeutic trial strongly suggested psychogenicity. | — | III |
| Van Borsel J, Van Lierde K, Oostra K & Eeckhaut C, 1997, 'The differential diagnosis of late onset stammering', in Lebrun Y (ed), *From the Brain to the Mouth*, Kluwer Academic Publishers, Dordrecht. | Expert opinion | — | — | — | IV |
| Mahr G & Leith W, 1992, 'Psychogenic stammering of adult onset', *Journal of Speech and Hearing Research*, 35 (2):283–86. | Expert opinion | — | The characteristic features of psychogenic stammering of adult onset are reviewed and four cases of this disorder are presented. | Psychogenic stammering of adult onset is best classified as a conversion reaction, and tentative criteria for this diagnosis are proposed. | IV |
| Helm-Estabrooks N, 1999, 'Stammering Associated with Acquired Neurological Disorders', in Curlee RF (ed), *Stammering and Related Disorders of Fluency*, Thieme Medical Publishers, New York. | Expert opinion | — | — | — | IV |

| Author(s) & Title | Design | Sample | Objective of study | Conclusions | Evidence Level |
|---|---|---|---|---|---|
| Baumgartner J, 1999, 'Acquired Psychogenic Stammering', in Curlee RF (ed), *Stammering and Related Disorders of Fluency*, Thieme, Medical Publishers, New York. | Expert opinion | — | — | — | IV |
| **Management** | | | | | |
| Stewart T & Grantham C, 1993, 'A case of acquired stammering: the pattern of recovery', *European Journal of Disorders of Communication*, 28 (4):395–403. | Case study | 21-year-old female | A case is presented of a 21-year-old student who demonstrated sudden onset of severe stammering speech. | The findings of speech assessments over a one year period post-onset are described and discussed. In addition, a comprehensive description of the client's own perceptions of her difficulties during the same time-scale is recounted. The case demonstrates a possible pattern of recovery and the profound psychological implications in the event of acquired stammering in adulthood. | III |
| Stewart T, 1997, 'Managing reconstruction in an adult with idiopathic stammering', *Journal of Clinical Speech & Language Studies*, 28:34–42. | Case study | 21-year-old female | This study focuses on the psychological issues arising from late onset of stammering in adults. These issues are discussed firstly in relation to one client who began stammering at age 21. In the second part of the paper the management of psychological issues are considered and a number of guidelines are proposed within a personal construct psychology framework. | — | III |

## DISORDERS OF FLUENCY

| Author(s) & Title | Design | Sample | Objective of study | Conclusions | Evidence Level |
|---|---|---|---|---|---|
| **Therapy Approaches** | | | | | |
| Market KE, Montague JC, Buffalo MD & Drummond SS, 1990, 'Acquired stuttering: descriptive data and treatment outcome', *Journal of Fluency Disorders*, 15 (1):21–33. | | 81 persons with acquired stammering | This study obtained biographical, dysfluency characteristics, etiology, treatment type, and therapy outcome information on 81 acquired stammerers throughout the USA. The subjects' age at onset of acquired stammering was 16 to 86 years. Most subjects were male; younger subjects (aged 16 to 30 years) were more likely to have head trauma, while older subjects (aged 31 to 86 years) were more likely to have had ischemic damage. Most subjects received either a slow rate, easy onset, or a combination of the two procedures as therapy type. | Therapy outcome was positive for 82 percent of subjects which suggests that traditional treatment procedures with acquired stammerers are highly successful. | III |
| Stewart T & Rowley D, 1996, 'Acquired stammering in Great Britain', *European Journal of Disorders of Communication*, 31:1–9. | | Questionnaire | There are a growing number of reports of late onset of stammering from clinicians but a lack of data concerning the nature, aetiology and outcomes of therapy. This research attempts to replicate in Great Britain a survey of clinicians carried out in the USA. Clinicians completed a questionnaire on their clients with acquired stammering. Details on possible cause, speech and language characteristics, and therapeutic outcomes were compared with the US study. | Results were similar in terms of aetiology and outcome measures despite reported differences in characteristics and treatment regimes offered. | III |
| Stewart T, 1997, 'Managing reconstruction in an adult with idiopathic stammering', *Journal of Clinical Speech & Language Studies*, 7:34–42. | Case study | 21-year-old female | This study focuses on the psychological issues arising from late onset of stammering in adults. These issues are discussed firstly in relation to one client who began stammering at age 21. In the second part of the paper the management of psychological issues are considered and a number of guidelines are proposed within a personal construct psychology framework. | — | III |

| Author(s) & Title | Design | Sample | Objective of study | Conclusions | Evidence Level |
|---|---|---|---|---|---|
| **CLUTTERING** | | | | | |
| **Assessment** | | | | | |
| Teigland A, 1996, 'A study of pragmatic skills of clutterers and normal speakers', *Journal of Fluency Disorders*, 21 (3–4):201–14. | Controlled study | 12 junior high school subjects ages 13:7 to 16:1 | In communication dyads, three junior high clutterers interacted verbally with three matched control subjects in a task that required one member of the dyad to explain a complicated route (from a marked map of a town centre) to the other (who had an unmarked map). Members played both roles in the dyads. These six subjects were compared with one group of normally speaking control subjects carrying out the same task. | Both quantitative and qualitative analyses indicate that, compared with normal speaking pupils, clutterers frequently manifested pragmatic errors and communication failures. | IIa |
| St Louis KO & Myers FL, 1997, *Cluttering: a clinical perspective*, Far Communications, Kibworth. | Expert opinion | — | — | — | IV |
| Ward D, 2003, 'Cluttering, speech rate and linguistic deficit. A case report', paper presented at the 4th World Congress on Fluency Disorders, Montreal, Canada. | Conference proceedings | — | — | — | IV |
| **Therapy** | | | | | |
| Thacker RC & De Nil LF, 1996, 'Neurogenic cluttering', *Journal of Fluency Disorders*, 21 (3–4):227–38. | Case study | 61-year-old | A case of acquired symptomatic cluttering in a 61-year-old patient with documented cortical, subcortical, cerebellar, and medulla lesions is presented. The subject's communication-related behaviours are described, and a comparison is made between this case, idiopathic cluttering, and the few cases of acquired symptomatic cluttering that have been reported. | — | III |

## DISORDERS OF FLUENCY

| Author(s) & Title | Design | Sample | Objective of study | Conclusions | Evidence Level |
|---|---|---|---|---|---|
| Craig A, 1996, 'Long term effects of intensive treatment for a client with both a cluttering and stammering disorder', *Journal of Fluency Disorders*, 21 (3-4):329–35. | Case study | 21-year-old man | This study presents data on the effects of an intensive smooth speech treatment programme for stammering on the speech and psychological status of a man, aged 21 years, who stammered and who was also diagnosed as a clutterer. Stammering was mild to moderate and consisted mostly of rapid repetitions with an occasional block. The client had stammered since the age of five years. Initial rate could not be determined with accuracy due to its irregularity and speed, but was estimated to be between 260 to 300 syllables per minute (SPM). Speech was also characterised by irregular quick bursts that were often unintelligible. There was no evidence of abnormal psychological traits. However, a higher than normal level of negative communication attitudes was evidenced. An intensive three-week smooth speech programme designed to reduce and control stammering was initiated. It was believed the training, which involved rate control, would control the cluttering symptoms as well. | After successful completion of the programme, stammering was greatly reduced, and the gains were maintained after 10 months. Speech rate was reduced to normal levels and was also maintained at the 10-month follow-up. Negative attitudes to communication, furthermore, were greatly reduced both in the short- and long-term. Consequently the cluttering symptoms after treatment were minimal. This case study suggests that an intensive treatment for stammering, which contains rate control, can also be a successful treatment for cluttering, at least for those who also stammer. | III |

| Author(s) & Title | Design | Sample | Objective of study | Conclusions | Evidence Level |
|---|---|---|---|---|---|
| Daly DA & Burnett ML, 1996, 'Cluttering: assessment, treatment planning and case study illustration', *Journal of Fluency Disorders*, 21 (3–4):239–48. | Case study | 9-year-old boy | Successful treatment of clients who present with a multitude of interrelated impairments is frequently dependent upon thorough and accurate diagnosis of the problems. Individuals who clutter often demonstrate a variety of speech and language deficits that make diagnosis difficult. Two clinical tools believed to be useful for obtaining and organising diagnostic data and for planning treatment with clients who show symptoms of cluttering are discussed. | The case study report illustrates the utility of these tools for collecting and organising all pertinent data. | III |
| Daly DA & Burnett ML, 1999, 'Cluttering: Traditional views and new perspectives' in Curlee RF (ed), *Stammering and related disorders of fluency*, Thieme Medical Publishers, New York. | Expert opinion | — | — | — | IV |
| St. Louis KO & Myers FL, 1997, 'Management of cluttering and related fluency disorders, in Curlee RF & Siegel G (eds), *Nature and Treatment of Stammering: New Directions*, 2nd edn, Allen & Bacon, Needham Heights, MA. | Expert opinion | — | — | — | IV |

# DISORDERS OF MENTAL HEALTH & DEMENTIA

| Author(s) & Title | Design | Sample | Objective of study | Conclusions | Evidence Level |
|---|---|---|---|---|---|
| **CHILDREN AND ADOLESCENT MENTAL HEALTH DISORDERS** | | | | | |
| **Core Speech & Language Skills** | | | | | |
| Baker L, Cantwell DP, 1987, 'Factors associated with the development of psychiatric illness in children with early speech/language problems', *Journal of Autism & Developmental Disorders* 17 (4):499–510. | Clinical study | 600 children aged between 2 and 6 years old selected from a community speech clinic | All children were given comprehensive speech and language evaluations and psychiatric evaluations. The correlates of psychiatric illness in children with speech and language disorders was investigated. | Of 600 two to six-year-olds selected from a community speech clinic, 50 percent had diagnosable psychiatric disorders according to *Diagnostic and Statistical Manual of Mental Disorders (DSM-III)* criteria. 'Psychiatrically ill' subjects were compared to 'psychiatrically well' subjects on a variety of developmental, socioeconomic, medical and psychosocial factors. Although some differences were found between the well and ill children in other factors, most differences, and the most highly significant differences, were found in areas of linguistic functioning. Clinical implications are discussed. | III |
| Giddan J, Milling L & Campbell NB, 1996, 'Unrecognised language and speech deficits in preadolescent psychiatric inpatients', *American Journal of Orthopsychiatry* 66(1). | Clinical study | Potential subjects consisted of 76 consecutive admissions to the child in-patient unit of a child and adolescent psychiatric hospital | During the first 10 days of admission, each child's speech and language functioning was assessed. After the tenth day each child was assigned a DSM-111-R diagnosis. | Of 55 psychiatrically hospitalised pre-adolescents with DSM-111-R diagnoses that are not commonly associated with language deficits, 60 percent were found to have language or speech deficits, although only 38 percent had ever received speech or language therapy. | III |
| **Variability in Performance** | | | | | |
| Greenspan SI, 1992, *Infancy and Early Childhood: The Practice of Clinical Assessment and Intervention with Emotional and Developmental Challenges*, International Universities Press, Madison, CT. | Expert opinion | — | — | | IV |

| Author(s) & Title | Design | Sample | Objective of study | Conclusions | Evidence Level |
|---|---|---|---|---|---|
| Lund N, 1993, in Duchan J (ed) *Assessing Children's Language in Naturalistic Contexts*, Prentice Hall Inc, Englewood Cliffs, NJ. | Expert opinion | — | — | — | IV |
| Tankersley M & Balan C, 1999, 'An overview of psychotropic drugs used in the treatment of behaviour in language disorders in Rogus', in Atkinson D & Griffith P (eds) *Communication Disorders in Children with Psychiatric and Behaviour Disorders*, Singular Publishing Group, San Diego. | Expert opinion | — | — | — | IV |
| **General Principles** | | | | | |
| Roth FP, 1999, 'Communicative intervention for children with psychiatric and communication disorders', *Child and Adolescent Psychiatric Clinics of North America* 8:137–52. | Literature review | — | This article describes language intervention for children with psychiatrically based communication disorders. | Specific therapy procedures are provided to illustrate strategies employed by Speech & Language Therapists as part of a multidisciplinary team effort to facilitate the acquisition of functional and socially appropriate communication skills. | IV |
| **Type and Method of Intervention** | | | | | |
| Jones J, 1995, 'Speech and language therapy in child psychiatry' in Chesson R & Chisholm (eds) *Child Psychiatric Units: At the Crossroads*, Jessica Kingsley, London. | Expert opinion | — | — | — | IV |
| Wintgens A, 2001, 'Child Psychiatry'm in France J & Kramer S (eds) *Communication in Mental Illness*, Jessica Kingsley, London. | Expert opinion | — | — | — | IV |

# DISORDERS OF MENTAL HEALTH & DEMENTIA

| Author(s) & Title | Design | Sample | Objective of study | Conclusions | Evidence Level |
|---|---|---|---|---|---|
| **ADULT MENTAL HEALTH DISORDERS (EXCLUDING DEMENTIA)** | | | | | |
| **Assessment of Communication Skills** | | | | | |
| Faber R, Abrams R, Taylor MA, Kasprison A, Morris C & Weisz R, 1983, 'Comparison of schizophrenic patients with formal thought disorder and neurologically impaired patients with aphasia', *American Journal of Psychiatry* 140 (10):1348–51. | Comparative study | 14 schizophrenic patients 13 neurologically impaired patients with aphasia | This study compares the speech and language of 14 schizophrenic patients having a formal thought disorder with 13 neurologically impaired patients with aphasia. Transcribed interviews with these patients were blindly assessed by five specialists for classification as schizophrenic or aphasic. | Three of the five specialists performed better than chance, but only one achieved high discriminating ability. Inter-rater reliability was poor. Five of the fourteen language abnormalities assessed differentiated the diagnostic groups. These findings suggest that schizophrenic patients share many language abnormalities with aphasic patients but do not exhibit a classic aphasic syndrome. | III |
| **Communication Interventions** | | | | | |
| Atkinson JM, Coia DA, Gilmour WH & Harper JP, 1996, 'The impact of education groups for people with schizophrenia on social functioning and quality of life', *British Journal of Psychiatry* 168 (2):199–204. | Randomised controlled trial | 146 adults with schizophrenia accepted a place in the group, 73 randomly allocated to the education group and 73 to the control condition | Education groups for people with schizophrenia have tended to concentrate on compliance with medication. This study examines impact on social behaviour and quality of life. A catchment-wide service was set up for community-based patients. Patients who indicated an interest in education groups were randomly allocated to either an education group or a waiting list control group. Those who attended groups were compared with the control group. | About one-quarter of community-based patients showed interest in attending education groups. Those who attended showed no change in mental state or compliance with medication (already high) but significant gains in quality of life, social functioning and social networks. | Ib |

| Author(s) & Title | Design | Sample | Objective of study | Conclusions | Evidence Level |
|---|---|---|---|---|---|
| Wong SE & Woolsey JE, 1989, 'Re-establishing conversational skills in overtly psychotic, chronic schizophrenic patients. Discrete trials training on the psychiatric ward', *Behavioural Modification* 13 (4):415–31. | Single subject design | 4 adults with schizophrenia | A discrete trials procedure incorporating graduated prompts; social and consumable reinforcement; corrective feedback; delay of reinforcement; and a chaining procedure was used to teach four actively psychotic, chronic schizophrenic patients rudimentary conversational skills. In a multiple-baseline design, training was sequentially applied to the target conversational skills of giving a salutation, addressing the trainer by his or her name, making a personal enquiry, and asking a conversational question. | Results showed systematic training effects in three of the four subjects. Training gains were reliable but slow, requiring over 70 trials to reach acquisition criterion on certain skills. The fourth subject exhibited only unstable gains on the first target response and minor improvements on the second target response, the latter of which disappeared when training procedures were withdrawn. All subjects displayed spontaneous recovery on the generalisation measure of answering a personal enquiry. | III |
| Hoffman RE & Satal S, 1993, 'Language therapy for schizophrenic patients with persistent "voices"', *British Journal of Psychiatry* 162:755–8. | Case series | 4 adults with schizophrenia | Four patients received language therapy. Three patients received 10 sessions of language therapy, each lasting approximately 45 minutes. This language therapy was designed to challenge and enhance novel discourse planning. | Three had significant, albeit temporary, reductions on the severity of their 'voices'. | III |

**Training**

| Author(s) & Title | Design | Sample | Objective of study | Conclusions | Evidence Level |
|---|---|---|---|---|---|
| Shulman MD & Mandel E, 1988, 'Communication training of relatives and friends of institutionalized elderly persons', *The Gerontologist* 28:797–9. | Qualitative study | Family members of residents in a home for the elderly | A series of workshops for family and friends of residents was designed to inform them of the nature of communication, how it is affected by the aging process, the psychological and neurological nature of communication impairments and how to manage situations in which communication breaks down. A questionnaire was administered pre- and post- the workshops. | The workshops resulted in increased understanding, increased satisfaction with visits and increased skills in using communication-facilitating techniques. | III |

## DISORDERS OF MENTAL HEALTH & DEMENTIA

| Author(s) & Title | Design | Sample | Objective of study | Conclusions | Evidence Level |
|---|---|---|---|---|---|
| **Assessment of Eating and Swallowing** | | | | | |
| Bach DB, Pouget S, Belle K, Kilfoil M, Alfieri M, McEvoy J & Jackson G, 1989, 'An integrated team approach to the management of patients with oropharyngeal dysphagia', *Journal of Allied Health* 18 (5):459–68. | Expert opinion | — | This paper describes a team approach to the assessment and management of patients with oropharyngeal dysphagia of neurologic origin. The team's major focus was to determine the need for adjustments to the patient's diet to maintain or restore the safety of oral feeding. This involved the development of a detailed radiographic examination and a series of dysphagia diets, in addition to comprehensive evaluations by an occupational therapist, physiotherapist and Speech & Language Therapist. | The effects of deteriorating swallowing ability on the physical, cognitive and emotional status of the patient are discussed in the context of a multidisciplinary approach. | IV |

## ADULT ORGANIC MENTAL HEALTH DISORDERS: DEMENTIA

| Author(s) & Title | Design | Sample | Objective of study | Conclusions | Evidence Level |
|---|---|---|---|---|---|
| **Assessment of Factors Contributing to Communication** | | | | | |
| Powell AL, Cummings JL, Hill MA & Benson DF 'Speech and Language Alterations in Multi-infarct Dementia', *Neurology* 38:717–19. | Comparative study | 18 individuals with multi-infarct dementia and 14 with dementia of the Alzheimer type | Speech and language functions were assessed in 18 individuals with multi-infarct dementia (MID) and 14 with dementia of the Alzheimer type (DAT). The age range and dementia severity of the two groups were comparable. We used a speech and language battery assessing 37 elements of verbal output to characterise alterations in the individuals. | MID patients had more abnormalities of motor aspects of speech, whereas DAT patients had empty speech, more marked anomia, and relative sparing of motor speech functions. The results demonstrate that speech and language differ in MID and DAT. | III |
| Azuma T & Bayles KA, 1997, 'Memory impairments underlying language difficulties in dementia', *Topics in Language Disorders* 18:58–64. | Expert opinion | — | The memory deficits associated with the dementia syndromes of Alzheimer's, Parkinson's and Lewy body disease are outlined and related to the language impairments that have been observed in patients with these disorders. | Based on the pattern of spared and impaired memory functions, specific strategies for facilitating language in dementia patients are proposed. | IV |

| Author(s) & Title | Design | Sample | Objective of study | Conclusions | Evidence Level |
|---|---|---|---|---|---|
| Purandare N, Allen NHP & Burns A, 2000, 'Behavioural and psychological symptoms of dementia', *Reviews in Clinical Gerontology* 10 (3):245–60. | Expert opinion | — | Review of the literature | Dementia is a syndrome which involves progressive disturbance of multiple cognitive functions, emotional control and social behaviour in clear consciousness. Behavioral and psychological symptoms are common in dementia | IV |

### Assessment of Communication Skills

| Author(s) & Title | Design | Sample | Objective of study | Conclusions | Evidence Level |
|---|---|---|---|---|---|
| Monsch AU, Bondi MW, Butters N & Salmon DP, 1992, 'Comparisons of verbal fluency tasks in the detection of the dementia of the Alzheimer type', *Archives of Neurology* 49:1253–8. | Comparative study | 43 male and 46 female subjects with probable dementia of the Alzheimer's type and 17 male and 36 female neurologically intact subjects | Compared performances of subjects with probable dementia of the Alzheimer's type and neurologically intact subjects on four categories of verbal fluency, to determine whether differential performance exists across tasks and to identify the fluency measure that best discriminates between these two groups. | Subjects with dementia showed impairment on numerous verbal fluency tasks. | III |
| Ripich DN, Carpenter BD & Ziol EW, 2000, 'Conversational cohesion patterns in men and women with Alzheimer's disease: a longitudinal study', *International Journal of Language and Communication* 35:49–64. | Comparative study | 31 women and 29 men with early to mid-stage Alzheimer's disease; and 47 non-demented elderly, 27 women and 20 men | The use of cohesion devices in conversations was examined in 60 individuals. | Those with Alzheimer's disease produced more referent errors than non-demented individuals, although both sets of subjects otherwise demonstrated similar use of cohesion devices. Although referencing errors differentiated early to mid-stage AD from NE, conversational discourse tasks alone may have limited clinical value to assess and monitor communication competence. | III |

### Variability of Performance

| Author(s) & Title | Design | Sample | Objective of study | Conclusions | Evidence Level |
|---|---|---|---|---|---|
| McKeith IG, Perry RH, Fairbairn AF, Jabeen S & Perry EK, 1992, 'Operational criteria for senile dementia of Lewy body type (SDLT)', *Psychological Medicine* 22 (4):911–22. | Clinical study | 58 case notes | Retrospective analysis of case notes of 21 autopsy patients with neuropathologically proven senile dementia of Lewy body type (SDLT) and 37 cases with neuropathologically proven Alzheimer's disease (AD) identified a characteristic clinical syndrome in SDLT. | Fluctuating cognitive impairment; psychotic features including visual and auditory hallucinations and paranoid delusions; depressive symptoms; falling and unexplained losses of consciousness were all seen significantly more often than in AD. | III |

## DISORDERS OF MENTAL HEALTH & DEMENTIA

### Communication Interventions in Early Dementia

| Author(s) & Title | Design | Sample | Objective of study | Conclusions | Evidence Level |
|---|---|---|---|---|---|
| Acton GJ, Mayhew PA, Hopkins BA & Yauk S, 1999, 'Communicating with individuals with dementia: the impaired person's perspective', *Journal of Geriatric Nursing* 25:6–13. | Qualitative study | Adults with dementia ranging in age from 55 to 84 | This study is a secondary analysis of a larger intervention study for individuals with dementia and their caregivers. The aims of this study were: 1 To identify meaningful communication episodes received from individuals with dementia. 2 To cluster meaningful communication episodes received from individuals into themes of meaning. | This study demonstrates that individuals with dementia are able to transmit meaningful communication and this communication can be interpreted by others, making client-centred interventions possible with this population. | III |
| Azuma T & Bayles KA, 1997, 'Memory impairments underlying language difficulties in dementia', *Topics in Language Disorders* 18:58–64. | Expert opinion | — | The memory deficits associated with the dementia syndromes of Alzheimer's, Parkinson's and Lewy body disease are outlined and related to the language impairments that have been observed in patients with these disorders. | Based on the pattern of spared and impaired memory functions, specific strategies for facilitating language in dementia patients are proposed. | IV |
| Lubinski, 1995, 'Nature and efficacy of communication management in dementia and communication' | Expert opinion | — | | — | IV |
| Erber NP, 1994, 'Conversation as therapy for older adults in residential care: the case for intervention', *European Journal of Disorders of Communication* 29:269–78. | Expert opinion | — | Social isolation resulting from sensory loss tends to reduce life satisfaction in older adults. Residence in a long-term care facility such as a nursing home does little to alleviate their communication needs. Potential communication partners are available but many need instruction, counselling and feedback to become therapeutically effective. | The Speech & Language Therapist's experience as both communication therapist and social facilitator can enhance consultation and staff training in this area. | IV |

| Author(s) & Title | Design | Sample | Objective of study | Conclusions | Evidence Level |
|---|---|---|---|---|---|
| **Communication Interventions in Later Dementia** | | | | | |
| Pietro MJS & Boczko F, 1998, 'The Breakfast Club: results of a study examining the effectiveness of a multi-modality group communication treatment', *American Journal of Alzheimer's Disease* 13:146–58. | Controlled study | 40 individuals with mid-stage Alzheimer's | Twenty individuals with mid-stage Alzheimer's participated for 12 weeks each in four groups of five in a five-day-a-week programme of structured multi-modality group communication intervention called 'The Breakfast Club'. Twenty matched patients participated in a standard conversation group and served as controls. The Breakfast Club attempted to incorporate all that was currently known about the residual communication strengths of Alzheimer's patients and about previous treatments shown to be effective with this population. | Results showed that Breakfast Club participants improved significantly on measures of language performance, functional independence and use of social communication, while control subjects did not. Breakfast Club members also showed significant increases in 'interest and involvement' and the use of procedural memories over the 12-week period. | IIa |
| **Partnership with Carer** | | | | | |
| Ripich DN, Ziol E, Fritsch T & Durand EJ, 1999, 'Training Alzheimer's disease caregivers for successful communication', *Clinical Gerontologist* 21:37–56. | Controlled study | 54 Alzheimer's disease caregivers were compared to a control group of 22 caregivers | A study of 54 Alzheimer's disease (AD) caregivers was conducted to investigate the effects of caregiver communication training. To improve communication – with their family members with AD – 32 caregivers participated in an eight-hour training program (FOCUSED). Ten of these were also given follow-up training (FOCUSEDBooster). The questioning patterns of the two groups of FOCUSED trained caregivers planning a menu with their family member with AD were compared to a control group of 22 caregivers. | Data were collected over three visits (entry, six months and 12 months). Analysis revealed that for all caregivers, open-ended questions, when compared with yes/no and choice questions, resulted in more failed responses by persons with AD. Following training, at six months, both FOCUSED and FOCUSED-Booster caregivers asked fewer open-ended questions compared to the control group. This suggests that communication partners of persons with AD can be trained to structure questions that result in more successful communication. | IIa |

## DISORDERS OF MENTAL HEALTH & DEMENTIA

| Author(s) & Title | Design | Sample | Objective of study | Conclusions | Evidence Level |
|---|---|---|---|---|---|
| Shulman MD & Mandel E, 1988, 'Communication training of relatives and friends of institutionalized elderly persons', *The Gerontologist* 28:797–9. | Qualitative study | Family members of residents in a home for the elderly | A series of workshops for family and friends of residents was designed to inform them of the nature of communication, how it is affected by the aging process, the psychological and neurological nature of communication impairments and how to manage situations in which communication breaks down. A questionnaire was administered pre- and post- the workshops. | The workshops resulted in increased understanding, increased satisfaction with visits and increased skills in using communication-facilitating techniques. | III |
| Greene VL & Monahan DJ, 1989, 'The effect of a support and education program on stress and burden among family caregivers to frail elderly persons', *The Gerontologist* 29:472–80. | Qualitative study | 208 individuals entered a support group 81 individuals acted as a control | 34 support groups were conducted over the 14-month life of the project. Each group met weekly for two hours over an eight-week period. | An eight-week professionally guided caregiver support group was found to produce statistically significant reductions in anxiety, depression and sense of burden among family caregivers to frail elderly persons living on the community. Effects were weaker four months after the intervention ended than immediately after, but reductions in anxiety and depression were still evident. | III |

| Author(s) & Title | Design | Sample | Objective of study | Conclusions | Evidence Level |
|---|---|---|---|---|---|
| Cavanaugh JC, Dunn NJ, Mowery D, Feller C, Niederehe G, Fruge E & Volpendesta D, 1989, 'Problem-solving strategies in dementia patient-caregiver dyads', *The Gerontologist* 29 (2):156–8. | Qualitative study | 45 families, of which 29 were involved with an older adult who had been diagnosed with dementia. Of these 29 participants, 16 involved a same-generation caregiver and 13 involved a younger-generation caregiver. The remaining 16 families were comparison families in which the target older adult was a normally ageing person. | The applicability of concepts of the zone of proximal development and scaffolding to the study of dementia were examined. Caregiver–patient dyads were compared to normal elderly dyads in the instructional strategies they used to complete the Block Design subtest of the WAIS- R. | The results showed that the use of a detailed behavioural coding scheme was successful in documenting systematic differences between the two groups. | III |

**Training**

| | | | | | |
|---|---|---|---|---|---|
| Bayles KA, Kaszniak AW & Tomoeda CK, 1987, *Communication and Cognition in Normal Aging and Dementia*, Taylor & Francis, London. | Expert opinion | — | — | — | IV |

**Environment**

| | | | | | |
|---|---|---|---|---|---|
| Lubinski R, 1995, 'Environmental considerations for elderly patients', *Dementia and Communication*, | Expert opinion | — | — | — | IV |

# DISORDERS OF MENTAL HEALTH & DEMENTIA

| Author(s) & Title | Design | Sample | Objective of study | Conclusions | Evidence Level |
|---|---|---|---|---|---|
| **Group Language Stimulation** | | | | | |
| Clark LW, 1995, 'Interventions for persons with Alzheimer's disease: Strategies for maintaining and enhancing communicative success', *Topics in Language Disorders* 15 (2): 47–65. | Literature review | — | Examines the challenge to identify and document effective non-medical communication interventions that will assist persons with Alzheimer's disease (AD) to function at their most optimal levels. Both direct (client-centred) and indirect (caregiver-oriented) interventions are described, and the intervention literature from disciplines other than speech and language pathology is reviewed. | Behavioural interventions and interventions for: 1) enhancing cognitive capacities, 2) non-verbal forms of expression, and 3) environmental orientation and responsiveness are described. Emphasis is placed on functional maintenance and prevention of excessive response to disability and learned helplessness. The authors argue for a paradigm shift from a focus on skills improvement to a broader quality-of-life orientation. | IV |
| **Assessment of Swallowing** | | | | | |
| Steele CM, Greenwood C, Robertson C, Sidmon-Carlson R, 1997, 'Mealtime difficulties in a home for the aged – not for dysphagia', *Dysphagia* 12:43–50. | Qualitative study | 349 residents of a home for the aged | A mealtime screening tool was administered to 349 residents of a home for the aged to determine the prevalence of mealtime difficulties. | An increased prevalence of mealtime difficulties was related to both the presence and degree of cognitive impairment. Oral intake was best among residents with severe cognitive impairment, many of whom received partial to total feeding assistance. In contrast, poor oral intake was associated with mild to moderate cognitive impairment, pointing to a need for more aggressive intervention with this group. The results clearly demonstrate that the prevalence of a wide range of eating-related problems far exceeds accepted estimates of dysphagia alone and support a multidisciplinary approach to mealtime interventions for the institutionalised elderly. | III |

| Author(s) & Title | Design | Sample | Objective of study | Conclusions | Evidence Level |
|---|---|---|---|---|---|
| Lund N, 1993, in Duchan J (ed) *Assessing Children's Language in Naturalistic Contexts*, Prentice Hall Inc, Englewood Cliffs, NJ. | Expert opinion | — | — | — | IV |
| Tankersley M & Balan C, 1999, 'An overview of psychotropic drugs used in the treatment of behaviour in language disorders in Rogus', in Atkinson D & Griffith P (eds) *Communication Disorders in Children with Psychiatric and Behaviour Disorders*, Singular Publishing Group, San Diego. | Expert opinion | — | — | — | IV |
| **General Principles** | | | | | |
| Roth FP, 1999, 'Communicative intervention for children with psychiatric and communication disorders', *Child and Adolescent Psychiatric Clinics of North America* 8:137–52. | Literature review | — | This article describes language intervention for children with psychiatrically based communication disorders. | Specific therapy procedures are provided to illustrate strategies employed by Speech & Language Therapists as part of a multidisciplinary team effort to facilitate the acquisition of functional and socially appropriate communication skills. | IV |
| **Type and Method of Intervention** | | | | | |
| Jones J, 1995, 'Speech and language therapy in child psychiatry' in Chesson R & Chisholm (eds) *Child Psychiatric Units: At the Crossroads*, Jessica Kingsley, London. | Expert opinion | — | — | — | IV |
| Wintgens A, 2001, 'Child Psychiatry'm in France J & Kramer S (eds) *Communication in Mental Illness*, Jessica Kingsley, London. | Expert opinion | — | — | — | IV |

# DISORDERS OF MENTAL HEALTH & DEMENTIA

| Author(s) & Title | Design | Sample | Objective of study | Conclusions | Evidence Level |
|---|---|---|---|---|---|
| **ADULT MENTAL HEALTH DISORDERS (EXCLUDING DEMENTIA)** | | | | | |
| **Assessment of Communication Skills** | | | | | |
| Faber R, Abrams R, Taylor MA, Kasprison A, Morris C & Weisz R, 1983, 'Comparison of schizophrenic patients with formal thought disorder and neurologically impaired patients with aphasia', *American Journal of Psychiatry* 140 (10):1348–51. | Comparative study | 14 schizophrenic patients 13 neurologically impaired patients with aphasia | This study compares the speech and language of 14 schizophrenic patients having a formal thought disorder with 13 neurologically impaired patients with aphasia. Transcribed interviews with these patients were blindly assessed by five specialists for classification as schizophrenic or aphasic. | Three of the five specialists performed better than chance, but only one achieved high discriminating ability. Inter-rater reliability was poor. Five of the fourteen language abnormalities assessed differentiated the diagnostic groups. These findings suggest that schizophrenic patients share many language abnormalities with aphasic patients but do not exhibit a classic aphasic syndrome. | III |
| **Communication Interventions** | | | | | |
| Atkinson JM, Coia DA, Gilmour WH & Harper JP, 1996, 'The impact of education groups for people with schizophrenia on social functioning and quality of life', *British Journal of Psychiatry* 168 (2):199–204. | Randomised controlled trial | 146 adults with schizophrenia accepted a place in the group, 73 randomly allocated to the education group and 73 to the control condition | Education groups for people with schizophrenia have tended to concentrate on compliance with medication. This study examines impact on social behaviour and quality of life. A catchment-wide service was set up for community-based patients. Patients who indicated an interest in education groups were randomly allocated to either an education group or a waiting list control group. Those who attended groups were compared with the control group. | About one-quarter of community-based patients showed interest in attending education groups. Those who attended showed no change in mental state or compliance with medication (already high) but significant gains in quality of life, social functioning and social networks. | Ib |

| Author(s) & Title | Design | Sample | Objective of study | Conclusions | Evidence Level |
|---|---|---|---|---|---|
| Wong SE & Woolsey JE, 1989, 'Re-establishing conversational skills in overtly psychotic, chronic schizophrenic patients. Discrete trials training on the psychiatric ward', *Behavioural Modification* 13 (4):415–31. | Single subject design | 4 adults with schizophrenia | A discrete trials procedure incorporating graduated prompts; social and consumable reinforcement; corrective feedback; delay of reinforcement; and a chaining procedure was used to teach four actively psychotic, chronic schizophrenic patients rudimentary conversational skills. In a multiple-baseline design, training was sequentially applied to the target conversational skills of giving a salutation, addressing the trainer by his or her name, making a personal enquiry, and asking a conversational question. | Results showed systematic training effects in three of the four subjects. Training gains were reliable but slow, requiring over 70 trials to reach acquisition criterion on certain skills. The fourth subject exhibited only unstable gains on the first target response and minor improvements on the second target response, the latter of which disappeared when training procedures were withdrawn. All subjects displayed spontaneous recovery on the generalisation measure of answering a personal enquiry. | III |
| Hoffman RE & Satal S, 1993, 'Language therapy for schizophrenic patients with persistent "voices"', *British Journal of Psychiatry* 162:755–8. | Case series | 4 adults with schizophrenia | Four patients received language therapy. Three patients received 10 sessions of language therapy, each lasting approximately 45 minutes. This language therapy was designed to challenge and enhance novel discourse planning. | Three had significant, albeit temporary, reductions on the severity of their 'voices'. | III |

## Training

| Author(s) & Title | Design | Sample | Objective of study | Conclusions | Evidence Level |
|---|---|---|---|---|---|
| Shulman MD & Mandel E, 1988, 'Communication training of relatives and friends of institutionalized elderly persons', *The Gerontologist* 28:797–9. | Qualitative study | Family members of residents in a home for the elderly | A series of workshops for family and friends of residents was designed to inform them of the nature of communication, how it is affected by the aging process, the psychological and neurological nature of communication impairments and how to manage situations in which communication breaks down. A questionnaire was administered pre- and post- the workshops. | The workshops resulted in increased understanding, increased satisfaction with visits and increased skills in using communication-facilitating techniques. | III |

# DISORDERS OF MENTAL HEALTH & DEMENTIA

| Author(s) & Title | Design | Sample | Objective of study | Conclusions | Evidence Level |
|---|---|---|---|---|---|
| **Assessment of Eating and Swallowing** | | | | | |
| Bach DB, Pouget S, Belle K, Kilfoil M, Alfieri M, McEvoy J & Jackson G, 1989, 'An integrated team approach to the management of patients with oropharyngeal dysphagia', *Journal of Allied Health* 18 (5):459–68. | Expert opinion | — | This paper describes a team approach to the assessment and management of patients with oropharyngeal dysphagia of neurologic origin. The team's major focus was to determine the need for adjustments to the patient's diet to maintain or restore the safety of oral feeding. This involved the development of a detailed radiographic examination and a series of dysphagia diets, in addition to comprehensive evaluations by an occupational therapist, physiotherapist and Speech & Language Therapist. | The effects of deteriorating swallowing ability on the physical, cognitive and emotional status of the patient are discussed in the context of a multidisciplinary approach. | IV |

## ADULT ORGANIC MENTAL HEALTH DISORDERS: DEMENTIA

| Author(s) & Title | Design | Sample | Objective of study | Conclusions | Evidence Level |
|---|---|---|---|---|---|
| **Assessment of Factors Contributing to Communication** | | | | | |
| Powell AL, Cummings JL, Hill MA & Benson DF 'Speech and Language Alterations in Multi-infarct Dementia', *Neurology* 38:717–19. | Comparative study | 18 individuals with multi-infarct dementia and 14 with dementia of the Alzheimer type | Speech and language functions were assessed in 18 individuals with multi-infarct dementia (MID) and 14 with dementia of the Alzheimer type (DAT). The age range and dementia severity of the two groups were comparable. We used a speech and language battery assessing 37 elements of verbal output to characterise alterations in the individuals. | MID patients had more abnormalities of motor aspects of speech, whereas DAT patients had empty speech, more marked anomia, and relative sparing of motor speech functions. The results demonstrate that speech and language differ in MID and DAT. | III |
| Azuma T & Bayles KA, 1997, 'Memory impairments underlying language difficulties in dementia', *Topics in Language Disorders* 18:58–64. | Expert opinion | — | The memory deficits associated with the dementia syndromes of Alzheimer's, Parkinson's and Lewy body disease are outlined and related to the language impairments that have been observed in patients with these disorders. | Based on the pattern of spared and impaired memory functions, specific strategies for facilitating language in dementia patients are proposed. | IV |

| Author(s) & Title | Design | Sample | Objective of study | Conclusions | Evidence Level |
|---|---|---|---|---|---|
| Wong SE & Woolsey JE, 1989, 'Re-establishing conversational skills in overtly psychotic, chronic schizophrenic patients. Discrete trials training on the psychiatric ward', *Behavioural Modification* 13 (4):415–31. | Single subject design | 4 adults with schizophrenia | A discrete trials procedure incorporating graduated prompts; social and consumable reinforcement; corrective feedback; delay of reinforcement; and a chaining procedure was used to teach four actively psychotic, chronic schizophrenic patients rudimentary conversational skills. In a multiple-baseline design, training was sequentially applied to the target conversational skills of giving a salutation, addressing the trainer by his or her name, making a personal enquiry, and asking a conversational question. | Results showed systematic training effects in three of the four subjects. Training gains were reliable but slow, requiring over 70 trials to reach acquisition criterion on certain skills. The fourth subject exhibited only unstable gains on the first target response and minor improvements on the second target response, the latter of which disappeared when training procedures were withdrawn. All subjects displayed spontaneous recovery on the generalisation measure of answering a personal enquiry. | III |
| Hoffman RE & Satal S, 1993, 'Language therapy for schizophrenic patients with persistent "voices"', *British Journal of Psychiatry* 162:755–8. | Case series | 4 adults with schizophrenia | Four patients received language therapy. Three patients received 10 sessions of language therapy, each lasting approximately 45 minutes. This language therapy was designed to challenge and enhance novel discourse planning. | Three had significant, albeit temporary, reductions on the severity of their 'voices'. | III |
| **Training** | | | | | |
| Shulman MD & Mandel E, 1988, 'Communication training of relatives and friends of institutionalized elderly persons', *The Gerontologist* 28:797–9. | Qualitative study | Family members of residents in a home for the elderly | A series of workshops for family and friends of residents was designed to inform them of the nature of communication, how it is affected by the aging process, the psychological and neurological nature of communication impairments and how to manage situations in which communication breaks down. A questionnaire was administered pre- and post- the workshops. | The workshops resulted in increased understanding, increased satisfaction with visits and increased skills in using communication-facilitating techniques. | III |

# DISORDERS OF MENTAL HEALTH & DEMENTIA

| Author(s) & Title | Design | Sample | Objective of study | Conclusions | Evidence Level |
|---|---|---|---|---|---|
| **Assessment of Eating and Swallowing** | | | | | |
| Bach DB, Pouget S, Belle K, Kilfoil M, Alfieri M, McEvoy J & Jackson G, 1989, 'An integrated team approach to the management of patients with oropharyngeal dysphagia', *Journal of Allied Health* 18 (5):459–68. | Expert opinion | — | This paper describes a team approach to the assessment and management of patients with oropharyngeal dysphagia of neurologic origin. The team's major focus was to determine the need for adjustments to the patient's diet to maintain or restore the safety of oral feeding. This involved the development of a detailed radiographic examination and a series of dysphagia diets, in addition to comprehensive evaluations by an occupational therapist, physiotherapist and Speech & Language Therapist. | The effects of deteriorating swallowing ability on the physical, cognitive and emotional status of the patient are discussed in the context of a multidisciplinary approach. | IV |

## ADULT ORGANIC MENTAL HEALTH DISORDERS: DEMENTIA

| Author(s) & Title | Design | Sample | Objective of study | Conclusions | Evidence Level |
|---|---|---|---|---|---|
| **Assessment of Factors Contributing to Communication** | | | | | |
| Powell AL, Cummings JL, Hill MA & Benson DF 'Speech and Language Alterations in Multi-infarct Dementia', *Neurology* 38:717–19. | Comparative study | 18 individuals with multi-infarct dementia and 14 with dementia of the Alzheimer type | Speech and language functions were assessed in 18 individuals with multi-infarct dementia (MID) and 14 with dementia of the Alzheimer type (DAT). The age range and dementia severity of the two groups were comparable. We used a speech and language battery assessing 37 elements of verbal output to characterise alterations in the individuals. | MID patients had more abnormalities of motor aspects of speech, whereas DAT patients had empty speech, more marked anomia, and relative sparing of motor speech functions. The results demonstrate that speech and language differ in MID and DAT. | III |
| Azuma T & Bayles KA, 1997, 'Memory impairments underlying language difficulties in dementia', *Topics in Language Disorders* 18:58–64. | Expert opinion | — | The memory deficits associated with the dementia syndromes of Alzheimer's, Parkinson's and Lewy body disease are outlined and related to the language impairments that have been observed in patients with these disorders. | Based on the pattern of spared and impaired memory functions, specific strategies for facilitating language in dementia patients are proposed. | IV |

| Author(s) & Title | Design | Sample | Objective of study | Conclusions | Evidence Level |
|---|---|---|---|---|---|
| **Communication Interventions in Later Dementia** | | | | | |
| Pietro MJS & Boczko F, 1998, 'The Breakfast Club: results of a study examining the effectiveness of a multi-modality group communication treatment', *American Journal of Alzheimer's Disease* 13:146–58. | Controlled study | 40 individuals with mid-stage Alzheimer's | Twenty individuals with mid-stage Alzheimer's participated for 12 weeks each in four groups of five in a five-day-a-week programme of structured multi-modality group communication intervention called 'The Breakfast Club'. Twenty matched patients participated in a standard conversation group and served as controls. The Breakfast Club attempted to incorporate all that was currently known about the residual communication strengths of Alzheimer's patients and about previous treatments shown to be effective with this population. | Results showed that Breakfast Club participants improved significantly on measures of language performance, functional independence and use of social communication, while control subjects did not. Breakfast Club members also showed significant increases in 'interest and involvement' and the use of procedural memories over the 12-week period. | IIa |
| **Partnership with Carer** | | | | | |
| Ripich DN, Ziol E, Fritsch T & Durand EJ, 1999, 'Training Alzheimer's disease caregivers for successful communication', *Clinical Gerontologist* 21:37–56. | Controlled study | 54 Alzheimer's disease caregivers were compared to a control group of 22 caregivers | A study of 54 Alzheimer's disease (AD) caregivers was conducted to investigate the effects of caregiver communication training. To improve communication – with their family members with AD – 32 caregivers participated in an eight-hour training program (FOCUSED). Ten of these were also given follow-up training (FOCUSEDBooster). The questioning patterns of the two groups of FOCUSED trained caregivers planning a menu with their family member with AD were compared to a control group of 22 caregivers. | Data were collected over three visits (entry, six months and 12 months). Analysis revealed that for all caregivers, open-ended questions, when compared with yes/no and choice questions, resulted in more failed responses by persons with AD. Following training, at six months, both FOCUSED and FOCUSED-Booster caregivers asked fewer open-ended questions compared to the control group. This suggests that communication partners of persons with AD can be trained to structure questions that result in more successful communication. | IIa |

## DISORDERS OF MENTAL HEALTH & DEMENTIA

| Author(s) & Title | Design | Sample | Objective of study | Conclusions | Evidence Level |
|---|---|---|---|---|---|
| Shulman MD & Mandel E, 1988, 'Communication training of relatives and friends of institutionalized elderly persons', *The Gerontologist* 28:797–9. | Qualitative study | Family members of residents in a home for the elderly | A series of workshops for family and friends of residents was designed to inform them of the nature of communication, how it is affected by the aging process, the psychological and neurological nature of communication impairments and how to manage situations in which communication breaks down. A questionnaire was administered pre- and post- the workshops. | The workshops resulted in increased understanding, increased satisfaction with visits and increased skills in using communication-facilitating techniques. | III |
| Greene VL & Monahan DJ, 1989, 'The effect of a support and education program on stress and burden among family caregivers to frail elderly persons', *The Gerontologist* 29:472–80. | Qualitative study | 208 individuals entered a support group 81 individuals acted as a control | 34 support groups were conducted over the 14-month life of the project. Each group met weekly for two hours over an eight-week period. | An eight-week professionally guided caregiver support group was found to produce statistically significant reductions in anxiety, depression and sense of burden among family caregivers to frail elderly persons living on the community. Effects were weaker four months after the intervention ended than immediately after, but reductions in anxiety and depression were still evident. | III |

| Author(s) & Title | Design | Sample | Objective of study | Conclusions | Evidence Level |
|---|---|---|---|---|---|
| Cavanaugh JC, Dunn NJ, Mowery D, Feller C, Niederehe G, Fruge E & Volpendesta D, 1989, 'Problem-solving strategies in dementia patient-caregiver dyads', *The Gerontologist* 29 (2):156–8. | Qualitative study | 45 families, of which 29 were involved with an older adult who had been diagnosed with dementia. Of these 29 participants, 16 involved a same-generation caregiver and 13 involved a younger-generation caregiver. The remaining 16 families were comparison families in which the target older adult was a normally ageing person. | The applicability of concepts of the zone of proximal development and scaffolding to the study of dementia were examined. Caregiver–patient dyads were compared to normal elderly dyads in the instructional strategies they used to complete the Block Design subtest of the WAIS- R. | The results showed that the use of a detailed behavioural coding scheme was successful in documenting systematic differences between the two groups. | III |

### Training

| | | | | | |
|---|---|---|---|---|---|
| Bayles KA, Kaszniak AW & Tomoeda CK, 1987, *Communication and Cognition in Normal Aging and Dementia*, Taylor & Francis, London. | Expert opinion | — | — | — | IV |

### Environment

| | | | | | |
|---|---|---|---|---|---|
| Lubinski R, 1995, 'Environmental considerations for elderly patients', *Dementia and Communication*, | Expert opinion | — | — | — | IV |

## DISORDERS OF MENTAL HEALTH & DEMENTIA

| Author(s) & Title | Design | Sample | Objective of study | Conclusions | Evidence Level |
|---|---|---|---|---|---|
| **Group Language Stimulation** | | | | | |
| Clark LW, 1995, 'Interventions for persons with Alzheimer's disease: Strategies for maintaining and enhancing communicative success', *Topics in Language Disorders* 15 (2): 47–65. | Literature review | — | Examines the challenge to identify and document effective non-medical communication interventions that will assist persons with Alzheimer's disease (AD) to function at their most optimal levels. Both direct (client-centred) and indirect (caregiver-oriented) interventions are described, and the intervention literature from disciplines other than speech and language pathology is reviewed. | Behavioural interventions and interventions for: 1) enhancing cognitive capacities, 2) non-verbal forms of expression, and 3) environmental orientation and responsiveness are described. Emphasis is placed on functional maintenance and prevention of excessive response to disability and learned helplessness. The authors argue for a paradigm shift from a focus on skills improvement to a broader quality-of-life orientation. | IV |
| **Assessment of Swallowing** | | | | | |
| Steele CM, Greenwood C, Robertson C, Sidmon-Carlson R, 1997, 'Mealtime difficulties in a home for the aged – not for dysphagia', *Dysphagia* 12:43–50. | Qualitative study | 349 residents of a home for the aged | A mealtime screening tool was administered to 349 residents of a home for the aged to determine the prevalence of mealtime difficulties. | An increased prevalence of mealtime difficulties was related to both the presence and degree of cognitive impairment. Oral intake was best among residents with severe cognitive impairment, many of whom received partial to total feeding assistance. In contrast, poor oral intake was associated with mild to moderate cognitive impairment, pointing to a need for more aggressive intervention with this group. The results clearly demonstrate that the prevalence of a wide range of eating-related problems far exceeds accepted estimates of dysphagia alone and support a multidisciplinary approach to mealtime interventions for the institutionalised elderly. | III |

| Author(s) & Title | Design | Sample | Objective of study | Conclusions | Evidence Level |
|---|---|---|---|---|---|
| Feinberg MJ, Ekberg O, Segall L & Tully J, 1992, 'Deglutition in elderly patients with dementia: findings of videofluorographic evaluation and impact on staging and management', *Radiology* 183 (3):811–14. | Clinical study | 131 individuals | Oral and pharyngeal function in 131 institutionalised elderly patients with advanced dementia was evaluated by means of videofluoroscopic deglutition examination (VDE). Evaluation of VDE findings prompted a change in clinical staging (degree of impairment) in 40 patients and substantial alteration in treatment planning in 28. | Findings were normal in only nine (7 per cent) patients. Oral-stage dysfunction was observed in 93 (71 percent) patients, pharyngeal dysfunction in 56 (43 percent) and pharyngoesophageal-segment abnormalities in 43 (33 percent). Multiple-stage dysfunction was noted in 55 (42 per cent) patients. Major aspiration of contrast medium was present in 31 patients, and minor aspiration in 66. Dementia is often associated with oral and pharyngeal impairment, and VDE can be important in diagnosis and treatment. | III |

### Management of Swallowing

| Author(s) & Title | Design | Sample | Objective of study | Conclusions | Evidence Level |
|---|---|---|---|---|---|
| Littlewood et al, 1997, 'Meal times: a missed opportunity?', *Journal of Dementia Care* July/Aug 18–20. | Qualitative study | 23 adults with dementia<br>21 staff | A questionnaire and an observation form were compiled to assess the following:<br>■ Patient's choices at mealtimes<br>■ Mealtime environment<br>■ Interactions between patients and with nursing staff<br>■ General mealtime atmosphere<br>Data was collected by two observers over a five-week period. | 15 out of 23 (65 percent) of patients participated in the questionnaire survey.<br>18 out of 21 (85 percent) of staff completed the questionnaire.<br>Changes have been made to the organisation of the ward subsequent to the study. | III |
| Finucane TE, Christmas C & Travis K, 1999, 'Tube feeding in patients with advanced dementia: a review of the evidence', *JAMA* 282 (14):1365–70. | Literature search | — | MEDLINE, 1966 through March 1999, was searched, to identify data about whether tube feeding in patients with advanced dementia can prevent aspiration pneumonia, prolong survival, reduce the risk of pressure sores or infections, improve function or provide palliation. | We found no published randomised trials that compare tube feeding with oral feeding. We found no data to suggest that tube feeding improves any of these clinically important outcomes, and some data to suggest that it does not. Further, risks are substantial. The widespread practice of tube feeding should be carefully reconsidered, and we believe that for severely demented patients the practice should be discouraged on clinical grounds. | IV |

## DISORDERS OF MENTAL HEALTH & DEMENTIA

| Author(s) & Title | Design | Sample | Objective of study | Conclusions | Evidence Level |
|---|---|---|---|---|---|
| **Behavioural Strategies** | | | | | |
| Coyne ML & Hoskins I, 1997, 'Improving eating behaviours in dementia using behavioural strategies', *Clinical Nursing Research* 6 (3):275–90. | Randomised controlled trial | 24 subjects from a dementia unit were randomly selected and randomly assigned to three experimental groups and three control groups | The purpose of this experimental pilot study was to determine the short- and long-term efficacy of directed verbal prompts and positive reinforcement on the level of eating independence (LEI) of elderly nursing-home patients with dementia. Short-term effects were assessed on two consecutive days following treatment (t2) and long-term effects on two consecutive days, seven days following treatment. | Significant differences were found in eating performance but not in frequency. Experimental groups retained treatment at both post-tests. The dementia diagnosis should not preclude the possibility that eating skills may be reacquired. | Ib |
| Kayser-Jones J & Schell E, 1997, 'Clinical outlook. The mealtime experience of a cognitively impaired elder: ineffective and effective strategies', *Journal of Gerontology Nursing* 23 (7):33–39. | Case study | 86-year-old woman with Alzheimer's disease | 100 residents of nursing homes were observed for six months or longer by graduate students in nursing and sociology. Each resident was observed weekly at all three meals noting how, when and what food was served, what the resident ate and a variety of interactions. This paper presents a case study of one woman and reports on effective and ineffective mealtime strategies. | Recommendations for positive strategies are suggested. | III |

| Author(s) & Title | Design | Sample | Objective of study | Conclusions | Evidence Level |
|---|---|---|---|---|---|
| Osborn CL & Marshall MJ, 1993, 'Self-feeding performance in nursing home residents', *Journal of Gerontology Nursing* 19 (3):7–14. | Qualitative study | 23 residents in a nursing home who were identified as partially dependent in feeding and had moderate to severe cognitive impairment | The study involved observations of the residents' self-feeding behaviours during two meals. Each resident was assessed individually at one meal for capability and at another meal for performance. Resident–staff interaction was also observed. Excess disability was found in the specific mealtime task of drinking liquids and among those eating a pureed diet. | Nursing home staff tended to rely on spoon feeding – a process in which the resident is a passive recipient of care rather than an active participant – as an intervention among residents who were partially able to feed themselves. Feeding techniques other than spoon feeding – including verbal and non-verbal prompts, and physical guiding – can support residents' participation in feeding even when independence is no longer possible. | III |

## DYSARTHRIA

| Author(s) & Title | Design | Sample | Objective of study | Conclusions | Evidence Level |
|---|---|---|---|---|---|
| **Multidisciplinary Team Working** | | | | | |
| Mitchell PR & Mahoney G, 1995, 'Team management for young children with motor speech disorders', *Seminars in Speech & Language* 16 (2):159–71. | Expert opinion | — | Describes the various forms of team-working and illustrates this with information from their own setting. | — | IV |
| **Perceptual Assessment** | | | | | |
| Netsell R & Daniel B, 1979, 'Dysarthria in adults: physiologic approach to rehabilitation', *Archives of Physical Medicine & Rehabilitation* 60 (11):502–8. | Case study | 20-year-old man, post-road traffic accident | A case study is used to illustrate a physical approach to the speech rehabilitation of adults with dysarthria. The approach emphasises the component-by-component analysis of the peripheral speech mechanism, where the selection and sequencing of treatment procedures follow directly from the physiologicalnature and severity of involvement in each component. | The case illustration is of a young man injured in an auto accident whose speech intelligibility improves from approximately 5–10 percent to 95 percent during the rehabilitation period. Effects of treatment upon individual components of the speech mechanism are illustrated. | III |
| Duffy JR, 1998, 'Stroke with dysarthria: evaluate and treat; garden variety or down the garden path?', *Seminars in Speech and Language* 19 (1):93–101. | Case study | 71-year-old man | The case of a man who initially presented to an emergency room with an isolated dysarthria is reviewed in order to demonstrate how history, clinical context and clinical observations can lead to accurate or inaccurate diagnosis. | The diagnostic process in this case illustrates, among others, the role of the history and clinical context in diagnosis, but their occasional capacity to mislead; the use of deductive strategies and pattern recognition in speech diagnosis; and the importance of diagnostic vigilance. | III |

| Author(s) & Title | Design | Sample | Objective of study | Conclusions | Evidence Level |
|---|---|---|---|---|---|
| **Communication Skills Profile** | | | | | |
| Yorkston KM, Strand EA & Kennedy MRT, 1996, 'Comprehensibility of dysarthric speech: implications for assessment and treatment planning', *American Journal of Speech Language Pathology* 5 (1):55–66. | Literature review | — | This paper describes the concept of comprehensibility, and how it is an important construct in the assessment and treatment of dysarthric speech. Intelligibility and comprehensibility are differentiated in terms of their definition, measurement and approaches to treatment. Specifically, comprehensibility is defined within the World Health Organisation model of chronic disease as a factor in disability affecting speech performance in physical and/or social contexts. The literature related to comprehensibility of dysarthric speech is reviewed. | — | IV |
| Berry W & Saunders S, 1983, 'Environmental Education: the universal management approach for adults with dysarthria', in Berry W (ed) *Clinical Dysarthria*, Pro-Ed, Austin, TX. | Expert opinion | — | — | — | IV |
| **Perception of Dysarthria** | | | | | |
| Fox CM & Ramig LO, 1997, 'Vocal sound pressure level and self-perception of speech and voice in men and women with idiopathic Parkinson disease', *American Journal of Speech Language Pathology* 6 (2):85–94. | Comparative study | 30 subjects with PD (15 men, 15 women) and 14 healthy comparison subjects (7 men, 7 women) | This study compared vocal sound pressure level and self-perception of speech and voice in men and women with idiopathic Parkinson disease with that in healthy men and women. They performed a variety of speech and voice tasks, and carried out perceptual self-ratings of nine speech and voice characteristics. To assess performance stability, subjects repeated the data collection procedures on three different days. | Results revealed that subjects with PD rated themselves as statistically significantly more severely impaired than HC subjects on all nine self-rated perceptual variables examined. | III |

## DYSARTHRIA

| Author(s) & Title | Design | Sample | Objective of study | Conclusions | Evidence Level |
|---|---|---|---|---|---|
| **Differential Diagnosis** | | | | | |
| Murdoch B (ed), *Dysarthria: A Physiological Approach to Assessment and Treatment*, Nelson Thornes, Cheltenham. | Expert opinion | — | — | — | IV |
| Yorkston KM, Beukelman DR & Bell KR, 1987, *Clinical Management of Dysarthric Speakers*, Taylor & Francis, London. | Expert opinion | — | — | — | IV |
| **Competing Environmental Stimuli** | | | | | |
| Yorkston KM, Strand EA & Kennedy MRT, 1996, 'Comprehensibility of dysarthric speech: implications for assessment and treatment planning', *American Journal of Speech Language Pathology* 5 (1):55–66. | Literature review | — | This paper describes the concept of comprehensibility, and how it is an important construct in the assessment and treatment of dysarthric speech. Intelligibility and comprehensibility are differentiated in terms of their definition, measurement and approaches to treatment. Specifically, comprehensibility is defined within the World Health Organisation model of chronic disease as a factor in disability affecting speech performance in physical and/or social contexts. The literature related to comprehensibility of dysarthric speech is reviewed. | — | IV |
| **Psychosocial Impact of Dysarthria** | | | | | |
| Yorkston KM, Bombardier C & Hammen VL, 1994, 'Dysarthria form the viewpoint of individuals with dysarthria', in Till J, Yorkston KM & Beukelman DR (eds) *Motor Speech Disorders – Advances in Assessment and Treatment*, Paul Brooks Publishing, Baltimore, MD. | Qualitative study | 33 adults with dysarthria with a range of severities | A 100-item questionnaire was developed to solicit information in the following areas: characteristics of the disorder; situational difficulty; compensatory strategies; and perceived reactions of others. | Results demonstrated that there was little difference among the groups for the numbers of speech characteristics endorsed, type and frequency of situations felt to be difficult and the number of compensatory strategies found to be beneficial. The clearest distinction between the severity groups was found to be in the perceived reactions of others. | III |

| Author(s) & Title | Design | Sample | Objective of study | Conclusions | Evidence Level |
|---|---|---|---|---|---|
| **Conversational Partners** | | | | | |
| King JM & Gallegos-Santillan P, 1999, 'Strategy use by speakers with dysarthria and both familiar and unfamiliar conversational partners', *Journal of Medical Speech-Language Pathology*, 7 (2):113–16. | Comparative study | 7 adults with dysarthria resulting from a CVA/TBI/cerebral palsy  14 adults with normal speech and language skills acted as either an unfamiliar or a familiar conversational partner | This study describes the types of strategies used by speakers with dysarthria (26–73 year olds) and their partners to improve the success of a communicative exchange. Speakers conversed with both a familiar communication partner and an unfamiliar communication partner. | The speakers with dysarthria tended to use more strategies with the unfamiliar communication partner than the familiar communication partner. The unfamiliar communication partners used more strategies with the speaker than the familiar communication partners. | III |
| **Physiological Approaches** | | | | | |
| Katsikitis M & Pilowsky I, 1996, 'A controlled study of facial mobility treatment in Parkinson's disease', *Journal of Psychosomatic Research* 40 (4):387–96. | Randomised controlled study | 16 individuals (mean age 69.94 yrs) with Parkinson's disease | Evaluated the effects of orofacial physiotherapeutic treatment on the facial mobility of individuals with Parkinson's disease. 16 individuals were allocated randomly to either the treatment group or to the control group. A short interview with each individual was videotaped, and 10 random frames of the videotape were used in the facial expression (FE) assessment. A facial outline was obtained, as well as 12 facial measures. The FE assessment was performed at baseline (pre-treatment), post-treatment and 4 weeks later. | Members of the treatment group were found after treatment to open their mouths to a greater extent than did those in the control group. Similarly, mid-top-lip measure; lower-lip thickness measure; top eyelid/iris intersect measure; and lower eyelid/iris intersect measure were significant across time in the treatment group only. | Ib |

## DYSARTHRIA

| Author(s) & Title | Design | Sample | Objective of study | Conclusions | Evidence Level |
|---|---|---|---|---|---|
| Ramig L, Countryman S, Thompson L & Horii Y, 1995, 'Comparison of two forms of intensive speech treatment for Parkinson Disease', *Journal of Speech Hearing Research* 38:1232–51. | Randomised controlled trial | 45 individuals with idiopathic Parkinson's disease | This study investigated the effects of two forms of intensive speech treatment: respiration (R), and voice and respiration (LSVT). Forty-five individuals completed 16 sessions of intensive speech treatment, four times per week for one month, on the speech and voice deficits associated with idiopathic Parkinson disease (IPD). A range of variables were assessed pre- and post-treatment. | Significant pre/post-treatment improvements were observed for more variables, and were of greater magnitude, for the individuals who received the LSVT. Only those who received the LSVT rated a significant decrease post-treatment on the impact of IPD on their communication. | Ib |
| Robertson SJ & Thomson F, 1984, 'Speech therapy in Parkinson's disease: A study of the efficacy and long term effects of intensive treatment', *Language & Communication Disorders* 36 Suppl:292–297, 2001. | Controlled study | 12 patients (aged 50–82 years) with Parkinson's disease. Six other parkinsonian patients (aged 53–78 years) served as controls. | The study evaluated the efficacy, and assessed the long-term effects, of intensive speech therapy in 12 patients with Parkinson's disease. Six other Parkinsonian patients served as controls. Experimental subjects participated in a two-week intensive speech therapy programme in which they were taught techniques designed to improve method, capacity and control of respiration; coordination and control of voice production; articulatory muscular control and strength; control of speech rate; and communication intelligibility. | Subjects were assessed pre- and post-therapy and at three months follow-up on the Dysarthria Profile. Results indicate that subjects improved in almost every aspect of motor production of speech and related activities, and that they were able to maintain this improvement at three months follow-up. | IIb |

| Author(s) & Title | Design | Sample | Objective of study | Conclusions | Evidence Level |
|---|---|---|---|---|---|
| Le Dorze G, Dionne L, Ryalls J, Julien M & Ouellet L, 1992, 'The effects of speech and language therapy for a case of dysarthria associated with Parkinson's disease', *European Journal of Disorders of Communication* 27 (4):313–24. | Single subject design | 74-year-old woman presenting with Parkinson's disease | The results of a single-subject multiple baseline across behaviours experiment on a 74-year-old woman presenting with Parkinson's disease are reported. Her speech was typical of a hypokinetic dysarthria. The main features of her dysarthric speech were: a restriction in the modulation of fundamental frequency, an inappropriate pitch level and a rate disturbance. Three measures of prosody were operationally defined as follows: 1) linguistic modulation of fundamental frequency; 2) mean fundamental frequency; and 3) rate. Treatment focused on ameliorating these aspects employing a multiple baseline design. | Measures during and post-therapy documented improvement for each of these three aspects of prosody. Independent judges were also more capable of understanding her speech and her speech prosody after therapy. Upon follow-up measures 10 weeks later, most of the improvement was maintained. | III |
| Robertson S, 2001, 'The efficacy of oro-facial and articulation exercises in dysarthria following stroke', *International Journal of Language & Communication Disorders* 36:292–7. | Conference proceedings | — | This study investigates the efficacy of traditional exercise therapy for eight clients. A clinic-based therapy programme and an exercise routine for home practice were agreed by a group of Speech & Language Therapists. | The results indicate not only the value of the therapy but also of a realistic and viable programme for clients to carry out at home. | IV |

**Compensatory Approaches**

| Author(s) & Title | Design | Sample | Objective of study | Conclusions | Evidence Level |
|---|---|---|---|---|---|
| Yorkston KM, Hammen VL, Beukelman DR & Traynor CD, 1990, 'The effect of rate control on the intelligibility and naturalness of dysarthric speech', *Journal of Speech Hearing Disorders* 55 (3):550–60. | Controlled study | 8 dysarthric individuals whose habitual sentence intelligibility was less than 90 percent 4 individuals with no history of neurological disorder served as controls | Speaking rates of individuals with severe ataxic dysarthria (n=4) and severe hypokinetic dysarthria (n=4) were reduced to 60 percent and 80 percent of habitual rates using four different pacing strategies (additive metered; additive rhythmic; cued metered; and cued rhythmic). Effects of rate control on sentence and phoneme intelligibility and speech naturalness were examined. | Sentence intelligibility improved for both groups, with metered pacing conditions associated with the largest improvement in scores. Similar improvements were not seen for the phoneme intelligibility task as speaking rates were reduced; however, one must recognise that sentence and phoneme intelligibility tasks are different. Slowing the rate of dysarthric speakers did not have as marked an impact on speech naturalness as it did for normal speakers whose naturalness decreased at slowed rates. Metered rate control strategies were associated with the lowest ratings of naturalness for all subject groups. | IIa |

## DYSARTHRIA

| Author(s) & Title | Design | Sample | Objective of study | Conclusions | Evidence Level |
|---|---|---|---|---|---|
| Workinger MS & Netsell R, 1992, 'Restoration of intelligible speech 13 years post-head injury', *Brain Injury* 6 (2):183–7. | Case study | 28-year-old male | This case study demonstrates the efficacy of treatment of a patient with severe dysarthria long after the accepted period of 'neurological recovery'. A physiological approach to treatment was utilised and resulted in a change from non-verbal communication to functional verbal communication. | — | III |
| Berry W & Saunders S, 1983, 'Environmental education: the universal management approach for adults with dysarthria', in Berry W (ed) *Clinical Dysarthria*, Pro-Ed, Austin, TX. | Expert opinion | — | — | | IV |

| Author(s) & Title | Design | Sample | Objective of study | Conclusions | Evidence Level |
|---|---|---|---|---|---|
| **Augmentative Approaches** | | | | | |
| Garcia JM & Dagenais PA, 1998, 'Dysarthric sentence intelligibility: contribution of iconic gestures and message predictiveness', *Journal of Speech, Language & Hearing Research* 41:1282–93. | Comparative study | 4 individuals with dysarthria 96 inexperienced listeners | This study examined changes in the sentence intelligibility scores of speakers with dysarthria in association with different signal-independent factors (contextual influences). This investigation focused on the presence or absence of iconic gestures while speaking sentences with low or high semantic predictiveness. The speakers were four individuals with dysarthria, who varied from one another in terms of their level of speech intelligibility impairment, gestural abilities and overall level of motor functioning. Ninety-six inexperienced listeners (24 assigned to each speaker) orthographically transcribed 16 test sentences presented in an audio plus video or audio-only format. The sentences had either low or high semantic predictiveness and were spoken by each speaker with and without the corresponding gestures. The effects of signal-independent factors (presence or absence of iconic gestures, low or high semantic predictiveness, and audio plus video or audio-only presentation formats) were analysed for individual speakers. | Not all signal-independent information benefited speakers similarly. Results indicated that use of gestures and high semantic predictiveness improved sentence intelligibility for two speakers. The other two speakers benefited from high predictive messages. The audio plus video presentation mode enhanced listener understanding for all speakers, although there were interactions related to specific speaking situations. Overall, the contributions of relevant signal-independent information were greater for the speakers with more severely impaired intelligibility. | III |

## DYSARTHRIA

| Author(s) & Title | Design | Sample | Objective of study | Conclusions | Evidence Level |
|---|---|---|---|---|---|
| Garcia JM & Cannito MP, 1996, 'Influence of verbal and nonverbal contexts on the sentence intelligibility of a speaker with dysarthria', *Journal of Speech Hearing Research* 39 (4):750–60. | Single case study | 62-year-old man with a history of CVA | The influence of verbal and non-verbal contextual factors on intelligibility was examined using sentences produced under varying conditions by a speaker with severe flaccid dysarthria. Contextual factors included: a) concurrent production of communication gestures; b) predictiveness of message content; c) relatedness of sentences to specific situational contexts; and d) prior familiarisation with the speaker. Sentences produced by the speaker were audio- and video-recorded and presented to 96 listeners/viewers who were assigned to three different methods of presentation of the stimuli: a) audio plus video, b) audio-only, or c) video-only conditions. | Results indicated that gestures, predictiveness and context influenced intelligibility; however, complex interactions were observed among these factors and methods of presentation of the stimuli. Results were interpreted in light of Lindblom's 'mutuality model', indicating that when signal fidelity is poor, as in the present speaker with dysarthria, differing combinations of signal-independent information may be employed to enhance listener understanding of spoken messages. | III |
| Beliveau C, Hodge MM & Hagler PH, 1995, 'Effects of supplemental linguistic cues on the intelligibility of severely dysarthric speakers', *Augmentative & Alternative Communication* 11 (3):176–86. | Comparative study | 3 female dysarthric speakers, with dysarthria ranging in severity from moderately severe to profound. 2 speakers had cerebral palsy and the third had a traumatic brain injury. | The purpose of this investigation was to determine if any of three types of linguistic cues (first letter, word class, combined first letter and word class) aided listeners in their ability to understand three speakers with different severity levels of dysarthria. Speech intelligibility was judged by four panels of 10 unfamiliar listeners (n=40) using a word transcription task. A two-factor (4 x 3) mixed design was used to determine the effects of cueing conditions and severity of dysarthria on speech intelligibility scores expressed as the number of correctly transcribed single words. The two factors were linguistic cue, having four levels (no cue, first-letter cue, word-class cue, combined first-letter and word-class cue), and speaker severity level, having three levels (profound/severe/moderately severe). | Significant main effects were found for the two independent variables. A significant first-order interaction was found for cueing condition by speaker severity. All three supplemental cueing conditions increased speech intelligibility scores, with the combined cueing condition providing the greatest enhancement of scores. Results are discussed with reference to the most effective cueing condition for each speaker severity level. The findings support the use of a combination of linguistic cues to augment the speech intelligibility of severe and profoundly dysarthric speakers. | III |

| Author(s) & Title | Design | Sample | Objective of study | Conclusions | Evidence Level |
|---|---|---|---|---|---|
| Hustad KC & Beukelman DR, 2002, 'Listener comprehension of severely dysarthric speech: Effects of linguistic cues and stimulus cohesion', *Journal of Speech Language & Hearing Research* 45 (3):545–88. | Comparative study | 4 women (aged 19 to 46 years) with severe dysarthria | This study examined the effects of experimentally imposed topic cues, alphabet cues and combined cues on listener comprehension of severely dysarthric speech produced by four women (aged 19 to 46 years) with severe dysarthria secondary to cerebral palsy. In addition, the relationship between intelligibility and comprehension was examined for each cue and stimulus cohesion condition. | Consistent with intelligibility results, the present study found that combined cues resulted in higher comprehension scores than any other cue condition and that no cues resulted in lower comprehension scores than any other cue condition for both related and unrelated sentences. In addition, comprehension scores were higher for alphabet cues than for topic cues in the related-sentences condition. | III |
| Garcia JM & Cobb DS, 2000, 'The effects of gesturing on speech intelligibility and rate in ALS dysarthria: A case study', *Journal of Medical Speech-Language Pathology* 8 (4):353–7. | Case series | 4 individuals with dysarthria | This study examined changes in the sentence intelligibility scores of speakers with dysarthria in association with different signal-independent factors (contextual influences). This investigation focused on the presence or absence of iconic gestures while speaking sentences with low or high semantic predictiveness. The speakers were four individuals with dysarthria, who varied from one another in terms of their level of speech intelligibility impairment, gestural abilities and overall level of motor functioning. Ninety-six inexperienced listeners (24 assigned to each speaker) orthographically transcribed 16 test sentences presented in an audio plus video or audio-only format. The sentences had either low or high semantic predictiveness and were spoken by each speaker with and without the corresponding gestures. The effects of signal-independent factors (presence or absence of iconic gestures, low or high semantic predictiveness, and audio plus video or audio-only presentation formats) were analysed for individual speakers. Not all signal-independent information benefited speakers similarly. | Results indicated that use of gestures and high semantic predictiveness improved sentence intelligibility for two speakers. The other two speakers benefited from highly predictive messages. The audio plus video presentation mode enhanced listener understanding for all speakers, although there were interactions related to specific speaking situations. Overall, the contributions of relevant signal-independent information were greater for the speakers with more severely impaired intelligibility. | III |

## APHASIA

### Effectiveness of Aphasia Therapy

| Author(s) & Title | Design | Sample | Objective of study | Conclusions | Evidence Level |
|---|---|---|---|---|---|
| Greener J, Enderby P & Whurr R, 2004, 'Speech and language therapy for aphasia following stroke', *Cochrane Database of Systematic Reviews* 2. | A search of the Cochrane Stroke Group Trials Register (last searched: March 1999) and reference lists of relevant articles to December 1998. Academic institutions and other researchers were also contacted to identify further published and unpublished trials. The *International Journal of Disorders of Communication* (known by other names in the past) was searched by hand, from 1969 to 1998. Date of most recent searches: January 1999. | Randomised controlled trials comparing: 1 Any type of formal speech and language therapy in any setting administered by trained speech and language therapists, versus no treatment. 2 Any type of formal speech and language therapy in any setting administered by trained speech and language therapists, versus any type of informal support for aphasia, given by speech and language therapists or volunteers, whether these were trained or untrained. | The objective of this review was to assess the effects of formal speech and language therapy and non-professional types of support from untrained providers for people with aphasia after stroke. | We considered 60 studies in detail, from which we identified 12 trials suitable for the review. Most of these trials were relatively old, with poor or unassessable methodological quality. None of the trials was detailed enough for us to complete description and analysis. We could not determine whether formal speech and language therapy is more effective than informal support. The main conclusion of this review is that speech and language therapy treatment for people with aphasia after a stroke has not been shown either to be clearly effective or clearly ineffective within a RCT. Decisions about the management of patients must therefore be based on other forms of evidence. Further research is required to find out if effectiveness of speech and language therapy for aphasic patients is effective. If researchers choose to do a trial, this must be large enough to have adequate statistical power, and be clearly reported. | I |

| Author(s) & Title | Design | Sample | Objective of study | Conclusions | Evidence Level |
|---|---|---|---|---|---|
| | | | 3. One type of speech and language therapy versus another type. Outcome measures included measures of any type of communication, other measures of functioning, numbers of drop-outs, and other non-clinical outcomes. | | |
| Robey RR, 1998, 'A meta-analysis of clinical outcomes in the treatment of aphasia', *Journal of Speech Language & Hearing Research*, 41(1):172–87. | An extensive search of aphasia-treatment literature yielded 55 reports of clinical outcomes satisfying the essential criteria for inclusion in a meta-analysis. | — | | The results confirmed those of an earlier meta-analysis in demonstrating the utility of aphasia treatments, generally considered, for bringing about desirable clinical outcomes. Beyond the general case, the new findings address clinical utility in finer detail than was previously possible. Effects of treatment for aphasia are synthesised and assessed for each of four important dimensions: amount of treatment; type of treatment; severity of aphasia; and type of aphasia. | II |

## APHASIA

| Author(s) & Title | Design | Sample | Objective of study | Conclusions | Evidence Level |
|---|---|---|---|---|---|
| **Key Aims of Intervention** | | | | | |
| Hilari K, Wiggins RD, Roy P, Byng S & Smith SC, 2003, 'Predictors of health-related quality of life (HRQL) in people with chronic aphasia', *Aphasiology*, 17(4): 365–81. | Cross-sectional survey study | 83 individuals (aged 21–92 yrs) diagnosed with chronic aphasia one year or more previously completed questionnaires and assessments concerning HRQL, emotional distress, daily activities, communication and social support. | Examined the main predictors of health-related quality of life (HRQL) in individuals with chronic aphasia following stroke. | Results show that 87 percent of subjects were able to self-report on all assessments. Emotional distress, involvement in home and outdoors activities, extent of communication disability, and number of co-morbid conditions explained 52 percent of the variance in HRQL. Stroke type, time post-onset and the demographic variables of gender, ethnicity, marital status, employment status, and socioeconomic status were not significantly associated with HRQL. It is concluded that increased distress, reduced involvement in activities, increased communication disability and co-morbidity predict poorer HRQL in those individuals with chronic aphasia after stroke. | II |
| Royal College of Physicians, 2004, *National Clinical Guidelines for Stroke*, prepared by The Intercollegiate Working Party for Stroke, London. www.rcplondon.ac.uk | Expert opinion | | | | IV |

| Author(s) & Title | Design | Sample | Objective of study | Conclusions | Evidence Level |
|---|---|---|---|---|---|
| Scottish Intercollegiate Guideline Network, 2002, 'Management of patients with stroke: Rehabilitation, prevention and management of complications, and discharge planning', *SIGN Guideline 64.* www.sign.ac.uk | Expert opinion | | | | IV |
| **Working in Partnership** | | | | | |
| NHS Executive, 1999, *Clinical Governance in the new NHS*, NHS Executive Quality Management Branch, London. | Expert opinion | | | | IV |
| Mayou R & Bryant B, 1993, 'Quality of Life in Cardiovascular Disease', *British Heart Journal*, 69 (5): 460–66. | Expert opinion | | | Review of the literature on quality of life and of use of quality of life assessment in relation to cardiovascular disease suggests basic principles about the ways in which these can be applied to research and clinical practice. High quality measures that have been properly chosen and not ad hoc token assessment, should be used. | IV |
| **Working in Partnership: Recommendation 1** | | | | | |
| Pound C, Parr S, Lindsay J & Woolf C, 2000, *Beyond Aphasia: Therapies for Living with Communication Disabilities*, Speechmark Publishing, Bicester. | Text | | | | IV |
| NHS Executive, 1999, *Clinical Governance in the new NHS*, NHS Executive Quality Management Branch, London. | Expert opinion | | | | IV |

## APHASIA

| Author(s) & Title | Design | Sample | Objective of study | Conclusions | Evidence Level |
|---|---|---|---|---|---|
| **Working in Partnership: Recommendation 2** | | | | | |
| Kagan A, Black S, Duchan J, Simmons-Mackie N & Square P, 2001, 'Training volunteers as conversational partners using "Supported Conversation for Adults with Aphasia" (SCA): A controlled trial', *Journal of Speech Language and Hearing Research*, 44: 624–38. | Randomised controlled trial | Twenty volunteers received SCA training and 20 control volunteers were merely exposed to people with aphasia. | This article reports the development and evaluation of a new intervention termed 'Supported Conversation for Adults with Aphasia' (SCA). The approach is based on the idea that the inherent competence of people with aphasia can be revealed through the skill of a conversation partner. The intervention approach was developed at a community-based aphasia centre where volunteers interact with individuals with chronic aphasia and their families. The experimental study was designed to test whether training improves the conversational skills of volunteers, and, if so, whether the improvements affect the communication of their conversation partners with aphasia. Twenty volunteers received SCA training, and 20 control volunteers were merely exposed to people with aphasia. Comparisons between the groups' scores on a Measure of Supported Conversation for Adults with Aphasia provide support for the efficacy of SCA. | Trained volunteers scored significantly higher than untrained volunteers on ratings of acknowledging competence and revealing competence of their partners with aphasia. The training also produced a positive change in ratings of social and message exchange skills of individuals with aphasia, even though these individuals did not participate in the training. Implications for the treatment of aphasia and an argument for a social model of intervention are discussed. | I |
| McClenahan R, Johnston M & Densham Y, 1992, 'Factors influencing accuracy of estimation of comprehension problems in patients following cerebrovascular accident, by doctors, nurses and relatives', *European Journal of Disorders of Communication*, 27(3): 209–19. | Correlation study | Doctors, nurses, and relatives of 30 aphasic stroke inpatients | Doctors, nurses and relatives of 30 aphasic stroke patients estimated how patients would perform on the comprehension sections of the Functional Communication Profile and the Western Aphasia Battery. Possible factors influencing the accuracy of these judgements were studied, including confidence of the respondents, the severity of the patients' comprehension problems, the relatives' educational background, and the length of the relative–patient relationship. | Although doctors, nurses and relatives over-estimated patients' abilities on both tests, they were more accurate for patients with mild problems. Doctors and nurses who were more confident of their predictions were more accurate than those with less confidence, whereas relatives were equally inaccurate when giving high and low confidence judgements. Length of relationship and educational level did not predict relatives' accuracy. | II |

| Author(s) & Title | Design | Sample | Objective of study | Conclusions | Evidence Level |
|---|---|---|---|---|---|
| **Assessment** | | | | | |
| **Assessment: Recommendation 1** | | | | | |
| Kertesz A, 1994, 'Neuropsychological evaluation of language', *Journal of Clinical Neurophysiology*, 11(2): 205–15. | Expert opinion | | Neuropsychological evaluation of language may be based on the psychometric approach or on extensive exploration of modular functions according to cognitive or linguistic theory. Various approaches have several features in common, although some emphasise individual functions and others explore syndromes in brain-damaged populations. Systematic assessment of language has been developed according to the goals of various clinicians and researchers. Beyond the diagnostic need, prognosis and planning for therapy, there are important theoretical reasons to have standardised aphasia tests and complementary experimental explorations of language deficit. Objective quantitation of deficit allows the study of the anatomical and physiological organisation of language-related structures. It also contributes to the relationship of language and other modalities of cognition, hemispheric lateralisation, language development in children and language dissolution in degenerative disease. The requirements, content, standardisation and application of aphasia tests are discussed. | | IV |

## APHASIA

| Author(s) & Title | Design | Sample | Objective of study | Conclusions | Evidence Level |
|---|---|---|---|---|---|
| Holland A, 1998, 'Functional outcome assessment of aphasia following left hemisphere stroke', *Seminars in Speech & Language*, 19 (3): 249–60, 323–4. | Expert opinion | | This article discusses issues regarding the assessment of functional outcomes in individuals who have aphasia following stroke. | Some different approaches to functional outcome measurement are critically reviewed, ranging from general measures of stroke outcome to measures that have been designed specifically for aphasic individuals, to measurements focusing on aphasia's effects on quality of life. Examples of how to relate treatment of aphasia directly to functional outcomes assessment are also provided. | IV |

### Assessment: Recommendation 3

| | | | | | |
|---|---|---|---|---|---|
| Hilari K, Wiggins RD, Roy P, Byng S & Smith SC, 2003, 'Predictors of health-related quality of life (HRQL) in people with chronic aphasia', *Aphasiology*, 17 (4): 365–81. | Cross-sectional survey study | 83 individuals (aged 21–92 yrs) diagnosed with chronic aphasia one year or more previously completed questionnaires and assessments concerning HRQL, emotional distress, daily activities, communication and social support. | Examined the main predictors of health-related quality of life (HRQL) in individuals with chronic aphasia following stroke. | Results show that 87 percent of subjects were able to self-report on all assessments. Emotional distress, involvement in home and outdoors activities, extent of communication disability, and number of co-morbid conditions explained 52 percent of the variance in HRQL. Stroke type, time post-onset and the demographic variables of gender, ethnicity, marital status, employment status, and socioeconomic status were not significantly associated with HRQL. It is concluded that increased distress, reduced involvement in activities, increased communication disability and co-morbidity predict poorer HRQL in those individuals with chronic aphasia after stroke. | II |

| Author(s) & Title | Design | Sample | Objective of study | Conclusions | Evidence Level |
|---|---|---|---|---|---|
| Aftonomos LB, Steele RD, Appelbaum JS, Harris VM, 2001, 'Relationships between impairment-level assessments and functional-level assessments in aphasia: Findings from LCC treatment programmes', *Aphasiology*, 15 (10–11): 951–64. | Correlation study | 50 adults | This study reports an outcome study of persons with aphasia participating in community-based treatment programmes. Patients were assessed before and after treatment using: (i) a standardised test of impairment, the Western Aphasia Battery, administered by treating clinicians; and (ii) a standardised assessment of disability (functional communication), the Communicative Effectiveness Index, rated by family members. Pre-treatment and post-treatment means are calculated and compared, with matched t-tests utilised to probe statistical significance of improvements after treatment. Impairment- and functional-level means were calculated by aphasia diagnostic categories, assigning rank orders and calculating Spearman rank-order correlations. | Data analysis shows that, before treatment, patients spanned a wide range of times after onset, aphasia diagnostic types and severity levels at start of care. Following treatment, means of the 50 patients improved significantly on every measure administered at both the impairment and the functional levels. Before treatment, there is strong positive correlation between impairment-level and functional-level assessment means by diagnostic categories; after treatment, improvement means by these diagnostic categories show moderate negative correlation. Further examination shows that post-treatment improvements are found to be best viewed as functions of same-type severity levels pre-treatment, with patterns of improvement at the impairment and functional levels diverging distinctly. | III |

**Assessment: Recommendation 4**

| | | | | | |
|---|---|---|---|---|---|
| Aftonomos LB, Steele RD, Appelbaum JS, Harris VM, 2001, 'Relationships between impairment-level assessments and functional-level assessments in aphasia: Findings from LCC treatment programmes', *Aphasiology*, 15 (10–11): 951–64. | Correlation study | 50 adults | This study reports an outcome study of persons with aphasia participating in community-based treatment programmes. Patients were assessed before and after treatment using: (i) a standardised test of impairment, the Western Aphasia Battery, administered by treating clinicians; and (ii) a standardised assessment of disability (functional communication), the Communicative Effectiveness Index, rated by family members. Pre-treatment and post-treatment means are calculated and compared, with matched t-tests utilised to probe statistical significance of improvements after treatment. Impairment- and functional-level means were calculated by aphasia diagnostic categories, assigning rank orders and calculating Spearman rank-order correlations. | Data analysis shows that, before treatment, patients spanned a wide range of times after onset, aphasia diagnostic types and severity levels at start of care. Following treatment, means of the 50 patients improved significantly on every measure administered at both the impairment and the functional levels. Before treatment, there is strong positive correlation between impairment-level and functional-level assessment means by diagnostic categories; after treatment, improvement means by these diagnostic categories show moderate negative correlation. Further examination shows that post-treatment improvements are found to be best viewed as functions of same-type severity levels pre-treatment, with patterns of improvement at the impairment and functional levels diverging distinctly. | III |

## APHASIA

| Author(s) & Title | Design | Sample | Objective of study | Conclusions | Evidence Level |
|---|---|---|---|---|---|
| Davidson B, Worrall L & Hickson L, 2003, 'Identifying the communication activities of older people with aphasia: Evidence from naturalistic observation', *Aphasiology*, 17 (3): 243–64. | Comparative study | The daily communication activities of 30 adults (aged 63–80 yrs) were observed and recorded for a total of 240 hrs during this study. After each hour of observation, the researcher checked which ASHA FACS items had been observed. | This study describes and compares the everyday communication activities of older people with aphasia and healthy older people living in the community. This study also investigated the content validity of the American Speech-Language Hearing Association Functional Assessment of Communication Skills for Adults (ASHA FACS) for older Australians. | The most common communication activities were conversations at home and in social groups. Results indicate that older people with aphasia engage in similar communication activities as healthy older people although differences were evident in the frequency of communication and in specific activities. AHSA FACS items were generally relevant to older Australians living in the community. | III |
| Parr S, Byng S & Gilpin S, 1997, *Talking About Aphasia: Living with Loss of Language After Stroke*, Open University Press, Buckingham. | Expert opinion | | | | IV |

### Therapies focusing on Participation

### Recommendation 3

| Author(s) & Title | Design | Sample | Objective of study | Conclusions | Evidence Level |
|---|---|---|---|---|---|
| Parr S, 2001, 'Psychosocial aspects of aphasia: whose perspectives?', *Folia Phoniatrica et Logopedica*, 53 (5): 266–88. | Interview | 50 people | This paper reviews some different meanings of the term 'psychosocial' and identifies the different ways in which the social and psychological sequelae of aphasia can be explored. These include qualitative methods, which seem well suited to addressing such complex issues. Having outlined some features of qualitative research, the paper describes a study in which fifty people talked about the consequences and significance of their long-term aphasia. | Their 'insider perspective' on aphasia suggests its impacts are extensive, complex, direct and indirect, interconnected, systemic, dynamic and diversely experienced. The paper discusses the various implications of the study for clinicians and researchers concerned with the psychosocial aspects of aphasia and outlines how some of the issues raised in the interviews might be addressed. | III |

| Author(s) & Title | Design | Sample | Objective of study | Conclusions | Evidence Level |
|---|---|---|---|---|---|
| Chapey R, Ducan JF, Elman RJ, Garcia LJ, Kagan A, Lyon JG & Simmons-Mackie N, 2001, 'Life participation approach to aphasia: a statement of values for the future', in Chapey R (ed), *Language Intervention Strategies in Aphasia and Related Neurogenic Communication Disorders*, 4th edn, Lippincott Williams & Wilkins, Philadelphia. | Text | | | | IV |
| Pound C, Parr S, Lindsay J & Woolf C, 2000, *Beyond Aphasia: Therapies for Living with Communication Disabilities*, Speechmark Publishing, Bicester. | Text | | | | IV |
| Royal College of Physicians, 2004, *National Clinical Guidelines for Stroke*, prepared by The Intercollegiate Working Party for Stroke, London. www.rcplondon.ac.uk | Expert opinion | | | | IV |

## Therapies focusing on improving Language Functioning

### Single Word Auditory Processing: Recommendation 1

| Author(s) & Title | Design | Sample | Objective of study | Conclusions | Evidence Level |
|---|---|---|---|---|---|
| McClenahan R, Johnston M & Densham Y, 1992, 'Factors influencing accuracy of estimation of comprehension problems in patients following cerebrovascular accident, by doctors, nurses and relatives', *European Journal of Disorders of Communication*, 27 (3): 209–19. | Correlation study | Doctors, nurses, and relatives of 30 aphasic stroke inpatients | Doctors, nurses and relatives of 30 aphasic stroke patients estimated how patients would perform on the comprehension sections of the Functional Communication Profile and the Western Aphasia Battery. Possible factors influencing the accuracy of these judgements were studied, including confidence of the respondents, the severity of the patients' comprehension problems, the relatives' educational background, and the length of the relative–patient relationship. | Although doctors, nurses and relatives over-estimated patients' abilities on both tests, they were more accurate for patients with mild problems. Doctors and nurses who were more confident of their predictions were more accurate than those with less confidence, whereas relatives were equally inaccurate when giving high and low confidence judgements. Length of relationship and educational level did not predict relatives' accuracy. | II |

## APHASIA

| Author(s) & Title | Design | Sample | Objective of study | Conclusions | Evidence Level |
|---|---|---|---|---|---|
| Le Dorze G, Brassard C, Larfeuil C & Allaire J, 1996, 'Auditory comprehension problems in aphasia from the perspective of aphasic persons and their families and friends', *Disability & Rehabilitation*, 18 (11): 550–8. | Qualitative study (semi-structured interviews) | 29 aphasic persons with mild-moderate impairment and 26 non-aphasic relatives/friends | This study explored, using a qualitative approach, the experience of auditory comprehension problems from the perspective of aphasic persons and their families and friends. Semi-structured group interviews were held with 55 persons (29 aphasic and 26 non-aphasic) who were asked to describe the consequences of aphasia on their lives. | Most participants contributed some material to the topic of interest. They described problematic situations and the behaviours they said they adopted at those times; they also provided explanations of what those problems were. Some discrepancies between aphasic persons and their families and friends were also noted. The essential elements of the experience of an auditory comprehension problem, centre around speakers' rate of speech and situations in which aphasic persons feel they are incapable of understanding or of following, because of an unfavourable environment. | III |

### Single Word Auditory Processing: Recommendation 2

| Author(s) & Title | Design | Sample | Objective of study | Conclusions | Evidence Level |
|---|---|---|---|---|---|
| Behrmann M & Lieberthal T, 1989, 'Category-specific treatment of a lexical-semantic deficit: a single case study of global aphasia', *British Journal of Disorders of Communication*, 24 (3): 281–99. | Case study | 57-year-old male with aphasia following left middle cerebral artery infarct | The aim of this study was to improve the comprehension of single items in a subject with global aphasia. Existing models of semantic organisation were used to inform and guide the treatment programme. Detailed pre-therapy testing suggested a severe comprehension deficit with an inability to obtain a precise semantic specification of the items, irrespective of modality of input. A category-specific hierarchical treatment programme, including generic and specific details about items, was implemented through various exercises and drills. | Post-therapy testing revealed a significant improvement on treated and untreated items of treated categories, but limited generalisation to items in untreated categories. Improvement in the subject's general semantic abilities was also documented following treatment. The results, which are shown to be a direct consequence of the intervention programme, lend support to the categorical and hierarchical view of the organisation of semantics, and provide a basis for future rehabilitation studies in this area. | III |

| Author(s) & Title | Design | Sample | Objective of study | Conclusions | Evidence Level |
|---|---|---|---|---|---|
| Francis DR, Riddoch MJ, Humphreys GW, 2001, 'Cognitive rehabilitation of word meaning deafness', *Aphasiology*,15 (8): 749–66. | Case study | 67-year-old male with aphasia, following left parietal CVA. Four years post onset. | Theoretical accounts of pure word meaning deafness are rare: accounts of its rehabilitation are virtually non-existent. The effects of two therapies in a male patient with pure word meaning deafness are contrasted. One therapy required only implicit auditory access from the patient (silent reading comprehension exercises). The second required explicit auditory access (auditory comprehension exercises), and thus appeared to be more suited to the exact locus of the patient's impairment. | Improvement was observed after both types of therapy. However, improvement on implicit access therapy was influenced by the use of a compensatory strategy developed by the patient. In contrast, improvement on explicit access therapy was more durable, and appeared to be due to a direct effect on the audition–semantics link, rather than to compensation. It is concluded that pure word meaning deafness is amenable to treatment, and that cognitive models can be useful in designing such therapy studies | III |
| Franklin S, 1989, 'Dissociations in auditory word comprehension: Evidence from nine fluent aphasic patients', *Aphasiology*, 3: 189–207. | Case series | Nine fluent aphasic patients, aged 52–80. Eight following CVA, one following head injury. | Traditional aphasia classifications do not allow for a detailed description of auditory comprehension impairments. A cognitive neuropsychological model of lexical processing allows us to distinguish at least five different levels of impairment in single word auditory comprehension. It also specifies a more complex relationship between impairments in repetition and auditory comprehension. Nine fluent aphasic patients, with auditory comprehension disorders, were assessed using tests of phoneme discrimination, lexical decision, synonym matching, and word and non-word repetition. | The results of these tests, as predicted, indicated that there were five dissociable levels of impairment, although there was some evidence for interaction between levels. The patients showed qualitative differences between auditory and written comprehension. Four of the patients had impairments in repetition, despite having no impairment in phoneme discrimination tests. No two patients showed exactly the same pattern of impairment across all the tests administered. | III |
| Grayson E, Hilton R & Franklin S, 1997, 'Early intervention in a case of jargon aphasia: efficacy of language comprehension therapy', *European Journal of Disorders of Communication*, 32 (3): Spec Issue: 257–76. | Single subject design | 50-year-old man with aphasia, following left temporo-parietal CVA. First six months post onset. | A client with dysphasia was treated during the first six months following onset. A cognitive neuropsychological model of language processing was used to establish the levels of impairment in auditory comprehension. Three separate phases of therapy were administered: a semantic therapy; a period of therapy where both semantics and auditory processing were treated; and therapy designed to enhance the processing of words in a sentence. | Four assessments were used to measure changes between each therapy phase, and the results demonstrate that improvement occurred in a pattern which suggests specific effects of treatment. | III |

# APHASIA

| Author(s) & Title | Design | Sample | Objective of study | Conclusions | Evidence Level |
|---|---|---|---|---|---|
| Morris J, Franklin S, Ellis AW & Turner JE, 1996, 'Remediating a speech perception deficit in an aphasic patient', *Aphasiology*, 10 (2): 137–58. | Case study | 73-year-old male with aphasia, following left CVA. Eight months post onset. | This study describes the assessment and treatment of a 73-year-old aphasic patient, JS, who had multiple language deficits. In particular, pre-speech and speech-level perceptual processes were both found to be impaired. The availability of lip-reading information improved his performance on certain tasks of speech discrimination. Remediation based on the assessment findings was then undertaken. Therapy focused on auditory discrimination at a phonemic level, utilising lip-reading, and was based on minimal pairs contrasts. | JS showed improvement on tests of phoneme discrimination, and a trend of improvement was seen for the other auditory tasks. Performance on the pre-speech tests also showed improvement following therapy. Performance on tests of naming and written word comprehension did not change, indicating that the effects of therapy were specific to auditory input and were not the result of spontaneous recovery. | III |

## Single Word Auditory Processing: Recommendation 3

| Author(s) & Title | Design | Sample | Objective of study | Conclusions | Evidence Level |
|---|---|---|---|---|---|
| Grayson E, Hilton R & Franklin S, 1997, 'Early intervention in a case of jargon aphasia: efficacy of language comprehension therapy', *European Journal of Disorders of Communication*, 32 (3): Spec Issue: 257–76. | Single subject design | 50-year-old man with aphasia, following left temporo-parietal CVA. First six months post onset. | A client with dysphasia was treated during the first six months following onset. A cognitive neuropsychological model of language processing was used to establish the levels of impairment in auditory comprehension. Three separate phases of therapy were administered: a semantic therapy; a period of therapy where both semantics and auditory processing were treated; and therapy designed to enhance the processing of words in a sentence. | Four assessments were used to measure changes between each therapy phase, and the results demonstrate that improvement occurred in a pattern which suggests specific effects of treatment. | III |

| Author(s) & Title | Design | Sample | Objective of study | Conclusions | Evidence Level |
|---|---|---|---|---|---|
| Maneta A, Marshall J & Lindsay J, 2001, 'Direct and indirect therapy for word sound deafness', *International Journal of Language & Communication Disorders*, 36 (1): 91–106. | Case study | An aphasic man | This paper evaluates two therapy programmes conducted with PK, an aphasic individual with word-sound deafness. The first aimed directly to improve discrimination skills, using minimal pair tasks supported with lip-reading. Disappointingly, there were no changes on discrimination tests after this therapy, even when PK could benefit from lip-reading. The second, indirect, programme aimed to change the communication behaviours with PK's wife. Strategies such as writing and simplifying information were modelled and practised. | A detailed information booklet, outlining the target strategies and explaining PK's main strengths and weaknesses supported the programme. Evaluation of this therapy involved pre- and post-therapy analysis of interactions between PK and his wife, with biographical questions forming the basis of the interactions. There were several changes after therapy on this measure. The number and length of communication breakdowns were reduced, and more questions were answered accurately. This study suggests that, in some cases of severe word sound deafness, indirect therapies may be most effective. | III |

**Single Word Auditory Processing: Recommendation 4**

| Author(s) & Title | Design | Sample | Objective of study | Conclusions | Evidence Level |
|---|---|---|---|---|---|
| Behrmann M & Lieberthal T, 1989, 'Category-specific treatment of a lexical-semantic deficit: a single case study of global aphasia', *British Journal of Disorders of Communication*, 24 (3): 281–99. | Case study | 57-year-old male with aphasia following left middle cerebral artery infarct | The aim of this study was to improve the comprehension of single items in a subject with global aphasia. Existing models of semantic organisation were used to inform and guide the treatment programme. Detailed pre-therapy testing suggested a severe comprehension deficit with an inability to obtain a precise semantic specification of the items, irrespective of modality of input. A category-specific hierarchical treatment programme, including generic and specific details about items, was implemented through various exercises and drills. | Post-therapy testing revealed a significant improvement on treated and untreated items of treated categories, but limited generalisation to items in untreated categories. Improvement in the subject's general semantic abilities was also documented following treatment. The results, which are shown to be a direct consequence of the intervention programme, lend support to the categorical and hierarchical view of the organisation of semantics, and provide a basis for future rehabilitation studies in this area. | III |

## APHASIA

| Author(s) & Title | Design | Sample | Objective of study | Conclusions | Evidence Level |
|---|---|---|---|---|---|
| Francis DR, Riddoch MJ, Humphreys GW, 2001, 'Cognitive rehabilitation of word meaning deafness,' *Aphasiology*,15 (8): 749–66. | Case study | 67-year-old male with aphasia, following left parietal CVA. Four years post onset. | Theoretical accounts of pure word meaning deafness are rare: accounts of its rehabilitation are virtually non-existent. The effects of two therapies in a male patient with pure word meaning deafness are contrasted. One therapy required only implicit auditory access from the patient (silent reading comprehension exercises). The second required explicit auditory access (auditory comprehension exercises), and thus appeared to be more suited to the exact locus of the patient's impairment. | Improvement was observed after both types of therapy. However, improvement on implicit access therapy was influenced by the use of a compensatory strategy developed by the patient. In contrast, improvement on explicit access therapy was more durable, and appeared to be due to a direct effect on the audition-semantics link, rather than to compensation. It is concluded that pure word meaning deafness is amenable to treatment, and that cognitive models can be useful in designing such therapy studies | III |
| Grayson E, Hilton R & Franklin S, 1997, 'Early intervention in a case of jargon aphasia: efficacy of language comprehension therapy', *European Journal of Disorders of Communication*, 32 (3): Spec Issue: 257–76. | Single subject design | 50-year-old man with aphasia, following left temporo-parietal CVA. First six months post onset. | A client with dysphasia was treated during the first six months following onset. A cognitive neuropsychological model of language processing was used to establish the levels of impairment in auditory comprehension. Three separate phases of therapy were administered: a semantic therapy; a period of therapy where both semantics and auditory processing were treated; and therapy designed to enhance the processing of words in a sentence. | Four assessments were used to measure changes between each therapy phase, and the results demonstrate that improvement occurred in a pattern which suggests specific effects of treatment. | III |
| Morris J, Franklin S, Ellis AW & Turner JE, 1996, 'Remediating a speech perception deficit in an aphasic patient,' *Aphasiology*, 10 (2): 137–58. | Case study | 73-year-old male with aphasia, following left CVA. Eight months post onset. | This study describes the assessment and treatment of a 73-year-old aphasic patient, JS, who had multiple language deficits. In particular, pre-speech and speech-level perceptual processes were both found to be impaired. The availability of lip-reading information improved his performance on certain tasks of speech discrimination. Remediation based on the assessment findings was then undertaken. Therapy focused on auditory discrimination at a phonemic level, utilising lip-reading, and was based on minimal pairs contrasts. | JS showed improvement on tests of phoneme discrimination, and a trend of improvement was seen for the other auditory tasks. Performance on the pre-speech tests also showed improvement following therapy. Performance on tests of naming and written word comprehension did not change, indicating that the effects of therapy were specific to auditory input and were not the result of spontaneous recovery. | III |

| Author(s) & Title | Design | Sample | Objective of study | Conclusions | Evidence Level |
|---|---|---|---|---|---|
| **Single Word Auditory Processing: Recommendation 5** | | | | | |
| Maneta A, Marshall J & Lindsay J, 2001, 'Direct and indirect therapy for word sound deafness', *International Journal of Language & Communication Disorders*, 36 (1): 91–106. | Case study | An aphasic man | This paper evaluates two therapy programmes conducted with PK, an aphasic individual with word-sound deafness. The first aimed directly to improve discrimination skills, using minimal pair tasks supported with lip-reading. Disappointingly, there were no changes on discrimination tests after this therapy, even when PK could benefit from lip-reading information. The second, indirect, programme of therapy aimed to change the communication behaviours with PK's wife. Strategies such as writing and simplifying information were modelled and practised. | A detailed information booklet, outlining the target strategies and explaining PK's main strengths and weaknesses supported the programme. Evaluation of this therapy involved pre- and post-therapy analysis of interactions between PK and his wife, with biographical questions forming the basis of the interactions. There were several changes after therapy on this measure. The number and length of communication breakdowns were reduced, and more questions were answered accurately. This study suggests that, in some cases of severe word sound deafness, indirect therapies may be most effective. | III |
| **Spoken Word Production: Recommendation 1** | | | | | |
| Hillis A & Carramazza A, 1994, 'Theories of lexical processing and rehabilitation of lexical deficits', in Riddoch MJ & Humphreys GW (eds), *Cognitive Neuropsychology and Cognitive Rehabilitation*, Lawrence Erlbaum Associates, Hove. | Case series | Three adults with aphasia | A series of single-subject studies of brain-injured patients who each made semantic errors in naming is presented. Three forms of the 'diagnosis' / treatment relationship are illustrated: (1) two very different treatment approaches are equally appropriate with respect to a given locus of damage, but individual patients respond differentially to the two approaches; (2) a given treatment strategy is equally important for multiple levels of disruption, although different components of the treatment may affect separate levels of processing; and (3) one strategy is appropriate for one level of damage, and a different strategy is required for a different level of damage. | A cognitive analysis of performance in each case provides evidence for processing relatively selective impairment to one or more components of lexical processing. Studies of the effectiveness of treatment for these patients indicate that some patients with the same putative locus of impairment require different treatment, and some patients with different loci of impairment respond to the same treatment. | III |

## APHASIA

### Spoken Word Production: Recommendation 2

| Author(s) & Title | Design | Sample | Objective of study | Conclusions | Evidence Level |
|---|---|---|---|---|---|
| Howard D, Paterson K, Franklin S, Orchard-Lisle V & Morton J, 1985, 'Treatment of word-retrieval deficits in aphasia: a comparison of two therapy methods', *Brain*, 108: 817–29 | Controlled trial | 12 adults with aphasia | The effects of two therapy methods in the treatment of picture naming problems are compared, using a within-patient design with 12 adult patients with chronic acquired aphasia. We contrast techniques that require the patient to process the meaning corresponding to the picture name (semantic treatment) with those that provide the patients with information about the phonological form of the name (phonological treatment). With each method, patients either had four sessions of treatment over one week, or eight sessions of treatment over two weeks. | Both methods caused day-by-day improvement that was specific to the actual items treated. Both methods resulted in significant improvement in naming when this was measured one week after the end of treatment, with a small, but significant, advantage for the semantic treatment; this is mainly due to improvement that generalises to untreated items. It is concluded that specific and theoretically motivated treatment methods can cause significant improvement in the word retrieval ability of patients with chronic aphasia. | II |
| Hillis A, 1989, 'Efficacy and generalisation of treatment for aphasic naming errors', *Archives of Physical Medicine and Rehabilitation*, 70: 632–36. | Single subject design | 2 adults with aphasia | Two severely aphasic patients who made frequent semantic errors in verbal picture naming, as well as frequent errors in written naming, were studied. Contrasting patterns of errors across various language tasks provided evidence that the two patients' naming errors arose from different underlying deficits. The effectiveness of cueing hierarchies on improving each patient's written naming was demonstrated in single-subject experiments using a multiple baseline design. | Although both patients exhibited acquisition and maintenance of written naming, only one showed generalisation to verbal naming and to untrained stimuli. Different results are interpreted as a reflection of separate sources of the subjects' naming errors. It is concluded that determining the cognitive basis of an individual's naming difficulty may permit predictions concerning language behaviours that are likely to improve concurrently as a function of treatment. | III |

| Author(s) & Title | Design | Sample | Objective of study | Conclusions | Evidence Level |
|---|---|---|---|---|---|
| Marshall J, Pound C, White-Thompson M & Pring T, 1990, 'The use of picture/word matching tasks to assist word-retrieval in aphasic patients,' *Aphasiology*, 4: 167–84. | Single case studies and a group study | 3 adults with aphasia for the case studies; 7 adults with aphasia for the group | Three single case studies and a small group study were undertaken to examine the effects of using picture-to-word-matching tasks as a therapeutic technique in aiding word retrieval in different patients. | Two single case studies were successful, despite differences in the patient's abilities at the therapeutic task. The benefits of the therapy continued for periods after it was completed. The third case study was not successful, preventing any further conclusion from being drawn, and indicating the need for further study to determine which patients might benefit. The group study used a similar therapeutic task, but patients were asked to carry it out in their own homes and without a therapist present. Treated items showed significant gains compared with controls, there was evidence of some improvement on semantically-related untreated items and the gains continued to be significant one month after treatment ended. | III |
| Coehlo CA, McHugh RE & Boyle M, 2000, 'Semantic feature analysis as a treatment for aphasic dysnomia: A replication,' *Aphasiology*, 14 (2): 133–42. | Case study | 52-year-old man | Replicated the study by M Boyle and CA. Coelho (1995), in which semantic feature analysis (SFA), a treatment to improve lexical retrieval by increasing the level of activation within a semantic network, was applied with a mild non-fluent aphasic individual. This resulted in improved confrontation naming of trained and untrained items, but no generalisation to connected speech. The present study investigated whether comparable treatment effect could be demonstrated, and to what extent the severity and type of aphasia might affect the overall outcome. SFA was applied to a 52-year-old right-handed male with a moderate fluent aphasic dysnomia, secondary to a closed-head injury. | Gains in confrontation naming of both trained and untrained stimulus pictures were noted, as well as on measures of connected speech. SFA treatment and generalisation effects were maintained. | III |

## APHASIA

| Author(s) & Title | Design | Sample | Objective of study | Conclusions | Evidence Level |
|---|---|---|---|---|---|
| Nickels L & Best W, 1996, 'Therapy for naming disorders (Part II): Specifics, surprises and suggestions', *Aphasiology*, 2: 109–36. | Single subject design | 3 adults with aphasia | This study presents a series of therapy studies aimed at remediation of the word-retrieval deficits of three aphasic patients. All three patients are argued to have semantic deficits and are given semantic therapy in the form of word-to-picture matching tasks. | Two of the patients show improved naming as a result of the therapy, with generalisation to untreated items. The third patient does not improve as a result of the word-to-picture matching therapy, even though her pattern of deficits appears similar. However, she does show item-specific improvement in naming with a different therapy (lexical). The reasons for the differences between the patients in their response to therapy are discussed. In particular the effect of the production of the word during the therapy is considered, and the patient's ability to perform the task accurately. Additionally, the role of modality of input and generalisation across modality of output, and the use of different types of semantic therapy was investigated. | III |

### Spoken Word Production: Recommendation 3

| Author(s) & Title | Design | Sample | Objective of study | Conclusions | Evidence Level |
|---|---|---|---|---|---|
| Bruce C & Howard D, 1987, 'Computer-generated phonemic cueing: an effective aid for naming in aphasia', *British Journal of Disorders of Communication*, 22: 191–201. | Case series | 3 women and 2 men with aphasia | This study investigated whether computer-generated phonemic cues can be used in improving naming in five adult Broca's aphasics, either in treatment or as a prosthesis. The subjects were taught to use a microcomputer as an aid to generate phonemic cues over five sessions. | Four subjects were significantly better in naming with the aid, and improvement generalised to names that had not been involved in treatment. Four subjects were better at indicating the first letters of names of items in the treatment set than those in untreated control pictures. | III |
| Francis D, Clark N & Humphreys G, 2002, 'Circumlocution induced naming (CIN): A treatment for effecting generalisation in anomia?', *Aphasiology*, 16: 243–59. | Single case design | 79-year-old woman | This study investigated whether requiring a client to name pictures with minimal help from therapists would result in generalisation. A 79-year-old woman, MB, who was anomic subsequent to a stroke, participated in this study. Therapy sessions required MB to name a set of pictures. Instead of cues, she was required to describe and 'talk around' each picture until the name came to her, no matter how long it took. | Non-parametric statistical analysis was performed on pre- and post-test results. Results show that therapy produced improvement in untreated as well as in treated words, and there was also a qualitative change in error patterns in treated words. Performance in unrelated control tasks did not improve. | III |

| Author(s) & Title | Design | Sample | Objective of study | Conclusions | Evidence Level |
|---|---|---|---|---|---|
| Hickin J, Best W, Herbert R, Howard D & Osbourne F, 2002, 'Phonological therapy for word-finding difficulties: A re-evaluation', *Aphasiology*, 16: 981–99. | Case series | 8 adults with aphasia | This study set out to investigate whether the use of phonological and orthographic cues in the treatment of word-finding difficulties could produce lasting improvements in word retrieval. The response of the participants to phonological and orthographic cues in a facilitation study was also related to their response to treatment using similar cues. The study used a case series design. The participants were eight people with acquired aphasia who were all at least one year post-onset, had a single left CVA, and had word-finding difficulties as a significant aspect of their aphasia. Detailed assessment of each participant was carried out to identify the nature of their word-finding difficulties, and this was related to response to treatment. | Results are given for the eight participants, seven of whom benefited overall from treatment. Both phonological and orthographic cues were effective in improving word retrieval. For the group as a whole there was a significant correlation between the overall outcome of facilitation and response to treatment. | III |
| Hillis A, 1989, 'Efficacy and generalisation of treatment for aphasic naming errors', *Archives of Physical Medicine and Rehabilitation*, 70: 632–36. | Single subject design | 2 adults with aphasia | Two severely aphasic patients, who made frequent semantic errors in verbal picture naming, as well as frequent errors in written naming, were studied. Contrasting patterns of errors across various language tasks provided evidence that the two patients' naming errors arose from different underlying deficits. The effectiveness of cueing hierarchies on improving each patient's written naming was demonstrated in single-subject experiments using a multiple-baseline design. | Although both patients exhibited acquisition and maintenance of written naming, only one showed generalisation to verbal naming and to untrained stimuli. Different results are interpreted as a reflection of separate sources of the subjects' naming errors. It is concluded that determining the cognitive basis of an individual's naming difficulty may permit predictions concerning language behaviours that are likely to improve concurrently as a function of treatment. | III |

## APHASIA

| Author(s) & Title | Design | Sample | Objective of study | Conclusions | Evidence Level |
|---|---|---|---|---|---|
| Howard D, Patterson K, Franklin S, Orchard-Lisle V & Morton J, 1985, 'Treatment of word-retrieval deficits in aphasia: a comparison of two therapy methods', *Brain*, 108: 817–29 | Controlled trial | 12 adults with aphasia | The effects of two therapy methods in the treatment of picture naming problems are compared, using a within-patient design with 12 adult patients with chronic acquired aphasia. We contrast techniques that require the patient to process the meaning corresponding to the picture name (semantic treatment) with those that provide the patients with information about the phonological form of the name (phonological treatment). With each method, patients either had four sessions of treatment over one week, or eight sessions over two weeks. | Both methods caused day-by-day improvement that was specific to the actual items treated. Both methods resulted in significant improvement in naming when this was measured one week after the end of treatment, with a small, but significant, advantage for the semantic treatment; this is mainly due to improvement that generalises to untreated items. It is concluded that specific and theoretically motivated treatment methods can cause significant improvement in the word retrieval ability of patients with chronic aphasia. | II |
| Le Dorze G, Boulay N, Gaudreau J & Brassard C, 1994, 'The contrasting effects of a semantic versus a formal-semantic technique for the facilitation of naming in a case of anomia', *Aphasiology*, 8: 127–41. | Single subject design | 56-year-old man | This study investigated the relative contribution of information about the spoken or written form of the picture name to the facilitative effect of semantic techniques in a single-subject study of a 56-year-old male patient with moderately severe mixed aphasia and anomia. He had received regular therapy, and, at the beginning of the experiment, ten months had elapsed since he suffered a cerebrovascular accident. An alternating treatment design compared the effects on naming of a formal semantic facilitation technique (including the spoken or written word form in a semantic comprehension task) to a purely semantic facilitation technique (a semantic comprehension task without the word form). | Results indicate that naming improved significantly for the items treated with the formal-semantic technique, while there was no change in naming for the items treated with the purely semantic technique. | III |

| Author(s) & Title | Design | Sample | Objective of study | Conclusions | Evidence Level |
|---|---|---|---|---|---|
| Miceli G, Amitrano A, Capasso R & Caramazza A, 1996, 'The treatment of anomia resulting from output lexical damage: analysis of two cases', *Brain & Language*, 52: 150–74. | Case studies | 2 adults with anomia | This study describes a treatment project, carried out with two anomic subjects. RBO and GMA failed to name pictures correctly as a consequence of damage to phonological lexical forms; their ability to process word meaning was unimpaired. Words that were consistently comprehended correctly, but produced incorrectly by each subject, were identified. Some words were treated, whereas some served as the control set. A significant improvement was observed in both subjects. As predicted by the model of lexical–semantic processing used as the theoretical background for the study, improvement was restricted to treated items and did not generalise to untreated words – not even to words that were semantically related to those administered during treatment. | Improvement was long-lasting, as shown by the fact that, 17 months post-therapy, GMA's performance on treated words was still significantly better than before treatment. These results are discussed in relation to the claim that cognitive models can be profitably used in the treatment of language disorders. | III |
| Nickels L, 2002, 'Improving word finding: Practice makes (closer to) perfect?', *Aphasiology*, 16: 1047–60. | Case study | 60-year-old man with aphasia | The paper describes a single case study of JAW, a 60-year-old man with aphasia. JAW's picture naming had been observed to improve over time while other tasks remained stable. An investigation was performed to identify the source of this improvement. Three treatment tasks were used, attempting to name the picture, reading aloud and delayed copying of the picture names. In the 'attempted naming' condition, this priming occurred every time a picture name was successfully produced. As JAW was not perfectly consistent, on each attempt at naming some additional items were primed. | All three tasks significantly improved subsequent picture naming of the treated items despite the fact that no feedback or error correction was provided. It is argued that the source of this improvement is from priming of retrieval of the phonological form. | III |

## APHASIA

| Author(s) & Title | Design | Sample | Objective of study | Conclusions | Evidence Level |
|---|---|---|---|---|---|
| Spencer K, Doyle P, McNeil M, Wambaugh J, Park G & Carrol B, 2000, 'Examining the facilitative effects of rhyme in a patient with output lexicon damage', *Aphasiology*, 14: 567–84. | Case study | 47-year-old woman | A theory-driven treatment was designed to facilitate access to the impaired output lexicons of a 47-year-old woman with aphasia resulting from a left parietal haemorrhage. In the context of a multiple-baseline design, lists of rhymed word pairs from four semantic categories were trained, using a systematic cueing hierarchy. Performance measures were based on the subject's generation of targeted words, verbally and in writing, when presented with a rhyme of the target. | Results demonstrated positive acquisition, generalisation and maintenance effects for treated and untreated items across semantic categories. Delayed generalisation patterns may be explained by retrieval inhibition or lateral inhibition. | III |

### Spoken Word Production: Recommendation 4

| Author(s) & Title | Design | Sample | Objective of study | Conclusions | Evidence Level |
|---|---|---|---|---|---|
| Franklin S, Buerk F & Howard D, 2002, 'Generalised improvement in speech production for a subject with reproduction conduction aphasia', *Aphasiology*, 16: 1087–1114. | Single subject design | 83-year-old woman | This study investigated the effects of a treatment procedure involving the detection and correction of the errors in speech production with a single female subject, aged 83 years, MB. The authors also examined the nature of MB's underlying deficit, and show how it changed as a result of treatment. Treatment effects were investigated in a single case study using multiple baselines over tasks, materials, and time. An in-depth cognitive neuropsychological case study was used to investigate the nature of MB's speech production deficit. MB had impaired naming, repetition, and oral reading, particularly with longer words, but good word comprehension. Her errors were primarily phonological, with many repeated attempts. Production of non-words was less accurate than real words. | The treatment improved production in all modalities and across a variety of tasks (including non-word reading). Further analysis of assessment results suggest that MB's impairment was at the level of phonological encoding, and that therapy had improved phoneme production across all word positions. | III |

| Author(s) & Title | Design | Sample | Objective of study | Conclusions | Evidence Level |
|---|---|---|---|---|---|
| **Single Word Reading: Recommendation 1** | | | | | |
| Ellis A, Flude B & Young A , 1987 '"Neglect Dyslexia" and the early visual processing of letters in words and non-words', *Cognitive Neuropsychology*, 4: 439–64. | Case study | 81-year-old woman | Examined an 81-year-old female, non-aphasic patient who suffered a left-sided neglect that affected her reading (a condition known as 'neglect dyslexia'). In text-reading, she often read only the right halves of lines, and in single-word reading she made errors affecting the initial letters (eg, 'river' misread as 'liver'). Neglect errors to both words and nonwords involved substitution of initial letters, resulting in errors of the same length as the target words. Comprehension of misread words matched the error, rather than the target. Although her neglect sometimes prevented the encoding of leftmost letters for identity, it is proposed that processes involved in assigning positions to letters in strings on a left–right spatial basis still responded to the existence of those letters. | — | III |
| **Single Word Reading: Recommendation 2** | | | | | |
| Coltheart M, Masterson J, Byng S, Prior M & Riddoch J, 1983, 'Surface Dyslexia', *Quarterly Journal of Experimental Psychology*, 35A: 469–95. | 2 case studies | 2 individuals with dyslexia – one with developmental dyslexia and one with acquired dyslexia. | Two cases of surface dyslexia are described. When reading comprehension was tested, homophones were often confused with each other: for example, *soar* was understood as an instrument for cutting, and *route* was understood as being part of a tree. Spelling was also impaired, with the majority of spelling errors being phonologically correct: for example *search* was spelled *surch*. Orthographic errors in reading aloud were also noted. These errors were not due to defects at elementary levels of visual processing. | There was a close similarity in the reading and spelling performance of both individuals, which supports the view that surface dyslexia can occur both as a developmental and as an acquired dyslexia. A theoretical interpretation of surface dyslexia within the framework of the logogen model (including a grapheme-phoneme correspondence system for reading non-words) is offered: defects within the input logogen system, and in communication from that system to semantics, were postulated for most of the symptoms of surface dyslexia. | III |

## APHASIA

| Author(s) & Title | Design | Sample | Objective of study | Conclusions | Evidence Level |
|---|---|---|---|---|---|
| Funnell E, 1983, 'Phonological processes in reading: new evidence from acquired dyslexia', *British Journal of Psychology*, 74: 159–80. | Case studies | 2 adults with acquired dyslexia | This paper investigates the reading performance of two patients with acquired dyslexia. The first patient read aloud all classes of word (85–95 percent correct), including affixed words, but failed to read aloud non-words. In addition, semantic judgements about written words were shown to be significantly impaired, relative to the ability to read the words aloud. These dissociations support the view that two independent lexical routes are available for reading aloud familiar words, a semantic route and a lexical phonological route. While unable to read aloud non-words, this patient retained the ability to segment orthographic and phonological stimuli. | The reading of non-lexical material, therefore, does not appear to be mediated by lexical analogy procedures. Instead, it is suggested that a non-lexical phonological route exists that is clearly independent of lexical phonological procedures. This patient could process isolated written suffixes orthographically, but could only access complete phonological word forms. Suffixed words (but not isolated suffixes) appear to be represented in the phonological word store. The second patient read aloud non-words, but could not give phonetic sounds appropriate to single letters. This dissociation suggests that the reading aloud of non-words is not reliant upon grapheme-phoneme rules. | III |
| Patterson K & Kay J, 1982, 'Letter-by-letter reading: psychological descriptions of a neurological syndrome', *Quarterly Journal of Experimental Psychology*, 34A: 411–41. | Case studies | 4 adults with letter-by-letter reading | This paper presents a general description of the characteristics of letter-by-letter reading and a summary of previous explanations of this reading deficit in both neurological and psychological models. One central topic, addressed by experimental investigation, concerns comprehension of written words. A second central topic, addressed through analysis of reading errors, concerns procedures for word recognition. | No evidence was obtained for the hypothesis that comprehension of a word could occur prior to, or in the absence of, the letter-by-letter analysis required for oral reading. It appears that such patients must do sequential letter identification of a word in order both to understand it and to report it. Two of the four patients showed a 'pure' letter-by-letter syndrome with no difficulty in word recognition once the component letters had been identified. For the other two patients, an additional lexical deficit often prevented a correctly identified sequence of letters from achieving recognition as the correct word. | III |

| Author(s) & Title | Design | Sample | Objective of study | Conclusions | Evidence Level |
|---|---|---|---|---|---|
| Parr S, 1995, 'Everyday reading and writing in aphasia: role change and the influence of pre-morbid literacy practice', *Aphasiology*, 9: 223–38. | Qualitative – semi-structured interviews | 20 adults with aphasia | Twenty people with aphasia (aged 30–86 years) were interviewed, most with a partner or close family member, to establish factors that might affect the focus of functional reading and writing therapy. This was done by exploring aphasic subjects' level of premorbid and current involvement with roles in domestic, work, social, and leisure contexts and literacy practices associated with those roles. Aspects of premorbid literacy practice included use of social networks, drafting and editing in composition of text and use of technical aids. | Premorbid and current roles were variable, and gains and losses in roles were reported subsequent to onset of aphasia. Aphasia was most often cited as the main reason for loss of four activities: corresponding about property, using the phone, dealing with bills and reading for relaxation. Literacy practices had been shared by, and delegated to, social network members premorbidly in an idiosyncratic manner. | IV |
| Coltheart M, Patterson K E, & Marshall JC, 1980, *Deep Dyslexia*, Routledge and Kegan Paul, London. | Text | | | | IV |

### Single Word Reading: Recommendation 3

| Author(s) & Title | Design | Sample | Objective of study | Conclusions | Evidence Level |
|---|---|---|---|---|---|
| Byng S & Coltheart M, 1986, 'Aphasia therapy research: methodological requirements and illustrative results', *Advances in Psychology*, 34: 191–213. | Case study | 41-year-old man | A rehabilitation approach to aphasia is described and tested on one aphasic patient. This approach seeks to restore, partially or fully, the impaired specific communicative ability. The patient's sentence comprehension deficit and deficit in abstract word comprehension were treated by specially developed methods. | It is concluded that the positive effects noted for both these deficits can only be ascribed to the treatment given. | III |

## APHASIA

| Author(s) & Title | Design | Sample | Objective of study | Conclusions | Evidence Level |
|---|---|---|---|---|---|
| De Partz MP, 1986, 'Re-education of a deep dyslexic patient: rationale of the method and results', *Cognitive Neuropsychology*, 13 (6): 869–85. | Case study | 31-year-old man | A report on the re-education of a deep dyslexia patient with fluent speech is presented. Results of extensive pre-therapeutic testing suggested that the patient was using a direct access route to meaning, and that the grapheme to phoneme conversion rules were impaired. To re-educate the reading abilities of the patient, a reorganisational rationale was chosen, that is, the attempt was made to reorganise the impaired grapheme to phoneme process by using spared lexical knowledge as a relay between graphemes and their pronunciation. The therapy was divided into three stages: single grapheme–reading reconstruction by using word codes as an intermediary; complex grapheme–reading reconstruction by using a homophonic word code and learning grapheme contextual rules. | After a year of intensive practice to automate the new strategies, the patient was able to read slowly and correctly. | III |
| Friedman RB & Lott SN, 2002, 'Successful blending in a phonological reading treatment for deep dyslexia', *Aphasiology*, 16: 355–72. | Single subject design | 40-year-old man 20-year-old woman | The hypothesis of this study is that patients will be successful blending letter-to-sound correspondences into words if those correspondences are trained in context, rather than in isolation. The correspondences were trained, therefore, as *bigraph–phoneme* correspondences, rather than as individual grapheme–phoneme correspondences (eg, 'pa'-/pæ/ and 'at'-/æt/, rather than 'p'- /p/, 'a'-/æ/ and 't'-/t/). The study followed a single-subject multiple-baseline design in which three sets of bigraphs, and words composed of those trained bigraphs, were trained sequentially. Two subjects with deep alexia participated in the study. | Subjects LR and KT successfully blended trained bigraphs in order to read both trained and untrained words that were composed of the trained bigraphs. It is suggested that the patients are learning a new means of decoding words, and that the underlying phonologic processing deficit remains. In terms of clinical application, the bigraph approach offers a viable alternative approach for re-training reading for those patients who are unable to blend individual phonemes into words. | III |

| Author(s) & Title | Design | Sample | Objective of study | Conclusions | Evidence Level |
|---|---|---|---|---|---|
| Greenwald ML & Gonzalez-Rothi LJ, 1998, 'Lexical access via letter naming in a profoundly alexic and anomic patient: a treatment study', *Journal of the International Neuropsychological Society*, 4: 595–607. | Single case study | 72-year-old woman | The results of a letter-naming treatment designed to facilitate letter-by-letter reading in an aphasic patient with no reading ability are reported. Patient MR's anomia for written letters reflected two loci of impairment within visual naming: impaired letter activation from print (a deficit commonly seen in pure alexic patients who read letter by letter) and impaired access to phonology via semantics (documented in a severe multimodality anomia). Remarkably, MR retained an excellent ability to pronounce orally-spelt words, demonstrating that abstract letter identities could be activated normally via spoken letter names, and also that lexical phonological representations were intact when accessed via spoken letter names. | MR's training in oral naming of written letters resulted in significant improvement in her oral naming of trained letters. Importantly, as MR's letter-naming improved, she became able to employ letter-by-letter reading as a compensatory strategy for oral word reading. MR's success in letter-naming and letter-by-letter reading suggests that other patients with a similar pattern of spared and impaired cognitive abilities may benefit from a similar treatment. Moreover, this study highlights the value of testing the pronunciation of orally-spelt words in localising the source of prelexical reading impairment, and in predicting the functional outcome of treatment for impaired letter activation in reading. | III |
| Lott SN, Friedman RB & Linebaugh CW, 1994, 'Rationale and efficacy of a tactile-kinaesthetic treatment for alexia', *Aphasiology*, 8 (2): 181–95. | Case study | 67-year-old man | Patients with pure alexia typically read words by first naming each letter of the word, either aloud or silently. These patients do not show signs of phonological alexia (poor pseudoword and functor reading). Patient TL, a pure alexic patient with poor letter-naming abilities, had marked difficulty in reading functors and pseudowords, but not in spelling them or identifying them when they were spelled to him, a pattern which has been called 'modality-specific phonological alexia'. A multiple-baseline design was used to evaluate a tactile-kinaesthetic treatment programme designed to improve TL's letter-naming, thus enabling him to read in letter-by-letter fashion. | Results showed that the treatment was efficacious, with a 51 percent improvement achieved in trained word reading and a 40 percent increase in untrained word reading. Furthermore, the part-of-speech effect was no longer significant following treatment, a result that our hypothesis of TL's underlying impairment predicted. | III |

## APHASIA

| Author(s) & Title | Design | Sample | Objective of study | Conclusions | Evidence Level |
|---|---|---|---|---|---|
| Maher LM, Clayton MC, Barrett AM, Schober-Peterson D & Gonzalez-Rothi LJ, 1998, 'Rehabilitation of a case of pure alexia: exploiting residual abilities', *Journal of the International Neuropsychological Society*, 4: 636–47. | Single subject design | 43-year-old with pure alexia | A case study of a 43-year-old woman with chronic and stable pure alexia. Using a multiple baseline design, we report the results of two different interventions to improve reading. First, a restitutive treatment approach, using an implicit semantic access strategy was attempted. This approach was designed to exploit privileged access to lexical-semantic representations, and met with little success. Treatment was then switched to a substitutive treatment strategy, which involved using the patient's finger to pretend to copy the letters in words and sentences recognition. | Reading using this motor cross-cuing strategy was 100 percent accurate and doubled in speed after four weeks of intervention. We propose that this patient's inability to benefit from the implicit semantic access treatment approach may be in part related to her inability to suppress the segmental letter identification process of word. | III |
| Nickels L, 1992, 'The autocue? Self-generated phonemic cues in the treatment of a disorder of reading and naming', *Cognitive Neuropsychology*, 9: 155–82. | Single case study | 43-year-old with deep dyslexia | Describes a therapy programme that aimed to improve oral reading and spoken naming in a 43-year-old deep dyslexic patient by teaching the patient grapheme–phoneme correspondences. | Improvement was achieved not by a learned mechanism for sublexical reading, but instead by enabling the use of patient-generated phonemic cues. The therapy has enabled the patient to produce the phoneme associated with the initial letter of the word, which then acted as a phonemic cue facilitating reading of that word. Spoken naming was also facilitated, as information on the written form of the word could similarly be used to provide a phonemic cue for spoken production. | III |

| Author(s) & Title | Design | Sample | Objective of study | Conclusions | Evidence Level |
|---|---|---|---|---|---|
| Scott C & Byng S, 1989, 'Computer assisted remediation of a homophone comprehension disorder in surface dyslexia', *Aphasiology*, 3 (3): 301–20. | Case study | 24-year-old woman | An information-processing model of reading was used to identify the locus of a reading and spelling disorder. The patient was found to exhibit the symptoms of surface dyslexia with surface dysgraphia, with a reliance on phonological decoding of the printed word to achieve comprehension. As a result, many errors were made in comprehending homophones. A remediation programme presented on a microcomputer was implemented to retrain the recognition and comprehension of a set of written homophones. | The patient improved in her ability to both recognise and comprehend homophones, but no generalisation of the improvement to spelling of homophones took place. | III |

## Single Word Writing: Recommendation 1

| Author(s) & Title | Design | Sample | Objective of study | Conclusions | Evidence Level |
|---|---|---|---|---|---|
| Parr S, 1995, 'Everyday reading and writing in aphasia: role change and the influence of pre-morbid literacy practice', *Aphasiology*, 9: 223–38. | Qualitative – semi-structured interviews | 20 adults with aphasia | Twenty people with aphasia (aged 30–86 years) were interviewed, most with a partner or close family member, to establish factors that might affect the focus of functional reading and writing therapy. This was done by exploring aphasic subjects' level of premorbid and current involvement with roles in domestic, work, social, and leisure contexts and literacy practices associated with those roles. Aspects of premorbid literacy practice included use of social networks, drafting and editing in composition of text and use of technical aids. | Premorbid and current roles were variable, and gains and losses in roles were reported subsequent to onset of aphasia. Aphasia was most often cited as the main reason for loss of four activities: corresponding about property, using the phone, dealing with bills and reading for relaxation. Literacy practices had been shared by, and delegated to, social network members premorbidly in an idiosyncratic manner. | IV |

## APHASIA

### Single Word Writing: Recommendation 2

| Author(s) & Title | Design | Sample | Objective of study | Conclusions | Evidence Level |
|---|---|---|---|---|---|
| Behrmann M, 1987, 'The rites of righting writing: Homophone remediation in acquired dysgraphia', *Cognitive Neuropsychology*, 4: 365–84. | Single case study | 53-year-old woman | A homophone retraining programme with a 53-year-old female surface dysgraphic patient was implemented. Extensive pre-therapy testing suggested that lexical processing was impaired in writing but not in reading, resulting in difficulties in writing homophones and irregular words. The treatment procedure involved the pairing of the written homophone with its pictorial representation in order to link the orthography with the corresponding meaning, and to enhance direct lexical access. | Results reveal significant improvement in writing the treated homophones and untreated irregular words, but minimal generalisation to untreated homophones. | III |
| Deloche G, Dordan M & Kremins H, 1993, 'Rehabilitation of confrontation naming in aphasia: relations between oral and written modalities', *Aphasiology*, 7: 201–16. | Case study | 28-year-old woman 50-year-old woman | This study presents a microcomputer-assisted rehabilitation program for picture confrontation naming impairments. The results reported concern two aphasic patients with inverse pre-therapeutic dependencies between oral and written naming mechanisms. Written naming responses of one patient with surface dysgraphia were often mediated by access to phonological word-forms, whereas the oral responses of one patient with conductive aphasia often relied on covert finding of orthographic word-forms. The rehabilitation technique focused exclusively on written naming from the keyboard, without oral training. | Improvements were obtained in both cases, with various generalisations to non-drilled items, untrained (oral) modality and handwriting. These beneficial effects were still present one year after therapy. | III |

| Author(s) & Title | Design | Sample | Objective of study | Conclusions | Evidence Level |
|---|---|---|---|---|---|
| De Partz MP, Seron X & Van der Linden M, 1992, 'Re-education of a surface dysgraphia with a visual imagery strategy', *Cognitive Neuropsychology*, 9: 369–401. | Case study | 24-year-old | Presents a specific strategy for the re-education of a 24-year-old right-handed brain-damaged patient who presented a surface dysgraphia resulting from impairments of the lexical procedure of writing, arising from a deficit in the orthographic output lexicon. A two-stage therapeutic programme was implemented. In the first stage, the subject was re-taught some graphemic contextual rules in order to optimise the relatively spared phonological writing procedure. In the second stage, the subject was re-taught the spelling of some irregular and ambiguous words by means of a technique that took into account his relatively spared performance in visual memory tasks. | In post-therapy, a selective effect of this imagery strategy was observed in comparison with untrained words and with words trained with classical methodology. Results support cognitive-oriented therapeutic approaches. | III |
| Mortley J, Enderby P & Petheram B, 2001, 'Using a computer to improve functional writing in a patient with severe dysgraphia', *Aphasiology*, 15: 443–61. | Case study | 67-year-old man | This case study describes and evaluates the therapy administered to MF to improve his severe writing impairment caused by a stroke eighteen months prior to this therapy intervention. Therapy was based on developing a compensatory strategy using his residual skills of being able to spell a word orally. A detailed account of the sequence of therapy procedures is given, initially focusing on specific non-functional tasks, followed by therapy with a more functional focus. A computer was used throughout the intervention to facilitate intensive repetitive practice. | The intervention proved to be successful, both in terms of improvements on assessments and with evidence of functional benefits. The use of both a dictionary to support the strategy and an adaptive word processor to promote functional carry over is described. The role of the computer in therapy is discussed as a tool to facilitate repetitive practice of therapy, and to encourage the independent use of the strategy embodied in therapy. | III |

## APHASIA

### Sentence Processing: Recommendation 1

| Author(s) & Title | Design | Sample | Objective of study | Conclusions | Evidence Level |
|---|---|---|---|---|---|
| Crerar MA, Ellis AW & Dean AC, 1996, 'Remediation of sentence processing deficits in aphasia using a computer-based microworld', *Brain & Language*, 52 (1): 229–75. | Controlled study | 14 aphasic adults | In this study, 14 aphasic patients were selected for having problems with sentence–picture matching involving reversible verb and preposition sentences. These problems were shown to be stable across three pre-intervention assessments. All assessments were computer-based and involved the matching of written sentences to pictures. Before therapy began, all the patients were given an assessment battery which included a 40-item Verb Test and a 40-item Preposition Test. The patients were then divided into two groups, A and B. Group A received two one-hour sessions of therapy per week for three weeks, aimed at improving the comprehension of verb sentences; then a second full assessment, followed by the same amount of therapy aimed at improving the comprehension of preposition sentences; and finally a third assessment. Group B received the preposition therapy first, followed by the verb therapy. The therapy involved the patient and therapist interacting with the computer, either assembling pictures to match written sentences ('picture-building mode') or assembling sentences to match pictures ('sentence-building mode'). | Group A showed a classical 'cross-over' treatment outcome. Performance on treated verb sentences improved during verb therapy and was retained when therapy switched to preposition sentences. Performance on treated preposition sentences was unaffected by verb therapy, but improved when therapy switched to the processing of prepositions. Performance on untreated verb and preposition sentences showed a similar pattern, though the improvements observed were not as great. Improvement was also shown on a paper-based 'Real World Test' which involved a wider range of more naturalistic sentences. Performance on a third aspect of sentence comprehension which the patients also had difficulty with, namely the comprehension of morphology, remained unchanged throughout, providing further evidence that the effects obtained were treatment-specific. The results of Group B were less clear cut. Comprehension of both verb and preposition sentences improved during the period that prepositions were being treated, then remained static during verb treatment. Comprehension of morphology remained unchanged throughout. At the level of the individual patient, the majority of patients obtained higher scores on both the Verb Test and the Preposition Test after therapy, but only three patients showed improvements on both verbs and | II |

| Author(s) & Title | Design | Sample | Objective of study | Conclusions | Evidence Level |
|---|---|---|---|---|---|
| | | | | prepositions that were statistically significant. Six patients showed significant improvements on verbs, but not prepositions, while one showed the opposite pattern. Only three patients failed to show so much as a borderline improvement on either verbs or prepositions. Finally, seven of the patients returned for an additional assessment five months after completing the therapy. These patients, who had demonstrated significant improvements during the therapy, were shown to have maintained their improved comprehension skills. | |
| Byng S, Nickels L & Black M, 1994, 'Replicating therapy for mapping deficits in agrammatism: remapping the deficit', *Aphasiology*, 8: 315–41. | Case series | 3 agrammatic aphasic adults | Replicated an earlier study conducted by Byng, in which treatments were provided for two agrammatic patients. The deficit of these two patients was interpreted within the framework of the mapping deficit hypothesis of agrammatism. In the present study, three agrammatic aphasic patients received therapy intended to improve their ability to comprehend and produce sentences. The therapy comprised two principal phases. In the first stage, the emphasis was on the linguistic and nonlinguistic conceptualisation of events, whereas, in the second and third stages, production of structured utterances became the task focus. | All three subjects could name the verbs represented in action pictures more effectively after the therapy. However, none of them showed a significant improvement in naming of pictures of objects. There appeared to be some generalisation of the therapeutic effect. | III |

## APHASIA

| Author(s) & Title | Design | Sample | Objective of study | Conclusions | Evidence Level |
|---|---|---|---|---|---|
| Schwartz MF, Saffran EM, Fink RB, Myers JL & Martin N, 1994, 'Mapping therapy: A treatment programme for agrammatism', *Aphasiology*, 8 (1): 19–54. | Case series | 8 chronic non-fluent aphasics | This study describes a treatment programme ('mapping therapy') directed at the remediation of mapping operations, and reports the results of a study designed to assess the effects of this intervention on comprehension and production. Eight chronic non-fluent aphasics were trained to identify the verb, agent and patient/theme in sentences presented in a combined written-spoken format. Three types of sentences were used: active transitives with action verbs (Type A); active transitives with experiential verbs (Type B), and non-canonical sentence types (eg, passives) with action verbs (Type C). The first phase of training utilised Type A sentences, the second Type B, the third Type C. Generalisation to the untrained sentence types was tested by means of multiple-baseline/generalisation probes. Generalisation to standard comprehension and production tasks was assessed through a comprehensive Language Assessment Battery. | Acquisition and generalisation profiles differed across subjects. However, following training, most patients showed improved scores on predicted measures of sentence production, and two patients also showed improvement on syntactic comprehension tests. The best outcomes were seen in patients with relatively pure agrammatism. Those with more severe and more complicated impairments had poorer outcomes, in part, we believe, because of the resource demands of this particular training task. | III |
| Mitchum C, Greenwald M & Berndt R, 2000, 'Cognitive treatments of sentence processing disorders: What have we learned?', *Neuropsychological Rehabilitation*, 10 (3): 311–36. | Review of previous studies | | Several cognitive neuropsychological studies describing treatments of sentence processing disorders have been reported in recent years. The authors review the outcome of 10 studies that describe treatment outcomes for 17 aphasic patients. Although the studies used different approaches to intervention, they shared the goal of improving reversible sentence comprehension, and they targeted a hypothesised deficit of 'thematic mapping'. | Several trends in treatment outcomes were observed. In most cases, there was strong evidence that the treatments induced a change in the pattern of sentence processing. Moreover, the outcomes indicated that impaired reversible sentence comprehension can arise from a range of impairments, only some of which directly implicate structural and/or lexical deficits assumed to be the source of poor thematic mapping abilities. Patterns of post-therapy generalisation | IV |

| Author(s) & Title | Design | Sample | Objective of study | Conclusions | Evidence Level |
|---|---|---|---|---|---|
| | | | | within and across processing modalities appeared to be related, among other things, to the therapy approach and to the selection of treatment materials. These findings are discussed with regard to the theoretical implications of sentence processing treatment data. | |

**Sentence Processing: Recommendation 2**

| Author(s) & Title | Design | Sample | Objective of study | Conclusions | Evidence Level |
|---|---|---|---|---|---|
| Berndt R, Mitchum C, Haendiges A & Sandson J, 1997a, 'Verb retrieval in aphasia. 1. Characterising single word impairments', *Brain and Language*, 56: 68–106. | Case series | 11 chronic aphasic adults | The ability of aphasic patients to produce words from the grammatical classes of nouns and verbs was investigated in tasks that elicited these types of words in isolation. Eleven chronic aphasic patients produced nouns and verbs in picture naming, videotaped scene naming, sentence completion, naming from definition and oral reading. Comprehension of the meanings of nouns and verbs was tested in word/picture and word/video scene matching, and appreciation of noun/verb grammatical class differences was tested with two metalinguistic tasks. | Five patients demonstrated significantly more difficulty producing verbs than nouns, two patients were significantly more impaired producing nouns than verbs, and the remaining four patients showed no difference between the two classes. There was no improvement in verb production when naming actions presented on videotape, suggesting that selective verb impairments are not attributable to conceptual difficulty in identifying actions in static pictures. Selective noun impairments occurred in the context of severe anomia, as reported in previous studies. Selective verb impairments were demonstrated for both agrammatic and fluent (Wernicke) patients, indicating that such deficits are not necessarily associated with the nonfluent and morphologically impoverished production that is characteristic of agrammatism. There was no indication that single word comprehension was affected in these patients in a manner consonant with their production impairments. Results are interpreted in light of current models of lexical organisation and processing. | III |

## APHASIA

| Author(s) & Title | Design | Sample | Objective of study | Conclusions | Evidence Level |
|---|---|---|---|---|---|
| Berndt R, Mitchum C, Haendiges A & Sandson J, 1997b, 'Verb retrieval in aphasia. 2. Relationship to sentence processing', *Brain and Language*, 56: 107–37. | | 10 chronic aphasic adults | Sentence comprehension and production were evaluated for 10 chronic aphasic patients who have been shown to demonstrate one of three patterns in the relative ease of retrieval of nouns and verbs. Although these patterns of noun/verb production were not entirely predictable from patients' clinical classifications, they were found here to be significantly correlated with several structural indices of sentence production and with failure to comprehend semantically reversible sentences. Noun/verb retrieval patterns were not strongly correlated with speech fluency nor with morphological characteristics of sentence production. Patients with relative impairment in the production of verbs were found to rely on high frequency, semantically empty, 'light' verbs when producing sentences, and to favor simple syntactic structures in which verbs do not require inflections. When forced to produce substantive verbs (in picture and scene descriptions), verb retrieval continued to undermine the production of well-formed sentences for the verb-impaired patients. In addition, two out of five such patients also showed some evidence for poor realisation of noun arguments for verbs they could not produce. Results are interpreted as indicating multiple contribution to patients' sentence processing impairments, one of which may be selective difficulty retrieving verbs. | — | III |

| Author(s) & Title | Design | Sample | Objective of study | Conclusions | Evidence Level |
|---|---|---|---|---|---|
| Marshall J, Pring T & Chiat S, 1998, 'Verb retrieval and sentence production in aphasia', *Brain and Language*, 63: 159–83. | Case study | 52-year-old woman with aphasia | This paper presents a subject with a selective verb retrieval deficit. Nouns were produced more successfully than verbs in spontaneous speech, picture naming and when naming to definition. The word class effect was not observed in comprehension tasks, reading aloud or writing. This indicated that it was due to a specific problem in accessing verbs' phonological representations from semantics. The second part of the paper explores the implications of the verb deficit for sentence production. | Analyses of narrative speech revealed a typically agrammatic profile, with minimal verb argument structure and few function words and inflections. Two investigations suggested that the sentence deficit was at least partly contingent upon the verb deficit. In the first, the subject was asked to produce a sentence with the aid of a provided noun or verb. The noun cues were not effective in eliciting sentences, whereas verb cues were. The second investigation explored the effects of therapy aiming to improve verb retrieval. This therapy resulted in better verb retrieval and improved sentence production with those verbs. These findings suggest that an inability to access verbs' phonological representations can severely impair sentence formulation. | III |
| Shapiro K & Caramazza A, 2003, 'Grammatical processing of nouns and verbs in left frontal cortex?' *Neuropsychologia*, 41: 1189–98. | Case study | 65-year-old man | This paper reports the case of a man, RC, who is more impaired at producing grammatical forms of words and pseudo-words used as verbs (he judges, he wugs) than of the same words used as nouns (the judges, the wugs). This pattern of performance constitutes the first clear demonstration that grammatical knowledge about verbs can be selectively impaired following brain damage. | A comparison of RC's behavioural and neurological profile with that of a patient who shows similar difficulties with nouns suggests that nouns and verbs are processed by separate neural systems with components in the left frontal lobe. | III |

## APHASIA

| Author(s) & Title | Design | Sample | Objective of study | Conclusions | Evidence Level |
|---|---|---|---|---|---|
| Raymer A & Ellsworth T, 2002, 'Response to contrastive verb retrieval treatments: a case study', *Aphasiology*, 16: 1031–45. | Case study | — | This paper compared effects of sequential verb retrieval treatments in one participant, and analysed effects on sentence production. The study focused on a woman called WR, with non-fluent aphasia and mild verb retrieval impairment related to semantic dysfunction. She participated in three phases of verb retrieval treatment – semantic, phonologic and rehearsal – in a multiple-baseline crossover design. Accuracy of picture naming was examined, and sentence production for trained and untrained verbs. | All treatments resulted in significantly improved naming of trained verbs, some generalised sentence production, and no improvement for untrained verbs. No difference was evident in effects across treatments. Unlike earlier studies, the repetition and phonologic treatments were as effective as semantic treatment for improving sentence production. These positive findings for all three treatments may relate to the semantic activation that occurs whenever a word is retrieved in the context of picture presentation, thereby fundamentally altering semantic activation patterns, and making the word more easily accessible in subsequent retrieval attempts, whether in isolation or in sentences. | III |

### Sentence Processing: Recommendation 3

| Author(s) & Title | Design | Sample | Objective of study | Conclusions | Evidence Level |
|---|---|---|---|---|---|
| Byng S, Nickels L & Black M, 1994, 'Replicating therapy for mapping deficits in agrammatism: remapping the deficit', *Aphasiology*, 8: 315–41. | Case series | 3 agrammatic aphasic adults | Replicated an earlier study conducted by Byng, in which treatments were provided for two agrammatic patients. The deficit of these two patients was interpreted within the framework of the mapping deficit hypothesis of agrammatism. In the present study, three agrammatic aphasic patients received therapy intended to improve their ability to comprehend and produce sentences. The therapy comprised two principal phases. In the first stage, the emphasis was on the linguistic and nonlinguistic conceptualisation of events, whereas, in the second and third stages, production of structured utterances became the task focus. | All three subjects could name the verbs represented in action pictures more effectively after the therapy. However, none of them showed a significant improvement in naming of pictures of objects. There appeared to be some generalisation of the therapeutic effect. | III |

| Author(s) & Title | Design | Sample | Objective of study | Conclusions | Evidence Level |
|---|---|---|---|---|---|
| Schwartz MF, Saffran EM, Fink RB, Myers JL & Martin N, 1994, 'Mapping therapy: A treatment programme for agrammatism', *Aphasiology*, 8 (1): 19–54. | Case series | 8 chronic non-fluent aphasics | This study describes a treatment programme ('mapping therapy') directed at the remediation of mapping operations, and reports the results of a study designed to assess the effects of this intervention on comprehension and production. Eight chronic non-fluent aphasics were trained to identify the verb, agent and patient/theme in sentences presented in a combined written-spoken format. Three types of sentences were used: active transitives with action verbs (Type A); active transitives with experiential verbs (Type B), and non-canonical sentence types (eg, passives) with action verbs (Type C). The first phase of training utilised Type A sentences, the second Type B, the third Type C. Generalisation to the untrained sentence types was tested by means of multiple-baseline/generalisation probes. Generalisation to standard comprehension and production tasks was assessed through a comprehensive Language Assessment Battery. | Acquisition and generalisation profiles differed across subjects. However, following training, most patients showed improved scores on predicted measures of sentence production, and two patients also showed improvement on syntactic comprehension tests. The best outcomes were seen in patients with relatively pure agrammatism. Those with more severe and more complicated impairments had poorer outcomes, in part, we believe, because of the resource demands of this particular training task. | III |
| Mitchum C, Haendiges A & Berndt R, 1996, 'Treatment of thematic mapping in sentence comprehension: Implications for normal processing', *Cognitive Neuropsychology*, 12: 503–47. | Case study | 47-year-old man with aphasia | Describes a treatment approach to thematic mapping impairment that succeeded in improving auditory sentence comprehension in a chronic aphasic man with a long-standing comprehension deficit. He had suffered a cerebrovascular accident at the age of 47 years. | Generalisation of improvement to auditory comprehension of sentences with untreated verbs, to comprehension of written sentences, and to tests using pictorial and videotaped materials not used in treatment, places constraints on the range of possible interpretations of the functional locus of treatment effects. Two areas that did not show improvement following treatment were auditory comprehension of sentences lengthened with modifiers, and spoken production of active and passive sentences that express correct thematic roles. These null effects are considered relevant to the role of working memory in sentence comprehension and the nature of therapy mapping procedures in comprehension and production. | III |

## APHASIA

| Author(s) & Title | Design | Sample | Objective of study | Conclusions | Evidence Level |
|---|---|---|---|---|---|
| Crerar MA, Ellis AW & Dean AC, 1996, 'Remediation of sentence processing deficits in aphasia using a computer-based microworld', *Brain & Language*, 52 (1): 229–75. | Controlled study | 14 aphasic adults | In this study, 14 aphasic patients were selected for having problems with sentence–picture matching involving reversible verb and preposition sentences. These problems were shown to be stable across three pre-intervention assessments. All assessments were computer-based and involved the matching of written sentences to pictures. Before therapy began, all the patients were given an assessment battery which included a 40-item Verb Test and a 40-item Preposition Test. The patients were then divided into two groups, A and B. Group A received two one-hour sessions of therapy per week for three weeks, aimed at improving the comprehension of verb sentences; then a second full assessment, followed by the same amount of therapy aimed at improving the comprehension of preposition sentences; and finally a third assessment. Group B received the preposition therapy first, followed by the verb therapy. The therapy involved the patient and therapist interacting with the computer, either assembling pictures to match written sentences ('picture-building mode') or assembling sentences to match pictures ('sentence-building mode'). | Group A showed a classical 'cross-over' treatment outcome. Performance on treated verb sentences improved during verb therapy and was retained when therapy switched to preposition sentences. Performance on treated preposition sentences was unaffected by verb therapy, but improved when therapy switched to the processing of prepositions. Performance on untreated verb and preposition sentences showed a similar pattern, though the improvements observed were not as great. Improvement was also shown on a paper-based 'Real World Test' which involved a wider range of more naturalistic sentences. Performance on a third aspect of sentence comprehension which the patients also had difficulty with, namely the comprehension of morphology, remained unchanged throughout, providing further evidence that the effects obtained were treatment-specific. The results of Group B were less clear cut. Comprehension of both verb and preposition sentences improved during the period that prepositions were being treated, then remained static during verb treatment. Comprehension of morphology remained unchanged throughout. At the level of the individual patient, the majority of patients obtained higher scores on both the Verb Test and the Preposition Test after therapy, but only three patients showed improvements on both verbs and prepositions that were statistically significant. | II |

| Author(s) & Title | Design | Sample | Objective of study | Conclusions | Evidence Level |
|---|---|---|---|---|---|
| | | | | Six patients showed significant improvements on verbs, but not prepositions, while one showed the opposite pattern. Only three patients failed to show so much as a borderline improvement on either verbs or prepositions. Finally, seven of the patients returned for an additional assessment five months after completing the therapy. These patients, who had demonstrated significant improvements during the therapy, were shown to have maintained their improved comprehension skills. | |
| Marshall J, Chiat S & Pring T, 1997, 'An impairment in processing verbs' thematic roles: a therapy study', *Aphasiology*, 11: 855–76. | Case study | 51-year-old man | Describes a 51-year-old male patient who presented with a selective verb disorder after a cerebrovascular accident. Verb retrieval was impaired both in spontaneous speech and naming. When verbs were accessed, a striking dissociation emerged. Subcategorisation was surprisingly intact, while the assignment of verbs' thematic roles was poor. Verb comprehension was also impaired, particularly when tasks demanded an appreciation of thematic information. A remediation programme was administered which aimed to improve insight into the role structures and mapping requirements of three argument verbs. | The subject showed gains in the production of this type of verb, which generalised to untreated items. However, there was no generalisation to verbs of a different type. Progress was also suggested by a second evaluative procedure, in which observers judged the intelligibility of the subject's output, before and after therapy. | III |
| Weinrich M, Shelton JR, Cox DM & McCall D, 1997, 'Remediating production of tense morphology improves verb retrieval in chronic aphasia', *Brain & Language*, 58: 23–45. | Case series | 3 adults with severe aphasia | Production of tense markers in C-VIC, a computerised visual communication system, was utilised as a treatment for three patients with severe expressive aphasia. Patients practised constructing C-VIC tense-marked sentences and then producing English equivalents. | After training, all patients demonstrated significant improvements in English verb retrieval and production of correct tense morphology. Generalisation of morphological rules for past tense production was seen for regular, but not irregular verbs. | III |

## APHASIA

| Author(s) & Title | Design | Sample | Objective of study | Conclusions | Evidence Level |
|---|---|---|---|---|---|
| Linebarger MC, Schwartz MF, Romania JR, Kohn SE & Stephens DL, 2000, 'Grammatical encoding in aphasia: evidence from a processing prosthesis', *Brain & Language*, 75 (3): 416–27. | Case series | 6 adults with aphasia | Agrammatic aphasia is characterised by severely reduced grammatical structure in spoken and written language, often accompanied by apparent insensitivity to grammatical structure in comprehension. This paper poses the question – does agrammatism represent loss of linguistic competence or rather performance factors such as memory or resource limitations? A considerable body of evidence supports the latter hypothesis in the domain of comprehension. | Presented here is the first strong evidence for the performance hypothesis in the domain of production: an augmentative communication system that markedly increases the grammatical structure of agrammatic speech, while providing no linguistic information, functioning merely to reduce on-line processing demands. | III |
| Beveridge MA & Crerar MA, 2002, 'Remediation of asyntactic comprehension using a multimedia Microworld', *Brain & Language*, 82: 243–95. | Case series | 3 adults | An efficacy study involving three patients is reported. All three patients achieved statistically significant improvements in written sentence comprehension as a result of eight hours of treatment focusing on active, passive and object-cleft sentence structures. | Treatment effects generalised both to untreated Microworld sentences and to the more naturalistic sentences of the Philadelphia Comprehension Battery (Saffran, Schwartz, Linebarger, Martin, & Bochetto, 1988), with some further evidence of generalisation to spoken sentence comprehension. Treatment effects were obtained with minimal input from a clinician. | III |

| Author(s) & Title | Design | Sample | Objective of study | Conclusions | Evidence Level |
|---|---|---|---|---|---|
| **Sentence Processing: Recommendation 4** | | | | | |
| Schwartz MF, Saffran EM, Fink RB, Myers JL & Martin N, 1994, 'Mapping therapy: A treatment programme for agrammatism', *Aphasiology*, 8 (1): 19–54. | Case series | 8 chronic non-fluent aphasics | This study describes a treatment programme ('mapping therapy') directed at the remediation of mapping operations, and reports the results of a study designed to assess the effects of this intervention on comprehension and production. Eight chronic non-fluent aphasics were trained to identify the verb, agent and patient/theme in sentences presented in a combined written-spoken format. Three types of sentences were used: active transitives with action verbs (Type A); active transitives with experiential verbs (Type B), and non-canonical sentence types (eg, passives) with action verbs (Type C). The first phase of training utilised Type A sentences, the second Type B, the third Type C. Generalisation to the untrained sentence types was tested by means of multiple-baseline/ generalisation probes. Generalisation to standard comprehension and production tasks was assessed through a comprehensive Language Assessment Battery. | Acquisition and generalisation profiles differed across subjects. However, following training, most patients showed improved scores on predicted measures of sentence production, and two patients also showed improvement on syntactic comprehension tests. The best outcomes were seen in patients with relatively pure agrammatism. Those with more severe and more complicated impairments had poorer outcomes, in part, we believe, because of the resource demands of this particular training task. | III |
| Ballard K & Thompson C, 1999, 'Treatment and generalisation of complex sentence production in agrammatism', *Journal of Speech Language and Hearing Research*, 42: 690–703. | Single subject design | 5 adults with agrammatic aphasia | This study examines (a) the acquisition and generalisation of complex sentence production in agrammatism using Linguistic Specific Treatment (LST) and (b) the utility of syntactic therapy in guiding hypothesis of treatment effects. LST trains construction and production of complex sentence structures. Four sentence types were selected for study: object clefts and object-extracted matrix and embedded questions (which are non canonical with *wh*-movement), and embedded actives (which are canonical with no overt movement). | Three of five participants demonstrated generalisation from object cleft treatment to production of matrix questions. LST was effective in improving their ability to generate less complex sentences with *wh*-movement. Once production of object clefts and matrix questions was acquired, all five participants demonstrated generalisation from treatment to improved production of embedded questions and/or embedded actives. This generalisation involved improved ability to generate embedded clausal structure to form complex sentences but continuing inability to express overt material in the complementiser phase. Direct treatment for embedded questions did not result in accurate production of embedded actives or vice versa. | III |

## APHASIA

| Author(s) & Title | Design | Sample | Objective of study | Conclusions | Evidence Level |
|---|---|---|---|---|---|
| Jacobs B & Thompson C, 2000, 'Cross modal generalisation of effects of training non canonical sentence comprehension and production in agrammatic aphasia', *Journal of Speech, Language and Hearing Research*, 43: 5–20. | Single subject design | 4 individuals with agrammatic Broca's aphasia | The cross-modal generalisation effects of training complex sentence comprehension and complex sentence production were examined in four individuals with agrammatic Broca's aphasia who showed difficulty comprehending and producing complex, non-canonical sentences. Object cleft and passive sentences were selected for treatment because the two are linguistically distinct, relying on wh-and NP movement, respectively. Two participants received comprehension training, and two received production training using linguistic specific treatment (LST). LST takes participants through a series of steps that emphasise the verb and verb argument structure, as well as the linguistic movement required to derive target sentences. A single-subject multiple-baseline design across behaviours was used to measure acquisition and generalisation within and across sentence types, as well as cross-modal generalisation (ie, from comprehension to production and vice versa) and generalisation to discourse. | Results indicated that both treatment methods were effective for training comprehension and production of target sentences and that comprehension treatment resulted in generalisation to spoken and written sentence production. Sentence production treatment generalised to written sentence production only; generalisation to comprehension did not occur. Across sentence types, generalisation also did not occur, as predicted, and the effects of treatment on discourse were inconsistent across participants. These data are discussed with regard to models of normal sentence comprehension and production. | III |

| Author(s) & Title | Design | Sample | Objective of study | Conclusions | Evidence Level |
|---|---|---|---|---|---|
| Thompson C, Shapiro L, Kiran S & Sobecks J, 2003, 'The role of syntactic complexity in treatment of sentence deficits in agrammatic aphasia: the complexity account of treatment efficacy', *Journal of Speech Language and Hearing Research*, 46: 591–607. | Single subject design | 4 individuals with agrammatic aphasia | This experiment examined the hypothesis that training production of syntactically complex sentences results in generalisation to less complex sentences that have processes in common with treated structures. Four adults were trained to comprehend and produce filler-gap sentences with *wh*-movement, including, from least to most complex, object-extracted *who*-questions, objects clefts, and sentences with object-relative clausal embedding. Two participants received treatment first on the least complex structure (*who*-question), and two received treatment first on the most complex form (object-relative constructions), while untrained sentences and narrative language samples were tested for generalisation. When generalisation did not occur across structure, each was successively entered into treatment. | Results showed no generalisation across sentence types when *who*-questions were trained; however, as predicted, object-relative training resulted in robust generalisation to both object clefts and *who*-questions. | III |

## Sentence Processing: Recommendation 5

| | | | | | |
|---|---|---|---|---|---|
| Marshall J, 1999, 'Doing something about a verb impairment: Two therapy approaches', in Byng S, Swinburn K & Pound C (eds), *The Aphasia Therapy File*, Psychology Press. | Single case study | 52-year-old woman with aphasia | Describes two therapy approaches to therapy for verb impairment. | | III |

## APHASIA

| Author(s) & Title | Design | Sample | Objective of study | Conclusions | Evidence Level |
|---|---|---|---|---|---|
| Weinrich M, Shelton JR, Cox DM & McCall D, 1997, 'Remediating production of tense morphology improves verb retrieval in chronic aphasia', *Brain & Language*, 58: 23–45. | Case series | 3 adults with severe aphasia | Production of tense markers in C-VIC, a computerised visual communication system, was utilised as a treatment for three patients with severe expressive aphasia. Patients practised constructing C-VIC tense-marked sentences and then producing English equivalents. | After training, all patients demonstrated significant improvements in English verb retrieval and production of correct tense morphology. Generalisation of morphological rules for past tense production was seen for regular, but not irregular verbs. | III |

### Therapies Focusing on Compensatory Strategies : Recommendation 1

| Author(s) & Title | Design | Sample | Objective of study | Conclusions | Evidence Level |
|---|---|---|---|---|---|
| Holland A, 1982, 'Observing functional communication of aphasic adults', *Journal of Speech & Hearing Disorders*, 47(1): 50–56. | Observational study | 40 aphasic adults | Summarises data obtained by observing the functional communication of 40 aphasics (aged 32–74 years) who lived at home. Typical communication patterns are described by presenting three case histories and detailed reports of the actual observations. Effective communication strategies are noted, and detailed examples of three successful strategy users are presented. | | III |

| Author(s) & Title | Design | Sample | Objective of study | Conclusions | Evidence Level |
|---|---|---|---|---|---|
| Baker R, 2000, 'The assessment of functional communication in culturally and linguistically diverse populations', in Worrall & Frattali (eds), *Neurogenic communication disorders: A functional approach*, Thieme, New York. | Text | | | | IV |
| Davidson B & Worrall L, 2000, 'The assessment of activity limitation in functional communication: challenges and choices', in Worrall & Frattali (eds), *Neurogenic communication disorders: A functional approach*, Thieme, New York. | Text | | | | IV |
| Worrall L, McCooey R, Davidson B, Larkins B & Hickson L, 2002, 'The validity of functional assessments of communication and the activity/ participation components of the ICIHD-2: Do they reflect what happens in real life?', *Journal of Communication Disorders*, 35: 107–37. | Expert opinion | | This paper aims to provide a better understanding of the nature of functional communication activities so that assessment and treatment efforts are based on a theoretical framework and empirical data. Three sources of information are discussed. The first is the Activity/Participation dimensions of the World Health Organization's International Classification of Functioning, Disability and Health. The second source is existing assessments of functional communication. The final source is data obtained from observational studies conducted in our research unit. The studies have observed the everyday communication of people with aphasia, people with Traumatic Brain Injury (TBI), and patients in hospital. The simplification of real-life communication in the WHO classification scheme, the variability of item sampling in existing assessments, and the complexity of communication observed in real-life settings has led to the conclusion that there are three levels of functional communication assessment: generic, population-specific and individualised. Clinicians may choose which level suits their purpose. | IV |

## APHASIA

| Author(s) & Title | Design | Sample | Objective of study | Conclusions | Evidence Level |
|---|---|---|---|---|---|
| Holland A, 1998, 'Functional outcome assessment of aphasia following left hemisphere stroke', *Seminars in Speech & Language*, 19: 249–59. | Expert opinion | | This article discusses issues regarding the assessment of functional outcomes in individuals who have aphasia following stroke. Some different approaches to functional outcome measurement are critically reviewed, ranging from general measures of stroke outcome, to measures that have been designed specifically for aphasic individuals, to measurements focusing on aphasia's effects on quality of life. Examples of how to relate treatment of aphasia directly to functional outcomes assessment are also provided. | | IV |

**Therapies Focusing on Compensatory Strategies : Recommendation 2**

| Author(s) & Title | Design | Sample | Objective of study | Conclusions | Evidence Level |
|---|---|---|---|---|---|
| Cubelli R, Trentini P & Montagna CG, 1991, 'Re-education of gestural communication in a case of chronic global aphasia and limb apraxia', *Cognitive Neuropsychology*, 8 (5): 369–80. | Case study | 63-year-old woman | Reports the results of pantomimic training of a 63-year-old woman with chronic global aphasia and severe limb apraxia who had not shown any improvements following standardised speech re-education. Training aimed to focus her attention on critical features of gestures. After treatment the patient showed a significant improvement of gestural ability. | | III |

| Author(s) & Title | Design | Sample | Objective of study | Conclusions | Evidence Level |
|---|---|---|---|---|---|
| Sacchett C, Byng S, Marshall J & Pound C, 1999, 'Drawing together: evaluation of a therapy programme for severe aphasia', *International Journal of Language & Communication Disorders*, 34 (3): 265–89. | Single subject design | 5 males, 2 females, age range 47–66. | This paper reports a therapy study that aims to promote communicative drawing in a group of seven people with severe and long-standing aphasia. Therapy was conducted on an individual and group basis over 12 weeks, and entailed a range of techniques which are described in some detail. Treatment was evaluated using a novel generative drawing assessment in which subjects were required to draw absent items in response to photographic and conversational cues. Pre- and post-therapy assessments of untreated skills, such as comprehension, naming and gesture, were also conducted. | The results indicated that, as a group, the subjects' drawing improved. Unchanged performance on the other assessments indicated that the gains were specific to the content of therapy and could not be attributed to spontaneous recovery. Pre- and post-therapy interviews with carers (ie, relatives and close friends of the individuals) suggested that the effects of therapy were also being felt in the home. These results have important implications for therapy with people with severe aphasia. | III |
| Carlomagno S, Losanno N, Emanuelli & Cassadio P, 1991, 'Expressive language recovery of improved communication skills: effect of PACE therapy on aphasics' referential communication and story-retelling', *Aphasiology*, 5: 419–24. | Case series | 8 adults with aphasia | Eight adults with chronic aphasia received a PACE therapy programme. All patients received aphasia testing as pre/post therapy evaluation. In order to assess their communicative abilities in a face to face setting, referential communication and story retelling tasks were also given. | Results showed that aphasics' referential communication abilities improved whereas standard aphasia parameters did not. Furthermore, when story retellings were submitted to naïve listeners, those produced after treatment were judged to be more informative. It is suggested that PACE therapy can improve communicative skills even in those aphasia patients who do not show language improvement. | III |
| Pound C, Parr S, Lindsay J & Woolf C, 2000, *Beyond Aphasia: Therapies for Living with Communication Disabilities*, Speechmark Publishing, Bicester. | Text | | | | IV |

## APHASIA

### Therapies Focusing on Compensatory Strategies : Recommendation 3

| Author(s) & Title | Design | Sample | Objective of study | Conclusions | Evidence Level |
|---|---|---|---|---|---|
| Robson J, Marshall J, Chiat S, Pring T, 2001, 'Enhancing communication in jargon aphasia: a small group study of writing therapy', *International Journal of Language & Communication Disorders*, 36 (4): 471–88. | Case series | 10 adults with aphasia | This study treated written output and examined whether it assisted communication for these clients. In stage 1 of the study, anagram sorting, delayed copying and lexical decision tasks were used to investigate the residual knowledge of written words in a group of ten people with jargon aphasia. Evidence of the presence of orthographic knowledge was taken as an indication that writing might be a useful focus for therapy. This hypothesis was explored in stage 2 with six clients. A personally useful vocabulary was selected for each, and copying, word completion and written picture-naming tasks were used in therapy to improve written production of these words. | The clients made progress in written naming. However, they showed little change on a 'message' assessment that tested their ability to use the written words to convey messages. Stage 3 targeted communicative writing. Here, three of the clients received 'message therapy,' which encouraged them to relate treated words to functional messages and to communicate them to a partner. The clients improved on the message assessment and observation of their communication, and reports from relatives suggested that they made functional use of writing in a range of communication settings. | II |

| Author(s) & Title | Design | Sample | Objective of study | Conclusions | Evidence Level |
|---|---|---|---|---|---|
| Jackson-Waite K, Robson J & Pring T, 2003, 'Written communication using a Lightwriter in undifferentiated jargon aphasia: A single case study', *Aphasiology*, 17(8): 767–80. | Case study | 71-year-old woman | This study reports a woman, MA, who has undifferentiated jargon aphasia. Her spoken output had not responded to treatment, and therapy had failed to establish a non-verbal mode of communication. Her writing was impaired, and its slow and effortful execution hindered her progress. However, she retained some ability to access written words and was aware of her errors. Therapy aimed to improve access to written words, and to facilitate writing by using a Lightwriter. Three stages of therapy were conducted. Words selected by MA for their usefulness were treated. In stage 1, solving anagrams, copying, delayed copying, and written naming were used to improve access to their orthographies. Written naming improved, but only to the pictures used in therapy. In stages 2 and 3 further words were introduced, and steps taken to encourage generalisation. In stage 2 several different pictures of each item were used to overcome the picture-specific effect. In stage 3, written words were used to describe situations and answer questions in order to encourage their use in communication. | MA improved significantly in writing treated words, and her rate of acquisition accelerated as therapy progressed. Performance was largely maintained after periods without treatment or exposure to the treated items. MA made progress in using her written vocabulary to answer questions in therapy, but needed prompting to use the Lightwriter rather than speech, and rarely made functional use of it outside the clinic setting. MA's progress demonstrates the potential for treating writing in jargon aphasia. Her progress in accessing word orthographies allowed her to use the Lightwriter for communication. Her inability to use writing spontaneously suggests that further therapy is needed, and that it should include a regular partner to encourage functional use. | III |

## APHASIA

| Author(s) & Title | Design | Sample | Objective of study | Conclusions | Evidence Level |
|---|---|---|---|---|---|
| Lustig A P & Tompkins CA, 2002, 'A written communication strategy for a speaker with aphasia and apraxia of speech: treatment outcomes and social validity', *Aphasiology*, 16 (4–6): 507–22. | Single subject design | 52-year-old man, 10 years post onset | The purpose of this study was to train an individual (LG) with longstanding aphasia and apraxia of speech to substitute a self-initiated written word for protracted articulatory struggle, in three conversational settings. A multiple-baseline design across three different settings was utilised, providing an opportunity for strategy practice with both familiar and unfamiliar conversational partners. Topics were constructed to be relevant and meaningful to LG. Several subject-evaluated psychosocial measures, including locus of control, were employed, and social validity ratings were solicited from unfamiliar raters. | LG adopted and successfully used the strategy across all settings, with both familiar and unfamiliar partners, at performance levels well above baseline. The number of abandoned conversational targets decreased considerably with strategy use, and social validation ratings indicated beneficial effects pertaining to communicative efficiency and comprehensibility in shorter, but not longer, conversational segments extracted from treatment videotapes. Conclusions: the training protocol was successful in improving LG's facility with targeted compensatory strategy use across designated conversational contexts. However, the clinical significance and social value of LG's strategy use in these settings may be mitigated by the accompanying communicative variables affecting the conversational exchange as a whole. | III |
| Mortley J, Enderby P & Petheram B, 2001, 'Using a computer to improve functional writing in a patient with severe dysgraphia', *Aphasiology*, 15: 443–61. | Case study | 67-year-old man | This case study describes and evaluates the therapy administered to MF to improve his severe writing impairment caused by a stroke eighteen months prior to this therapy intervention. Therapy was based on developing a compensatory strategy using his residual skills of being able to spell a word orally. A detailed account of the sequence of therapy procedures is given, initially focusing on specific non-functional tasks, followed by therapy with a more functional focus. A computer was used throughout the intervention to facilitate intensive repetitive practice. | The intervention proved to be successful, both in terms of improvements on assessments and with evidence of functional benefits. The use of both a dictionary to support the strategy and an adaptive word processor to promote functional carry over is described. The role of the computer in therapy is discussed as a tool to facilitate repetitive practice of therapy, and to encourage the independent use of the strategy embodied in therapy. | III |

| Author(s) & Title | Design | Sample | Objective of study | Conclusions | Evidence Level |
|---|---|---|---|---|---|
| Bruce C, Edmundson A & Coleman M, 2003, 'Writing with voice: an investigation of the use of a voice recognition system as a writing aid for a man with aphasia', *International Journal of Language & Communication Disorders*, 38 (2): 131–48. | Case study | 57-year-old man | This study investigated whether a man with fluent aphasia could learn to use Dragon NaturallySpeaking® to write. A single case study of a man with acquired writing difficulties is reported. A detailed account is provided of the stages involved in teaching him to use the software. The therapy tasks carried out to develop his functional use of the system are then described. Outcomes included the percentage of words accurately recognised by the system over time, the quantitative and qualitative changes in written texts produced with and without the use of the speech-recognition system, and the functional benefits the man described. | The treatment programme was successful and resulted in a marked improvement in the subject's written work. It also had effects in the functional life domain, as the subject could use writing for communication purposes. The results suggest that the technology might benefit others with acquired writing difficulties. | III |

## APHASIA

### Therapies Focusing on Compensatory Strategies : Recommendation 4

| Author(s) & Title | Design | Sample | Objective of study | Conclusions | Evidence Level |
|---|---|---|---|---|---|
| Jackson-Waite K, Robson J & Pring T, 2003, 'Written communication using a Lightwriter in undifferentiated jargon aphasia: A single case study', *Aphasiology*, 17 (8): 767–80. | Case study | 71-year-old woman | This study reports a woman, MA, who has undifferentiated jargon aphasia. Her spoken output had not responded to treatment, and therapy had failed to establish a non-verbal mode of communication. Her writing was impaired, and its slow and effortful execution hindered her progress. However, she retained some ability to access written words and was aware of her errors. Therapy aimed to improve access to written words, and to facilitate writing by using a Lightwriter. Three stages of therapy were conducted. Words selected by MA for their usefulness were treated. In stage 1, solving anagrams, copying, delayed copying, and written naming were used to improve access to their orthographies. Written naming improved, but only to the pictures used in therapy. In stages 2 and 3 further words were introduced, and steps taken to encourage generalisation. In stage 2 several different pictures of each item were used to overcome the picture-specific effect. In stage 3, written words were used to describe situations and answer questions in order to encourage their use in communication. | MA improved significantly in writing treated words, and her rate of acquisition accelerated as therapy progressed. Performance was largely maintained after periods without treatment or exposure to the treated items. MA made progress in using her written vocabulary to answer questions in therapy, but needed prompting to use the Lightwriter rather than speech, and rarely made functional use of it outside the clinic setting. MA's progress demonstrates the potential for treating writing in jargon aphasia. Her progress in accessing word orthographies allowed her to use the Lightwriter for communication. Her inability to use writing spontaneously suggests that further therapy is needed, and that it should include a regular partner to encourage functional use. | III |

| Author(s) & Title | Design | Sample | Objective of study | Conclusions | Evidence Level |
|---|---|---|---|---|---|
| Sacchett C, Byng S, Marshall J & Pound C, 1999, 'Drawing together: evaluation of a therapy programme for severe aphasia', *International Journal of Language & Communication Disorders*, 34 (3): 265–89. | Single subject design | 5 males, 2 females, age range 47–66. | This paper reports a therapy study that aims to promote communicative drawing in a group of seven people with severe and long-standing aphasia. Therapy was conducted on an individual and group basis over 12 weeks, and entailed a range of techniques which are described in some detail. Treatment was evaluated using a novel generative drawing assessment in which subjects were required to draw absent items in response to photographic and conversational cues. Pre- and post-therapy assessments of untreated skills, such as comprehension, naming and gesture, were also conducted. | The results indicated that, as a group, the subjects' drawing improved. Unchanged performance on the other assessments indicated that the gains were specific to the content of therapy and could not be attributed to spontaneous recovery. Pre- and post-therapy interviews with carers (ie, relatives and close friends of the individuals) suggested that the effects of therapy were also being felt in the home. These results have important implications for therapy with people with severe aphasia. | III |
| Lustig AP & Tompkins CA, 2002, 'A written communication strategy for a speaker with aphasia and apraxia of speech: treatment outcomes and social validity', *Aphasiology*, 16 (4–6): 507–22. | Single subject design | 52-year-old man, 10 years post onset | The purpose of this study was to train an individual (LG) with longstanding aphasia and apraxia of speech to substitute a self-initiated written word for protracted articulatory struggle, in three conversational settings. A multiple-baseline design across three different settings was utilised, providing an opportunity for strategy practice with both familiar and unfamiliar conversational partners. Topics were constructed to be relevant and meaningful to LG. Several subject-evaluated psychosocial measures, including locus of control, were employed, and social validity ratings were solicited from unfamiliar raters. | LG adopted and successfully used the strategy across all settings, with both familiar and unfamiliar partners, at performance levels well above baseline. The number of abandoned conversational targets decreased considerably with strategy use, and social validation ratings indicated beneficial effects pertaining to communicative efficiency and comprehensibility in shorter, but not longer, conversational segments extracted from treatment videotapes. Conclusions: the training protocol was successful in improving LG's facility with targeted compensatory strategy use across designated conversational contexts. However, the clinical significance and social value of LG's strategy use in these settings may be mitigated by the accompanying communicative variables affecting the conversational exchange as a whole. | III |

# APHASIA

## THERAPIES FOCUSING ON THE SKILLS OF CONVERSATIONAL PARTNERS

### Working With Family Members/Carers Of People With Aphasia : Recommendation 1

| Author(s) & Title | Design | Sample | Objective of study | Conclusions | Evidence Level |
|---|---|---|---|---|---|
| Booth S & Swabey D, 1999, 'Group training in communication skills for carers of adults with aphasia', *International Journal of Language & Communication Disorders*, 34 (3): 291–309. | Qualitative study | 4 carers of adults with aphasia | This study describes a communication skills group programme for four carers of adults with aphasia that ran once a week for 6 consecutive weeks. The content of the group was based on an approach previously not described in the literature in any detail. Conversation analysis (CA) was used to guide individualised advice that was incorporated into the group by the use of written advice sheets. Intervention was motivated by the results of a newly developed assessment tool – the Conversation Analysis Profile for People with Aphasia (CAPPA) – and a quantitative and qualitative analysis of collaborative repair. The CAPPA utilises the methodology of conversation analysis (CA) as a means of both characterising and comparing the relationship between the carers' perception of the aphasia and what is occurring in natural conversation. During the group, accurate perceptions and strategies that minimised the disruption to the conversation were reinforced, while inaccurate perceptions and strategies that appeared to impede interaction were discouraged. The use of the CAPPA results and a quantitative/qualitative analysis of repair management to measure change pre- and post-group was explored. | The post-intervention analyses examined three questions in particular: (1) did the carers demonstrate more accurate perceptions of their relatives' aphasia?; (2) did the carers report a decrease in the problem severity of the aphasia?; and (3) was there a change in the time taken to repair a trouble source, and was this attributable to a change in the management of repair by the carer? The study was essentially an investigation of whether this type of approach was beneficial to the carers involved. The results suggested that focusing on individualised advice and targeting conversation management in the group setting was a useful way of providing advice to carers. Furthermore, the CAPPA and a quantitative/qualitative analysis of repair management seem to have the potential for motivating the individualised advice and measuring the effectiveness of an intervention. | III |

| Author(s) & Title | Design | Sample | Objective of study | Conclusions | Evidence Level |
|---|---|---|---|---|---|
| Hopper T, Holland A & Rewega M, 2002, 'Conversational coaching: treatment outcomes and future directions', *Aphasiology*, 16: 745–62. | Single subject design | Two couples (aged 76/70 and 41/39 years) | This study assessed the effects of conversational coaching to determine variables for consideration in future efficacy research of this treatment technique. Two couples (aged 76/70 and 41/39 years) participated in a single-subject experimental design across subjects. During baseline sessions, the aphasic subjects watched a videotaped story about a real-life event, and then attempted to share the content of that story with their spouses. During treatment sessions, the same procedure was used, but the clinician intervened and coached both subjects in the use of selected verbal and non-verbal strategies to improve the quality of the conversation. The primary dependent measure in the study was the number of main concepts successfully communicated during conversations. | Positive outcomes, including the subjects' perception of treatment effects, support further experimental study of this technique. Strategy selection, stimuli for conversational topics, and procedural specificity of the intervention were variables identified as necessitating further research in a controlled experiment design. | III |
| Maneta A, Marshall J & Lindsay J, 2001, 'Direct and indirect therapy for word sound deafness', *International Journal of Language & Communication Disorders*, 36 (1): 91–106. | Case study | An aphasic man | This paper evaluates two therapy programmes conducted with PK, an aphasic individual with word-sound deafness. The first aimed directly to improve discrimination skills, using minimal pair tasks supported with lip-reading. Disappointingly, there were no changes on discrimination tests after this therapy, even when PK could benefit from lip-reading information. The second, indirect, programme of therapy aimed to change the communication behaviours with PK's wife. Strategies such as writing and simplifying information were modelled and practised. | A detailed information booklet, outlining the target strategies and explaining PK's main strengths and weaknesses supported the programme. Evaluation of this therapy involved pre- and post-therapy analysis of interactions between PK and his wife, with biographical questions forming the basis of the interactions. There were several changes after therapy on this measure. The number and length of communication breakdowns were reduced, and more questions were answered accurately. This study suggests that, in some cases of severe word sound deafness, indirect therapies may be most effective. | III |

## APHASIA

| Author(s) & Title | Design | Sample | Objective of study | Conclusions | Evidence Level |
|---|---|---|---|---|---|
| Simmons N, Kearns K & Potechin G, 1987, 'Treatment of aphasia through family member training', in Brookshire R (ed), *Clinical Aphasiology Conference Proceedings*, BRK Publishers, Mineapolis. | Conference proceedings | | | | IV |

### Working With Volunteers: Recommendation 2

| Author(s) & Title | Design | Sample | Objective of study | Conclusions | Evidence Level |
|---|---|---|---|---|---|
| Kagan A, Black S, Duchan J, Simmons-Mackie N & Square P, 2001, 'Training volunteers as conversational partners using 'Supported Conversation for Adults with Aphasia' (SCA): A controlled trial', *Journal of Speech Language & Hearing Research*, 44: 624–38. | Randomised controlled trial | 40 volunteers | This article reports the development and evaluation of a new intervention termed 'Supported Conversation for Adults with Aphasia' (SCA). The approach is based on the idea that the inherent competence of people with aphasia can be revealed through the skill of a conversation partner. The intervention approach was developed at a community-based aphasia centre where volunteers interact with individuals with chronic aphasia and their families. The experimental study was designed to test whether training improves the conversational skills of volunteers, and, if so, whether the improvements affect the communication of their conversation partners with aphasia. Twenty volunteers received SCA training, and 20 control volunteers were merely exposed to people with aphasia. Comparisons between the groups' scores on a Measure of Supported Conversation for Adults with Aphasia provide support for the efficacy of SCA. | Trained volunteers scored significantly higher than untrained volunteers on ratings of acknowledging competence and revealing competence of their partners with aphasia. The training also produced a positive change in quality ratings of social and message exchange skills in individuals with aphasia, even though these individuals did not participate in the training. Implications for the treatment of aphasia and an argument for a social model of intervention are discussed. | I |

| Author(s) & Title | Design | Sample | Objective of study | Conclusions | Evidence Level |
|---|---|---|---|---|---|
| Rayner H & Marshall J, 2003, 'Training volunteers as conversation partners for people with aphasia', *International Journal of Language & Communication Disorders*, 38 (2): 149–64. | Qualitative study | Six volunteers | Six volunteers were trained in conversing with people with moderate or severe aphasia. The study aimed to evaluate whether training changed the volunteers' knowledge about aphasia and their interactions with people with aphasia. It also explored whether changes in the volunteers were matched by improved participation of the people with aphasia in conversation. Volunteers were recruited from a local aphasia group. They were trained as a group over three sessions (9 hours in total). The training drew on the techniques of Kagan. It included presentation of information using different media, group discussions, viewing of videos and role play. The course aimed to improve: (1) the volunteers' understanding of the nature of aphasia; (2) the volunteers' knowledge about communication strategies to use with people with aphasia; and (3) the skills of the volunteers in supporting people with aphasia in conversation. An additional aim was to increase the aphasic subjects' participation in conversation. Two evaluation methods were employed. Specially designed questionnaires were administered before and after training to evaluate the volunteers' knowledge and understanding. Volunteers were also videotaped in conversation with people with aphasia before and after training. The videos were rated by speech and language therapists, using nine-point rating scales, derived from Kagan (1999). | Significant improvements were seen on the questionnaire scores and in ratings of the volunteers' videos. The rating gains were attributed to the training course, since baseline scores were stable and improvements only occurred after the training period. There were comparable gains in the participation of the aphasic subjects, which again occurred after training. The study demonstrates that a short training course can change the knowledge and practice of experienced volunteers. The findings have implications for teaching generic skills to volunteers working with people with aphasia. | III |

# APHASIA

| Author(s) & Title | Design | Sample | Objective of study | Conclusions | Evidence Level |
|---|---|---|---|---|---|
| **GROUP THERAPY** | | | | | |
| **Group Therapy : Recommendation 1** | | | | | |
| Elman RJ & Bernstein-Ellis E, 1999a, 'The efficacy of group communication treatment in adults with chronic aphasia', *Journal of Speech, Language & Hearing Research*, 42 (2): 411–19. | Randomised controlled trial | 24 adults | This study examined the effects of group communication treatment on linguistic and communicative performance in adults with chronic aphasia. Participants were randomly assigned to two treatment and two deferred treatment groups. Groups were balanced for age, education level, and initial aphasia severity. Twenty-four participants completed the four-month treatment trial. While in the treatment condition, all participants received five hours of group communication treatment weekly, provided by a speech-language pathologist. The focus of treatment included increasing initiation of conversation and exchanging information using whatever communicative means possible. While awaiting group communication treatment, participants in the deferred treatment groups engaged in such activities as support, performance, or movement groups in order to control for the effects of social contact. Linguistic and communicative measures were administered to all participants at entry, after two and four months of treatment, and following four to six weeks of no treatment. In addition, participants in the deferred treatment groups received an additional administration of all measures just before their treatment trial. | Results revealed that participants receiving group communication treatment had significantly higher scores on communicative and linguistic measures than participants not receiving treatment. In addition, significant increases were revealed after two months of treatment and after four months of treatment. No significant decline in performance occurred at time of follow-up. | I |

| Author(s) & Title | Design | Sample | Objective of study | Conclusions | Evidence Level |
|---|---|---|---|---|---|
| Mackenzie C, 1991, 'An aphasia group intensive efficacy study', *British Journal of Disorders of Communication*, 26 (3): 275–91. | Controlled study | 5 adults with chronic aphasia | The response of five adults with chronic aphasia to a four-week intensive treatment course is presented. Using four language tests, pre-intervention stability was demonstrated over the month preceding the treatment programme. | Following the intervention period, two subjects showed improvement in one test, and more widespread changes occurred in three subjects. On further assessment one month after treatment had finished, one of the two subjects who had made the least progress performed better than at the end of the course, and one had returned to pre-treatment level. Although there were indications of regression in two of the three other subjects, this was not to pre-treatment level. Only one subject maintained the gains made fully. Given the short duration of the course, the changes in performance noted suggest that, providing transport is available, intensive treatment of aphasia should be available to patients with sufficient motivation and stamina. | II |
| Avent JR, 1997, 'Group treatment in aphasia using cooperative learning methods', *Journal of Medical Speech-Language Pathology*, 5 (1): 9–26. | Case series | 8 adults with acquired brain injury | The purposes of this paper are to outline the principles of cooperative learning, describe a new aphasia group treatment called Cooperative Group Treatment, and provide preliminary treatment efficacy data. The study included eight brain injured individuals. Using a single-subject, multiple-baseline across behaviours design, the effects of treatment were determined by examining content–information units produced in narrative and procedural discourse. | Results indicate treatment efficacy for individuals with mild aphasic impairments. | III |

## APHASIA

| Author(s) & Title | Design | Sample | Objective of study | Conclusions | Evidence Level |
|---|---|---|---|---|---|
| Bollinger RL, Musson ND & Holland A, 1993, 'A study of group communication intervention with chronically aphasic persons', *Aphasiology*, 7 (3): 301–13. | Case series | 10 adults with aphasia | This study is an investigation of the effects of a relatively more structured group treatment programme on the communication ability of 10 chronically aphasic patients. Subjects participated in a 60-week programme that included two series of 20 weeks of group treatment and 10 weeks of treatment withdrawal. | Subjects made gains in overall communication ability after 20 weeks of structured group treatment, and initial gains were retained throughout treatment withdrawal. Reinitiation of structured treatment after a no-treatment interval resulted in a significant gain in communication ability, as measured by the Porch Index of Communicative Ability (PICA). Significant Communicative Ability of Daily Living test gains were limited to the first treatment interval. | III |
| Elman RJ & Bernstein-Ellis E, 1999b, 'Psychosocial aspects of group communication treatment: preliminary findings', *Seminars in Speech & Language*, 20 (1): 65–72, 93–4. | Qualitative study | Adults with aphasia and their carers | This article discusses preliminary psychosocial data from an efficacy study on the effects of group communication treatment in adults with chronic aphasia. Using a qualitative interview approach, participants with aphasia and their relatives/caregivers reported many positive psychosocial changes following treatment. | The results suggest that group communication treatment had an impact on participants' home and community lives without direct treatment in those settings. Results are discussed in the context of managed care, group theory, and positive health. | III |

| Author(s) & Title | Design | Sample | Objective of study | Conclusions | Evidence Level |
|---|---|---|---|---|---|
| **Computer Supported Therapy : Recommendation 1** | | | | | |
| Katz RC & Wertz RT, 1997, 'The efficacy of computer-provided reading treatment for chronic aphasic adults', *Journal of Speech, Language & Hearing Research*, 40 (3): 493–507. | Randomised controlled trial | 55 adults with aphasia | This study examined the effects of computer-provided reading activities on language performance in chronic aphasic patients. Fifty-five aphasic adults were assigned randomly to one of three conditions: computer reading treatment, computer stimulation, or no treatment. Subjects in the computer groups used computers three hours each week for 26 weeks. Computer reading treatment software consisted of visual matching and reading comprehension tasks. Computer stimulation software consisted of non-verbal games and cognitive rehabilitation tasks. Language measures were administered to all subjects at entry and after three and six months. | Significant improvement over the 26 weeks occurred on five language measures for the computer reading treatment group, on one language measure for the computer stimulation group, and on none of the language measures for the no-treatment group. The computer reading treatment group displayed significantly more improvement on the Porch Index of Communicative Ability 'Overall' and 'Verbal' modality percentiles and on the Western Aphasia Battery Aphasia 'Quotient' and 'Repetition' subtest than the other two groups. The results suggest that: (a) computerised reading treatment can be administered with minimal assistance from a clinician; (b) improvement on the computerised reading treatment tasks generalised to non-computer language performance; (c) improvement resulted from the language content of the software and not stimulation provided by a computer; and (d) the computerised reading treatment we provided to chronic aphasic patients was efficacious. | Ib |
| Mortley J, Enderby P & Petheram B, 2001, 'Using a computer to improve functional writing in a patient with severe dysgraphia', *Aphasiology*, 15: 443–61. | Case study | 67-year-old man | This case study describes and evaluates the therapy administered to MF to improve his severe writing impairment caused by a stroke eighteen months prior to this therapy intervention. Therapy was based on developing a compensatory strategy using his residual skills of being able to spell a word orally. A detailed account of the sequence of therapy procedures is given, initially focusing on specific non-functional tasks, followed by therapy with a more functional focus. A computer was used throughout the intervention to facilitate intensive repetitive practice. | The intervention proved to be successful, both in terms of improvements on assessments and with evidence of functional benefits. The use of both a dictionary to support the strategy and an adaptive word processor to promote functional carry over is described. The role of the computer in therapy is discussed as a tool to facilitate repetitive practice of therapy, and to encourage the independent use of the strategy embodied in therapy. | III |

## HEAD & NECK CANCER

| Author(s) & Title | Design | Sample | Objective of study | Conclusions | Evidence Level |
|---|---|---|---|---|---|
| **Membership of Multidisciplinary Team** | | | | | |
| British Association of Otorhinolaryngologists (BAO-HNS), 1998, *Effective Head & Neck Cancer Management. Consensus Document.* | Expert opinion | — | — | — | IV |
| British Association of Otorhinolaryngologists (BAO-HNS), 2000, *Effective Head & Neck Cancer Management. Second Consensus Document.* | Expert opinion | — | — | — | IV |
| Machin J & Shaw C, 1998, 'A multidisciplinary approach to head and neck cancer', *European Journal of Cancer Care (Engl)* 7 (2):93–96. | Expert opinion | — | Expert opinion illustrated by a case study. | Head and neck cancer and its treatment can leave patients with impaired swallowing and ability to communicate. A multidisciplinary approach from the Speech & Language Therapist and dietician can help the patient maximise their function and identify when additional methods of support are required. | IV |
| Birchall M, Nettelfield P, Richardson A & Lee L, 2000, 'Finding their voice: a focus group study of patients with head and neck cancer and their carers', South & West Regional Cancer Organisation. | Service user consultation | — | — | — | IV |
| **Involvement Prior to Radiotherapy/Chemotherapy /Surgical Management** | | | | | |
| Dhillon RS, Palmer BV, Pittam MR & Shaw HJ, 1982, 'Rehabilitation after major head and neck surgery – the patients' view', *Clinical Otolaryngology* 7 (5):319–24. | Qualitative study | 49 patients who were free of tumour 5 months to 14 years after total laryngectomy or a commando procedure | Forty-nine patients were given questionnaires designed to obtain the patient's assessment of their resulting disability. Sixteen areas of disability were studied, grouped under five main headings: speech; eating; cosmetic; employment; and social. | Following laryngectomy more than half of the patients achieved successful communication by oesophageal speech. Success in this was usually associated with minimal problems in other areas. The disabilities after commando procedures were more varied and complex. More patients reported severe disability in more than one area. Difficulties with chewing and swallowing were prominent. The results are illustrated with patients' comments. Ways in which rehabilitation might be improved are considered. | III |

| Author(s) & Title | Design | Sample | Objective of study | Conclusions | Evidence Level |
|---|---|---|---|---|---|
| Natvig K, 1983, 'Laryngectomees in Norway. Study No. 2: pre-operative counselling and postoperative training evaluated by the patients and their spouses', *Journal of Otolaryngology* 12 (4):249–54. | Qualitative study | 189 laryngectomees 131 spouses | 189 laryngectomees and their spouses were invited to take part in an interview regarding the quality of pre-operative counselling and post-operative training they had experienced. | Twenty-six percent of 189 Norwegian laryngectomees considered pre-operative counselling to be unsatisfactory. Similarly, post-operative self-care training was rated unsatisfactory by 55 percent. The quality of the pre-operative counselling had a significant influence on the patients' ability to perceive post-operative training, which subsequently correlated with mastery of the laryngectomy event. Seventy percent of the spouses felt that they had not been offered adequate counselling. The problems endured at home for 60 percent of them could have been amenable to relief by improved counselling. | III |
| Johnson AF, Jacobson BH & Benninger MS, 1990, 'Management of voice disorders', *Henry Ford Hospital Medical Journal* 38 (1):44–47. | Expert opinion | — | — | It is important for clinicians from internal medicine, paediatrics and family practice to be able to identify those factors in the history or observed vocal symptoms which suggest need for referral for comprehensive voice evaluation, as well as to understand the distinct but complementary roles of the specific disciplines involved in diagnosis and treatment of patients with voice disorders. | IV |

## HEAD & NECK CANCER

| Author(s) & Title | Design | Sample | Objective of study | Conclusions | Evidence Level |
|---|---|---|---|---|---|
| Doyle PC, 1999, 'Postlaryngectomy speech rehabilitation: contemporary considerations in clinical care', *Journal of Speech Language Pathology and Audiology* 23 (3): 109–16. | Expert opinion | — | The removal of one's larynx due to cancer results in changes that cross anatomical, physiological and psychological boundaries. Oncologic safety is primary for those undergoing total laryngectomy; however, the immediate and complete loss of verbal communication results in significant challenges to one's well-being. In some instances, these changes may threaten the success of long-term rehabilitation outcomes. WHO recommends that any comprehensive rehabilitation plan include attention to the performance of, or barriers to, activities as well as social attitudes and potential social penalties due to disease and its treatment. | If post-laryngectomy rehabilitation is to be successful, professionals working with those who undergo laryngectomy must carefully consider, and seek to comprehensively address, the effects of post-laryngectomy changes in each of these areas. | IV |

**Pre- and Post-assessment**

| Author(s) & Title | Design | Sample | Objective of study | Conclusions | Evidence Level |
|---|---|---|---|---|---|
| Kreuzer SH, Schima W, Schober E, Pokieser P, Kofler G, Lechner G & Denk DM, 2000, 'Complications after laryngeal surgery: videofluoroscopic evaluation of 120 patients', *Clinical Radiology* 55 (10):775–81. | Case series | 120 patients with suspected complications after laryngeal resection | Videofluoroscopic assessment of the spectrum and incidence of swallowing complications after state-of-the-art laryngeal cancer surgery. A retrospective study of videofluoroscopic examinations of 120 patients (94 men, 26 women; mean age, 58 years) with suspected complications after laryngeal resection (partial laryngectomy, 65; total laryngectomy, 55). | Abnormalities were found in 110 patients, including strictures in nine, fistulas in six and mass lesions in 13 patients. Aspiration was found in 63 patients overall (partial laryngectomy, 61/65; total laryngectomy, 2/55), occurring before swallowing in 5, during swallowing in 34, after swallowing in 9 and at more than one phase in 15 patients. Pharyngeal paresis was detected in 3 and pharyngeal weakness in 19 patients. Pharyngo-oesophageal sphincter dysfunction was observed in 10 cases. | III |

| Author(s) & Title | Design | Sample | Objective of study | Conclusions | Evidence Level |
|---|---|---|---|---|---|
| Panchal J, Potterton AJ, Scanlon E & McLean NR, 1996, 'An objective assessment of speech and swallowing following free flap reconstruction for oral cavity cancers', *British Journal of Plastic Surgery* 49 (6):363–9. | Case series | Eight patients | Eight consecutive patients underwent excision of oral cavity cancer and reconstruction with a microvascular free flap. Six patients had one pre- and two post-operative assessments of speech and swallowing at four to six weeks and four to six months respectively. | The speech assessment consisted of an intelligibility score and an articulation score. The swallowing assessment consisted of a videofluoroscopic examination. Five patients had an excellent post-operative speech assessment score, two had a moderate and one a poor result. Videofluoroscopy demonstrated minor swallowing problems pre-operatively in one patient. Post-operatively, three patients had severe or moderate loss of control of bolus. The abnormalities of speech and swallowing were minor in the majority of the patients and the overall outlook was good. | III |
| De Leeuw JR, De Graeff A, Ros WJ, Hordijk GJ, Blijham GH & Winnubst JA, 2000, 'Negative and positive influence of social support on depression in patients with head and neck cancer: a prospective study', *Psycho-Oncology* 9 (1):20–8. | Qualitative study | 197 patients with an average age of 58 years | The aim of this prospective study is to examine the influence of different aspects of social support on the depressive symptomatology in head and neck cancer patients treated with surgery and/or radiotherapy. Patients completed a questionnaire relating to available and received support, the extent of the social network, depressive symptoms and general health complaints before and 6 months after treatment. | Received support was found to be associated with more depressive symptomatology at baseline and available support led to less depressive symptomatology. The relationship between social support and depressive symptoms was especially apparent in patients with few general health complaints. Whereas the availability of support seemed to be beneficial regardless of the situation, the effect of received support was equivocal. The provision of support should be tailored to the needs of the individual patient. | III |

## HEAD & NECK CANCER

| Author(s) & Title | Design | Sample | Objective of study | Conclusions | Evidence Level |
|---|---|---|---|---|---|
| Doyle PC, 1999, 'Postlaryngectomy speech rehabilitation: contemporary considerations in clinical care', *Journal of Speech Language Pathology and Audiology* 23 (3): 109–16. | Expert opinion | — | The removal of one's larynx due to cancer results in changes that cross anatomical, physiological and psychological boundaries. Oncologic safety is primary for those undergoing total laryngectomy; however, the immediate and complete loss of verbal communication results in significant challenges to one's well-being. In some instances, these changes may threaten the success of long-term rehabilitation outcomes. WHO recommends that any comprehensive rehabilitation plan include attention to the performance of, or barriers to, activities as well as social attitudes and potential social penalties due to disease and its treatment. | If post-laryngectomy rehabilitation is to be successful, professionals working with those who undergo laryngectomy must carefully consider, and seek to comprehensively address, the effects of post-laryngectomy changes in each of these areas. | IV |
| Yvonne E (ed), 1983, *Laryngectomy: Diagnosis to Rehabilitation*, Croom Helm, London. | Expert opinion | — | — | — | IV |
| Darley FL & Keith RL (eds), 1986, *Laryngectomee Rehabilitation*, Proceedings of the Mayo Clinic Laryngectomee Rehabilitation Seminar, College Hill Press, Houston, TX. | Expert opinion | — | — | — | IV |
| Salmon S, 1979, *Pre- and Post-Operative Conferences with Laryngectomised and their spouses*, Proceedings of the 5th Laryngectomee Rehabilitation Seminar, Mayo Clinic. | Conference Proceedings | — | — | — | IV |

| Author(s) & Title | Design | Sample | Objective of study | Conclusions | Evidence Level |
|---|---|---|---|---|---|
| **Pre-treatment Counselling and Information Giving** | | | | | |
| Natvig K, 1983, 'Laryngectomees in Norway. Study No. 2: pre-operative counselling and postoperative training evaluated by the patients and their spouses', *Journal of Otolaryngology* 12 (4):249–54. | Qualitative study | 189 laryngectomees 131 spouses | 189 laryngectomees and their spouses were invited to take part in an interview regarding the quality of pre-operative counselling and post-operative training they had experienced. | Twenty-six percent of 189 Norwegian laryngectomees considered pre-operative counselling to be unsatisfactory. Similarly, post-operative self-care training was rated unsatisfactory by 55 percent. The quality of the pre-operative counselling had a significant influence on the patients' ability to perceive post-operative training which subsequently correlated with mastery of the laryngectomy event. Seventy percent of the spouses felt that they had not been offered adequate counselling. The problems endured at home for 60 percent of them could have been amenable to relief by improved counselling. | III |
| Stam H, Koopmans J & Mathieson C, 1991, 'The psychosocial impact of a laryngectomy: a comprehensive assessment', *Journal of Psychosocial Oncology* 9 (3). | Qualitative | 51 laryngectomees | Fifty-one laryngectomees completed a structured interview composed of 111 questions. The questions were grouped as follows: Demographic data; illness and speech variables; social networks and support; preparation at the time of surgery; rehabilitation of communication and related problems; lifestyle changes; identity changes; quality of life; and psychosocial adjustment. | Gender, surgical variables and the extent of the patient's social support predicted the use of oesophageal speech. Pre-operative visits by fellow laryngectomees predicted later quality of life. Poor psychological adjustment was related to the length of time spent in the hospital after surgery, dissatisfaction with social support and changes in lifestyle after surgery. Changes in identity were also predictive of both psychological adjustment and quality of life. | III |
| Annunziata M, Foladore S, Magni DM, Grrivellari D, Feltrin A, Bidoli E & Veronesi A, 1998, 'Does the information level of cancer patients correlate with quality of life? A prospective study', *Tumori* 84 (6). | Qualitative | 175 patients with cancer | The aim of this study was to evaluate the impact of information level on quality of life in cancer patients previously studied for their information level. A questionnaire explored the degree of information on diagnosis and status of disease, the patient's interpretation of his/her disease status and his/her satisfaction with the information received. Quality of life was evaluated some months after evaluation of the information level. | Information for analysis was obtained on 53.7 percent of the sample. There was no difference in the quality of life of adequately versus inadequately informed patients. Satisfaction with the information received influenced quality of life. | III |

## HEAD & NECK CANCER

| Author(s) & Title | Design | Sample | Objective of study | Conclusions | Evidence Level |
|---|---|---|---|---|---|
| Zeine L & Larson M, 1999, 'Pre- & post-operative counselling for laryngectomees & their spouses: an update', *Journal of Communication Disorders* 32 (1):51–61. | Survey | — | This survey was developed to determine if pre-operative counselling services have improved since the 1978 Keith, Linebaugh & Cox study. The questions were aimed at obtaining information on the quality and quantity of support services available to laryngectomees and their spouses. Questions addressed the type, amount and content of information received. In addition, questions regarding post-operative counselling services for laryngectomees and spouses of laryngectomees were also included. | Results indicated that 21 percent of the laryngectomees were not aware that laryngectomy surgery would result in loss of voice. In addition, not all speech rehabilitation options were explained to the patients. Pre- and post-operative counselling services for laryngectomees continue to be inadequate. It appears that little change has been made to improve this situation. | III |
| Dhillon RS, Palmer BV, Pittam BV & Shaw HJ, 1982, 'Rehabilitation after major head and neck surgery – the patients' view', *Clinical Otolaryngology* 7 (5):319–24. | Qualitative study | 49 patients who were free of tumour 5 months to 14 years after total laryngectomy or a commando procedure | Forty-nine patients were given questionnaires designed to obtain the patient's assessment of their resulting disability. Sixteen areas of disability were studied grouped under five main headings: speech; eating; cosmetic; employment; and social. | Following laryngectomy more than half of the patients achieved successful communication by oesophageal speech. Success in this was usually associated with minimal problems in other areas. The disabilities after commando procedures were more varied and complex. More patients reported severe disability in more than one area. Difficulties with chewing and swallowing were prominent. The results are illustrated with patients' comments. Ways in which rehabilitation might be improved are considered. | III |

| Author(s) & Title | Design | Sample | Objective of study | Conclusions | Evidence Level |
|---|---|---|---|---|---|
| Doyle PC, 1999, 'Postlaryngectomy speech rehabilitation: contemporary considerations in clinical care', *Journal of Speech Language Pathology and Audiology* 23 (3):109–16. | Expert opinion | — | The removal of one's larynx due to cancer results in changes that cross anatomical, physiological and psychological boundaries. Oncologic safety is primary for those undergoing total laryngectomy; however, the immediate and complete loss of verbal communication results in significant challenges to one's well-being. In some instances, these changes may threaten the success of long-term rehabilitation outcomes. WHO recommends that any comprehensive rehabilitation plan include attention to the performance of, or barriers to, activities as well as social attitudes and potential social penalties due to disease and its treatment. | If post-laryngectomy rehabilitation is to be successful, professionals working with those who undergo laryngectomy must carefully consider, and seek to comprehensively address, the effects of post-laryngectomy changes in each of these areas. | IV |
| Mathieson CM, Henderikus J & Scott J, 1990, 'Psychosocial adjustment after laryngectomy: a review of the literature', *Journal of Otolaryngology* 19(5). | Literature review | — | This paper reviews the literature on the psychosocial outcomes of a laryngectomy. The largest group of studies focuses on factors that contribute to oesophageal speech acquisition, one important measure of rehabilitation outcome. | The research suggests that long-term adjustment for the laryngectomee is shaped by multiple variables, which include: extent of surgery; pre-operative visits by a fellow laryngectomee; illness variables; changes in lifestyle following surgery; patient satisfaction with social support; chronic pain; and ability to communicate. It concludes that psychosocial variables contribute substantially to successful post-surgical adjustment. | IV |
| McQuellon RP & Hurt GJ, 1997, 'Psychosocial impact of the diagnosis and treatment of laryngeal cancer', *Otolaryngolic Clinics of North America* 30 (2):231–41. | Expert opinion | — | The diagnosis and treatment of laryngeal cancer involves psychosocial stress for most patients because the disease can be life-threatening and treatment is potentially disfiguring. Since voice is essential to psychological identity, laryngectomy may pose significant short- and long-term adjustment problems. Risk for psychological disturbance and problems at the initiation of treatment and adaptation following treatment can be predicted based on certain patient information. | The integration of a multidisciplinary team at the outset of treatment planning is crucial in helping patients adjust to the impact of laryngeal cancer. | IV |

## HEAD & NECK CANCER

### Meeting Others

| Author(s) & Title | Design | Sample | Objective of study | Conclusions | Evidence Level |
|---|---|---|---|---|---|
| Stam H, Koopmans J & Mathieson C, 1991, 'The psychosocial impact of a laryngectomy: a comprehensive assessment', *Journal of Psychosocial Oncology* 9 (3). | Qualitative | 51 laryngectomees | Fifty-one laryngectomees completed a structured interview composed of 111 questions. The questions were grouped as follows: demographic data; illness and speech variables; social networks and support; preparation at the time of surgery; rehabilitation of communication and related problems; lifestyle changes; identity changes; quality of life; and psychosocial adjustment. | Gender, surgical variables and the extent of the patient's social support predicted the use of oesophageal speech. Pre-operative visits by fellow laryngectomees predicted later quality of life. Poor psychological adjustment was related to the length of time spent in the hospital after surgery, dissatisfaction with social support and changes in lifestyle after surgery. Changes in identity were also predictive of both psychological adjustment and quality of life. | III |
| De Leeuw JR, De Graeff A, Ros WJ, Hordijk GJ, Blijham GH & Winnubst JA, 2000, 'Negative and positive influenced of social support on depression in patients with head and neck cancer: a prospective study', *Psycho-Oncology* 9 (1):20–8. | Qualitative study | 197 patients with an average age of 58 years | The aim of this prospective study is to examine the influence of different aspects of social support on the depressive symptomatology in head and neck cancer patients treated with surgery and/or radiotherapy. Patients completed a questionnaire relating to available and received support, the extent of the social network, depressive symptoms and general health complaints before and six months after treatment. | Received support was found to be associated with more depressive symptomatology at baseline and available support led to less depressive symptomatology. The relationship between social support and depressive symptoms was especially apparent in patients with few general health complaints. Whereas the availability of support seemed to be beneficial regardless of the situation, the effect of received support was equivocal. The provision of support should be tailored to the needs of the individual patient. | III |
| Johnson AF, Jacobson BH & Benninger MS, 1990, 'Management of voice disorders', *Henry Ford Hospital Medical Journal* 38 (1):44–47. | Expert opinion | — | — | It is important for clinicians from internal medicine, paediatrics and family practice to be able to identify those factors in the history or observed vocal symptoms that suggest a need for referral for comprehensive voice evaluation, as well as to understand the distinct but complementary roles of the specific disciplines involved in diagnosis and treatment of patients with voice disorders. | IV |

| Author(s) & Title | Design | Sample | Objective of study | Conclusions | Evidence Level |
|---|---|---|---|---|---|
| Doyle PC, 1999, 'Postlaryngectomy speech rehabilitation: contemporary considerations in clinical care', *Journal of Speech Language Pathology and Audiology* 23 (3): 109–16. | Expert opinion | — | The removal of one's larynx due to cancer results in changes that cross anatomical, physiological and psychological boundaries. Oncologic safety is primary for those undergoing total laryngectomy; however, the immediate and complete loss of verbal communication results in significant challenges to one's well-being. In some instances, these changes may threaten the success of long-term rehabilitation outcomes. WHO recommends that any comprehensive rehabilitation plan include attention to the performance of, or barriers to, activities as well as social attitudes and potential social penalties due to disease and its treatment. | If post-laryngectomy rehabilitation is to be successful, professionals working with those who undergo laryngectomy must carefully consider, and seek to comprehensively address, the effects of post-laryngectomy changes in each of these areas. | IV |
| Birchall M, Nettelfield P, Richardson A & Lee L, 2000, 'Finding their voice: a focus group study of patients with head and neck cancer and their carers', South & West Regional Cancer Organisation. | Service user consultation | — | — | — | IV |

## Selection of Communication Methods

| Author(s) & Title | Design | Sample | Objective of study | Conclusions | Evidence Level |
|---|---|---|---|---|---|
| Carr MM, Schmidbauer JA, Majaess L & Smith RL, 2000, 'Communication after laryngectomy: an assessment of quality of life', *Otolaryngology Head Neck Surgery* 122 (1):39–43. | Questionnaire | 74 laryngectomees | The purpose of this study was to examine quality of life for laryngectomees using different methods of communication. A survey was mailed to all the living laryngectomees in Nova Scotia. Patients were asked to rate their ability to communicate in a number of common situations, to rate their difficulty with several communication problems and to complete the EORTC QLQ-C30 quality-of-life assessment tool. | Sixty-two patients responded (return rate of 84 percent); 57 percent were using electrolaryngeal speech, 19 percent oesophageal speech and 8.5 percent tracheoesophageal speech. These groups were comparable with respect to age, sex, first language, education level and years since laryngectomy. There were very few differences between these groups in ability to communicate in social situations and no difference in overall quality of life as measured by these scales. The most commonly cited problem was difficulty being heard in a noisy environment. Despite the fact that tracheoesophageal speech is objectively most intelligible, there does not seem to be a measurable improvement in quality of life or ability to communicate in everyday situations over electrolaryngeal or oesophageal speakers. | III |

## HEAD & NECK CANCER

| Author(s) & Title | Design | Sample | Objective of study | Conclusions | Evidence Level |
|---|---|---|---|---|---|
| Natvig K, 1983, 'Laryngectomees in Norway. Study No. 2: pre-operative counselling and postoperative training evaluated by the patients and their spouses', *Journal of Otolaryngology* 12 (4):249–54. | Qualitative study | 189 laryngectomees 131 spouses | 189 laryngectomees and their spouses were invited to take part in an interview regarding the quality of pre-operative counselling and post-operative training they had experienced. | Twenty-six percent of 189 Norwegian laryngectomees considered pre-operative counselling to be unsatisfactory. Similarly, post-operative self-care training was rated unsatisfactory by 55 percent. The quality of the pre-operative counselling had a significant influence on the patients' ability to perceive post-operative training which subsequently correlated with mastery of the laryngectomy event. Seventy percent of the spouses felt that they had not been offered adequate counselling. The problems endured at home for 60 percent of them could have been amenable to relief by improved counselling. | III |
| Zeine L & Larson M, 1999, 'Pre- & post-operative counselling for laryngectomees & their spouses: an update', *Journal of Communication Disorders* 32 (1):51–61. | Survey | — | This survey was developed to determine if pre-operative counselling services have improved since the 1978 Keith, Linebaugh & Cox study. The questions were aimed at obtaining information on the quality and quantity of support services available to laryngectomees and their spouses. Questions addressed the type, amount, and content of information received. In addition, questions regarding post-operative counselling services for laryngectomees and spouses of laryngectomees were also included. | Results indicated that 21 percent of the laryngectomees were not aware that laryngectomy surgery would result in loss of voice. In addition, not all speech rehabilitation options were explained to the patients. Pre- and post-operative counselling services for laryngectomees continue to be inadequate. It appears that little change has been made to improve this situation. | III |

### Provision and Planning of Alternative Communication

| | | | | | |
|---|---|---|---|---|---|
| Karnell LH, Funk GF & Hoffman HT, 2000, 'Assessing head and neck cancer patient outcome domains', *Head Neck* 22 (1):6–11. | Survey | — | The purpose of this study was to assess the relative importance to patients' lives of multiple outcomes resulting from the management of head and neck cancer (speech; eating; aesthetics; pain/discomfort; and social/role functioning). | Logistic regression indicated that speech and eating best predicted quality of life. These data demonstrated that, for this group of patients, speech has the most impact on well-being. | III |

| Author(s) & Title | Design | Sample | Objective of study | Conclusions | Evidence Level |
|---|---|---|---|---|---|
| Carr MM, Schmidbauer JA, Majaess L & Smith RL, 2000, 'Communication after laryngectomy: an assessment of quality of life', *Otolaryngology Head Neck Surgery* 122 (1):39–43. | Questionnaire | 74 laryngectomees | The purpose of this study was to examine quality of life for laryngectomees using different methods of communication. A survey was mailed to all the living laryngectomees in Nova Scotia. Patients were asked to rate their ability to communicate in a number of common situations, to rate their difficulty with several communication problems and to complete the EORTC QLQ-C30 quality-of-life assessment tool. | Sixty-two patients responded (return rate of 84 percent); 57 percent were using electrolaryngeal speech, 19 percent oesophageal speech and 8.5 percent tracheoesophageal speech. These groups were comparable with respect to age, sex, first language, education level and years since laryngectomy. There were very few differences between these groups in ability to communicate in social situations and no difference in overall quality of life as measured by these scales. The most commonly cited problem was difficulty being heard in a noisy environment. Despite the fact that tracheoesophageal speech is objectively most intelligible, there does not seem to be a measurable improvement in quality of life or ability to communicate in everyday situations over electrolaryngeal or oesophageal speakers. | III |
| Edels Y (ed), 1983, *Laryngectomy: Diagnosis to Rehabilitation*, Croom Helm, London. | Expert opinion | — | — | — | IV |

### Selection of appropriate treatment strategies

| Author(s) & Title | Design | Sample | Objective of study | Conclusions | Evidence Level |
|---|---|---|---|---|---|
| Pauloski BR, Rademaker AW, Logemann JA & Colangelo LA, 1998, 'Speech and swallowing in irradiated and non-irradiated post-surgical oral cancer patients', *Otolaryngology Head Neck Surgery* 118 (5):616–24. | Comparative study | 18 patients 9 patients received surgical intervention and post-operative radiation therapy 9 patients received surgical intervention only | The effect of radiation on speech and swallowing function was assessed for 18 patients surgically treated for oral and oropharyngeal cancer. Nine patients received surgical intervention and post-operative radiation therapy, and nine received surgery only. | Statistical testing indicated that overall speech function did not differ between the irradiated and non-irradiated patients. Irradiated patients had significantly reduced oral and pharyngeal swallowing performance. Specifically: longer oral transit times on paste boluses; lower oropharyngeal swallow efficiency; increased pharyngeal residue; and reduced cricopharyngeal opening duration. Impaired function may be the result of radiation effects such as edema, fibrosis and reduced salivary flow. Increased use of tongue range-of-motion exercises during and after radiation treatment may reduce the formation of fibrotic tissue in the oral cavity and may improve pharyngeal clearance by maintaining adequate tongue base-to-pharyngeal-wall contact. | III |

## HEAD & NECK CANCER

| Author(s) & Title | Design | Sample | Objective of study | Conclusions | Evidence Level |
|---|---|---|---|---|---|
| Sonies BC, 1993, 'Remediation challenges in treating dysphagia post head/neck cancer. A problem-oriented approach', *Clinical Communication Disorders* 3 (4):21–26. | Single case study | A post head/neck surgery patient with a hematologic condition | A problem-oriented approach to dysphagia treatment was developed. Treatment was graded so that a hierarchical approach was used for all problems. Passive and resistive exercises preceded active exercise, and sensory stimulation preceded motion tasks. | After three months of treatment using an oral sensory motor stimulation paradigm and graded series of lip and tongue strengthening and motion exercises, swallowing had improved so that total nutritional intake was by mouth and weight was restored to normal. | III |
| Logemann JA, Pauloski BR, Rademaker AW & Colangelo LA, 1997, 'Speech and swallowing rehabilitation for head and neck cancer patients', *Oncology (huntingt)* 11 (5):651–56, 659. | Literature review | — | This paper reviews the literature on speech and swallowing problems in various types of treated head and neck cancer patients. | Pilot data support the use of range of motion (ROM) exercises for the jaw, tongue, lips and larynx in the first three months after oral or oropharyngeal ablative surgical procedures, as patients who perform ROM exercises on a regular basis exhibit significantly greater improvement in global measures of both speech and swallowing, as compared with patients who do not do these exercises. | IV |

### Alaryngeal Voice Therapy: Oesophageal, Artificial Larynx, Surgical Voice Restoration

| Author(s) & Title | Design | Sample | Objective of study | Conclusions | Evidence Level |
|---|---|---|---|---|---|
| Kalb MB & Carpenter MA, 'Individual speaker influence on relative intelligibility of oesophageal speech and artificial larynx speech', *Journal of Speech & Hearing Disorders* 46 (1):77–80. | Comparative study | 15 proficient male laryngectomised speakers divided into three groups | Comparisons were made of the relative intelligibility of oesophageal and artificial larynx speech. Five used only oesophageal speech, five used only artificial larynx speech and five produced both forms of speech. | Differences in intelligibility between oesophageal and artificial larynx speech resulted when data comparisons were based on different speaker groups. However, differences were not evident when data from the same speakers were compared. The results were interpreted to highlight the possible influence of individual speaker characteristics, rather than differences between communication methods. | III |

| Author(s) & Title | Design | Sample | Objective of study | Conclusions | Evidence Level |
|---|---|---|---|---|---|
| Carr MM, Schmidbauer JA, Majaess L & Smith RL, 2000, 'Communication after laryngectomy: an assessment of quality of life', *Otolaryngology Head Neck Surgery* 122 (1):39–43. | Questionnaire | 74 laryngectomees | The purpose of this study was to examine quality of life for laryngectomees using different methods of communication. A survey was mailed to all the living laryngectomees in Nova Scotia. Patients were asked to rate their ability to communicate in a number of common situations, to rate their difficulty with several communication problems and to complete the EORTC QLQ-C30 quality-of-life assessment tool. | Sixty-two patients responded (return rate of 84 percent); 57 percent were using electrolaryngeal speech, 19 percent oesophageal speech and 8.5 percent tracheoesophageal speech. These groups were comparable with respect to age, sex, first language, education level and years since laryngectomy. There were very few differences between these groups in ability to communicate in social situations and no difference in overall quality of life as measured by these scales. The most commonly cited problem was difficulty being heard in a noisy environment. Despite the fact that tracheoesophageal speech is objectively most intelligible, there does not seem to be a measurable improvement in quality of life or ability to communicate in everyday situations over electrolaryngeal or oesophageal speakers. | III |
| Finizia C, Hammerlid E, Westin T & Lindstrom J, 1998, 'Quality of life in patients with laryngeal cancer: a post treatment comparison of laryngectomy v radiotherapy', *Laryngoscope* 910:1566–73. | Comparative study | 14 irradiated laryngeal speakers with preserved larynx were matched with 14 salvage-surgery laryngectomised patients speaking with tracheoesophageal prosthesis | This study was designed to compare the voice and the quality of life (QOL) of laryngeal cancer patients receiving treatment with radical radiotherapy with or without laryngectomy as salvage surgery. It also compared the patients' own perceptual ratings of their voice to the perceptual ratings of a group of listeners. | The perceptual ratings of speech intelligibility, voice quality and speech acceptability showed a significant difference between the treatment groups. Both the patients who received treatment with radiotherapy and the listeners rated the irradiated laryngeal voices higher than the tracheoesophageal speech. The laryngectomised patients scored significantly better than the patients treated with radical radiotherapy on the question about hoarseness. No other significant difference was found for the QOL functions and symptoms. When patients treated with radiotherapy were compared with patients treated with laryngectomy as salvage surgery, QOL was similar, only small differences being found in the perceptual speech evaluation. | III |

## HEAD & NECK CANCER

| Author(s) & Title | Design | Sample | Objective of study | Conclusions | Evidence Level |
|---|---|---|---|---|---|
| St Guily JL, Angelard B, El-Bez M, Julien N, Debry C, Fichaux & Gondret R, 1992, 'Postlaryngectomy voice restoration', *Archives Otolarygol Head Neck Surgery* 118. | Prospective comparative study | 83 patients who underwent total laryngectomy | Voice restoration was studied in 81 patients: oesophageal voice was used by 19 patients, a tracheoesophageal procedure by 41 and 21 patients had no voice restoration. | Results were assessed according to voice quality and usage. Tracheoesophageal speech had a success rate of 73 percent (good voice, daily use) after I month, while oesophageal voice proved to have only a 5 percent success rate. Thirty patients (37 percent) remained without a substitute voice. The reasons for their exclusion are presented; they include a high rate of refusal. Long-term results regarding usage and quality are also presented. | III |

### Selection of Surgical Voice Restoration with Laryngectomee

| Author(s) & Title | Design | Sample | Objective of study | Conclusions | Evidence Level |
|---|---|---|---|---|---|
| Bertino G, Bellomo A, Miani C, Ferrero F & Staffieri A, 1996, 'Spectrographic differences between tracheal-oesophageal and oesophageal voice', *Folia Phoniatr Logop* 48 (5):255–61. | Controlled study | 18 total laryngectomy patients<br><br>10 had oesophageal voice<br><br>8 had undergone primary voice rehabilitation with a tracheal – oesophageal voice button applied<br><br>10 normal adult males acted as controls | In order to evaluate the results of voice and speech rehabilitation after total laryngectomy, some acoustic parameters (fundamental frequency, waveform perturbation) were examined in 18 total laryngectomy patients. Eight of these subjects had previously been surgically rehabilitated with a tracheal-oesophageal phonatory valve, while 10 had been submitted to oesophageal speech rehabilitation. | Analysis of results has shown that tracheal-oesophageal voices are more likely to provide a stable fundamental frequency, there is also a tendency toward more clearly defined harmonics. Jitter and shimmer are more similar to the values of normal subjects compared with those observed in oesophageal speech. Such results seem to depend on a more regular vibration pattern in the pharyngeal-oesophageal segment, due to the more efficient expiratory flow in tracheal-oesophageal speech. Moreover a correlation between the objective parameters evaluated and the subjective score on speech acceptability was demonstrated. | IIb |

| Author(s) & Title | Design | Sample | Objective of study | Conclusions | Evidence Level |
|---|---|---|---|---|---|
| Robbins J, Fisher HB, Blom ED & Singer MI, 1984, 'Selected acoustic features of tracheoesophageal, oesophageal, and laryngeal speech', *Arch Otolaryngol* 110 (10):670–2. | Comparative study | Three groups of 15 male speakers. Group 1: tracheoesophageal speakers Group 2: 15 oesophageal speakers Group 3: 15 normal laryngeal speakers | Voice samples of 15 laryngeal, oesophageal, and tracheoesophageal speakers using the Blom-Singer voice prosthesis were analysed for intensity, frequency and rate. | Results indicate that characteristic values for tracheoesophageal speech are more similar to laryngeal speech than oesophageal speech, demonstrating the powerful advantage of this pulmonary-supported method of alaryngeal voice. | III |
| Clements KS, Rassekh CH, Seikaly H, Hokanson JA & Calhoun KH, 1997, 'Communication after laryngectomy. An assessment of patient satisfaction', *Arch Otolaryngol Head Neck Surgery* 123 (5):493-6. | Survey | 41 patients who had undergone total laryngectomy | To determine the satisfaction of patients with their current method of alaryngeal communication. To focus primarily on the patients' perception of their own speech. Forty-seven patients underwent total laryngectomy for cancer and survived. Thirty-one of the 47 patients responded to the survey. Patients were divided into four groups by their current method of communication: 1) tablet writers; 2) oesophageal speech; 3) electrolarynx; and 4) tracheoesophageal speech. | Patients in Group 4 were significantly more satisfied with their speech (perceived their speech to be of better quality), had improved ability to communicate over the telephone and had less limitation of their interactions with others. Patients in Group 4 also rated their overall quality of life higher. | III |
| RCSLT, 1999, 'Tracheo-oesophageal puncture procedures', *Guidelines from the Royal College of Speech & Language Therapists*. | Expert opinion | — | — | — | IV |

# Appendix 2
# Data Extraction Forms

# ANALYTIC COHORT / ONE SAMPLE LONGITUDINAL CHECKLIST FORM

## STUDY IDENTIFICATION

Author

Title

Reference                                    Year of publication

Checklist completed by

## Section 1  OBJECTIVE

| Evaluation criteria | Comments |
| --- | --- |
| 1.1  Outline the aim of this study | |
| 1.2  Is the hypothesis clearly defined? <br> *If no, explain why and reject* | Yes ☐ No ☐ |
| 1.3  Is the design appropriate to the objective? <br> *If no, explain why and reject* | Yes ☐ No ☐ |

## Section 2  SAMPLE

| | |
| --- | --- |
| 2.1  Is the diagnostic criteria clearly stated? <br> *If no, explain why* | Yes ☐ No ☐ Not stated ☐ |
| 2.2  Is the diagnostic criteria adequate? <br> *If no, explain why* | Yes ☐ No ☐ Not stated ☐ |
| **Exposed group?** | |
| 2.3  Inclusion criteria (please state) | |
| 2.4  Exclusion criteria (please state) | |
| 2.5  How were exposed recruited? | |
| 2.6  Indicate if controls were used | |
| 2.7  Is the method of statistical analysis appropriate? | |
| **Non-exposed group?** | |
| 2.8  Inclusion criteria (please state) | |
| 2.9  Exclusion criteria (please state) | |
| 2.10  Were the non-exposed cohort selected from the same population as exposed? | Yes ☐ No ☐ Not stated ☐ |
| 2.11  How were non-exposed recruited? | |
| 2.12  Are power calculations included? Was the number required the actual number recruited? | Yes ☐ No ☐ Not stated ☐ |

## Section 3 EXPOSURE

### 3.1   What was measured?

*1*

*2*

*3*

*4*

*5*

---

### 3.2   Who carried out the measurement(s)?

*1*

*2*

*3*

*4*

*5*

---

### 3.4   What were the measurement tool(s)?

*1*

*2*

*3*

*4*

*5*

---

### 3.5   Were the tool(s) validated?

*1* Yes ☐ No ☐ Not stated ☐

*2* Yes ☐ No ☐ Not stated ☐

*3* Yes ☐ No ☐ Not stated ☐

*4* Yes ☐ No ☐ Not stated ☐

*5* Yes ☐ No ☐ Not stated ☐

---

## Section 4  OUTCOME

4.1  What was measured and how often?

*1*

*2*

*3*

*4*

*5*

4.2  Who carried out the measurements?

*1*

*2*

*3*

*4*

*5*

4.3  What were the measurement tool(s)?

*1*

*2*

*3*

*4*

*5*

4.4  Were the tool(s) validated?

*1* Yes ☐ No ☐ Not stated ☐        *2* Yes ☐ No ☐ Not stated ☐        *3* Yes ☐ No ☐ Not stated ☐

*4* Yes ☐ No ☐ Not stated ☐        *5* Yes ☐ No ☐ Not stated ☐

4.5  Were the data collectors blinded to exposure status of subjects?

*1* Yes ☐ No ☐ Not stated ☐        *2* Yes ☐ No ☐ Not stated ☐        *3* Yes ☐ No ☐ Not stated ☐

*4* Yes ☐ No ☐ Not stated ☐        *5* Yes ☐ No ☐ Not stated ☐

4.6  Length of follow-up?

4.7  Time-frame for ascertainment of outcome appropriate?

Yes ☐ No ☐ Not stated ☐

## Section 5  ANALYSIS

5.1  Were 80 percent of those followed up included in
the analysis?                                       Yes ☐ No ☐ Not stated ☐

5.2  Losses to follow-up differ from those contacted?   Yes ☐ No ☐ Not stated ☐

5.3  Attrition rate? Specify number

5.4  Statistical analysis adequate and appropriate?

5.5  Unit of analysis?

5.6  Method of analysis?

5.7  Confounding satisfactorily dealt with?         Yes ☐ No ☐

## Section 6  DESCRIPTION OF THE STUDY

6.1  Are the findings transferable to the guideline population?   Yes ☐ No ☐

6.2  Are there clinically important differences in outcome?   Yes ☐ No ☐

6.3  Do the benefits outweigh harms risk?           Yes ☐ No ☐

## Section 7  GENERAL NOTES & COMMENTS

Author's comments

Do you agree with the author's conclusions?        Yes ☐ No ☐

List specific reservations (if any)

Is the paper to be included as evidence?           Yes ☐ No ☐

# CASE CONTROL / CASE SERIES CHECKLIST FORM

## STUDY IDENTIFICATION

Author

Title

Reference | Year of publication

Checklist completed by

## Section 1  OBJECTIVE

| Evaluation criteria | How well is this criterion addressed? Use the notation as outlined in the key at the end of the form. |
|---|---|
| 1.1  Does the study address an appropriate and clearly focused question? | |
| **Selection of subjects** | |
| 1.2  Are the cases and controls taken from the same source population? | |
| 1.3  Are the same exclusion criteria used for both cases and controls? | |
| 1.4  What percentage of each group (cases and controls) participated in the study? | |
| 1.5  Is there any comparison of participants and non-participants to establish their similarities or differences? | |
| **Assessment** | |
| 1.6  Are cases clearly defined and differentiated from controls? | |
| 1.7  Is it clearly established that controls are non-cases? | |
| 1.8  Is there evidence that the method of assessment was comparable between cases and controls? | |
| **Confounding** | |
| 1.9  Are the main potential confounders considered and assessed appropriately? | |
| **Statistical analysis** | |
| 1.10  Are the same data processing methods used for cases and controls? | |

| | |
|---|---|
| 1.11 Is the method of statistical analysis appropriate? | |
| 1.12 Is any measure of precision given? | |
| 1.13 Is a measure of goodness of fit of any multivariate model given? | |
| 1.14 Has a correction been made for multiple statistical testing (where appropriate)? | |

**Causal Relationships**

| | |
|---|---|
| 1.15 Is there positive evidence of a causal relationship? | |

### Section 2  SAMPLE

| | |
|---|---|
| 2.1 How well was the study carried out to minimise the risk of bias or confounding, and to establish a causal relationship between intervention and effect? (Code ++, + or −) | |
| 2.2 Taking into account clinical considerations and your evaluation of the methodology used, and the statistical power of the study, are you certain that the overall effect is due to the factor(s) investigated in this study? | |
| 2.3 Are the results of this study directly applicable to the client group targeted by this study? | |

### Section 3  DESCRIPTION OF THE STUDY

3.1    What intervention/approaches or prognostic factors are considered?


3.2    What outcomes are considered?


3.3    What are the characteristics of the study population? (eg, age, sex)


3.4    What are the characteristics of the study setting?

## Section 4  GENERAL NOTES & COMMENTS

**List specific reservations (if any)**

Do you agree with the author's conclusions?  Yes ☐ No ☐

Is the paper to be included as evidence?  Yes ☐ No ☐

___

### KEY FOR 'How well is this criterion addressed?'

**Section 1**
- Well covered
- Adequately addressed
- Poorly addressed
- Not addressed
- Not reported
- Not applicable

___

**Section 2**

**++**  **All** or **most** of the criteria have been fulfilled.
  Where they have not been fulfilled the conclusions of the study or review are thought *very unlikely* to alter.

**+**  **Some** of the criteria have been fulfilled.
  Those criteria that have not been fulfilled or not adequately described are thought *unlikely* to alter the conclusions.

**−**  **Few** or **no** criteria fulfilled.
  The conclusions of the study are though *likely or very likely* to alter.

___

# CROSS-SECTIONAL / SURVEY CHECKLIST FORM

*(All questions do not apply to both designs – if not appropriate, please record N/A)*

## STUDY IDENTIFICATION

Author

Title

Reference                                    Year of publication

Checklist completed by

## Section 1  OBJECTIVE

| Evaluation criteria | Comments |
| --- | --- |
| 1.1  Does the study address an appropriate and clearly focused question? State which type of study design was used, eg, survey, prevalence data. | |
| 1.2  Are the reasons for and the aims of the study clearly stated? | |
| 1.3  Is the design described in enough detail and is it appropriate to the aims of the study? | |
| 1.4  Are the criteria for selecting the sample clearly defined? Does it constitute the full range of likely participants? | |
| 1.5  Describe the setting in which the study takes place | |
| 1.6  Outline the inclusion criteria | |
| 1.7  Outline the exclusion criteria | |
| 1.8  What sampling method was used? | |
| 1.9  When was the study conducted? | |

### Data collection

| | |
| --- | --- |
| 1.10  What was measured? | |

| | |
|---|---|
| 1.11  Who carried out the measurements? | |
| 1.12  What were the measurement tool(s)? | |
| 1.13  Were they validated? | |

**Data analysis**

| | |
|---|---|
| 1.14  Describe how the data was analysed | |
| 1.15  What was the response rate? | |
| 1.16  Describe the results | |
| 1.17  Are the analysis and interpretation procedures discussed? | |
| 1.18  Are the results credible and if so, are they important in practice? | |

**Section 2  SAMPLE**

| | |
|---|---|
| 2.1  Taking into account clinical considerations and your evaluation of the methodology used, and the data analysis, are you certain that the overall effect is due to the factor(s) investigated in this study? | |
| 2.2  Are the results of this study directly applicable to the client group targeted by this study? | |

| 2.3 | Are the limitations of the methodology and biases discussed? | |
| --- | --- | --- |
| 2.4 | Is the risk of bias low, moderate or high? | |

## Section 3  DESCRIPTION OF THE STUDY

3.1   Are the findings transferable to the guideline population?


3.2   Does the evidence support the researcher's claims?


3.3   Are the conclusions drawn justified by the results?


## Section 4  GENERAL NOTES & COMMENTS


**List specific reservations (if any)**


Do you agree with the author's conclusions?        Yes ☐ No ☐

Is the paper to be included as evidence?        Yes ☐ No ☐

# RANDOMISED CONTROLLED TRIAL CHECKLIST FORM

## STUDY IDENTIFICATION

Author

Title

Reference                                        Year of publication

Checklist completed by

## Section 1  OBJECTIVE

| Evaluation criteria | How well is this criterion addressed? Use the notation as outlined in the key at the end of this form. |
|---|---|
| 1.1  Does the study address an appropriate and clearly focused question? | |
| 1.2  Was the assignment of subjects to treatment groups randomised? | |
| 1.3  Was an adequate concealment method used? | |
| 1.4  Were the subjects and investigators kept 'blind' about treatment allocation? | |
| 1.5  Apart from the treatment under investigation, were the groups treated equally? | |
| 1.6  What percentage of the individuals recruited into the study are included in the analysis? (*>80 percent = well covered, otherwise rate as poorly covered*) | |
| 1.7  Were all subjects analysed in the groups to which they were randomly allocated? | |
| 1.8  Were the treatment and control groups similar at the start of the trial? | |
| 1.9  Are the results homogeneous between sites? (*This only applies to multi-centre /multi-site studies*) | |

## Section 2  OVERALL ASSESSMENT OF THE STUDY

| | |
|---|---|
| 2.1  How well was the study done to minimise bias? Code ++, + or − | |
| 2.2  If coded as + or −, what is the likely direction in which bias might affect the study results? | |

| | |
|---|---|
| 2.3 Taking into account clinical considerations and your evaluation of the methodology used, and the statistical power of the study, are you certain that the overall effect is due to the study intervention? | |
| 2.4 Are the results of this study directly applicable to the client group targeted by this study? | |

## Section 3 DESCRIPTION OF THE STUDY

3.1 What intervention/approaches are considered?


3.2 Are the intervention/approaches aimed at individuals or populations?


3.3 What outcomes are considered?


3.4 What are the characteristics of the study population? (eg age, sex)


3.5 What are the characteristics of the study setting?


3.6 How many groups/sites are there in the study?

## Section 4 GENERAL NOTES & COMMENTS

**List specific reservations (if any)**

Do you agree with the author's conclusions?   Yes ☐ No ☐

Is the paper to be included as evidence?   Yes ☐ No ☐

---

**KEY FOR 'How well is this criterion addressed?'**

**Section 1**

■   Well covered
■   Adequately addressed
■   Poorly addressed
■   Not addressed
■   Not reported
■   Not applicable

---

**Section 2**

++   **All** or **most** of the criteria have been fulfilled.
Where they have not been fulfilled the conclusions of the study or review are thought *very unlikely* to alter.

+   **Some** of the criteria have been fulfilled.
Those criteria that have not been fulfilled or not adequately described are thought *unlikely* to alter the conclusions.

−   **Few** or **no** criteria fulfilled.
The conclusions of the study are though *likely or very likely* to alter.

---

# SINGLE SUBJECT DESIGN CHECKLIST FORM

## STUDY IDENTIFICATION

Author

Title

Reference                                        Year of publication

Checklist completed by

## Section 1 OBJECTIVE

| Evaluation criteria | Comments |
|---|---|
| 1.1 Does the study address an appropriate and clearly focused question? | |
| 1.2 Are the reasons for and the aims of the study clearly stated? | |
| 1.3 Is the hypothesis clearly defined? | |
| 1.4 Is the design described in enough detail and is it appropriate to the aims of the study? | |

### Population

| | |
|---|---|
| 1.5 What are the characteristics of the study population? (eg, age, sex) | |
| 1.6 What are the characteristics of the study setting? | |

### Assessment

| | |
|---|---|
| 1.7 Is/are the baseline measurement(s) and results adequately described? | |
| 1.8 Are the baseline assessment tools appropriate and fully described? | |
| 1.9 Is there evidence that all incidental variables have been controlled? | |
| 1.10 Is/are the experimental intervention(s) described in enough detail to allow full replication? | |
| 1.11 Are the post-experimental assessment tools appropriate and fully described? | |

| **Statistical analysis** | |
|---|---|
| 1.12 Is the method of statistical analysis adequate and appropriate? | |
| 1.13 Is any measure of precision given? | |
| 1.14 Has a correction been made for multiple statistical testing (where appropriate)? | |
| **Causal relationship** | |
| 1.15 Is there positive evidence of a causal relationship? | |

## Section 2  OVERALL ASSESSMENT OF THE STUDY

| | |
|---|---|
| 2.1 How well did the study minimise the risk of bias or confounding, and to establish a causal relationship between intervention and effect? | |
| 2.2 Taking into account clinical considerations and your evaluation of the methodology used, and the statistical power of the study, are you certain that the overall effect is due to the factor(s) investigated in this study? | |

## Section 3  DESCRIPTION OF THE STUDY

3.1   What influencing factors are considered?

3.2   What outcomes are considered?

3.3   Are the conclusions justified?

3.4   Are the findings generalisable to the guideline population?

## Section 4 GENERAL NOTES & COMMENTS

**List specific reservations (if any)**

Do you agree with the author's conclusions?        Yes ☐ No ☐

Is the paper to be included as evidence?        Yes ☐ No ☐

# SYSTEMATIC REVIEW & META-ANALYSIS CHECKLIST FORM

## STUDY IDENTIFICATION

Author

Title

Reference                                    Year of publication

Checklist completed by

## Section 1  OBJECTIVE

| Evaluation criteria | How well is this criterion addressed? Use the notation as outlined in the key at the end of this form. |
|---|---|
| 1.1  Does the review address an appropriate and clearly focused question? | |
| 1.2  Was the literature search sufficiently rigorous to identify all relevant studies? (*eg, Did it cover multiple databases? Was any hand searching done?*) | |
| 1.3  Were the criteria used to select articles for inclusion appropriate? | |
| 1.4  Was the validity of individual studies included in the review appraised? | |
| 1.5  Was it reasonable to combine the studies? (*eg, Are the populations comparable? Are the methods used the same? Are the outcomes comparable?*) | |
| 1.6  Are the data summarised to give a point estimate of effect and confidence intervals (if applicable)? | |
| 1.7  Do the conclusions flow from the evidence reviewed? | |

## Section 2  OVERALL ASSESSMENT OF THE STUDY

| | |
|---|---|
| 2.1  How well did the study minimise bias? Code ++, + or – | |
| 2.2  If coded as + or –, what is the likely direction in which bias might affect the study results? | |
| 2.3  Taking into account clinical considerations and your evaluation of the methodology used, are you certain that the overall effect is due to the study intervention? | |
| 2.4  Are the results of this study directly applicable to the client group targeted by this study? | |

## Section 3 DESCRIPTION OF THE STUDY

3.1   What types of study are included in the review?

3.2   What intervention/approaches are considered?

3.3   Are the intervention/approaches aimed at individuals or populations?

3.4   What outcomes are considered?

3.5   Are potential confounding factors considered?

3.6   What are the characteristics of the study population? (eg, age, sex)

3.7   What are the characteristics of the study setting?

## Section 4  GENERAL NOTES & COMMENTS

**List specific reservations (if any)**

Do you agree with the author's conclusions?     Yes ☐ No ☐

Is the paper to be included as evidence?     Yes ☐ No ☐

---

**KEY FOR 'How well is this criterion addressed?'**

---

**Section 1**

■     Well covered

■     Adequately addressed

■     Poorly addressed

■     Not addressed

■     Not reported

■     Not applicable

---

**Section 2**

++     **All** or **most** of the criteria have been fulfilled.
        Where they have not been fulfilled the conclusions of the study or review are thought *very unlikely* to alter.

+     **Some** of the criteria have been fulfilled.
        Those criteria that have not been fulfilled or not adequately described are thought *unlikely* to alter the conclusions.

−     **Few** or **no** criteria fulfilled.
        The conclusions of the study are though *likely or very likely* to alter.

---

# QUALITATIVE STUDIES CHECKLIST FORM

## STUDY IDENTIFICATION

Author

Title

Reference                                      Year of publication

Checklist completed by

## Section 1  OBJECTIVE

| | **Evaluation criteria** | **Comments** |
|---|---|---|
| 1.1 | Does the study address an appropriate and clearly focused question? | |
| 1.2 | Are the reasons for and the aims of the study clearly stated? | |
| 1.3 | Is the design described in enough detail and is it appropriate to the aims of the study? | |
| 1.4 | Describe the qualitative method used | |
| 1.6 | Are the criteria for selecting the sample clearly defined? Does it constitute the full range of likely participants? | |
| 1.7 | Describe the setting in which the study takes place? | |
| 1.8 | Outline the method of recruitment (*eg, is an account given of where, who and how those potentially included in the sample were contacted?*) | |
| 1.9 | Describe the sample characteristics (*eg, age, gender, ethnicity and other relevant characteristics*) | |
| | **Data collection** | |
| 1.10 | Is the fieldwork adequately described? Is there an account of where data were collected, by whom and in what context? Describe | |

1.11  Are methods of data collection adequately described?
      Is the time-scale outlined; are the data-collection
      methods appropriate for gaining the information
      required; were standardised research protocols used?
      Describe

      Tick which data collection method was used:

      ■ Unstructured interviews ☐
      ■ Semi-structured interviews ☐
      ■ Focus groups ☐
      ■ Participant observation ☐
      ■ Non-participant observation ☐
      ■ Existing documents ☐
      ■ Free written text or drawings ☐
      ■ Other (describe) ☐

1.12  Was the data collected systematically? Is there
      evidence of consistent use of interview guide/study
      protocol?

**Data analysis**

1.13  Describe how the data was analysed. (*eg, Were
      responses to individual questions categorised and the range
      of categories reported? Was coding used? Was it presented
      as a loose collection of descriptive material with little
      analysis?*)

1.14  What was the response rate?

1.15  Describe the results

| | |
|---|---|
| 1.16 Are the analysis and interpretation procedures discussed? | |
| 1.17 Is there evidence of efforts to establish validity? (*eg, evidence that accounts of the phenomenon reflect it accurately*) | |
| 1.18 Is there evidence of efforts to establish reliability? (*eg, evidence that accounts of the phenomenon are consistent over time and between researchers*) | |
| 1.19 What was the researcher's perspective and has this been taken into account? | |
| 1.20 Are the results credible and if so, are they important in practice? | |

## Section 2 OVERALL ASSESSMENT OF THE STUDY

| | |
|---|---|
| 2.1 Taking into account clinical considerations and your evaluation of the methodology used, and the data analysis, are you certain that the overall effect is due to the factor(s) investigated in this study? | |
| 2.2 Are the results of this study directly applicable to the client group targeted by this study? | |
| 2.3 Are the limitations of the methodology and biases discussed? | |
| 2.4 Is the risk of bias low, moderate or high? | |

## Section 3  DESCRIPTION OF THE STUDY

3.1    Are the findings transferable to the guideline population?

3.2    Does the evidence support the researcher's claims?

3.3    Are the conclusions drawn justified by the results?

## Section 4  GENERAL NOTES & COMMENTS

**List specific reservations (if any)**

Do you agree with the author's conclusions?          Yes ☐ No ☐

Is the paper to be included as evidence?          Yes ☐ No ☐

# Appendix 3
# Levels of Evidence &
# Grading of Recommendations

## Interpretation of the Grading Structure

It is vital to recognise that the grade does *not* relate to the importance of the recommendation but to the methodological strength of the supporting evidence, using the grading system below.

### LEVELS OF EVIDENCE

| Level | Type of evidence (based on AHCPR 1992) |
|---|---|
| Ia | Evidence obtained from meta-analysis of randomised controlled trials |
| Ib | Evidence obtained from at least one randomised controlled trial |
| IIa | Evidence obtained from at least one well-designed controlled trial without randomisation |
| IIb | Evidence obtained from at least one other type of well-designed quasi-experimental study |
| III | Evidence obtained from well-designed non-experimental descriptive studies, such as comparative studies, correlation studies and case-control studies |
| IV | Evidence obtained from expert committee reports or opinions and/or clinical experience of respected authorities |

### GRADING OF RECOMMENDATIONS

| Grade | Recommendations (based on AHCPR 1994) |
|---|---|
| A (Evidence levels Ia, Ib) | Requires at least one randomised-controlled trial as part of the body of literature, of overall good quality and consistency, addressing the specific recommendation. |
| B (Evidence levels IIa, IIb, III) | Requires availability of well-conducted clinical studies but no randomised clinical trials on the topic of recommendation. |
| C (Evidence level IV) | Requires evidence from expert committee reports on opinions and/or clinical experience of respected authorities. Indicates absence of directly applicable studies of good quality. |

# Appendix 4
# Membership of
# Project Advisory Group

Ms Grainne Asher
Educational Psychologist
Harrow Psychology Service
Middlesex

Professor Sally Byng
Chief Executive Officer
Connect – Communication Disability Network
London

Dr Paul Carding
Councillor for Research for RCSLT
Speech & Language Therapy Dept
Newcastle Royal Infirmary

Professor Pam Enderby
Dean of the Medical School
Sheffield University

Dr Marcia Kelson
Senior Research Fellow
College of Health
London

Dr Finbar Martin
St Thomas' Hospital
London

Ms Judy Mead
Chartered Society of Physiotherapists
London

Dr Sue Roulstone
Director of Speech & Language Therapy
Research Unit
Bristol

Mrs Debby Rossiter
Vice- President of RCSLT
Chief Speech & Language Therapist
King's College Hospital
London

Ms Christine Sealey-Lapes
College of Occupational Therapists
London

Ms Sian Williamson
Clinical Effectiveness Support Unit
Cardiff

# Appendix 5
# Membership of
# Expert Groups

## PRE-SCHOOL CHILDREN WITH COMMUNICATION, LANGUAGE & SPEECH NEEDS EXPERT GROUP MEMBERS

Ms Gillian Bolton

Dr Gina Conti-Ramsden

Ms Tessa Gittens

Ms Norma Ham

Ms Celia Harding

Ms Lorraine Kelly-Atherton

Ms Claire Lewis

Ms Julia Scotland

Ms Chris Sherlock

## SCHOOL-AGED CHILDREN WITH SPEECH, LANGUAGE & COMMUNICATION DIFFICULTIES EXPERT GROUP MEMBERS

Ms Maureen Aarons

Ms Melanie Abba

Ms Liz Baldwin

Ms Philomena Cleary

Ms Lorraine Coulter

Ms Carol Everingham

Ms Gila Falkus

Ms Carolyn Letts

Ms Diana McQueen

Ms Jennifer Reid

Ms Liz Royall

Ms Liz Shaw

Ms Alison Stewart

Ms Catherine Sutcliffe

Ms Lesley Unwin

## AUTISTIC SPECTRUM DISORDERS EXPERT GROUP MEMBERS

Ms Maureen Aarons

Ms Eileen Burke

Ms Tessa Gittens

Ms Celia Harding

Ms Julia Scotland

## CLEFT PALATE & VELOPHARYNGEAL ABNORMALITIES EXPERT GROUP MEMBERS

Ms Liz Albery

Ms Lisa Crampin

Ms Denise Dive

Dr Anne Harding

Ms Caroline Hattee

Ms Christine Hayden

Ms Anthea Masarei

Ms Roz Razzell

Dr Jane Russell

Dr Debbie Sell

Dr Triona Sweeney

Ms Melanie Walsh

Ms Rosemary Wyatt

## CLINICAL VOICE DISORDERS EXPERT GROUP MEMBERS

Ms Frances Ascott

Dr Eva Carlson

Ms Lesley Cavalli

Ms Christine Currie

Ms Eryl Evans

Ms Sue Jones

Ms Myra Lockhart

Ms Lesley Mathieson

Ms Kate MacFarlane

Ms Eimear McCrory

Ms Kaye Radford

Ms Emer Scanlon

Ms Jane Thornton

## DEAFNESS/HEARING LOSS EXPERT GROUP MEMBERS

Ms Maria Cameron

Ms Gill Close

Ms Judy Halden

Ms Liz Hole

Ms Susan Howden

Ms Caitie McKenna

Ms Frances McMenemy

Ms Janet O'Keefe

Ms Anne O'Sullivan

Ms Alison Peasgood

Ms Fiona Wilson

## DISORDERS OF FEEDING, EATING, DRINKING & SWALLOWING (DYSPHAGIA) EXPERT GROUP MEMBERS

Ms Julie Dick

Dr Catherine Dunnet

Ms Jay Ellis

Ms Virginia Hale

Ms Alison Humphrey

Ms Annette Kelly

Ms Sue McGowan

Ms Helen Mould

Ms Jenny Moultrie

Ms Jacqueline Newell

Ms Sue Pownall

Ms Gail Robertson

Ms Catherine Russell

Ms Sue Strudwick

Ms Shana Taubert

Ms Kate Wilson

## DISORDERS OF FLUENCY EXPERT GROUP MEMBERS

Dr Shelagh Brumfitt

Ms Frances Cook

Ms Rosemarie Hayhow

Ms Roberta Lees

Ms Isabel O'Leary

Dr Trudy Stewart

Ms Melanie Wade

Ms Kate Williams

Ms Louise Wright

# DISORDERS OF MENTAL HEALTH & DEMENTIA EXPERT GROUP MEMBERS

Ms Julia Binder

Ms Debra Borsley

Ms Karen Elliott

Ms Kathleen Gilmour

Ms Joy Harris

Ms Jane Jones

Ms Jackie Kindell

Ms Sandra Polding

Ms Victoria Ramsey

Ms Barbara Tanner

Ms Susan Wallace

Ms Jeanne Yitshaki

## DYSARTHRIA EXPERT GROUP MEMBERS

Ms Sarah Barnes

Ms Morag Bixley

Mr Paul Jones

Ms Jayne Lyndsay

Ms Alison MacDonald

Ms Gwen Margree

Ms Janet Moar

Ms Sandra Robertson

Dr Margaret Walshe

# APHASIA EXPERT GROUP MEMBERS

Katerina Hilari

Ruth Nieuwenhuis

Debby Rossiter

Carol Sacchett

Anne Whateley

Celia Woolf


The significant contributions of the following is also acknowledged:

Lisa Hirst

Jon Hunt

and a wider group of SLTs who contributed to earlier work on the guideline.

## HEAD & NECK CANCER EXPERT GROUP MEMBERS

Ms Frances Ascott

Dr Eva Carlson

Ms Lesley Cavalli

Ms Christine Currie

Ms Eryl Evans

Ms Sue Jones

Ms Myra Lockhart

Ms Lesley Mathieson

Ms Kate MacFarlane

Ms Eimear McCrory

Ms Kaye Radford

Ms Emer Scanlon

Ms Jane Thornton

# Appendix 6
# Voluntary Organisations Involved in Service User Consultation

## VOLUNTARY ORGANISATIONS INVOLVED IN SERVICE USER CONSULTATION

AFASIC

Cleft Lip and Palate Association

Down's Syndrome Association

MENCAP

Motor Neurone Disease Society

Multiple Sclerosis Society

Parkinson's Disease Society

Speakability

Stroke Association

The British Stammering Association

The National Association of Laryngectomee Clubs

The National Autistic Society

The National Deaf Children's Society

Alzheimers Association

MIND

# Appendix 7
# Focus Groups as Organised
# by Clinical Guideline

# FOCUS GROUPS AS ORGANISED BY CLINICAL GUIDELINE

Aphasia

Autistic Spectrum Disorder

Cleft Palate & Velopharyngeal Abnormality

Disorders of Fluency

Head & Neck Cancer

Pre-School Children with Communication, Language & Speech Needs

School-Aged Children with Speech, Language & Communication Difficulties

# Appendix 8
# User Questionnaire

# USER QUESTIONNAIRE

Please answer each of the following questions. Please continue overleaf if necessary.

**1. What *has* been done well for you?**




**2. What has *not* been done well for you?**




**3. What *should* be done for you?**



*In order to help analyse the responses, I would appreciate it if you could also complete the following:*

## FOR INFORMATION ONLY

1. Who completed this questionnaire?

   ☐ User     ☐ Carer/Parent     ☐ Other

2. Please state briefly the reason you need to attend speech and language therapy



3. Which part of Great Britain are you from?



4. Please indicate your age range:

   ☐ 0–16     ☐ 16–40     ☐ 40–65     ☐ 65+

# Appendix 9
# Information Gathered from
# Focus Groups & Questionnaire

# PRE-SCHOOL AND SCHOOL-AGED CHILDREN

*There were three main approaches to consulting with the users:*

- *Inviting representatives from voluntary organisations to attend meetings of the expert groups.*
- *Focus groups with service users or their parents/carers.*
- *Postal questionnaire.*

*The following information is based upon an analysis of the service user questionnaires and the issues raised at focus groups. Examples of individual comments are included and grouped under common themes.*

*What was done well for you?*
- **Therapy**
    - Mainstream-school staff were trained. There was effective integration of all members of the team.
    - Child observed in a naturalistic setting over a period of several weeks.
    - Well developed and effectively implemented home and playgroup programmes
    - Full, detailed and demonstrable explanations of what occurred in therapy session was given to parent.

- **Speech & Language Therapist**
    - Team-working by the Therapist and the teacher was excellent. Parent did not realise the role distinction, as both professionals 'worked in a circular fashion'. Very effective communication.
    - Written information and access to reports was provided for teachers and friends, as appropriate.

- **Service Provision**
    - Information and training was available from a parent course – parental attitudes to the communication disorder have changed.

*What was not done well for you?*
- **Service Provision**
    - There was conflict between Health and Education regarding provision of service.
    - There is not enough therapy provision.
    - The length of time between being referred to the Speech & Language Therapist and acknowledgement of acceptance to service was too long.

- **Therapy**
    - Assessments which are perceived as failure-based; trying to find out what is wrong with the child.
    - The child was not placed on a waiting list as the parent was given a sheet of advice that was seen as intervention. The parent was unaware of this situation, and had expected the child to be placed on a waiting list.

*What should be done for you?*
- **Service Provision/Therapy**
    - Continuity of care is required.
    - There must be sensitivity to both child and parent when placing within a group setting.
    - There should be written information from the Speech & Language Therapist regarding explanation of the disorder.
    - Collaboration between all professionals involved in child's care
    - The Speech & Language Therapist should provide a working 'diagnosis' concerning the child's communication.
    - Any therapy information given to the parents, eg, tasks, should be modelled by the therapist first.

## AUTISTIC SPECTRUM DISORDERS

*There were three main approaches to consulting with the users:*

- *Inviting representatives from voluntary organisations to attend meetings of the expert groups.*
- *Focus groups with service users or their parents/carers.*
- *Postal questionnaire.*

*The following information is based upon an analysis of the service user questionnaires and the issues raised at focus groups. Examples of individual comments are included and grouped under common themes.*

*What was done well for you?*

- **Speech & Language Therapist**
  - Therapist has particular expertise in this area and has therefore given very specific advice.

*What was not done well for you?*

- **Service Provision**
  - There is not enough therapy provision.
  - Too many changes of staff and therefore difficult for the child and parent to gain confidence in the Therapist.
  - Waiting list too long.

*What should be done for you?*

- **Service Provision/Therapy**
  - Continuity of care is required.
  - Collaboration between all professionals involved in child's care.
  - Group therapy required for development of 'communication' skills.

## CLEFT PALATE & VELOPHARYNGEAL ABNORMALITIES

*There were three main approaches to consulting with the users:*

- *Inviting representatives from voluntary organisations to attend meetings of the expert groups.*
- *Focus groups with service users or their parents/carers.*
- *Postal questionnaire.*

*The following information is based upon an analysis of the service user questionnaires and the issues raised at focus groups. Examples of individual comments are included and grouped under common themes.*

*What was done well for you?*
- **Therapy**
  - Speech therapy after operation corrected the few remaining problems. Child handled with care and concern, and therapy was made fun.
  - The ability to predict a trend for future operations based on speech therapy.
  - Technical, anatomical explanations were very revealing and helpful.

- **Speech & Language Therapist**
  - Speech & Language Therapist at hospital very accommodating and willing to arrange appointments on request.
  - Excellent Speech & Language Therapist.
  - Therapist has done everything asked for – and more!

- **Service Provision**
  - Communication between local speech therapy and hospital is good.

*What was not done well for you?*
- **Service Provision**
  - Long waits for therapy, and long intervals between sessions.
  - Constant changes of staff.
  - No cover provided when Therapist on extended leave, eg, maternity leave.
  - Telephone 'assessments'.
  - Distance required to travel to see Therapist.

*What should be done for you?*
- **Service Provision**
  - Continuity of care.
  - Group therapy – not so isolated by disability.

## DEAFNESS/HEARING LOSS

*There were three main approaches to consulting with the users:*

- *Inviting representatives from voluntary organisations to attend meetings of the expert groups.*
- *Focus groups with service users or their parents/carers.*
- *Postal questionnaire.*

*The following information is based upon an analysis of the service user questionnaires and the issues raised at focus groups. Examples of individual comments are included and grouped under common themes.*

*What was done well for you?*
- **Therapy**
  - Staff used signing in home surroundings and played signing games.
  - Child has also been encouraged to use voice.
  - Taught me how to breathe, to control speech, set targets. Support when needed.
  - Good follow-through procedure subsequent to cochlear implant.

- **Speech & Language Therapist**
  - Showed respect for child.
  - Excellent Speech & Language Therapist.

*What was not done well for you?*
- **Service Provision**
  - Long waits for therapy, and long intervals between sessions.
  - Constant changes of staff.
  - Very difficult to persuade Local Education Authority that speech and language therapy was needed.

*What should be done for you?*
- **Therapy**
  - More written/video help for parents to maintain therapy at home.
  - Therapy in mainstream school would help school awareness – better than taking child to clinic.

- **Service Provision**
  - Need more Speech & Language Therapists to work with deafness.

## DISORDERS OF FLUENCY

*There were three main approaches to consulting with the users:*

- *Inviting representatives from voluntary organisations to attend meetings of the expert groups.*
- *Focus groups with service users or their parents/carers.*
- *Postal questionnaire.*

*The following information is based upon an analysis of the service user questionnaires and the issues raised at focus groups. Examples of individual comments are included and grouped under common themes.*

*What was done well for you?*
- **Therapy**
  - Was shown how to deal with physical aspects, eg, neck muscle tension, speech dysfluency.
  - Child has been taught to mouth one word at a time – used to become very angry when we could not understand him.
  - Consistent therapy lasting for periods over 1 hour.
  - Play area outside room helped put my child at ease.

- **Speech & Language Therapist**
  - Therapist very flexible in approach. Open to discussion on methods.
  - Very good at tailoring exercises to individual children; very tactful.
  - The amount of support, and the fact that it was done on a 1:1 basis.
  - Flexible with appointment times.
  - Staff very caring and knowledgeable.

- **Impact upon individual/carer**
  - Took account of demands on all family members; involved both parents with exercises for child.
  - Able to discuss problem openly for first time. Better understanding.
  - Helped me gain confidence.

*What was not done well for you?*
- **Service Provision**
  - Six months from GP referral to initial appointment.
  - Long waiting lists.
  - Had to take child out of local area due to shortage of service provision.
  - Difficulty in accessing information about stammering services.

- **Speech & Language Therapist**
  - Therapist did not have specialist skills in stammering.

*What should be done for you?*
- **Service Provision**
  - More local intensive courses.
  - Should be information from therapist regarding centres of excellence, support networks.
  - Therapists should be aware of the importance of each appointment to the individual and family.

## DISORDERS OF FEEDING, EATING, DRINKING & SWALLOWING (DYSPHAGIA)

*There were three main approaches to consulting with the users:*

- *Inviting representatives from voluntary organisations to attend meetings of the expert groups.*
- *Focus groups with service users or their parents/carers.*
- *Postal questionnaire.*

*The following information is based upon an analysis of the service user questionnaires and the issues raised at focus groups. Examples of individual comments are included and grouped under common themes.*

### *What was done well for you?*
- **Speech & Language Therapist**
  - Therapist has given me the confidence to deal with the feeding/swallowing problems.
  - Given a good lesson on physiology and anatomy.
  - Therapist really good listener who has helped me come to terms with problems.

### *What was not done well for you?*
- **Service Provision**
  - More therapy required.

### *What should be done for you?*
- **Service Provision**
  - More therapy provision.
  - Collaborative working between therapist and dietician.
  - Better community facilities.

# HEAD & NECK CANCER

*There were three main approaches to consulting with the users:*

- *Inviting representatives from voluntary organisations to attend meetings of the expert groups.*
- *Focus groups with service users or their parents/carers.*
- *Postal questionnaire.*

*The following information is based upon an analysis of the service user questionnaires and the issues raised at focus groups. Examples of individual comments are included and grouped under common themes.*

*What was done well for you?*
- **Speech & Language Therapist**
  - Everything the Speech & Language Therapist has done, and shown me, was done well – very supportive.
  - Therapist made me feel good about myself after my operation.
  - Speech & Language Therapist arranged for me to meet other laryngectomees before my operation, which helped a lot.
  - Between having my operation and having the first valve fitted, was taught to speak.
  - Have had excellent service for the past 11 years, and have a standard of life I would not have imagined before.
  - Full explanation of 'Do's' and 'Don'ts' regarding diet, medication and exercises.
  - Had all the help I needed to help me learn to talk again.
  - Therapist 'bonded' with me, even before my operation, and gave me confidence.
  - Through the help I received, I have made a remarkable recovery.

*What was not done well for you?*

*What should be done for you?*
- **Service Provision**
  - Six-monthly or annual reviews would be reassuring, and act as confidence boosters.